MW00667455

Beyond the Golden Door

A New Life In America

by

Elisa Palombo Sapienza

Author's Note

Born Elisa Costanza Palombo, the author's first name was Americanized into Alice by her first grade teacher, as was often done in 1926. Later, she married Salvatore Sapienza and, after being widowed in 1974, married John Donnelly. She is currently recognized as Alice Sapienza Donnelly, but chose as her pen name, Elisa Palombo Sapeinza.

SECOND EDITION

SECOND PRINTING

Copyright 2002, 2007 by Alice Sapienza Donnelly
Elisa Palombo Sapienza (pen name)

ISBN number 978-0-9723654-0-6

All rights reserved. No part of this book may be reproduced, stored in a retrieval system, or transmitted by any means, electronic (including the internet), mechanical, photocopying, recording, or otherwise, without written permission from the author.

DEDICATION

This book is dedicated to all immigrants who shaped America's twentieth century. Although it focuses on the Italian immigrant experience, it can be appreciated by people of other ethnic roots whose ancestors built America.

The struggle and prejudice they faced in their efforts at assimilation are a testimony to immigrant grit and tenacity. Their story reflects ethnic pride, connects us with our past, and promotes understanding of our differences and similarities. It is a legacy to my children and their progeny as a reminder of their splendid past.

CONTENTS

Part IV — Epilogue

ACKNOWLEDGEMENTS

I gratefully acknowledge University of Pittsburgh History Professor, Dr. Jonathan Levine, who suggested that I write this true narrative, which was born in his Genealogy Class in 1972.

This story is a post-mortem tribute to my parents, Paolo and Maria Giuseppa, and my siblings Gracia, Silvio, Domenico and Luigi Palombo, to my husband Salvatore and his parents, Sebastiano and Rosa Sapienza. I thank my children, Rosette, Tom, Jimmy and Frank for their views, and brother-in-law Lee, who shared family photos.

Jacques Millard merits thanks for his proofreading skills. Kudos also to Roey, his wife, to Nicolas Ciotola, Italian Curator at Heinz Hall, and my friend Mary Ann Capezuto. Italian Professor Jan "Gianna" Vairo, O.P.B. and Professor Margaret Bozenna Goscilo deserve credit for their editing skills, and my friend Rick Harris for his Cover design and photography.

Finally, I value the research of eminent historians who have helped verify facts about hardships and prejudices immigrants suffered in their efforts to assimilate. *Grazie Tutti!*

ACCOLADES

Writer's Digest   Category: Inspirational

11thAnnual International Self-Published Book Evaluation

Beyond the Golden Door, by Elisa Palombo Sapienza

"What an amazing recollection of this immigrant Italian family. The author carries the reader along with well told details, anecdotes and dialogue to make these stories immediate. This is interesting valuable history, not just of this one Italian family and the Pennsylvania community they settle in. But, Elisa has done a masterful job of capturing the difficult immigrant experience, the ship passage, going through Ellis Island, assimilating into American culture. She vividly retells this family's hardships, emotional adjustments, discriminations, setbacks and determination to live the good life and overcome such problems. We Americans so often take for granted the good comfortable life we are free to enjoy in the U.S.
This book recounts a vastly important slice of American life, the immigrant experience that helped to lay our nation's foundation – and these experiences should never be forgotten. At least, this is a wonderful family legacy of interest to family members and Italian communities. But this book is much more. Inside there are stories within stories and many people involved in these tales....**This is the stuff of mini-series, family sagas that are often popular in novels and on TV....**"

A *Writer's Digest* reviewer answers this question, "What impressed you most about *Beyond the Golden Door?*"

Ms. Sapienza's book is a nostalgic treasure that families involved will cherish for generations to come. A tale well told with storyteller's flair for detail, dialog, personality and emotion. Her characters come to life from the pages. The addition of humorous anecdotes along with incidents of grief, uncertainty and calamity give this book color and verve....The book's largest and most enthusiastic audience is going to be descendents of thousands of immigrants whose family experiences mirror those in this book...."

The Statue of Liberty lifts her lamp "beside the Golden Door."

INTRODUCTION
From Europe to America

The restless nature of homo sapiens has spurred humans to travel the length and breadth of Planet Earth. But nothing has equalled the force that propelled the greatest numbers to America since the Declaration of Independence. By the nineteenth century, ten to twenty percent who came to America did not survive the Atlantic crossing; and those who did had no guarantee that they would be admitted. The fate of immigrant hopefuls lay in New York Harbor, a half-mile beyond the Statue of Liberty, on three and a half barren acres of Ellis Island. But by the time the statue was in place in 1886, its comforting welcome to immigrants was already out-of-date. For since the 1790 Naturalization Act and the 1798 Alien and Sedition Act, admission and citizenship had become difficult. And being deported was a certainty for anyone judged to be a threat to the peace and safety of America.

The first sight of the Statue of Liberty evoked various emotions among immigrant hopefuls. The enormous impressive statue, officially named *Liberty Enlightening the World*, was the work of Frédéric Auguste Bartholdi, born August 2, 1834 in Colmar, Eastern France. She evolved from a half dozen small-scale models to become the spike-crowned, toga-clad lady with upraised arm bearing Liberty's torch. (Bartholdi actually shifted her torch from her left to her right hand.) When the statue was finished, the Steamer *Isere* entered New York Harbor on June 17, 1885, bearing France's gift of friendship, packed in eighty-some crates. The Lady and the Lamp, universally known as the symbol of freedom, came to rest on Bedloe's Island.

At her dedication ceremony, a poem by Whittier was read. The search for a permanent inscription for her base ended two decades later when the words from Emma Lazarus' poem *The New Colossus* gained attention. The Mother of Exiles cries with silent lips:

> Give me your tired, your hungry, and your poor,
> Your huddled masses yearning to breathe free,
> The wretched refuse of your teeming shores,
> Bring these the homeless tempest-tossed to me,
> I lift my lamp beside the golden door.

Despite the poetic welcome, however, many disappointments waited on Ellis Island in the red-brick Victorian and Byzantine buildings at the threshold of the Golden Door. Once a naval arsenal, this island next to Bedloe's Island opened in 1892 as the immigration reception center to process newcomers to America. For those seeking a new life with better opportunity and freedom from poverty or oppression, this processing involved dread, because a failed physical exam or political test could deny them entry to America.

The most frightening part of the entry process lay at the top of the long slate stairs in the center of the Great Hall. Thousands of immigrant feet clanged their way up to the Board of Doctors, who waited to examine hopeful entrants. They looked for those who limped, had trouble breathing, or scratched at lice. They examined for signs of trachoma, an eye disease, or for presumed signs of mental instability shown by confused frightened immigrants. Newcomers were branded, like cattle, with yellow or blue chalk. Those marked with "E" for eye problems, "L" for limp, "H" for heart, or "M" for mental problems were separated from their loved ones to be re-examined. Those who failed a second examination were stopped on the very doorstep of America, doomed to be deported!

Moreover, although Lady Liberty lifted her lamp beside the Golden Door to welcome those "yearning to breathe free," some Americans were ambivalent about accepting even strong healthy immigrants. Most, who understood why foreigners were needed to populate the country, welcomed them. But those who favored native-born Americans over foreign-born people, in other words nativists, objected to the immigration. Their animosity had begun with early Anglo-Saxon settlers, whose belief in the "Nordic Myth" prejudiced them against dark-haired, brown-eyed foreigners. Early and late nativists openly defamed non-Nordics as inferior and led anti-immigrant movements to stop their entry. Nativism developed in three periods. The first was anti-Catholic, spanning from the 1830's to the mid 1850's, and targeting Irish and German Catholics. Until the mid-twentieth century, anti-Catholicism never completely died out.

The second phase was anti-Asian. It thrived from the early 1870's and culminated in the Chinese Exclusion Act passed in 1882. By President Roosevelt's recommendation, Congress repealed the act in 1943. Later anti-Asian movements were directed against Filipinos and Japanese from

1905 until 1924. Then World War II fueled further Japanese hatred. The anti-Asian phase, like the anti-Catholic phase, was still evident into the mid-twentieth century.

By 1907, more than fourteen million newcomers had been registered, and immigration had become a powerful political issue filled with restrictions and resentment. The third phase, which rejected *all* immigrants, began in the mid-1880's and lasted until the triumph of a general restriction in the passage of the Immigration Act of 1924. Clearly, America had been hostile to the same immigrants that it had officially welcomed.

In 1918, one of the leading nativist propagandists was Madison Grant, whose book *The Passing of a Great Race* popularized the earlier concept of Nordic supremacy. Grant argued that Nordics are superior because they have a light skin, a narrow skull, light hair, and blue eyes. He prophesied all the ills that would befall America "on account of the increase of dark-eyed types." But Edmund Traverso, his contemporary, disagreed. He thought Grant's book created dangerous mischief. In his publication, *Immigration — A Study of American Values*, Traverso censured it as a "dithyrambic praise of the blonde, blue-eyed White and his achievements," calling the book "about as fine an example of dogmatic piffle as has ever been written." Unfortunately, Traverso's clearsightedness was the exception, so there was scarsely a time when nativist attitudes did not exist in American society.

EXPLODING THE "WRETCHED REFUSE" MYTH

Nativists believed or assumed that most immigrants, pushed by catastrophic conditions at home, were rejects who came here with limited skills seeking better lives but offering little in return. Considering this historical view, one can understand Emma Lazarus' derogatory view, expressed in verse beneath Lady Liberty's feet. No doubt, influenced by accepted nativist dogma, she saw the "poor huddled masses" as the "wretched refuse."

Conversely, modern social historians explode this myth. Instead, they confirm that immigrants from every European ethnic group came each with their own talents and expectations, and with the ability and will to survive the animosity that awaited them. For instance, social scientist E.G. Ravenstein studied various ethnic groups. In his 1889 essay "Laws of Migration," he dispelled the myths about immigrants being second-rate, and established that only a minority migrated from their homelands because conditions were intolerable.

Modern immigration historians like Roger Daniels agree with Ravenstein that most felt the "pull" because they sought economic improvement and because their talents fit available opportunities here. Moreover, Daniels disputes nativist beliefs that immigrants had inferior intellects. Preconceived notions about foreigners' lack of intellectual abilities did not square with the "wretched refuse" concept. Immigrant students in America often quit school in early grades, not because of their inferior intellects, but because the language barrier caused them to become discouraged, and because they felt awkward.

The growth of the notion of Nordic European superiority began after the voyages of Columbus and other explorers. Daniels notes that, in the Age of Discovery, not only did Europeans "arrogantly assume their own superiority, but they also disregarded the legitimacy of the civilizations and cultures they encountered," declaring that their contempt "would soon evolve into modern racism." Daniels leaves this admonition: "We who write of the triumphs of modern immigration to America must never forget the societies and peoples whom the newcomers conquered and sometimes exterminated."

PREMIGRATION ITALIANS

One-hundred and fifty years before Pilgrim Fathers stepped upon Plymouth Rock, Massachusetts, in 1620, early Italian seamen explorers had already introduced America to Europe. They were Genoese explorer, Christopher Columbus, who "discovered" America; Florentine navigator, Amerigo Vespucci, for whom America was named; Venetian navigator, Giovanni Caboto [John Cabot], who co-founded New England; and Giovanni da Verrazano, who first sailed into New York Harbor.

Yet, in telling the story of immigration, early American historians have ignored preexisting Old World cultures, and have given their own misinterpretations of immigrant abilities and quality of life in European countries. For example, politically and culturally developed Northern Italians came to America in the 1600's: merchants, physicians, actors, musicians, seamen, stone masons, artists, and sculptors. Venetian glassblowers came as early as

1622. Early migrants brought cross-cultural fables, fairy tales, and stories from European literature.

Roger Daniels records that a surprising number of Italian intellectuals came during the eighteenth and nineteenth centuries. Among the most significant arrivals was Filippo Mazzei, a physician and scholar. Benjamin Franklin convinced Mazzei to go to Virginia and establish Italian agriculture — wine grapes and olives. Mazzei settled near Thomas Jefferson and influenced him and Thomas Paine with his theory on the equality of man, which was written into the Bill of Rights. Jefferson had a broad relationship with Italian immigrants. He recruited Italian masons to build Monticello, his home, and enlisted Italian musicians to help form the United States Marine Band.

Italians made important contributions in the Arts. After his arrival here in 1805, Lorenzo da Ponte, Mozart's libretist and professor of Italian at Columbia University, supervised the building of America's first opera house. Constantino Brumidi has been called the Michelangelo of the United States Capitol. At age seventy, working 180 feet above the floor, he painted the frescoes in the Capitol dome. His fresco of Washington at Yorktown graces the House of Representatives dining room.

In Italy, many premigration Italians were highly respected land owners, *proprietari terriero*. They were town-dwellers who traveled to their farms to cultivate their land. Those who worked under them as peasant farmers were *contadini*, or had followed respectable trades. Some kept a *negozio*, or business. The *calzolaio* fabricated shoes. The *sarto* made clothing. The miller ground grain into flour at the *mulino*, thus the name Mulinaro. Surnames derived from family characteristics, trades, or areas of origin. Ferrante was the iron worker or smith. Sapienza denoted wisdom, Capo Bianco signified a white head, and Romano identified one from Rome.

Thus immigrants coming to America often bore names that indicated their status back home or their respective trades. But inspectors at Ellis Island, who could not understand their names or them, registered distorted surnames. If a foreigner was illiterate or unaware, the new name stuck. Sensing this as an obstacle, some deliberately Anglicized their names to calm their apprehension and escape the rampant prejudice held by self-appointed, superior *americani*. Facetiously, then, the translation of the name Maria Giuseppa Ferrante could yield the Anglicized name, Mary Jo Smith.

Unlike families who changed their names to escape prejudice, the Palombos and Sapienzas, who are the focus of this story, would not corrupt their names. Besides devaluing Italians' status with name changes, Americans assumed that they were illiterate. But contrary to popular myth, most Italian immigrants were not nor did they devalue education. They prized it to varying degrees. Though in many foreign cultures schooling was a matter of choice, social historians confirm in pre-migration history that most Italians were literate. By the 1900's some had even learned to speak and read English before their arrival in America.

PITTSBURGH—ETHNIC PATCH QUILT

The thousands of Europeans who came to the New World in the seventeenth and eighteenth centuries saw opportunites for gain. The growth of industry in the nineteenth century brought mass immigration to industrial cities like Pittsburgh. In its surrounding areas, each nationality settled in ethnic enclaves where the Allegheny and Monongahela Rivers converged to form the Ohio River at a point called the "Golden Triangle." By the 1930's, over sixty-five percent of Pittsburgh's residents were either immigrants or children of immigrants. Each group brought particular skills and customs. Between 1880 and 1910, the two largest immigrant groups to enter Pittsburgh were Poles and Italians. Blacks, Croatians, Czechs, Finns, Germans, Hungarians, Irish, Jews, and Serbs also formed ethnic patch quilts throughout the inner city and in mill towns along the Allegheny and Monongahela Rivers. They lived and shopped in company-built houses, and stores.

German immigrants lived on the North Side. Between the two rivers, Polish immigrants settled on Pittsburgh's Polish Hill. East of the heart of the city, Italian immigrants and Blacks settled in Pittsburgh's Hill District along with Jewish immigrants. By the 1920's the Jewish community had moved east to Oakland. Italians and Blacks had moved from the Hill to East Liberty and Homewood. The Irish located in Garfield, Lawrenceville and Homewood. Italians from Abruzzi settled in Bloomfield, where they have lived since early 1900. An Italian mix populated Homewood-Brushton. By 1920, more than 14,000 Italians lived in the city.

With the development of trolley lines, newcomers broke the cultural mold and left the inner city to live in the upper-class neighborhoods of

Homewood, where elite financial and industrial tycoons Andrew Carnegie, John Heinz II, Henry Clay Frick, Andrew Mellon, and George Westinghouse had settled between 1860—1910. "Millionaire's Row" eventually became Point Breeze. By 1980, multiethnic Homewood was a Black Community.

ADAPTERS AND SURVIVORS

Work dominated the lives of immigrants to the Steel City. The ability to secure jobs was the key to surviving and improving the family's upward mobility. Pittsburgh's steel mills attracted large numbers of Polish and Italian immigrants at the turn of the century. Laborers in the mills helped acculturate them into industry. About two thirds of the Poles became mill hands with little opportunity to move up the corporate hierarchy. Italian men experienced the same lack of upward mobility; but by 1910 many had deserted the mills in favor of construction work.

Through the *Padrone* system, Italian labor contractors provided jobs for a fee. Because discrimination hampered their advancement, precocious Italians were driven to succeed. Using their Mediterranean talents, they created new businesses in the building trades, in landscape gardening, and in wholesale and retail food stores.

Family and ethnic bonds were strong. Each nationality formed mutual aid societies that provided benefits for illness and death. They built ethnic churches and parochial schools, promoted social functions and nurtured Old World traditions. Relatives and friends accommodated immigrants with living space. Those who could not weather the obstacles returned home defeated. Successful immigrants took risks, adapted and survived. Their concept of America, contrary to the legendary "streets paved with gold," was realistic. They had learned, and taught their children, that the way to success was working hard and sacrificing present desires for future gains. This was the very philosophy embraced by their early Anglo-Saxon forebears, whose descendants failed to see the commonality.

This philosophy was shared by the Palombo and Sapienza families, who migrated to pursue the "American dream." They brought proud and turbulent histories and the tenacity to succeed. Like many immigrants, they walked into Anglo-American "arrogant superiority" and challenged its obstacles. They came to Pittsburgh, Pennsylvania, a mosaic of cultures and classes living harmoniously side by side in Homewood. And, like earlier elite upper-class Homewood suburbanites, they helped establish their own ethnic version of the American dream. Their experiences parallel those reported by historians who recorded the social history of Italians and other newcomers who lived "in the shadow of the mills." This anecdotal social history is a tribute to all immigrants, each group with its unique stories, who have collectively contributed to the rich history of immigration that has made America the great country that she is. Well done! *Bravi tutti!*

Part I: The Early Years

Chapter 1

The Dream and the Distant Magnet

This account of a bygone era begins in the Italian region once called Abruzzi — later re-named Abruzzo e Molise, and rests in America where many hopeful immigrants overcame the obstacles that awaited them in the New World on Ellis Island and beyond the Golden Door. An immigrant's daughter reveals the attitudes of twentieth century America as she presents its social history through family experiences and true anecdotes. Who has not been fascinated by four enchanting words that often begin a story?

"Once upon a time," in the village of Castellino Sul Biferno, nestled in the Abruzzi hills, lived Maria Giuseppa Ferrante and Paolo Palombo, two young people who would one day share a common destiny. Their village in Provincia Campo Basso had changed little since the Middle Ages, when in 1011 its Latin name was Castrum Eudolini. Feudal Baron Andrea di Isernia, under the reign of King Ruggero, won title to the lands in 1140. When its citizens won certain rights of possession in 1300, the *paese* became Castellino di Lino, and finally Castellino Sul Biferno, meaning little castle above the Biferno River, and referring to an ancient castle atop the village, where the visibility was seven miles — not an unlikely lookout point against possible intruders.

The name and setting hold the implication of a fairy tale, where boy and girl meet and live happily ever after. Their story, however, is not make-believe. Rather it is a tale of their immigration to the New World that begins before the turn of the century.

Maria Giuseppa lived with her sister, Arcangela, and their mother, Mamma Maria Luigi. The girls played and scampered up and down the village hillside, tending their little flock of sheep in bare feet, saving their only shoes for Sunday Mass. Their father, Domenico Ferrante, the village metal craftsman, died when they were young. The orphans scarcely remembered their Papa. Of necessity, Mamma Maria Luigi remarried and was soon widowed a second time.

Maria Giuseppa's *paesano,* Paolo Palombo, son of Pietro Paolo Palombo and grandson of Nicolo Palombo, was orphaned at age five when he and his sister Nicola lost their mother, Filomena, during childbirth in 1886. Ten-year-old Nicola became his surrogate mother for two years until their father remarried a widow whose daughter was six years old.

Paolo, *il povero sfortunato*, was orphaned again when his father died a hero's death. At age twelve he assumed the responsibility of manhood. Pietro had left him with a strong sense of the value of hard work and an indelible memory of bravery. The story of his death became a legend.

Villagers mourned for their hero. Pietro had saved many *paesani* and their sheep from certain death when the waters from the swollen *fiume* unexpectedly flooded the peninsula where their sheep grazed. Courageously, Pietro had carried townspeople and sheep one by one on his broad shoulders to safety, before the waters could claim them. With each struggle toward shore, his six-foot frame bent further, until he fell exhausted in his little stone hut not far from the *fiume*. He was too spent to climb the steep hillside to his house. For several days, he lay gravely ill and finally yielded his life to *pulmonite* — pneumonia.

When his father died, the work that fell to Paolo was not alien. He had been accustomed to doing farm chores before and after his school day. And now, with his stepmother, sister, and villagers who rotated their help, Paolo farmed the land, tended the animals, preserved smoked meats, and made olive oil, wine, and cheese.

One day as he worked, Paolo reminisced about the time that Cico, the frisky family mule, had balked against moving up the vertical hillside to the *piazza*. Each time his father had prodded Cico to carry his heavy cargo, the mule had refused to move. Pietro had given him a smart slap on the rump and pulled his ears. Hard! From that day forward, the mule would kick wildly at Pietro who, in the end, had to keep his distance. The mule became a safe haven when Paolo felt his father's menacing wrath. He smiled through tears at the memory.

Between farm chores, he worked resolutely at his studies. School for every child began at age seven, and for four years was rigorous and compulsory. At the end of those primary grades, students knew arithmetic, and could spell and read well enough to lift them from illiteracy. The parish priest sometimes helped children in the rudiments of advanced reading and figures to better prepare them for the strict *maestri* in the secondary grades.

Reading was a prized distinction. Most villagers learned to read Latin in order to respond to the Latin Mass. Religious songs and stories, the Gospels, and letters from friends and relatives in America were incentives for learning. Paolo himself hoped one day to attend school in Milano, as his father had intended. The plan was abandoned when tragedy struck again.

His sister, Nicola, was soon to be married. She had only a modest dowry — certainly less than the generous *dote* Papa Pietro would have given her. Life with their stepmother had been hard for Paolo and Nicola. To rescue him from her abuse, Nicola had planned to take Paolo to live with her and her new husband. But her groom adamantly refused to take the boy. She was not in a position to bargain. At the thought of leaving her *Paolino* behind, a deeply depressed Nicola grieved. And grieved. On the eve of her wedding day, Nicola died — of a broken heart, it was later said. She had cared deeply about *Paolino*'s future and his education.

However, as things worsened after Nicola's death, *Il povero orfanello* had to finally be taken in by his father's brother, *Zio* Valentino Palombo. A determined Paolo completed the eight grades of secondary school to qualify him for higher schooling in Milano. But here his formal education ended, because the money his father had set aside for his education had been depleted by his stepmother.

Paolo set his own course for education. He borrowed books from the parish priest and read the history of two great Italian men: Amerigo Vespucci and Cristoforo Colombo. Their voyage to a new world intrigued young Paolo, and he dreamed about America. He read famous literary stories. Because of the strong oral tradition of storytelling, Paolo recounted these to village children — as he would eventually tell them to his own children. He read family Bibles, written in Italian and Latin.

By the time he was twenty, Paolo's stepmother had died, and her daughter had married. But, the resourceful Paolo had accumulated enough *soldi* to buy the land alongside the land bequeathed him from his father. By the 1800's, when nearly 2,000 *paesani* populated the hills in the Abruzzi provinces, the valley had been enriched for centuries by the mountain water from their hillsides above the Fiume Biferno. It splashed over the rocks into the fertile valley, then fell into the Biferno and flowed to the Adriatic Sea. Maria Nascia of Boiana recorded that by the mid 1800's, the government had accessed the water from the *fiume* and piped it to the Abruzzi villages of Boiana, Montavano, Petrelle, Morrona, Lucite, Castello Buttaccio, Aquilla, Ateleta, and Molisano.

Pietro would have been proud of his son, for, by village standards, Paolo became highly respected as a *proprietario* — landowner. Since ancient times, land had been valued above money. Paolo's farm lands were lush with vegetables, fig trees, olive groves, and vineyards. To supply meats for his table, he kept a family of animals: several piglets, chickens, and lambs. Sheep and goats were a resource for cheeses. While he did not live in poverty, Paolo lived simply, and happily, with his wife, Maria Giuseppa, and their little Grazia.

Maria Giuseppa Ferrante had become his secret *biondina* — blonde sweetheart — years ago. Her eyes were as blue as his own. He had teased her, carried her slate to school, and thought of marrying her one day. His attraction began in childhood. The memory of an incident when Maria was five years old amused Paolo and gained his admiration thereafter. Nearly every day Maria stole into the schoolroom to hear *la maestra* read stories. She memorized them and decided that she would learn to read. On examination day the province schoolmaster came to test the students. He asked for a volunteer to read. Maria, crouched in her favorite corner, impulsively shot her hand into the air and begged to read: *"Signor Maestro, voglio leggere."*

The startled schoolmaster spied Maria, pondered about the little girl with the dirty face and asked, *"Ma chi è questa ragazza con la faccia sporca?"* He gestured her to come forward and offered Maria the book. She recited the page — perfectly. The amused schoolmaster knew she was not reading, but rewarded her with a little sack full of *dolci*. Maria snatched the sweets, and hastily curtsied her thanks, *"Grazie, signor maestro."* She ran home as fast as she could, to avoid the children who would surely follow like a swarm of bees.

Paolo had kept careful watch over this bright spirited little girl. As his admiration grew, so did his love for her. When he was convinced that his early thoughts about having her for a wife were exactly right, Paolo engaged his friends to help serenade her at her window. Among them was his best *amico* Domenico Stanziano. Paolo's intentions were clear — and public.

Maria would live in his house. Paolo knew she would have a small dowry to bring to the marriage. He had planned ahead and acquired new towels, pots, pans, and cutlery. He built a handsome wide shelf above the hearth to hold their Bibles and new housewares. And made a handsome wide bench for their hearth place.

An Italian girl in those days began to prepare her *dote* early. Since Maria had been orphaned, her dowry would be modest. She sewed two dresses, several new aprons and undergarments for her wardrobe. She and Mamma had frugally saved *spiccioli* to barter many eggs and a piglet to acquire the cotton to make four sheets and covers for four feather pillows. Maria edged these in beautiful lace. She and Mamma made a new feather mattress, covered in coarse muslin, and six tovagliette to serve as kitchen towels. For her bridal bed, Maria gave the beautiful heavy lace spread she had crocheted as a younger *signorina*. With her dowry, she brought her most precious gift. From her small flock of sheep, Maria sheared the wool, spun and dyed the threads — red and black — and wove a huge plaid blanket. She edged the top in black velvet and embroidered her initials, M. G. F. She and Mamma sewed her long, brown wool wedding skirt and made a white silk *camicetta* and white lace *sciarpa* to cover her head and shoulders. New hightop shoes, Mamma's gold cross and earrings, and *un mazzolino di fiore* from Mama's flower bed, completed Maria's wedding attire.

The village band would accompany the newlyweds from the church to an outdoor feast. Paolo had slaughtered a lamb and piglet to roast over a *carboni* and wood fire, and brought cheeses and fruits for the *festa*. Mamma had prepared *pasta fatto a mano con salsa, e insalata verde con pomodori, e olive* — homemade *pasta* with sauce, a green salad with tomatoes and olives.

Mamma Luigi was proud of her daughters. It was time now to help Arcangela prepare her *dote*, for from all signs, Antonio Palumbo, not related to Paolo, would soon serenade *her*.

Paolo promised his new *sposa* that Mamma Maria Luigi would always be cared for. He vowed to move Mamma into his house one day, and to build Maria Giuseppa a new stone house with a fine balcony.

Paolo was able — and adventurous. He knew that his family's future in Italy extended no further than the livelihood that his lands provided. For the intelligent young man, whose opportunities had been thwarted by misfortune, this was not future enough for his family. Paolo had been conditioned by his father to expect more than farming as his life's work. Although he felt remorse that his dream for more education was shattered, he was an eternal optimist.

And so was Maria Giuseppa. Together, they considered the opportunity of one day building a new dream beyond the boundaries of Abruzzi. Paolo had grown more curious about America each time he read letters from townsmen who had migrated to the *terra d'oro.* They wrote about immigrants who spoke many tongues. Through the village *giornale,* he learned more about the New World discovered by Cristoforo Colombo. America beckoned.

One day when Paolo and his donkey had transported fresh fruits and vegetables up the steep hillside to the *piazza,* villagers gathered to hear the latest information from their *paesani*, recently returned from America. Some *ritornati* were migrants who had made several trips across the Atlantic between 1904 and 1907, when immigration from Naples had peaked. Temporary migration was typical at that time. But some men, preferring to stay in America, never returned to the wives who were identified as *vedove bianche*, widows who dressed in white. Others only migrated to gain temporary advantage for their families in Italy.

Townsmen assailed the *ritornati* with questions. As they listened, excitement about opportunities in America increased. Paolo Palombo, imbued with the spirit of Marco Polo, Amerigo Vespucci, and Cristoforo Colombo, listened with heightened curiosity and enthusiasm, and confirmed his desire to emigrate. Like many migrants, he saw America as an opportunity to make a good life even better for his family in Italy by earning money to send home.

The adventurous risk-taker and his wife planned his first voyage. By the grace of God and Vittorio Emanuele III, Re D'Italia, he would leave after spring planting in 1904. Paolo and Maria, experienced at adapting to challenges, were confident that she could manage the farm. As the *padrona*, Maria would oversee wine-making and food processing. The peasant farmers — *contadini* — would help harvest vegetables, grapes, figs, and olives. Mamma Maria Luigi would help nurture little Grazia.

The day before his departure was a special occasion that called for eating meat. Maria prepared homemade pasta and chicken soup over the hearth fire. The outdoor oven was filled with bread, *pizza* and *biscotti*. Cheeses, dried meats, figs, and olives, together with new wine for the adults, and goat's milk for the children, completed the bon-voyage meal they shared with family and friends. They sang and danced. They cried and prayed to *Dio* and *Santa Lucia*, patron saint of travelers.

Early that morning, Paolo and Maria had climbed the steps of the Via San Piedro, with their townsmen, to the Santa Chiesa, where they received the priest's blessing and Holy Communion, and prayed for Paolo's safe journey. Paolo reminisced about the Good Fridays when he had tramped along that same Path of St. Peter, in the *Via Croce*. He had portrayed Paul, Christ's disciple, in the procession of the Way of the Cross. His Maria had personified the tortured Blessed Mother searching for her Son. Paolo remembered her beautiful, soulful voice chanting compassionately, to processioners along the way, *"Il figlio mio dov'e?"*

Paolo cleared his throat and crossed himself. They would not sing *a cappella* at Holy Mass for a long time. For comfort, Paolo thought about reuniting with his *amici* in America. As Maria and Paolo lay close in warm embrace, Maria remembered an Italian adage that Mamma spoke when she cautioned that one who takes a new road and leaves the old behind, knows what he leaves but knows not what he will find: *"Caro Paolo, chi lascia la strada vecchia, per quella nuova, sa quello che lascia, ma non quello che trova."* There was little sleep that night.

Chapter 2

La Porta d' Oro — The Golden Door

Paolo Palombo would carry his father's name proudly to America. Pietro had taught him always to carry it proudly and honorably. Pietro Paolo Palombo, son of Genario Palombo, was descended from post-feudal landowners, a respected distinction when owning land was a measure of prosperity. Paolo was proud of his father's legacy — a respect for learning. One of his uncles had become a priest, one the town's *sindaco* — mayor, another was a musician who played in the village band, and cousin Carmella became a nun and teacher.

Paolo was also proud of his name, officially recorded in ancient heraldic archives and depicted on his coat of arms as a *colomba*, a pigeon or dove. In Catholic liturgy, the dove has been a symbol of the Holy Ghost, a symbol of peace. Surnames defined a person's personal traits, occupation, or place of residence. Paolo remembered hearing that immigrants' names, when they reached America, were sometimes distorted, or misspelled. He decided, before he went to the Naples port of embarkation, that the *americani* would not misspell or corrupt his name.

Before his first crossing in 1904, Paolo learned that those who appeared to be physically or mentally impaired, or were perceived to be political dissenters, would be turned away. Although there were fewer limits on immigration, there were still various restrictions. *Paesani* at the *piazza* had described how in the examining rooms men stripped to the waist to be examined, and women underwent hair inspections for lice. Eyelids were turned inside out and examined for trachoma. Armed with knowledge, he carefully planned his strategy.

In Naples, he went to the *Opera Assistenza Emigranti.* At the Immigrant Office he arranged passage, then joined hundreds of immigrants with whom he would share steerage on the crowded boat. Paolo recorded expenses, observations, stories about America, and his reactions so that he might learn from his experience. Maria would be anxious for every detail when he sent her letters.

Being foresighted, Paolo already had places to stay in America. There were *paesani* in Niles, Ohio; in Pittsburgh, Pennsylvania; and the village of Clyde, New York. He was sure his voyage to America would help him realize a dream to improve his family's future in Italy. There might even be the possibility of a future in America. Life had taught him to take risks, have courage, and adapt.

On shipboard, the outgoing adventurer made many friends, and absorbed all the information he could extract from immigrants who had crossed before. Since the assassination of President McKinley in 1903 by an American Anarchist with a foreign-sounding name, Congress had demanded a probe of the political opinions of incoming immigrants. Paolo, unaware of the law, only knew that *americani* Customs officials were strict about political attitudes. He had asked the *ritornati* about questions he would have to answer, taking care to record and study them carefully. And he memorized essential American words. The new language fascinated him. Paolo was ready.

He explored the vessel and conversed with shipmen. He was fascinated by the "dit dit da-dit" of wireless telegraphy and nodded his head vigorously when one of the shipmen said the familiar name Marconi, who had discovered wireless telegraphy. One day, he was destined to hear those sounds again on an unforgettable date with Fate.

Paolo was like a curious child, eager to learn, but limited by language, and somewhat humiliated that he could not fluently express his thoughts. Perhaps his *paesano* Domenico Angelo in Niles, Ohio, would help him. Paolo had selected his destination carefully from the descriptions he had heard, and decided New York City would not be one of them. Niles seemed to be more like his own farm land. He already anticipated hard work. But he was accustomed to it and unafraid. He reminisced about the joyous times with *paesani* at harvest time. The sharks swimming about the boat, as they looked for food or dead bodies, startled him out of his reverie. He wrote Maria about the fish that were bigger than horses.

Fifteen days later, he was fascinated to watch seagulls dive toward the water, with eyes intent on luckless fish. He remembered the seagulls that flew over the coast of the Adriatic Sea when he and Maria visited cousins in Campo Basso, and missed her.

Suddenly, land appeared amid cries of *"Ecco la terra!"* Paolo saw *la magnifica Statua della Libertà*, as the ship sailed into New York Harbor. The statue symbolized *la porta oro* — "the golden door" to America, characterized in the poem inscribed at her feet. The ship's horns blasted mightily. He was overwhelmed. Tugs and ferry boats slipped among large ships. He waited eagerly for the boat that would ferry him to Ellis Island — the place immigrants had come to dread for fear of being branded "undesirable" as *alleged* political or health hazards.

But Paolo was not afraid. He stood tall and confident under his brimmed hat and smoothed the lapels of his only suit. Coming from sunny Italy, he owned no overcoat. He sat patiently on the long bench between the unending maze of iron rails, waiting for his health exam and for his Immigration Health Inspection Card to be stamped "APPROVED." He remembered that immigrants had to be physically and mentally sound to pass, and pulled himself even taller as he approached the physician.

Paolo was relieved to pass the exam and be chalk-marked with a bold yellow letter. Those who were chalk-marked in blue letters, such as "H" for heart trouble, or "LPC," likely to become a public charge, were to be deported. Those who pleaded their case were sent to the Board of Special Inquiry room. Paolo envisioned his own Maria Giuseppa and children in that predicament, cleared his throat — and prayed for those unfortunate passengers.

His next hurdle was customs. His modest neatly-packed valise passed quickly through customs inspection. He smiled and said "Allo" and answered questions pleasantly. Paolo was ready when the inspector asked, "Are you an Anarchist?"

"No *Anarchista!* Me want be *Americano*," he answered firmly. The customs inspector smiled and tapped his shoulder. Paolo crossed himself and thanked God and the saints for a safe landing and clearance. He soon found himself herded through the turnstile toward the green door and the boat that would ferry him to land. America at last!! *Grazie, Dio!*

There would be several hours to explore New York City before he boarded the train for Niles, Ohio. Paolo walked among the towering buildings. He came upon rows and rows of steps that fronted rows and rows of doors, and windows stacked high, where clothes hung from the sky. There were horses and wagons, fruit stalls and shop fronts, noisy children and adults who seemed to be running everywhere and nowhere. A man with a push-cart was selling fruit. Another man, with a little monkey scurrying at the end of his leash, cranked a huge box on wheels that produced organ music. *"Ecco, Ecco!"* he cried in Italian as he shook his cup for change. What a terrible way to make a living, Paolo thought as he deposited several precious American coins in the cup.

He would write to Maria: *"New York e un bosco di grande edifici — e puzza! Non è per me."* Paolo saw New York as a stench-filled forest of big structures, and decided that it was not the place for him. Already he missed his farm. At the station Paolo met red-capped friendly men with black, smiling faces. Paolo smiled back and said, "Allo!"

In Niles, Ohio, he was reunited with his *amico*, Domenico Angelo, where he shared a modest room in a private boarding house owned by an Italian family. There he met Italians from central and southern Italy, all with their own dialects. He was happy to find newspapers printed in Italian, and became absorbed in American politics, and especially Teddy Roosevelt's election.

The new arrival found it easy to get work. Jobs were plentiful, if one would accept anything that was offered. What choice was there for a man who spoke no English? Most immigrants started out as manual laborers. One of the great changes of the century was industrialization. With the introduction of machines, skilled workers were needed to produce hardware items such as nails, nuts, bolts and chains. Workers were hired to fabricate small parts for machines. Paolo found work in a factory where he was trained in the manufacture of small parts. In the summer, he worked part-time as a farm hand, in order to save money enough to send home to Maria and Mamma. His needs were simple, and he sometimes sacrificed necessities in order to save. Fellow immigrants sacrificed just as intensely. Some shared overcoats when they worked staggered shifts. Being cheerful by nature, Paolo did not complain. He wrote Maria colorful details about American life, and told her about the comfort he felt in attending Holy Mass.

The Latin Mass was universal, his link to home. The ritual and vestments were familiar. No matter how tired he felt, he looked forward to Sundays. When the priest lifted the gold chalice, Paolo joyously chanted the Latin responses. Although Latin hymns were part of the Catholic Mass, many non-Italian Catholic immigrants did not sing Latin. During Benediction his clear tenor voice sang out *"O Salutaris Ostia!"* He was bewildered when

American faces turned and looked. He thought of Maria and how they sang the Latin and Italian hymns.

On his first Christmas in America, Paolo missed hearing the *Pastorale*. It was the traditional story of the Nativity that he and Maria sang in harmony. He imagined his *paesani* reliving the story of Bethlehem. Paolo reminisced how *campanelli* pealed joyously, as shepherd *zampognari* played their bagpipes among the hills and led the holy procession toward the *presepio*. At the manger scene, huge statues with delicate faces waited for the arrival of *Bambino Jesu*. He missed home.

Paolo found more *paesani* when he explored Pittsburgh, Pennsylvania. Although Pittsburgh's dark, smokey skies did not appeal to him, there was abundant work of every kind. Here he could earn enough money to send home. Some immigrants did hard labor for $1.25 a day. Paolo earned $2.50 a day ($15 a week) and set aside $5 for room and board, $3 to spend for himself, and sent home $7 a week — a decent sum then. Any extra money he earned went into an American bank account.

Before leaving America, Paolo decided to visit the little village of Clyde, New York, where Maria's cousins, the Di Lisios, lived. Rafaelo, Frederico, Carolina, and Filomena had settled on small farms that reminded Paolo of home.

When he met Carolina DiSanto's little son Alessandro, he thought of Grazia, unaware that one day the two children's paths would cross. He asked many questions of the cousins — and toyed with the idea of making America his new home. In two years Paolo had saved a good nest egg. It was time to return to Abruzzi.

He had made many new friends and had learned enough English so that he could feel more confident the next time he came. He would not forget Americans' fascination with the Wild West, nor their love for George Washington, who was like their king, he thought, and for President Teddy Roosevelt, who wore big cowboy hats. Most of all, he would not forget his newest love, grand opera. Paolo was overwhelmed! Operas had never been performed in his village. He had taken a train to Chicago to hear the great Italian tenor Enrico Caruso, and was spellbound by his powerful voice singing *arias* from *Aida*. He bought the *libretto* to take to Maria Giuseppa. One day he and Maria would sing the love song *Celeste Aida,* he decided. Paolo learned that Italian operas, like *Lucia di Lammermoor* and others, had been performed in the American West one hundred years before. He was proud of Italy's musical gift to America.

The mood of the time was upbeat, perhaps a reflection of Teddy Roosevelt's energetic and optimistic "can do" influence. It was a time of opportunity and confidence. Historians had recorded it variously as the "Age of Optimism," the "Cocksure Era" and the "Age of Innocence." And although life for immigrants was hard, the work ethic "you must earn what you have" was like his own. Men dominated the workplace and retreats such as saloons and barbershops, where they could exchange news, gain helpful leads to jobs, and get a shave and a haircut for "two bits" (25 cents.) To naive Paolo, these retreats were a surprise. There were no saloons or barbershops in his village.

Paolo considered the possibility that Maria might enjoy the opportunities here. He would have to prepare her for a monumental transition. He knew that she would not want to leave Mamma. He wrote her about fascinating things he had never seen: the telephone, the typewriter, the sewing machine, and conveyances that moved about the city without being drawn by horse or donkey (although rare, the first automobiles had made their debut at the turn of the century.) He wrote Maria about *negozi* where people who did not have farms could buy vegetables, eggs, meat, and ready-baked bread. To entice her further, he told her about very big *negozi* where one could buy every manner of ready-made clothing and *mobilia*, furniture, including a *gabinetto* that magically kept food cold to keep it from spoiling.

Paolo could hardly contain himself from telling about entertainments. He described vaudeville, and the circus with animals much bigger than the live monkeys that the traveling expositions brought to Castellino. But he stopped short of describing the Can-Can chorus girls at the *teatro*. She had never seen a theater performance, or chorus girls. He decided that if Maria ever came to America, he definitely would play a practical joke on her. The playful Paolo formed a mischievous idea for *un grande scherzo*. Paolo sold hard. He wrote that she would feel at home in America because his fellow Italians and immigrants from other countries had brought their customs with them. He assured her that while the streets were not made of gold, opportunities were.

He prepared for his voyage home in 1906. He would pack neatly, have his travel papers in order and shop for presents. For Maria, he bought a pair of high-button shoes. She had traced her tiny foot pattern on paper for him. His gift for Grazia was an American baby doll, and for Mamma and Arcangela he bought stockings. Tonight Paolo would have a *festa di buon viaggio* with his *amici* and drink *vino di casa* made from bought grapes. He was a moderate man; he would stop short of becoming *ubbriaco* — drunk.

Paolo was fascinated with the many languages spoken by fellow immigrants. He had begun to learn some of their phrases and greeted them in their language. He accepted his Americanized first name, Paul. America was a truly amazing mix. He liked what he had found and decided that one day he would return with his family. The lure to America was powerful.

Chapter 3

The Magnetic Pull Unites Two Families

The Corso and the Sapienza families from Sicily were pulled to America by the same distant magnet. One day their paths would cross with the Palombo family from Abruzzi. But beyond the Golden Door, they would face the anti-immigrant attitudes which had been greeting newcomers to America since the days of the Massachusetts Bay colony.

For over four centuries, Colonists had formed strong prejudices and suspicions about how foreigners from certain parts of Europe behaved and looked. They favored fair, Nordic-looking people, believing them to be a superior race. Southern Italians, they believed, were less educated and skilled than their northern counterparts, and were "dark and swarthy" and somehow inferior. Anglos were unaware that, given the heterogeneous nature of Sicily, many were fair-skinned, red-haired, Nordic-looking and gifted.

In the face of strong prejudice against them, a few early newcomers had turned to illegal activity to survive, thereby casting a negative stigma upon honest Sicilians for several generations. In the mid-twentieth century, films about Prohibition Era gangsters, the *Cosa Nostra*, and the *Mafia* created an enduring image of Italians as international criminals. Of course, immigration historian Professor Roger Daniels has recently noted that "the notion of an international Mafia conspiracy dominating all Italian American crime is a foolish one." He demonstrates that, contrary to popular impressions, Sicilians have proven to be honest, astute in business, and talented in the arts. But the stereotype was far from being challenged back in the first year of the twentieth century.

It was into this climate of animosity toward Mediterraneans that fair-skinned, red-haired Francesco Corso, an enterprising tradesman from Palermo, Sicily, came to America and became a successful *mercante*. In 1895, Francesco's father, Liborio, had visited America to investigate the possibility of establishing business in the New World. *Paesani* invited him to Pittsburgh, which was humming with industry. But Liborio, preferring the beauty of sunny Sicily to the gray smokey American city, returned to his prosperous livelihood and family in Sicily.

However his sons, Francesco and his brother Santo, developed an attraction to America. In 1906, they came with their wives, followed by their sister Maria and her husband, and their brothers Giuseppi and Antonino. The intelligent brothers could not tolerate the lowly laborers' jobs available to them. Out of necessity, they made their own opportunities, and like their father, were forced to succeed as *mercanti,* with their wives who worked beside them.

Their little sister Rosa, a generation younger, lived in Palermo with their parents, in a stone and marble three-story home in affluent Termini Alto, a beautiful *paese* overlooking the Mediterranean Sea. Rosa was proud and quick to distinguish it from Termini Basso, the fishing village below. The architecture reflected Spanish influence: tile roof, marble floors, stairs and balustrades. The rooftop garden was filled with colorful flowers and miniature potted lemon trees, and housed pigeons, where squabs were raised as a gourmet delicacy.

Rosa's father, Liborio Corso, had been successful in business since the 1800's. Like his father Santo, he transported vegetables, fruits and other staples by mule caravan along the *corso* throughout the surrounding countryside. His wife, Salvatrice, a sharp business woman, kept a well-stocked *negozio* of fresh foods, staples and variety goods. To keep her accounts accurate, she used an abacus to total her customers' purchases. One word fittingly describes their lifestyle. *Abbondanza* — abundance.

In another Sicilian city, Lentini, there lived a young musician who would change Rosa Concetta Corso's life. He was Sebastiano Sapienza. For centuries, the Sapienza family had roots in Lentini, the home of Plato, ambassador to the Athenian Senate in Greece. Their surname, a highly respected name for centuries, combined *sapere (*to know) and *saggezza* (wisdom,) like the Greek name Sophia. The human species is called *homo sapiens,* the scientific name for modern man. The Italian university is *la sapienza,* and the name has been chanted in the Latin Mass — *"salis sapienza."*

It is logical to conclude that there was genetic co-mingling, for Sicily, at the tip of the Italian boot, was easily accessible to Greece from across the Ionian Sea. Commuting between the two areas was commonplace during the Golden Age, when the greatest minds converged in Sicily — not always by choice. Philosophers and teachers who challenged the gods and accepted beliefs were banished from Greece to Sicily. Or, condemned to die like Socrates, were given a cup of poison hemlock.

Greek culture had influenced Sicily since before 600 B.C. Accessible from the Strait of Messina, and the Mediterranean and Ionian Seas, it attracted seafarers from Africa and greater Europe. Inter-cultural evidence found in the ruins on the Sicilian Plain of the Greeks indicates that it had also been inhabited by Arabs, Phoenicians, and Spaniards. A rich cultural mixture would come together with the Sapienza and the Corso family, who had Spanish roots.

The city of Lentini was noted for its lively markets, artisans and street musicians. As an artisan, Salvatore hand-fashioned shoes and, as a musician, played baritone saxhorn in the town band. Marianna and Salvatore were teachers at heart. Marianna, exceptionally talented in tailoring and needle-work, instructed her daughter Vincenzina, who became a *Maestra Singera* — a name derived from the Singer sewing machine. Vincenzina taught tailoring, embroidery, crocheting and related crafts. She made altar scarves for the Basilica in Rome. In gratitude, the Holy Father sent her beautiful towels embroidered with the Sacred Heart.

Salvatore taught his sons music when they were very young. He began teaching Sebastiano, at age seven, to play the baritone saxhorn. The instrument was heavy for the budding musician. When he first heard arpeggios being played on the clarinet, he abandoned the cumbersome horn. He became so attached to his clarinet that he took it to his bed to play and play.

Sebastiano's love of music attracted him to an early professional career. At age fourteen he performed in local bands and for silent films in theater orchestras. Sebastiano was an achiever. He studied English and enrolled at the University of Palermo Music School, where he studied theory and began composing. To earn his tuition, he worked for an attorney as a translator of Italian/English. His creativity, reflected in his beautiful handwriting, led him to practice calligraphy. This talent would serve him well one day.

After finishing his music study at the university, he left home when he was eighteen to audition at Caltanasetta, and won a position in the opera house orchestra. His performance in the quartet from *Rigoletto* moved the audience and brought a warm reaction. That evening, Sebastiano's dynamics and interpretation so impressed the conductor of the Termini Imerese Opera House that the *Maestro* offered him a position in Palermo as clarinet soloist.

His move to Termini Imerese sealed his destiny. As Sebastiano practiced his music, a signorina who lived across the *strada* sat on her balcony and listened. Rosa, daughter of Liborio Corso and Salvatora Diega Corso, attracted Sebastiano's notice. He charmed the dark-haired, hazel-eyed beauty with his music. Sebastiano composed a song, *Rosa,* whose sweet melody told his love for her. A proposal soon followed. They planned to be married in the Chiesa Santa Madre in Termini Imerese.

Since their sons and daughter had settled in America, the Corso parents found their home empty. Rosa, born to her parents late in life, was passionately close to them. They filled her every wish and welcomed the prospective newlyweds to live in their spacious house. The union would bring together two families who were talented in the arts and astute in business.

At her wedding, on June 11, 1911, Rosa wore a floor-length wedding dress, handmade for her by Vincenzina Sapienza. She had also made the traditional *abito d'otto giorno* — a dress for the eighth day that brides traditionally wore when they emerged from seclusion after the wedding.

Salvatrice kissed her daughter and pushed a jeweled bone comb into Rosa's upswept hair. Salvatore's biggest cart and donkey, pronounced *"sheko"* in Sicilian dialect, was adorned with bright flowers, and waited to carry the bride to the nearby church.

The musicians had gathered on the *strada*. Sebastiano, his brothers Delfino, Francesco, and their father would join them when festivities began after the wedding and *Santa Messa.* In the dining hall, tables were piled high with dried meats, cheeses, nuts, olives, a variety of pasta, and delicacies from sunny Sicily's lush farms: enormous oranges, lemons, grapefruit, peaches, figs, and grapes. Candy *confetti,* pastries and special wines were ready for a feast befitting the daughter of a prosperous *mercante.*

Salvatrice Diega Corso, of royal lineage, was happy for her daughter — and hopeful that Rosa might produce a son to inherit the Diega fortune. The bequest, valid for five generations, had been left specifically for a son to use for his education to the priesthood. It would be worthless to Rosa's brothers, who had emigrated to America. Salvatrice prayed that Rosa might produce a son in this fifth generation to qualify for the legacy.

Rosa Corso Sapienza was proud of the rich cultural legacy her groom brought to their marriage. What a fitting name, Sapienza! History validates it as a mark of the family's intelligence. Salvatore and Marianna Sapienza's children, Carmelina, Lavinia, Vicenzina, Delfino and Luigi had migrated to professional careers in Florence, Rome, Pisa, Milan and Tripoli. Their grandchildren subsequently proved their success in careers as teachers, lawyers, and multilingual professionals.

Rosa adored her handsome talented and popular Sebastiano, and secretly worried about other women when he was away performing. One evening when she was attending the opera, she saw admiring women soliciting his attention. Rosa Concettina fumed! At the next performance when the *signorinas* approached Sebastiano, she walked boldly up to their little circle, hugged him and brazenly lit a cigarette! And later threatened to do it again! The gentle, vanquished Sebastiano fell into line.

If Rosa was an ardent wife, she was an even more devoted mother. When their first baby's birth was imminent, Dr. Giardino attended her. The labor was long and painful. The infant, born with the umbilical cord wrapped around her neck, suffocated before the doctor could free her. Rosa could not be reconciled. She was angry at the *Bella Madonna*. Her mother was devastated. A year later Rosa gave birth to a grandson. Salvatrice was ecstatic!

As was the custom, he was baptized Salvatore — Savior — for his paternal grandfather, and nicknamed "Toto" — a handle that stuck for years. There was great celebration in Termini and in Lentini at the birth of a grandson. *Zia* Vicenzina had crocheted Toto a beautiful christening dress, slip and hat. Rosa treasured and saved it, hoping that her grandchildren and great-grandchildren would wear it one day. *Nonno* Sapienza, Sebastiano and his brothers, and their musician friends played the infant soothing music.

How Rosa wished her brothers and sister in America could see her *bambinedo,* Sicilian dialect for baby boy. At least, Toto would have his uncle Francesco Sapienza, who lived with them. Every morning when Rosa awakened Francesco for work, she called his nickname *"Ciccio!"* One morning as she held baby Toto, his little face reddened and he called "Cheeecheeo!" — the first word he spoke. Rosa repeated the story for years, reflecting her obvious joy in being a mother. Rosa gave her baby scrupulous care, nourishing him with Scott's Emulsion and cod liver oil imported from America.

Toto became a strapping tall boy, who was extremely bright and adventurous. He frequently ran off, only to be captured at the convent or church parish house. Mother and grandmother were sure that he had an attraction toward religion and the priesthood. At last the family inheritance would educate Toto for that vocation. One afternoon when he disappeared for nearly a day, they found him happily stuffed to the ears with sweets — an acquired daily habit. Their dreams of *Padre* Salvatore Sapienza went up in smoke!

Nonna Marianna Sapienza was amazed at his intelligence and was sure that he would grow up to become a philosopher. The talented Marianna made little suits for Salvatore and her second grandson, Liborio. She fashioned smart dresses and lace collars for her daughter-in-law. Rosa Concettina adored her sisters and brothers-in-law, but kept a respectful arms-length from her mother-in-law, holding to traditional "mother-in-law myths."

Rosa was passionately close to her parents. Although they filled her every wish, Rosa yearned for her brothers and sister, who were far away in America. She was intrigued by their letters, but could not be attracted to travel across the Atlantic as long as she had her parents.

Soon misfortune would hound her, when Italy was drawn into World War I. It took her Sebastiano into service. She wrote letters copiously, keeping him encouraged. In one letter she wrote that their third son Delfino, then two years old, had bitten an almond in half and given it to his mother to send to his Papa. Rosa was astounded at his intelligence and was convinced that this child was special.

During Sebastiano's absence, first her Papa and then Mamma died. Rosa lived in fear that Sebastiano might die. But because of his professional skills, he served safely behind the front lines as an officer and was able to inform Rosa when the troop train would be passing through Termini. Rosa and her Toto, Libo and little Delfino were at the station to welcome the soldiers and receive a fleeting hug from their Papa. It would be the last time he saw his little Delfino.

The baby developed a serious infection from a huge neck boil; the lesion infected his bloodstream. Delfino died of blood poisoning. Rosa could bear no more. Sebastiano was gone; she had lost her parents and several friends in the war, and now her little Delfino. Her grief deepened when news from America came that a great flu epidemic had claimed her sister's life. The only family she had left was four brothers in America.

Rosa's prayers for Sebastiano's safe return from war were answered. He was home again in 1919, months after the Armistice was signed on November 11, 1918. As time passed, her obsession to be with her own family in America intensified. Contrary to America's negative perception of immigrants, abject poverty or political pressure did not drive Rosa to emigrate.

She was adamant. She had nothing to lose, she decided. Her brothers would protect her. Rosa's grief and self-indulgent desire clouded the realization that if they were to emigrate, Sebastiano would have to leave his own family and two successful careers. Sebastiano had no idea what futile arguments and emotional frustrations lay ahead with his intractable wife! Her dynamic force would propel them toward the distant magnet that had pulled her brothers and sister across the Atlantic. Finally, Sebastiano capitulated.

Chapter 4

Ben Venuto e Ciao! — Welcome and Goodbye!

In the early 1900's, adventurous immigrants who did not fear deportation made several crossings. Nevertheless, Paolo was happy to be home from his first voyage. Townspeople filled the *piazza* to greet their returning voyagers.

Paolo had added another *valigia* to his baggage. It held a few more modest presents. For Grazia, Arcangela, and Mamma, Paolo had brought silk head scarves to wear to Mass. For Maria, he brought a light blue silk blouse to complement her eyes, and an American hat which she felt too timid to wear.

He could hardly wait to sit next to Maria at Mass and sing an *a cappella* duet. And he wanted to hold his little blonde blue-eyed Grazia, who was surely growing too rapidly for him to enjoy.

That night the *paesani* gathered at his house to feast and listen to stories from America. Paolo loved the familiar smells of herbs and garlic. Tonight there was homemade pork sausage. He remembered with great amusement that when he had first married Maria, she had not known how to cook meat. In desperation, the astonished Paolo had stepped outside their door and shrieked the news: *"Dio mio! Ho sposato 'na donna che non sa' cucinare la carne!"* He watched Maria bring a heaping *piatto* full of sausage and chicken to the table, and gave his startled wife a resounding kiss. Their guests laughed. Maria turned beet red and wished the guests were gone!

Before daybreak, he and Maria went to the little stone hut by the Biferno where Pietro had died. Paolo crossed himself and said a prayer for his father's soul — and pulled Maria inside.

Later, as he moved among the fig trees, olive groves and vineyards, he was happy to feel the warm sun on his face and to touch again the rich black soil of his beloved farmland. But he was happiest to tease Maria until she pretended to be annoyed. And tease he did, until she blushed crimson, laughed and called him a teaser. *"O, Paolo, se' cimentuso!"* Paolo sang and whistled as he worked. Maria, toiling beside him, sang along as their slim strong bodies bent to the earth.

Occasionally, Paolo thought about Pittsburgh, where he had found his *amici* in a place called Homewood. He had described to Maria its houses, from the most humble made of wood, or built of *mattone* or brick, and those made from stone that looked like *castelli*. Maria was astonished when he wrote about horseless trolley cars attached at the end of long poles to overhead *corde*. And amazed that they traveled on *binari* right down the middle of the *strada*. Paolo described how, on those same streets, horse-drawn wagons brought food and goods for sale from house to house, and horseless carriages called auto-mo-bile carried rich people about. He could not put America out of his mind.

But there was much to be done here and now. He would build a new stone house with a balcony. Stone was plentiful and Paolo was skillful. He had to learn more than one trade in a self-sustaining small town. And necessity was a great teacher. He was a farmer, miller, stonecutter/builder, and best of all, storyteller. Townspeople gathered nightly to hear his stories about the New World — and months later to admire Paolo's new balcony.

Mamma was proud of her son-in-law. But she grew apprehensive as her Arcangela prodded her own husband Antonio to consider making the voyage to America one day. In Paolo's absence, Maria Giuseppa had managed his affairs well. She had saved most of the money he had sent. Paolo was so proud of his beautiful *Rossa*, a nickname she earned because of her rose-red complexion. He wanted to take her beyond the village of Castellino, and decided they would visit Paolo's cousins in Campo Basso.

Once there, Paolo looked out over the Adriatic Sea and felt a strong urge to sail to America again. He thought about the opportunities that lay ahead. He remembered that his friends in Homewood had much work in the building trades. His perceptions had been keen. He explained to Maria that America offered many new work opportunities for immigrants.

There were jobs in manufacturing steel for trolley cars, railroad trains, and tracks. These were in settlements around Pittsburgh, Pennsylvania. And there were many more jobs beyond Pittsburgh, since Henry Ford had invented the automobile. Immigrants worked hard as laborers in different occupations. New settlements mushroomed near large cities like Detroit, New York, and Chicago. Homewood, populated by an elite and a growing middle class, was such a community in Pittsburgh. Paolo liked Homewood. Maria became fascinated with America.

The more Paolo recounted his experiences in America, the more restless he became. His desire for his family's improvement pulled him toward the distant magnet. By December 1907, Paolo had completed plans to sail again for America. After Christmas he packed his Bible and his clothing. He would include the coat he bought in America. He reviewed his notes and studied English, remembering that Americans called him Paul. His destination would certainly be Hazelwood in Pittsburgh where his boyhood friend Domenico Stanziano lived.

The restless adventurer set sail again early in January 1908 and joined his *amico* for shared room and board. Domenico had come to America in 1902 and found it urgent to learn the English language if he were to succeed as an Italian. He studied hard to lose his accent. His reward came when he was hired as Pittsburgh's first Italian trolley car conductor. Domenico became Dom, and he called Paolo Paul.

The two friends spent evenings reminscing about Holy Day feasts, boyhood pranks and balcony serenades to their sweethearts. Dom helped Paul learn English. Work was plentiful. Paolo found a job in a steel mill, but the hours were long. Pittsburgh steel mills belched out their black smoke twenty-four hours a day. He toiled alongside immigrants of other nationalities. He wrote his thoughts to Maria: *"Lavoro nella bocca dell' inferno! Non è per me!"* Work before the open hearth was like working in the mouth of hell, Paolo reflected and decided it was not for him. To those Italians who loved the land and to those who enjoyed being creative, blast furnaces left much to be desired. Paolo decided to change jobs. He would search carefully for his next one. Dom directed him to friends in Homewood.

By habit, the curious traveler always asked many questions and explored the environment around him. He learned that the prosperous Pittsburgh factories that he detested produced great wealth for their owners, who built country estates with elaborate gardens. These fabulously wealthy industrialists, George Westinghouse, Henry Frick, Andrew Carnegie, John Heinz and others chose to live beyond Pittsburgh's inner city, which had become a ghetto for immigrants. Homewood, beyond the railroad tracks, had become a suburb for the elite. Paolo reasoned that the people of this class would hire workers to keep their elaborate homes and gardens beautiful.

His hunch proved correct. He moved to Homewood, where he found Maria's cousin Giovanni Ferrante, who lived on Tioga Street. Paolo's

English had improved. He found work as a gardener at one of the country estates. Owners of these estates employed dozens of servants to maintain their elaborate homes and lifestyles. These servants lived in obscure parts on the premises. Other domestic workers and their families settled not too far away in the developing middle-class Homewood-Brushton area, located between the train tracks and trolley tracks, on Susquehanna and Tioga Streets, and on Hamilton Avenue. When the working-class immigrants and Blacks first invaded Homewood, they encountered social and religious opposition, just as they had encountered in first coming to America. Prejudice had many faces. No group of immigrants suffered greater abuse than African slaves whose importance to history has been largely ignored, until recently, by early historians who did not view slave trade as immigration.

Eventually, however, Homewood-Brushton became a rich mixture of nationalities, races, and religions where working people lived in harmony side by side. However, the class status was clear by location. The elite, who lived on the "right side" of the railroad tracks, was a tight-knit community of residents who rode commuter trains or automobiles, worked together in business, worshipped in the same non-Catholic churches, and intermarried. Those from the "wrong side" of the tracks lived in smaller, often rented, houses. Some still had outhouses instead of indoor toilet facilities, and no electricity.

Paolo explored the surrounding neighborhoods where larger brick homes with well-kept gardens, neat lawns and trees gave a hint of the countryside. The streetcars that traveled through Homewood and Brushton had definitely changed these communities from country to city. English, Irish and German blue-collar workers with specialized trades lived here, and fit well into the largely Protestant, Northern European character of its residents. In contrast to mill workers who, out of economic necessity, had to live within walking distance to work, Homewood-Brushton residents could commute anywhere. As he walked beyond the trolley lines on paved sidewalks and along a grid of planned streets, Paolo knew he would remember this kind of neighborhood.

Giovanni Ferrante, who had a prospering construction business in Homewood, offered him work. Paolo noted that many Italians worked at construction. It was a natural transition. Some worked with marble, making cemetery monuments. Others, like Frank Donatelli, built elaborate walls and houses.

Still others paved streets and sidewalks. Proud artisans even stamped their names into their work. Fond of gardening, the ambitious immigrant hatched a plan to work at both. He accepted every job from digging foundations to cement finishing and stonecutting. As he worked, he often thought of his new stone house and balcony in Italy. He was happy in his work — if one could call hard labor happiness.

His burdens were lightened by the thought of a second child to be born. According to custom, his name, if it was a boy, would honor Paolo's father Pietro. A man wanted at least one son.

Paolo promised that the boy would never work as hard as he had. Long hours at hard labor were inhuman. Paolo decided that little Pietro and all his children would have whatever education their intelligence could command. Paolo recalled his sorrow at having been denied a higher education.

Working alone, and the limited pleasure he found with his friends, did not satisfy Paolo. Like them he had little energy after long hours of work. And although they had established a social life, they missed their church and religious customs. The Latin Mass was simple enough to understand, but sermons in English were not satisfying to most. Paolo read his Gospels in Italian and attended Mass at Holy Rosary, the nearest Catholic church. He understood more of the English language as he listened to the sermons. Those who could not understand English or read Italian felt alienated.

Some sought more than their modest little homes and patches of gardens. Homewood-Brushton and surrounding eastern areas had developed into communities of German, Irish, Polish and Jewish ethnic churches, which had formed their own social cliques and kept alive their Old World customs. The Homewood-Brushton Italians longed for this same social and spritual communion, and looked for an answer to their dilemma.

They approached Father Malady, pastor of Holy Rosary Church in Homewood. The diocese, no doubt, understood that their frustration was not unique. Catholic immigrants of other nationalities had sought to bond together and looked to their church as a haven to communicate in their own languages. They were oblivious to the non-Catholics who believed that the Church actually worked against their assimilation into American society.

More specifically, Protestants criticized Catholics for their persistence in using foreign languages in Church and schools. They believed that by grouping aliens together, the church impeded their Americanization and encouraged Catholic hostility to naturalization. Similarly, when the Protestants came to America, they, too, had grouped themselves by *their* religion and nationality. And, like ethnic groups before them, their own religion had once played a key role in their socialization.

The Italians of Homewood-Brushton showed great joy when they learned that soon an Italian priest would arrive to help them to organize their parish, and provide them with the spiritual comfort they sought in a language they could understand. Despite the variety of dialects spoken by most, formal Italian would be used for church services, along with Latin. Most were literate in formal Italian, but never lost their dialect.

In late September 1907, Father Florindo De Francesco arrived from Abruzzi — without the Abruzzese dialect; and he spoke fluent English. The new priest became the guest of Father Malady at Holy Rosary Church for a few months. This hospitality was noteworthy because association between Italian and Irish Catholics was uncommon when there was prejudice within the church. Italian Catholicism was different than Irish, Polish or German Catholicism. Irish Catholics did not understand the Italian way of worship through feast days that honored the Madonna or special saints. They looked down upon Italians. Father Malady was an exception.

It was truly a day of thanksgiving when the first Mass was celebrated in an old vacant storeroom on Oakwood Street in Brushton. Arriving in America again in late January 1908, Paolo was happy to find a priest in Brushton. Although Mass was celebrated in Latin, the Gospel and sermon were in Italian. Paolo prayed and wept for joy with the parishioners when they heard their own beautiful language once again. Father De Francesco was an eloquent and dramatic speaker. Like Father Malady, his charisma helped knit the community. His strict discipline commanded respect and awe. Also, Paolo, who rarely spoke formal Italian for fear of offending those who could not, now enjoyed non-dialectic conversations with Father De Francesco.

Paolo's letter to Maria would be a long one. He wrote that now there was a new goal to achieve — the goal of contributing generously toward developing the new Italian parish. He hoped that one day she would come to America and attend Mass in the new church that his fellow Italians were building with their money and skills.

In May 1908, at the corner of Bennet and Hale Streets in Brushton, ground was broken for Mother of Good Counsel Church, *Madre del Buon Concillio.* The Italian laborers were capable and built a simple oblong church with a steeple roof. A white wooden altar and large statues of their favored saints gave the immigrants the comfort of home. Understandably, *Sant' Antonio*, patron of orphans, was Paolo's favorite saint. Italian artist Attilio Martone became the Michelangelo Buonarroti of the new church when he painted the ceiling with religious Renaissance art. His work adorned a number of Catholic churches throughout Pittsburgh and surrounding areas.

Paolo thought of Maria as he sang the first Latin responses and hymns in the new Italian church. Father Malady helped celebrate the first Mass and dreamed of building his own big church one day. Diocesan plans were in progress for constructing the grand Gothic cathedral on Lang Avenue in Homewood. Ground would be broken, appropriately, on St. Patrick's Day in 1928. Although both edifices would be standing through the last decade of the millenium, by mid-century Mother of Good Counsel Church parishoners would construct a larger church a few blocks away on Bennet Street and Brushton Avenue to accomodate its growing congregation.

Meanwhile, in the Brushton community, a small congregation of Italian Protestants had joined the church on Hale Street, which was located next to Mother of Good Counsel's original church. Two Tedesco families worshipped on Hale Street. One family was Catholic, the other was Protestant. Paolo found it amazing that all Italians were not Catholic and did not celebrate the saints' feast days with a Mass on Italian religious holy days. Curiously, none of them were his *paesani.*

In his next conversation with Father DeFrancesco, Paolo asked questions about these Italians. He learned that their conversion from Catholicism was rooted in the history of the unification of North and South Italy after *il Risorgimento.* Paolo was familiar with the Revival of the Arts, which began in the early nineteenth century and led to the proclamation of the Kingdom of Italy and its eventual unification in 1871. He knew that the Italians of the North and South were opponents before the *Risorgimento.* Although he did not agree, Paolo then understood why some converted their religion.

Social historians recorded that prior to the unification, when economic conditions were deplorable in Southern Italy, many Italians left, never intending to return to Italy. They brought with them a strong anti-clerical attitude. When they came to America, faced with immigrant prejudice, they felt excluded. When American Protestants mounted a drive to include them, they abandoned their Italian Catholic tradition. Protestants converted them by approaching Italian women. They taught their recruits to read English, and helped them to assimilate. Colonists had begun to recruit Italians as early as 1656 when more than one-hundred Italian Protestants were brought to New York and Delaware by the Dutch. These were the Waldensians, religious dissenters led by Peter Waldo, a merchant of Lyons, France, who founded his own church about 1170. They were excommunicated by Pope Lucius III. Although nearly all Italian immigrants remained Catholics, only a small number became Protestant.

America was a curious place. Paolo would have so much to tell Maria. He could not possibly write it all in his next letter. He imagined his next live conversation with his *Bella Rossa,* and his thoughts turned to the child they were expecting. He had been gone only seven and a half months. Like the magnet that pulled him to America, an equally strong force was now pulling him home. Paolo was a practical and foresighted man. He saw that new opportunities in America were growing sparse. Newspapers reported that immigration ranks had kept swelling since 1892. Nearly a million immigrants a year had passed through Ellis Island. Consequently, work was becoming more difficult to find. America was even sliding into an economic slump. As the tide of newcomers grew, immigrants who could not find work talked of leaving. Although Paolo had work, he was torn *fra due amori*, America and *Italia*, his two loves. Ultimately, he decided he must return home.

Chapter 5

Torn Between Two Loves

In the fall of 1908, Paolo gathered his few possessions and his money, and planned his return to Italy. He hoped he would arrive in time to greet his new infant. It was an early, dreary fall morning when the ship left the great New York harbor. On every deck, passengers were waving their last good-byes along the crowded rails. The great ship coughed out three deep earsplitting bellows as she sailed through the narrows past Ellis Island; and Paolo thought sadly about those who had never been privileged to be admitted onto American soil. He watched the New York shoreline move away as they approached the Great Lady of Bedloe Island. He would never forget the sight of her raised arm holding the torch. As he watched her grow smaller, the dismal wail of foghorns in the distance made him melancholic.

He was hardly surprised to find his second return passage was more crowded than the first. Paolo learned about the dilemmas and rejections that immigrants had faced in their attempts to blend into American society. Some had been welcome, others had been met with open resistance and made to feel inferior. The foreigners did not connect their rejections with the seventeenth century Anglo-Saxon attitudes that had shaped Colonial American thinking. They were unaware of the anti-immigrant feelings that had often been expressed by political leaders. For example, Thomas Watson complained that "the scum of creation has been dumped upon us."

By the late nineteenth century, "... the growth of the notion of European superiority was quite clear," said modern historian Roger Daniels. Nativists were convinced that, of all European races, Anglo-Saxons, Aryan, Teutonic or Nordic were the best, with superior inborn characteristics and intelligence. They even assumed that political institutions could thrive best among *them*. In fact, in 1894, young Harvard men pressured for change in America's immigration policy and formed the Immigration Restriction League. Its chief political spokesman, Senator Henry Cabot Lodge, whose own Italian ancestor Giovanni Caboto helped found the Massachusetts Bay Colony, considered certain immigrants to be inferior people whose prolific reproduction threatened the foundation of Anglo-American civilization. Italian-Anglo

Congressman Lodge, who scorned his Italian heritage, even worked for implementing a literacy test to improve the quality of new immigrants.

Paolo sensed the anti-immigrant attitudes from his conversations with disillusioned fellow Italian passengers. Some Americans had ridiculed their habits and seen them as subhuman creatures. "We were treated little better than *animali* — like *ignoranti,*" they complained. "Because we cannot speak their language they think we are stupid!" The immigrants spoke in disdain of tobacco-chewing men with dirty spitting habits, and Americans who ate potatoes that in Italy even the poor threw to the pigs. Some talked about filthy streets that were never cleaned, crowded living in New York ghettos with smelly water, *sorci,* and *cimici* — rats and bedbugs.

Other passengers verified their claims. Those who had lived in Chicago complained about living near smelly slaughterhouses. And women, who had been used to working outdoors, found it hard to keep order indoors. Others protested about hard work at hot furnaces for long hours and small pay. Some feared the gangs of angry men who refused to work for little pay and fought their bosses. From newspapers, they learned the word *strike*. Newcomers were bewildered about the equally hostile *Negri* who fought other workers. They did not understand that to keep labor in line, powerful industrialists used these Black men, alongside Italians, as tools to break strikes.

But Italians were not alone in their complaints. Paolo heard similar discontent from passengers of other nationalities. Those immigrants who had not been well received were bewildered. They did not realize that American bigotry was so deep-seated, with fixed prejudices about how people worshipped and looked. Eighteenth century America was heavily Protestant and colonists resembled Anglo-Saxons. A large majority, like Paolo, who had light hair and were fair-skinned, and blue-eyed, were accepted differently from dark-haired, dark-skinned people. Nordic influence was clear.

New England in the 1600's had fewer brunettes and more people with light hair and gray and blue eyes. Historian Edmund Traverso noted, "Nordic blood was kept pure in the colonies because (. . .) among Protestant peoples, there was a strong race feeling about ethnic mixtures and religious beliefs, which persisted into the mid-twentieth century" and beyond. Anti-Catholicism was strong. Paolo, from a strictly Catholic *paese*, was not aware that there were suspicions about how Catholic immigrants worshiped. Protestant religious philosophy conflicted with Catholic philosophy and its dogma, and unsuspecting Italians were particular targets for bigotry, because the Pope and his hierarchy in Rome were Italian. They believed that Catholics owed their allegiance to the Pope and posed a danger to American government.

Protestant animosity against Irish Catholics was obvious, too. The New York Evening Post advertised on September 4, 1830: "Wanted chambermaid . . . must be American, Scotch, Swiss or African — no Irish." When a canal was dug in New Orleans, the South even preferred that the Irish accept high mortality jobs rather than risk the lives of slaves whose labor there, and in sugar and cotton fields, was cheap.

But despite America's imperfections and the immigrants' complaints, Paolo was not disillusioned. America had treated him well. The curious adventurer had learned much and had become absorbed with American politics and the idea of democracy. *Il Progresso* and later the *Sentinella* newspaper had kept him well informed. He was optimistic. And he was certain that one day he would return to America.

To save money, Paolo traveled steerage class, later called third class. He wore his best American clothes and ventured among passengers who traveled second class. He spoke his best Italian, and some English. In America, Paolo had developed a love for opera. He loved to sing, and so did Maria. Since his first trip, he had wanted desperately to take her to the opera so that she could learn the songs and they could sing together.

He imagined that when she came to live in America, she would have many things like those he had seen in the "wish book" that *americani* called the Sears Roebuck catalog. He would buy her beautiful clothes and big hats with plumes and shell hairpins for her braids. And they would have a handsome *fornello di cuccina* made of iron where Maria could cook from the top and, from the bottom, keep the room warm with *carboni*. She would no longer have to cook over a hearthfire or gather firewood, or go outside to get well water. And Paolo would buy a machine that would sew, and a wooden ice box where the food could stay cold. And he fancied telling Maria about men who flew through the air like birds. He had so much to relate. Poor Paolo was sorry to leave America, but happy at the prospect and vision of his reunion with Maria and Grazia — and the thought of a new *bambino*. He wished for a son.

He looked over the ship's rail at the ocean and his thoughts, like a pendulum, alternated between America and Italy. What a critical situation he faced! He hoped he would arrive in time for the baby's birth. Passing his hand across his forehead, he uttered his thoughts, *"Ma che situazione critica! E tempo di cogliere l'uva! Devo fare il vino!"* It was time to harvest, time to pick grapes and make wine.

Paolo became preoccupied with phases of the moon. His child would be born at the full moon, he mused. A big moon would help ferment the wine. But if the grapes are picked too early, the sugar that turns to alcohol is too low and the *vino* sours. If the grapes are picked too late and the weather turns warm, the grapes get too ripe and ferment on the vine! And if it rains! Unthinkable! The vines absorb the water and dilute the sugar in the grapes! *Santa Maria,* what trouble!

"O Santa Maria! Che guaio! O Santa Lucia! . . . Santa Lucia . . ." Paolo began to sing the song: *"Sul mare lucica . . . l'astro argento . . ."* And as his tenor voice grew *crescendo,* a few of his fellow Italian passengers closed about him and sang along. Paolo thought of the wine flask that Domenico had pushed into his *valigia,* and went to retrieve the *fiasco di vino.* He shared it with his *amici.* As the *vino* disappeared, the singers sang *ad alta voce,* Caruso style. They sang every Italian folk song imaginable from Abruzzi, Napoli, Calabria and Sicilia, each in their own dialects:

"Ohi Mareeee," and *"Ce la luna mezz' oooo mare . . ."* and *"O sole mio . . ."* Yes, they did what any Italian does when there is trouble, pray or sing. Paolo slept well that night.

The happy visionary arrived in Castellino Sul Biferno several days before the birth of his first son. There was much feasting and rejoicing when Silvio Pietro Palombo received his *Santo Battesimo.*

Paolo had brought more American gifts for his family. To hold the money he had saved for the family's passage to America, he opened another Italian bank account in the *Provincia di Campobasso, Casa Di Risparmio, Libretto N. 00876.* "Soma day — *se Dio vuole,*" he said, crossing himself and planting *un grande bacio* on Maria's red cheek.

The villagers had gathered each evening to hear news about their friends in America and about the new Italian Padre Florindo DeFrancesco. Excitement grew, especially when Paolo told his *paesani* that one could not tell a *contadino* from a *signore,* a peasant from a gentleman. He himself sported a new American suit, highly-polished shoes, a new brimmed hat, and a moustache — just like his revered President Teddy Roosevelt's. He had sent home copies of the Italian-American *Sentinella,* which Maria had neatly folded on the fireside shelf, near her Bibles and the Sears Roebuck Catalog. The *giornale* helped to instill in Maria a sense of identification with, and vicarious pride in, this land of opportunity.

Paolo kept busy improving the family's houses. He gained new respect for Maria's ability and hard work at sustaining the many chores in his absence. Together, they harvested fruits and vegetables, and grain to grind into flour. They crushed olives for oil and strung fresh figs and peppers to dry. Paolo made pork sausage and *prosciutto, ricotta,* and *formaggio* from goat's milk.

Most of all, Paolo loved harvesting grapes from his lush vineyard; and he enjoyed the singing, dancing and feasting as the women stomped the grapes into *vino.*

Often as he worked, Paolo reminisced about America. He found himself whistling *The Star-Spangled Banner* and singing it in fractured English. While he did not think the American National Anthem was quite as stirring as the French one, he loved and respected it. To him it represented a land which gave him opportunity and would one day help him improve his life. He had to think very hard to remember whether he whistled his own Italian National Anthem as often.

He continued to correspond with his friends in America, who wrote that work was now once more plentiful and immigrants welcomed to perform many kinds of labor. The great American magnet pulled him again. For Paolo the decision was easy. He would continue to inspire Maria, relying on the Sears Roebuck catalog to strengthen his appeal and weaken her resistance.

As Maria Giuseppa's excitement about America grew, so did her frustrations. She was consumed with the sorrow of leaving Mamma Maria Luigi and her sister Arcangela. But stories and news of American life fascinated Maria, and she agreed to consider the idea of going to the *terra nuova.*

Inherently, Paolo and Maria were risk takers. He continued to caution her that if they expected to succeed, they must adapt — accommodate — and work hard. Their lives had been one adjustment after another. Life had taught them this lesson early. It became their philosophy for survival. They would teach it to their children. American philosophy was like their own. They would fit well into American social life. Maria was prepared. It was definite. They would go to America!

Paolo would make the crossing again to prepare for their arrival. He had been home only two years. Certainly their separation this time would not be as long. But the random hand of Fate held another challenge for the young idealists.

Chapter 6

Destino Crudele — Cruel Fate

By 1910, Paolo had crossed the Atlantic four times. He anticipated that this voyage to America would be his last. With his *Passaporto Per l' Estero, S.S. Luisiana, 218* in hand, Paolo said a fond *addio* to his family, expecting to be reunited with them in America within two years. The *Luisiana* would leave the port of Naples on February 28. Parting with Mamma, his *paesani*, and all that he held dear, took great courage and caused Paolo deep grief. He imagined what it would be like for Maria and Mamma, and turned his back on them to hide tears. But experience had taught him that opportunity lay in the New World.

He set out with high aspiration. But the *S.S. Luisiana* was ill-fated. About ten days out to sea, she caught fire and, as a result, developed a serious leak in her lower hull. She began to list, even as crewmen frantically did repairs to keep her afloat. Working against the heavy demands of the sea, they finally succeeded in saving the *Luisiana* by weighting the side opposite the damaged hull so that the impaired section would rise above the water level.

Years later, Paolo relived the terror when he described the horror and panic of his fellow steerage passengers being tossed about the crowded open decks. In many languages, they raised their cries in frantic appeals to heaven. He related how desperately voyagers fought for life jackets and pushed to scramble into the lifeboats. Some of the crewmen and male passengers were assigned to man boats. Others battled to keep the March sea from flooding the *Luisiana*, for she was tilting so badly that those unaccustomed to the sea could not remain upright. Chairs, trunks, clothing and all items not battened down or obstructed by obstacles slid to the lower side. Many items slid through the broken rails into the churning sea. Two helpless passengers slid into the water. Crewmen began the daunting task of rescuing them. One was saved. The other fell victim to sharks. Some of the ship's cargo was lost. Paolo lost all of his possessions except the *bursa* that held his passport, papers, and money, which caution had taught him to keep in the inside pocket of his jacket.

The busy crew worked resolutely aboard as lifeboats, filled with terrified immigrants, were lowered into the water. Male passengers worked alongside of them to assist in the rescue. Paolo stayed on board and heard the Morse Code S.O.S. signal of distress. From hearing it on his first passage, he recognized its rapid high staccato bleats and thought about Marconi, and spoke a blessing: *"Benedetto Dio! E benedetto Marconi!"* For years to come Paolo could never hear the deep mournful wail of a foghorn without feeling anew the terror of his experience.

As passengers were helped to their lifeboats, the ship's captain barked out orders for oarsmen to remain within sight of the *Luisiana*, yet far enough away to avoid colliding with her. And then, her foghorn began a deep incessant wail *come un' anima disperata* — like a desperate soul. Paolo thought about Maria and his children and their uncertain destinies. Finally, he crossed himself and climbed into the last lifeboat.

He thought of his children as orphans, and invoked the Holy Mother to save them. He prayed frantically that they would not sink: *"Mio poveri orfanelli! Santa Maria, O Dio mio! Salvaci! Non ci fare affondare!"* Although he could not understand all the languages of the distressed cries, he knew that all voices were raised in common supplication. Paolo took his place with other oarsmen. Rowing required great strength against the unyielding sea, but kept him reasonably warm. However, his feet were wet and cold from the white saltwater that washed overboard from the crest of the waves. Those who were not rowing spent time bailing out water with their hats. Occasionally there was a startling swish alongside the boat as a shark cut through the water like a long gleaming sword — *come una spada lunga e lucente* — as Paolo later described. Its huge tail hurled a foaming spray over the helpless lifeboats. Passengers were terrified and cried out their prayers.

"Silenzio!" someone warned. The passengers bailed out water less noisily, but not less fearfully. If the big ship had made some of them seasick, the lifeboat was even less merciful. Where once the sea had seemed blue-green and friendly, it now appeared clay-gray and terrorizing. The *Luisiana* and the bobbing lifeboats were the only break in the monotonous scenery of sea and sky, which blended together at the end of Paolo's vision. The immigrants fell into unison as someone led the *Pater Noster* in Latin. Their

prayers reminded Paolo that it was *Quaresima*. During Lent, the villagers at home prayed frequently.

Through those many fearful hours of waiting, Paolo thought of the agony of Jesus in the Garden of Gethsemane where He began His suffering. Paolo offered his own agony in contrition. *"O Signore Jesu! Santa Maria!"* he cried. *"A morire a venti-nove anni? Che peccato! Che destino crudele! Mia povera moglie senza marito! Mia poveri orfaneli! Ascolta, Madre Dolorosa!"* He bargained with the Sorrowful Mother that it would be a sin to die at twenty-nine years and leave his wife widowed and his children orphaned. Paolo thought sadly of his own life without his father and mother. Now his dreams for his children would be broken as his own had been. Life in those hours became precious, its flaws unimportant. If only God would spare him, he would be a better person, he vowed.

Night fell upon the sea and swallowed the water's surface. Even the occasional sweep of the *Luisiana's* searchlights did not penetrate the black veil between water and sky. The truly "tempest-tossed" later compared the eerie experience to being suspended in *un cavo nero,* a black hole. A voice in the darkness, believing that this is what hell must be, lamented *"Così sarà l'inferno."* Another desperate soul beseeched *"Dio Mio, Abbi Pieta di noi!* My God, have mercy on us!" A litany of prayers broke forth.

Darkness dropped like a shroud over the crippled ship obscuring her from sight. Only intermittent light beams from the *Luisiana*, an occasional flicker from her portholes, and the measured deep mournful voice of her horn cut throught the black pitch about them. Adults and children huddled together and pulled further into their clothes to keep out the cold damp air. Hunger and thirst were not as important as the common effort of keeping the *Luisiana* within sight and bailing out water from the wildly tossing lifeboats. Children who cried from hunger and thirst finally surrendered to sleep, exhausted. One surrendered its life.

Paolo was sleepless. At dawn the sea and the sky were of a common gray hue. He had to become accustomed once again to the dizzying panorama. An incessant wail from one of the boats revealed a distraught mother cradling the lifeless body of her infant. The crazed woman snapped and, clutching her dead child hysterically, flung herself overboard. Within minutes predators and the sea devoured them. Stunned silence gripped the voyagers.

The *Luisiana* made a curious spectacle navigating slowly askew. Crewmen had lowered her anchor and weighted down her undamaged side sufficiently enought to keep her afloat. Paolo spotted crewmen in the crow's nest atop her mast peering through their binoculars.

Several hours later, a small speck appeared against the blue sky. Paolo marked the vision in his memory. He noted that the sunlight behind a huge cloud shone halo-like around its rim. *"Ecco il Spirito Santo!* Here comes the Holy Ghost!" An American passenger cried. *"Benedetto Dio!* Blessed be God!"

"E Benedetto Suo Santo Nome!" came the response in unison. "And blessed be His Holy Name!" Passengers cried and prostrated themselves in humble gratitude. Paolo, like his fellow passengers, had looked at death. Their faces reflected it. He marked this in his memory, too. The ordeal was not over for several hours until lifeboats and passengers were lifted to safety.

The crippled *Luisiana*, sailing slowly atilt, caused the rescue ship, navigating alongside, several days delay in reaching America. Once aboard the crowded vessel, Paolo made a solemn oath never to make another crossing. Maria and the family must come to him. Their future was decided by the fate of the *Luisiana*. Surely their crossing would be a safe one, just as his other crossings had been. He would not write Maria the news, and prayed the incident would not reach her ears. He did not want her to become afraid to make the voyage.

If steerage accommodations had been scarcely adequate before, they were less so now, but no one complained. Passengers shared their clothing with the rescued. Paolo later remembered thinking that food and water were a benediction from God. He broke his first piece of bread and kissed it. This gesture became a habit until he died!

Weary passengers cheered when they saw *la Statua di Liberta*. With his fellow voyagers, Paolo knelt in a prayer of thanksgiving. He had come home! He wept when he set foot on American soil — and kissed *la terra santa*. New York looked wonderful! Pittsburgh looked magnificent!

During the crossings from the 1890's to the 1920's, immigrants endured various hardships that are each worthy of its own story. Thousands died from contagious skin diseases, tuberculosis or pneumonia. Exclusion was *mandatory* for immigrants who were found to have trachoma, the eye disease. Families were split, for example, if a child was found to be infected. One of the parents had to return to the native country with the rejected child. Many, overcome with fear from the crossing or rejection for entry, committed suicide. There were no psychologists then to help them recover from their trauma, and certainly there were none for the *Luisiana* immigrants. The event would leave its scar; but to survive they would have to adjust and move bravely ahead.

Paolo did not want Maria Giuseppa to suffer trauma if she heard about the disaster. When he arrived in Homewood, he greeted his friends with great emotion and cautioned them not to write home about his terrifying experience. The telling of his frightening ordeal reduced him to tears, and again he begged his friends not to write home about his *grande scossa e spavento* — his big shock and fear.

But weeks later, a letter from Maria told him that she had read the news in the *Italo-Americana Gazetta* sent home to her townsmen. Don Alfonso, her cousin in Italy, offered a Mass in thanksgiving for the survivors of the *Luisiana*. At Mother of Good Counsel Church, Father De Francesco offered a Mass in *grazie a Dio*. Paolo decided to be patient about urging Maria to cross to America.

Five months after his arrival, Paolo received news that his second son, Domenico, was born on August 12. He was named for Maria's father. He was grateful that the *bambino* was not born an orphan and happy to have another son to carry the Palombo name. He decided that he must work even harder now.

In 1910, economic conditions were better in Pittsburgh than years earlier. Upon his return, Paolo had little difficulty finding work and was surprised to learn that some of his unskilled friends had suffered heavy financial losses to already meager incomes. Paolo scouted the upper middle-class neighborhoods of Homewood and secured work as a gardener, accepting whatever labor his strength would allow, no matter how menial. His aim was to buy a home and save money for his family's passage to America. He continued to provide for Mamma Luigi, sending home *denari*, which were deposited in Arcangela's name at *la Casa Di Risparmio Postali*.

Paolo knew that he would forever be American. Therefore, he had much catching up to do on American news and politics. There was a new president now, William Howard Taft. But he had preferred the colorful Teddy Roosevelt, he decided. He decided, too, that he would improve his English.

Languages fascinated Paolo, and in his encounters at various jobs, he had managed to absorb a few basic ethnic phrases from the Hungarians, the Poles, and the Germans. Most of all, he enjoyed hearing the musical brogue of the Irish and retained his own accent until he died at seventy-five. Just as he had done on previous visits to America, Paolo developed a comradeship and respect for all nationalities. He was especially anxious to help new arrivals.

Through news channels and letters sent to the Old World, America's growing prosperity and its need for laborers attracted more and more arrivals from all parts of Europe between 1910 and 1920. By then there were almost four hundred thousand Italian immigrants in and around New York City alone. Others ventured South to New Orleans, West to large industrialized cities, and as far as California where they comprised more than ten percent of the population. America had opened her portals wide until the 1920's, and then drastic changes in immigration quotas imposed new restrictions and drastically cut entry for Italians, who were the highest group denied admittance.

Paolo knew that his brother-in-law, Antonio, was saving to come to America. And he knew that his Arcangela would suffer the same distress as Maria had at the thought of leaving Mamma Luigi. By 1913, Antonio could no longer resist. He emigrated, leaving Arcangela and their son behind. Paolo would help him seek work and get established.

When Antonio arrived, he found room and board in Homewood. Soon he became "Tony." He also became one of the Italians who, unable to find work as craftsmen in the building trades, worked for government agencies doing public works jobs. Provided with a secure job, Tony would one day bring his family to America and two sisters would be reunited.

But Paolo was growing impatient to bring his own family across. Their arrival was long past due. Once again, events beyond his control would affect his destiny. Gathering war clouds in Europe would determine his fate. By 1914, conditions in Europe made war inevitable. On July 28, 1914, Austria declared war against Serbia. Before the signing of the Armistice on November 11, 1918, twenty-eight nations were engaged in World War I.

The war caused a boom in American industries. Factories became hungry for the least amount of knowledge and skill that would be useful in the steel mills. Pittsburgh-area blast furnaces belched out thick columns of black smoke. Paolo's friends urged him to go back to the steel mills, where they were engaged in making steel for American products and war implements for Europe. But Paolo refused to return to work at the "mouth of hell."

A Triple Alliance with France, Russia and Great Britain was formed against the "German menace." When negotiations failed with Russia, the German Chancellor dispatched an ultimatum on July 31, 1914; and on August 1, Germany declared war on Russia. Europe became a tinderbox. Many battles were fought bewteen the first battle of the Marne in 1914 and the second battle of the Marne in 1918. When Italy joined the Allies in 1915, the war had expanded over Western Europe. Italians followed the news closely and learned that crossing the Atlantic had become perilous, because Germany was torpedoing ships without warning.

When the British liner *Sussex* was torpedoed, killing several American citizens, President Wilson won Congressional approval on April 19, 1916, to threaten severance of diplomatic relations. Germany relented for a time, but fearful of losing the war, its military party reverted to unrestricted attacks by submarines. Germany knew that the United States would have no choice but to enter the war.

The Italian *Gazetta* was filled with war news, which showed that sentiments in Italy were divided between nations in the Triple Alliance and Germany. Italo-Americans were, in the main, sympathetic to the Allies, as were the Poles, Czechs, and Slovaks. Their sentiments were so strongly nationalistic that they sent money back home to support the Allied cause. Some returned to their homeland for conscription. Paolo was eligible to be conscripted, but his experience on the *Luisiana* had so terrified him that he truly did not want to sail again. His family must come to him. He reasoned and believed, as he had at the outset, that America would offer greater opportunities for them.

Finally, spurred by patriotism for America, he gave in to his conscience and went back to industry, but not to the inferno. He remembered his experience of working in hardware manufacture in Niles, Ohio. This helped him to get hired by National Tube in Hazlewood, where he worked at making ammunition for the war. There was no overtime pay for working twelve-hour days for little more than $2.50 a day.

His commitment to America was strong. By now he felt that he was progressing well in English, and having met the minimum seven-year residency requirements, he filed for his first citizenship papers and studied for his coveted goal. After his evening prayer ritual, Paolo planned to write to Maria Giuseppa about his intent to become a *cittadino americano*; and he would urge her to leave Italy before wartime immigration quotas closed.

Tonight his prayers would be critical. He decided to bypass praying to *Santa Maria* and the saints, and go directly to *Dio Omnipotente* and say a *preghiera per ottenere due favori speciali*— he would ask for two special favors: guidance to help him convince Maria that she absolutely *must* leave Italy, and assurance that her journey on the perilous sea would be safe.

As Paolo sat at his bedroom window, the evening sun cast a long slanted ray of amber light across his Bible. He recited the Lord's Prayer, in Italian: *"Padre nostro, che sei nei'cieli, sia santificato il tuo nome . . ."* And then, raising his tenor voice, sang it in Latin: *"Pater noster qui es in coelis, sanctificetur nomen tuum . . ."* Every evening Paolo selected a favored Italian or Latin hymn to sing, depending upon the occasion or holy day. He imagined his *Bella Rossa* back home saying her evening prayers with Mamma Luigi, his *bambini* and Arcangela, and he raised his voice in glorious praise: *"Pange Lingua Gloriosi, Corporis mysteriu . . ."* Oh how glorious it would be to sing with Maria again, he thought!

Chapter 7

Addio!

When the war began, the major goal of opposing sides was to destroy their enemy's supply lines. The French armada and the British Royal navy held a lead over the German fleet. Having won control of the seas, they drove German merchant shipping from the ocean, leaving the Germans with one weapon to stop the French and British blockade — the submarine.

All areas in the Atlantic were in danger since the *Lusitania,* the largest British ship afloat, had been torpedoed by Germany, without warning, on May 7, 1915 at Kinsale Head off the Irish coast. In twenty minutes 1,198 lives were lost; over one-hundred were Americans. Following several more such incidents, a storm of resentment erupted. When America protested, the German government promised Wilson that it would stop sinking merchant ships without warning, but threatened to resume unrestricted submarine warfare if the enemy did not moderate the terms of the blockade.

Nonetheless, rampant submarine warfare continued and put many American ships in peril, bringing anti-German feeling to a climax and America's imminent break with Germany. The war frenzy had strengthened the nativist mood and spurred a spirit of nationalism. Everywhere posters of a serious Uncle Sam, pointing a convincing forefinger, commanded: "UNCLE SAM WANTS YOU!" Wilson urged all American residents — citizens and non-citizens — to be deeply concerned about world oppression. He asserted that those who had come to America because this was a land of opportunity and freedom should be willing to fight to "make the world safe for democracy."

Paolo was strongly influenced by his message. Like him, many immigrants in the United States were trapped. Their families at home felt doomed. But hard work and hope sustained the new patriot until he would see peace and embrace his little family once again. He feared for their safety because submarines posed an increasing threat. He remembered the sinking of the *Lusitania* — and prayed.

Paolo feared greatly as news on both sides of the Atlantic repeatedly warned that immigration quotas would close. He begged Maria to act quickly before their passports expired. It was Mamma Luigi, bedridden with arthritis and complications of aging, who urged her daughter to hasten preparations. Mamma commanded her to go quickly with God's blessing: *"Va, figlia mia. Va presto. Dio vi benedica."* She admonished Maria that she and Paolo had been separated too long, advising her that a wife belongs with her husband, and children belong with their father. Mamma reassured her daughter that Arcangela would be with her until her last days. She promised that one day Arcangela would join her Antonio and Maria's family in America.

Maria prayed and wept, knowing that she would never again see her *cara Mamma.* Grazia, now thirteen years old, was very close to her *Nonna* and *Zia* Arcangela. Her grief was as great as theirs. She wondered which saint she should implore to protect them from that dreaded *mostro sottomarino* that prowled beneath the waters. For years to come, Grazia would remember their final painful parting.

Although Maria kept abreast of war news from letters and from any newspapers she could secure, she was not aware of the growing anti-immigrant movement in America. By 1916, Congress had proposed a series of restrictions for prospective newcomers. Admission through Ellis Island would eventually be denied to criminals, persons with various diseases, paupers, illiterates or anyone who was perceived as a political threat. Paolo, aware about immigration restrictions, had carefully schooled Maria to demonstrate that she was not illiterate, and had taught her a few American courtesy words.

She gathered her Bibles and the bank books from *Casa di Risparmo Postali.* She would leave Arcangela her Sears Roebuck catalog and some of her dowry. Finally, Maria began distributing her other possessions among her friends. She would be allowed only one trunk in passage, so she selected carefully. She would take one-half dozen embroidered sheets, one dozen lace-edged pillow cases, her hand-crocheted shawl, two hand-crocheted lace bed covers, and the big red and black plaid blanket, which she had spun from the wool that she had sheared from her sheep. Soon she would take her last walk along the Biferno. She beseeched the Sorrowful Mother for help: *"Bella Madre Dolorosa aiutami!"*

Early on the day before their departure for America, Maria Giuseppa and her little family went to Holy Mass. After she attended to her bedridden Mamma, Maria mounted Cico, her faithful donkey, and rode him sidesaddle down the steep hillside. Toppo, her piglet, scrambled close behind. Today she would take her last walk among her olive groves and vineyards.

The Biferno River was peaceful in the early morning mist. Maria's straight thin figure made a graceful silhouette against the fog. As she walked barefoot along its banks, she and Cico and Toppo created a curious tableau. Today would be the last time Maria would gather wood chips for the fire. She filled her big coarse scarf, tied it securely, and balanced the bundle on her head. Tomorrow she and her three *ragazzi* would leave for America. Tomorrow would bring her one day closer to Paolo. Her face flushed crimson. She burned with excitement at the thought of their reunion. Maria removed the bundle from her head, pushed her little hatchet into the straw basket hanging from Cico's back, and dropped to the ground. She drank in the beauty of her lush farmland near the Biferno, and felt sad to know this would be her final walk on the land she loved.

Maria Giuseppa had never left Castellino Sul Biferno, except when she and Paolo had visited cousins in Campo Basso. Her daydream carried her to memories of the pencil-line horizon of the Adriatic Sea, where restless billows rolled in from the blue sky and gathered momentum behind the incoming surf. She laughed aloud, remembering her shock and glee at being catapulted into a bed of seaweed. The ocean had fascinated and frightened her. She prayed that she and her little family would arrive safely in America.

Maria blinked away the tears. She wanted tomorrow to come quickly. And she wished it never would. The thought of crossing the ocean filled her with horror. *"Bella Madonna, prego che arrivamo sani e salvi."* She prayed that they would arrive whole and safe.

Her fear had grown steadily since she had heard the news that, last May 7, a German submarine had torpedoed and sunk the *Lusitania*. News had reached her little town that even neutral ships were not safe to travel. It was now April 30, 1916, nearly a year later, and conditions were growing worse.

Maria came out of her reverie abruptly and pulled herself to her feet. She lifted the bundle of chips to her head and turned her attention to the hillside, which rose in layers above the *fiume*. Tiny stone houses were sprinkled among the slopes as though some unseen hand had spilled them from a huge salt shaker, causing them to fall and rest in random clusters. Maria looked up and thought about their stone house with the balcony that Paolo had so happily built. She searched the bluff for the old castle that dominated the skyline, and remembered how the village earned its name, Castellino Sul Biferno.

Tomorrow she must say goodbye to Toppo and Cico. She scratched her piglet's snout and said, *"Poverini Toppo e Cico. Domani vi dico addio."* The piglet grunted back at the sound of her voice. She stopped to pull gently at Cico's long gray ears and rub his nose, remembering how faithfully he had carried bundles of wood for the fire and baskets of grapes, and olives, and vegetables to the *piazza*. Cico was growing old. He brayed softly and nudged Maria's nose, nearly knocking the bundle of chips off her head. She wept softly and comforted herself that Cico and Topo would be happy with Arcangela, secure that she would take care of them and Mamma Luigi, and care for the goat herd so that there would be plenty of milk and cheese. Arcangela would look after the farm and the harvesting — and . . . Suddenly, she felt guilty that she was leaving her sister too much work. *"Santa Maria!"* she exclaimed. *"La lascio troppo lavoro!"*

Maria's breast swelled with emotion when she thought of parting with Mamma and Arcangela. Mamma Luigi, crippled with rheumatism, seldom left her bed these days, except to use the tall crock chamber pot. *"Povera Mamma,"* she whispered. Maria worried about how lonely it would be for them. And she remembered how Mamma had wept quietly when she heard Paolo's letter from America begging Maria to come with the *bambini*.

"Cara mia," he had written, *"Bisogni venire subito. La guerra si fa più critica."* In his final letter he insisted that she *must* come immediately because the war was growing more critical. Paolo emphasized that if America and Italy entered the war, passage to America would stop! Twice before Paolo had implored Maria to come. Each time that she had thought of leaving Mamma nearly alone and helpless, she had resisted the temptation to leave.

Yesterday Maria had gone to Don Alfonso, her priest, for comfort. He had assured them that they would be safe, for the Madonna would keep them in Her care. But Don Alfonso's encouraging words had disguised his anxiety about the menacing voyage. They had toured the little church, stopping before each saint to beseech their protection. Don Alfonso had prayed with them and advised that a family belonged together. Maria Giuseppa had faith. Tomorrow she would return to the *Cappella* and pray, and leave her gold locket at the feet of the Madonna as her parting gift.

Addio!

The cold water at the river's edge licked at her bare toes. She sat on a flat rock and pushed her feet into the clear foam, remembering again the Adriatic Sea. Would America have a sea so beautiful? She recalled how the waves leaped onto the beach and rearranged the sand in shimmering layers . . . and how the wind, piercing and cool, sprayed sea mist that caught the sun and scattered glittering chips about her. She blushed at the memory of the sea spray dampening the strawberry blonde curls at her ears kinking them into tiny sausages, of Paolo whispering, *"mia bella rossa"* and kissing her passionately.

It had been six years since Paolo had left Abruzzi for the third time to make his fortune in America. The separation had been painful. And now for Maria, the separation from her dear family and friends would be painful. She stroked the sun-bleached rock where she had often washed her family's clothes. *"Mamma mia,"* she sighed. And shook her head sadly, reminiscing about how she and her friends gathered to visit and wash. *"Domani diciamo addio!"* Tomorrow they would say goodbye! Her blue eyes misted. She pulled herself to her feet, blinked away the tears, and kicked at broken shells and pebbles. Cico nudged her rump. She came out of her reverie. They would soon approach the footpath that wound up the steep hillside.

"Fermo, Cico," she said as she withdrew the little hatchet from his saddle pack. He brayed. She laughed. And cried. And searched the nearby cove for vagrant vegetation, and gathered twigs for Arcangela to use for her hearth fire.

Ahead of her, a lone set of footprints stretched along the river's edge, marring the perfection of the wet shore. They were Grazia's footprints. Grazia would soon be thirteen. Maria was proud of her eldest child. She had been a great comfort and help during Paolo's absence. While Maria Giuseppa had tended the olive groves and vineyards, and supervised the workers at planting and harvest time, Grazia had kept house and cared for Silvio Pietro, little Domenico and Mamma. She recalled how she and Grazia had tied the baby's cradle high in a tree to protect it from animals and snakes. Paolo had said that in America they did not do this.

Maria spotted Grazia stopping by a rocky cove in the hillside. From a wild fig tree growing along the footpath above it, a young man leaped to the ground. It was Giovanni. Maria pulled Cico's harness to halt him, sensing that she must keep her distance. Cico slackened his pace. The piglet walked ahead. *"Vieni! Vieni subito, Toppo!"* she commanded softly. He obeyed and came quickly.

Grazia and Giovanni were absorbed in serious conversation. Grazia's head scarf had slipped down around her shoulders. The morning sun caught the golden highlights of her long blonde hair. Maria noted with pride her daughter's slim figure and high firm bosom. Giovanni took Grazia's hand and kissed it. He untied her scarf and dabbed her eyes, and they continued their conversation.

Maria became lost in reverie. This particular cove always brought back pleasant and exciting memories. She stopped walking and reminisced about an episode that had occurred here fifteen years ago while she tended her small flock of sheep.

She recalled the day that she had gone about her daily task of gathering firewood as she scrambled up and down the hillside, like a mountain goat, attempting to herd her flock to lush grazing ground along the bottom slope. As she foraged in the thick underbrush for wood chips, a huge thorn pierced her foot, causing it to bleed and soil her dress.

It was high noon, and the breeze was warm. Maria felt the hot sun on her bosom and shoulders as she she stripped herself down to her *mutandine*. She walked to the river to bathe her foot and wash her dress in the foaming water. Just as she hung it on the edge of a rock that jutted over the cove, a small green fig from the tree overhead fell and hit her back.

She knew that only ripe figs fall from their tree and speculated that these were small and green, and she mumbled, *"Questa è piccola e verde."*

She looked up and discovered that a grinning Paolo had been peering down at her from among the wide fronds. *"Santa Maria!"* she cried — and crossed herself.

Then, worried that Paolo had seen her, exclaimed *"Mi vede cosi! Non dirlo a nessuno, o rimango scandalizzata!"* ("Say nothing about seeing me this way or I will be scandalized!")

"E il nostro segreto per sempre, mia bella Rossa. Prometto Dio." Paolo had promised God that it would remain their secret forever.

Maria blushed crimson at the memory. This characteristic, and her rosy complexion, had justly earned her the pseudonym *la rossa* — Red. It had become Paolo's favorite nickname.

That night Paolo, Domenico Stanziano, and several of their friends serenaded her at her window. Now that Paolo's intentions had been made clear — and public, *la proposta di matrimonio* would soon follow. It had seemed such a short time ago, Maria thought. And now, here stood her Grazia by that same cove.

Cico and Toppo were growing restless. Maria would have to move closer to the young couple. She watched Giovanni draw Grazia to him. He lifted her face and kissed her long and tenderly. Maria turned her back, blinked away the tears, adjusted the long straw baskets at Cicco's sides, and slid the hatchet into place.

Toppo nudged at her toes. Suddenly she stooped down and slapped the piglet's fat rump. *"Va via! Va via!"* she ordered. He squealed, obeyed and ran away.

"Ecco Toppo! Buon giorno, Signora Maria Giuseppa," Giovanni greeted the piglet and Maria. *"Sono venuto a dire l'ultimo addio!"* He had come to say his last goodbye.

"Ah, e addio a Grazia," she laughed. Maria took note that his hair was chestnut brown and his eyes were deep blue like Paolo's.

A melancholic Giovanni said, *"Signora, per favore, desidero un piccolo ricordo dalla famiglia Palombo."* He wished for a little rememberance to keep.

Maria thought for a moment and retrieved the little hatchet from Cico's side pouch and offered it. *"Va bene, Giovanni,"* she agreed. *"Ecco quest' accetta per ricordo"*

"Tante grazie!" he exclaimed and promised to return it when he came to America to marry Grazia. *"La porto in America quando vengo sposare Grazia,"* he jested, barely able to conceal his emotion.

"Prego," Maria said. She laughed. And cried. And teased, wondering whether this was a serious proposal. *"È questa una proposta di matrimonio?"* she asked. Giovanni did not answer.

He secured the hatchet into his belt and ran toward the Biferno without looking back. He plunged into the river and swam until Maria and Grazia saw only a small dot above the water. Grazia would never see her *caro* Giovanni again.

The wind whipped their skirts high. The women and the animals began their climb up the long winding path to the village. There would be many sad *addios* ahead. Maria's heart was heavy. Very heavy.

That evening there would be one last visit to cousin Don Alfonso for his blessing. Maria and Grazia, Silvio and Domenico knelt before him and wept quietly. Finally, Don Alfonso tried to discourage Maria from making the trip. Privately, he reminded her that German submarines could sink their ship and the sharks would eat them. He implored her to leave the children behind. But Maria scolded her cousin for his lack of faith and declared that God would see them safely to America, with the help of *everyone's* prayers. She and Grazia laid their gold jewelry at the foot of the Holy Mother as a final tribute of their faith. They kept only the gold earrings and crosses that they wore, and Maria's wedding ring, which she never removed from her finger.

Paesani came to Mamma Luigi's to say their last goodbye to their beloved friends. "It was like a wake," Grazia recalled years later. "Like a funeral. No celebration. Everyone cried and prayed. Everyone feared for us because of the war and the German submarines."

Early on the morning of their departure, the little family went to say their last painful goodbye to Mamma Luigi. Maria, Grazia, Silvio, and Domenico covered her face with wet kisses and tears. Mamma quietly unclasped their hands from about her neck and calmly gave them her last blessing and sent them away. Moments later Maria returned to admonish Arcangela to take good care of their Mamma. She heard Mamma Luigi shriek *"come un' anima disperata"* -- like a desperate soul — a chilling scream that would haunt her for years to come.

Zio Costanzo accompanied them in the carriage to Campo Basso, the province capital, where travelers from other provinces would also travel to the port of embarkation. Along the way, Maria carried the sound of Mamma's final piercing outcry. She straightened her back, held her head high and gathered her courage, determined not to be overcome with grief.

Upon their arrival at Naples, *Zio* Costanzo found a kindly male passenger, pressed a few *spiccioli* in his hand, and appealed to him to look after Maria and her *bambini*. Frederico Antonio DiFabio solemnly promised Costanzo that he would. Maria, in turn, extracted promises from *Zio* Costanzo to take care of her Mamma, and assured him that she would name one of her children after him. *Zio* Costanzo tucked a prized holy medal into

Maria's palm, kissed her goodbye, and they parted with his blessing — and a final appeal and thanks to Frederico.

Maria's passport had been issued on April 6, 1915, "*In Roma DI Sua Maesta Vittorio Emaneuele III, Re D'Italia,*" His Majesty the King of Italy. The year until the following April had been a long, torturous wait. From Campo Basso, voyagers would go to Naples to sail on the *S.S. Il Duca d' Aosta.* If all went well, they were due to arrive in New York Harbor by May 13, 1916.

Maria surveyed the passengers who crowded the ship's rail, and thought compassionately about the many immigrants from other countries who would leave their homelands forever, and gasped from emotion and fear. She tried not to think of the menace ahead. Instead she fixed her attention on the beautiful blue Bay of Naples and thought of Paolo's deep blue eyes. Three mighty blasts from the ship's horn startled her. As *Il Duca d' Aosta* pulled away from port, Maria finally wept, *"Addio mia bella Mamma! Addio mia bell' Italia!"*

Courtesy Elio and Irma Colaizzi

The hills of Abruzzo, Italia.

Paolo Palombo after his
first trip home from America in 1904.

Courtesy Steamship Historical Society of America Collection, Langsdale Library, University of Baltimore

S.S. Luisiana built in Riva Trigoso, Italy, 1905. Speed 14 knots; 381 feet long, 47 feet wide. Passengers 1625 (25 first class, 1600 third class). Torpedoed and sunk off Spain by a German submarine in 1917.

Paolo Palombo's passport for his last crossing on the *S.S. Luisiana.*

Courtesy Library of Congress, Prints and Photographs Division, Detroit Publishing Company Collection

Immigrant men often made more than one crossing to America.

Courtesy Library of Congress, Prints and Photographs Division, Detroit Publishing Company Collection

Immigrants, approved for entry, wait to disembark
from the ferry boat to America's shore.

Courtesy Library of Congress, Prints and Photographs Division, Detroit Publishing Company Collection

Ellis Island — ferry boats transport immigrants from ship
to Ellis Island and onto American shore.

Courtesy Library of Congress, Prints and Photographs Division, Detroit Publishing Company Collection

New York, in the early 1900s, impressed Paolo as a forest of
tall buildings and "clothes hanging from the sky."

Maria's Public Health Service card was stamped at Ellis Island for approval to enter America.

Maria Giuseppa Palombo's passport. Maria sailed on the Duca d' Aosta with her children in 1916.

Courtesy Steamship Historical Society of America Collection, Langsdale Library, University of Baltimore

The *S.S. Duca d' Aosta*. Built by Cantieri Navale Siciliani, Palermo, Italy, 1908. Speed 16 knots; 476 feet long, 53 feet wide. Passengers 1836 (80 first class, 16 second class, 1740 third class). Scrapped in 1929.

Before leaving Castellino Sul Biferno, Italy, Maria Giuseppa posed with Zio Costanzo and her children, Silvio, Domenico and Grazia.

Maria's sister, Archangela Palumbo, photographed with her little Domenico before they sailed to America in 1919. Her husband, Antonio Palumbo, was not related to Maria's husband Paolo Palombo.

Part II — Ethnic Enclaves

Chapter 8

Allora Questa è l'America? — So *This* is America?

Since immigrants were permitted only one clearly labeled trunk to take on their voyage, many came aboard burdened like jack-horses. Maria and the *bambini* each carried a suitcase instead of cloth bundles aboard *Il Duca d' Aosta*. Paolo had observed that many immigrants who carried cloth bundles reminded him of *zingari* — gypsies who carried bundles and were viewed as cunning vagabonds. *Signore* Frederico carried the *mezzito*, a half-bushel, which Maria had secured from the *piazza*. This held their food. Maria was not sure that her children would like the ship's food.

Paolo had warned of the problems of traveling in steerage with a mass of humanity jammed onto every inch of deck space. He had described the rank odor of the toilet facilities and had warned Maria that after a few days *puzzano*. She and *Signore* Frederico surveyed the area to avoid the smelly section, and selected a space near the sleeping quarters.

Maria gathered her brood close and cautioned them to stay within the orderly section she had prepared for their comfort. She pulled the *mezzito* close to her. It was tightly packed with fresh figs, grapes, olives, loaves of bread, *prosciutto, formaggio di capra* — the children loved goat cheese— two flasks of red wine, and a crock of *fettucini fatta a mano, con salsa*. The handmade fettucini with tomato sauce would be their first meal. Each person carried a flask of well water.

Maria Giuseppa was surprised and relieved that the ship was not as crowded as she had envisioned. But when the steamer arrived at Gibraltar, several hundred Greek passengers boarded. Confusion erupted. Noisy children scurried about. Parents shouted them into obedience. The confusion and babble caused Maria to hold her head and exclaim, *"Ma che babilonia!"*

Since ships had no balancers to steady them in those days, the vessel rolled with the turbulence of the sea. In steerage, the voyage was very rough. Maria was beginning to feel *mal di mare*. For those who were not seasick, meals were served at long tables — in two shifts. Maria could not eat, but nibbled on a bit of bread instead.

After supper, *Signore* Frederico scouted for their sleeping area. Women and small children slept in bunk beds stacked by twos around the walls. Men were in separate quarters. On the first night, Maria's children slept from sheer exhaustion. Nights were spent huddled in darkness for fear that lights from *Il Duca d' Aosta* might betray their presence to some enemy ship; and when night fell upon the sea, Maria was terrified. Except for an occasional whimper from a sleepless child, only an intermittent faint burst of cannon fire was heard in the distance. Maria prayed her rosary. And had her customary colloquial conversation with the Blessed Mother. Her Italian became very formal when she bargained with *Dio Omnipotente*.

During the day there were survival drills. Captain and crew helped passengers practice donning life jackets and getting into the lifeboats. The drills brought an uneasy recollection of what it must have been like for Paolo adrift all night away from the *Luisiana*. There was little gaiety and much praying.

Poor Maria — her seasickness did not relent. Grazia ate little. But Domenico and Silvio Pietro, seemingly unaffected by the rolling ship, had good appetites. They eventually consumed the food that Maria had packed into the *mezzito*. The mischievous imps threw the empty container over-board. It overturned. As it bobbed up and down over the waves, it was mistaken for a submarine about to surface. A frightened passenger cried out, *"Il sottomarino!! Il sottomarino!! O Dio mio! Il sottomarino!!"* The drill siren screeched its piercing high-pitched wail! Panic broke out. But Grazia, who had seen the *mezzito* fly overboard, reported this to *Signore* Frederico, who alerted the crewmen before the lifeboat rescue maneuvers got underway. After the bobbing object was identified, the siren stopped. When calm was restored, the frightened pair of blonde blue-eyed imps received a non-stop Italian tongue-lashing that subdued them for a few hours. The crimson-faced, mortified Maria apologized profusely to any and all who would listen.

Early in the voyage, Grazia had asked permission to go and play games with a group of little Greek girls. She wore the pretty lace shawl that *Nonna*

Maria Luigi had made. The girls tried it on all around. When Grazia returned from play, Maria noticed that the beautiful *scialle* was crawling with lice. She became petrified that if Grazia caught *pidocchi* they could be deported! Maria immediately tore it from Grazia's head and tossed it overboard! She watched it disappear into the water, and imagined she heard her precious Mamma's last piercing shriek. But Maria did not even have time to cross herself, or pray, or cry. She hustled Grazia into the bathing area. *"Santa Maria! Santa Maria! Pidocchi!"* she exclaimed as she washed her hair with soap. And then she remembered that those who became infested were deloused with a strong-smelling liquid. Maria searched, found, and recognized the bottle she had seen marked *"per pidocchi,"* and washed Grazia's hair again.

Sanitary conditions among the immigrants were difficult to maintain. Maria noticed that some passengers never sponge-bathed the entire trip. Some at least bathed on the day of landing. The idea revolted her. She thought of the clear sparkling water of the *fiume* and grew sad.

There was illness on board. And death. One day Grazia noticed that a nearby passenger became very ill and died. Soon crewmen came and wrapped the corpse in a sheet. She followed the sailors and saw them tie heavy bags around the body and put it on a long board. They lifted it to the rail and tilted it. Grazia recalled seeing it fall into the sea with a loud swoooosh! When sharks appeared alongside the vessel, passengers knew that another death had occurred. One remarked, *"C' è stata un 'altra morte."* The spectacle haunted Grazia. Sharks terrified her. They were plentiful and followed the ships, preying for food.

But sharks fascinated little Domenico. While Maria comforted Grazia at their appearance, Domenico climbed the rail and leaned over to get a better look at them. Just as he lost his footing and was about to plunge overboard, an alert immigrant caught at his feet. The bewildered Domenico could not understand the commotion about him as his mother cried, and crewmen and passengers shook their fingers at him. The fearsome sharks, the sea sickness, the fear of death by torpedoes, and the thought of Domenico's and her father's near escapes from death at sea were a traumatic experience for Grazia. Like Paolo, the frightened *signorina* vowed that she would never again cross the water. And she did not.

The voyage was fifteen endless days long. *Il Duca d' Aosta* was due in New York Harbor in three days. On the eve of landing, Maria Giuseppa organized and packed her possessions. As if the ocean had not made her ill enough, the fear that they might not pass physical inspection on Ellis Island increased her malaise. She remembered Paolo's description of the sad voyagers who were marked with blue chalk letters and directed to a holding area.

Before sunrise on the day of arrival, Maria thoroughly sponge-bathed herself and dressed in a neatly tailored suit. She bathed the children, combed their hair and dressed them in their best clothes. Finally she pinned their name and destination tags securely to each of their lapels. Maria was prepared to read them for the inspectors, to prove that she was literate. Paolo had schooled her well. She had put her documents in neat order in her American *bursa*. He had arranged for her passage, including railroad tickets on the Pennsylvania Railroad, destined for East Liberty in Pittsburgh, where they would meet again. This arrangement was the most practical one. It saved Paolo precious time from work and train fare to New York.

Maria gathered their bags, secured her purse on her arm and pulled the little family to the deck. They found their places against the rail to watch the land rise out of the water. People cheered and cried and prayed in relief. *"Benedette Dio! La Statua Liberta! Grazie, Signore!"* And suddenly there she was — huge and majestic. Maria's children, accustomed to much smaller statues in their church, were awestruck. *"Santa Maria!"* cried Maria, overcome with joy. Little Domenico, believing that this was the Holy Mother, crossed himself and dropped to his little knees. In the harbor narrows, tugboats, barges, and ferry boats sounded a cacophony of whistles and horns in a greeting ritual. The children held their ears.

After being ferried to Ellis Island, passengers were hustled to the Immigrant Receiving Station, where they entered the huge baggage room area to find their trunks and check belongings. Papa had warned Maria about con men who lined the entrance, intent on enticing naive "greenhorns" to part with their baggage. Some unwittingly parted with train tickets and money.

Years later, Grazia remembered hearing "lots of feet climb up the long noisy stairs" in the center of the giant hall with ceilings higher than her church. She remembered the doctors who waited at the top, ready to examine their eyes and hair. Most of all, Grazia remembered the fear they had at being marked with the blue chalk Papa had told about. Maria had instructed her children to smile, stand tall, walk straight, be well-mannered — and NOT SCRATCH— no matter where they itched — so that they would not make *una brutta figura,* a bad impression, on the feared medical and customs inspectors.

Grazia never forgot the happy look on her mother's face as the inspector chalked each of their arms in yellow. He smiled when Grazia curtsied to him and said, "Tank you!" Maria smiled brightly, adjusted her beautiful hat, tilted her head and repeated, "Tank you," in grateful relief that her little family had made *una buona figura.* Making a good impression was important.

But Maria's joy was marred when she looked toward the holding area where unhappy passengers sat in various stages of grief. She crossed herself and gasped, *"O Dio! Poveri sfortunati!"* sad for the poor unfortunates.

"America! *Finalmente!*" Maria cried as they pushed their way through the green door to the ferry that would take them to New York City. *"Grazie, Bello Dio!"* she said as she kissed her fingers and touched them to the earth.

Maria was touched by the embraces and greetings of reunited families and imagined her own reunion with her *caro* Paolo — and blushed. On their way to the station, they marveled at the forest of tall buildings, which were much taller than their Papa had described. Maria was fascinated by the hubbub along the streets. She looked for clothes that "were hanging from the sky" between buildings.

At the station, they thanked *Signore* Frederico, said goodbye, and climbed aboard. The train lurched, and they moved. Small clumps of gray wooden houses whizzed by the window. Maria Giuseppa was sorry that she had left her sunny Castellino with its white stone houses. *"Allora, questa è l'America?"* If *this* was America, she was not impressed.

As the train gained momentum the whistle shrieked several high-pitched blasts. She remembered Mamma Luigi's shriek and grew sadder. But it had been six years since she had seen Paolo and the thought of their reunion comforted and excited her.

Soon a Black man came along the aisle. Although Paolo had told Maria about the *Negri* in America, she was, nonetheless, startled and curious when she saw him. He nodded and smiled broadly at her and the children. She smiled back. He punched holes into her tickets and touched his hard red cap, smiled again, and moved on. Maria liked him.

Believing that his face was dirty, Silvio Pietro whispered, *"La facia è sporca."* His mother, explaining that God had made him that way, answered, *"Cosi l' ha fatta Dio."* She explained further that he was like one of the three Kings who stood in the *presepio* in front of *il Bambino Jesu.*

"Oh, allora serà un Santo." Pietro had concluded that he must be a saint. He was satisfied. Mother and children chattered away in the only language they knew as the scenery rolled by and redeemed some of Maria's first negative impression. The weary little family slept away the darkness on their way to Pittsburgh. Due to arrive in East Liberty at 1:00 p.m., they neverthe-less wakened early to prepare for Papa. Maria wanted to look beautiful for Paolo. She patted her neatly-braided blonde crown and tugged at the little curls next to her gold earrings. And blushed crimson at the thought of their reunion. She smoothed her American-tailored suit, put on the matching deep-brimmed hat, and adjusted Paolo's locket over her blue silk blouse. Judging from pages of hats she had seen in the Sears Roebuck catalog, Maria reasoned that women always wore hats when they walked outdoors or went to Mass. She hoped Paolo would remember his first gifts to her from America, and was pleased that she had left her prized Sears catalog with Arcangela.

The journey had been one surprise after another. They were not prepared to experience the smell of grey air filled with thick smoke from nearby steel mills. Both Maria and Grazia felt the urge to be back in sunny Italy. Nearly three weeks had passed. Maria missed Mamma Luigi. Grazia yearned for her Giovanni. The beautiful America they had heard and read so much about impressed them as being dirty. Neither of them spoke their thoughts until long after their arrival. For now, having Papa again was payment enough for their disappointment.

The black iron horse whistled its way into the bustling downtown Pennsylvania Station to discharge passengers and pick up those bound for points East. Stations were busy with commuters whose only mode of transportation to their jobs was the railroad. The ticket taker examined their lapel tags, shook his head, and pointed forward. Maria had listened intently for the familiar name as the redcap swayed his way along the aisles calling out destinations. Soon she heard him call *"Avanti!* East Liberty!" The engine coughed its last stream of smoke and hissed to a stop. *"Ragazzi, Venite! Venite, subito!"* They scrambled for suitcases and cloth bags. The redcap *"con la faccia scura"* flashed his last toothy smile and helped the voyagers down the steep iron steps.

The station was crowded with people on their way to work, some well dressed, others in dirty-looking work clothes. The new arrivals searched for their Papa among the crowd. Suddenly, little Domenico thought that he recognized Papa. He pointed his forefinger, pulled at Maria's skirt and said, *"Questo serà Papa."* And it was! Paolo crushed Maria to him, and they both laughed and wept. He hugged his little brood and covered them with kisses. Grazia later remembered that his moustache had pinched her.

Papa followed the baggage wagons along the platform, secured their large trunk and paid to have it delivered by wagon to 7315 Tioga Street in Homewood. They climbed the long iron steps leading to the street. Grazia thought about the "noisy steps" on Ellis Island. The newcomers saw their first automobile and were astounded. A Black man wearing a square cap held open the door as an elegant lady got inside. Grazia commented: *"Serà ricca,"* concluding that she was probably rich.

As they walked toward the streetcar tracks, Papa laughed and announced that soon they would have another ride on a little train Americans called a "strrreeetcarrr." Maria remembered that Paolo had once explained that it traveled on *binari* that ran down the middle of the *strada*. Paolo promised that one day soon they would ride it again to visit Domenico Stanziano's family in Hazelwood. Paolo explained that Dom was a streetcar conductor, in fact, the first Italian in Pittsburgh to be hired as a *conduttore*. Maria smiled and remembered Domenico's and Paolo's serenade to her on the eve of Paolo's proposal. The family chattered happily as they rode the trolley. Paolo reminded them that soon they would be reunited with *Zio* Antonio and *paesani* in Homewood. Maria sighed in happy relief. *Finalmente* — they were home!

Chapter 9

New Americans — The Ethnic Patchquilt

The May afternoon was cool and bright in Homewood. Paolo whistled happily as the family walked from the 76 Frankstown car line to their cousin's home on Tioga Street. Maria and Grazia were pleased that the air was smoke-free. Unlike mill towns situated near heavy industry, Homewood was bordered by light manufacturing plants and several city parks. Its respectable middle-class tone attracted both white-collar and blue-collar residents. Multinational immigrants and Blacks lived among middle-class Americans not far from Homewood's elite upper class.

Homewood had evolved into a streetcar suburb of country estates and new middle-class neighborhoods. A network of car lines, built in the 1890's by profits from factories and manufacturing plants, ran between downtown and East End. Early immigrants, who no longer desired to live in the downtown area or along the rivers, envied the elite who could live in the green, pollution-free East End. Although they could not afford to build elaborate country estates, they moved nearby, where they built moderate detached frame and brick houses. This enabled them to travel to work, to town, and to amusements. Trolley rides became a social experience.

The wealthy industrial barons — Henry Clay Frick, H. J. Heinz, Andrew Carnegie — traveled by train and maintained their own private railroad cars, which were held on private tracks near the Homewood station. Though trains were normally punctual, business magnates could literally slow down or stop a train. One local tycoon, George Westinghouse, did just that by pointing his umbrella at the approaching engineer. (In lieu of a cane Mr. Westinghouse, copying the style of upper-class Englishmen, always carried an umbrella, rain or shine.)

Now, as the newcomers walked along Homewood Avenue past Bennet and Kelly Streets, they approached the Hamilton Avenue streetcar track. Pietro spied a horse-drawn ice delivery wagon creaking alongside the rails. He watched children hop onto its rear running board to retrieve pieces of ice. Curious to know what it was he asked, *"Ma che cos' è?"* The boys had never seen ice and begged to taste it. Paolo obliged them and gave Maria and Grazia a taste, too. They saw girls skipping rope and boys kneeling on one knee beside a chalk circle playing marbles. Paolo explained the games. There was so much to learn.

They arrived at 7315 Tioga Street, where he had found lodging at the home of *Signore* Martone. True to the practice that immigrants helped newer immigrants, his friend had made room in their six-room house to accommodate them in their parlor and enclosed porch, until Paolo found space of their own. In the Petrucci family's house across the street, Filomena, Maria Giuseppa's first cousin, had prepared a welcoming feast. *"Benedetto Dio!"* Filomena wept as she embraced Maria and her children. Grazia and her brothers enjoyed the warm greeting from their second cousins, Annie, Dom and Joe.

Soon *paesani* came to welcome the new family and hear news from home. *"Benvenuti! Benvenuti, cari,"* each visitor exclaimed amid a cacophony of questions, laughter, and tears. This emotional scenario recurred among immigrants from every country with new arrivals. They brought food to celebrate the occasion.

Space was precious in their modest homes, but friends and relatives temporarily accommodated as many newcomers as possible. At the Martone house, all rooms served as bedrooms except the kitchen. Maria used the kitchen table to write her first two letters to Italy. Her letter to Mamma related details about their journey and news about their *paesani* in America. Her letter to Don Alfonso reproached him for not believing in the protection of God.

Weeks later, Don Alfonso's reply bore the horrifying news that Maria Luigi had died on May 5. Maria recalled that, on that *very* day, she had heard her mother's grieved shriek as the sea swallowed Mamma's *scialle!* Inconsolable, she blamed herself for her mother's death. Paolo, deeply grieved, tried to comfort her. They went to Father DeFrancesco to arrange for a requiem Mass. Maria was grateful for a priest whose prayers and Italian discourse helped ease her grief. She and Paolo went into the little church that they had grown to love, and lit candles. Maria prayed to be forgiven for deserting Mamma.

In their new environment, like most European immigrants, Maria found comfort, security, and familiarity in the ethnic churches, religious customs and benefit societies. Homewood women joined Mother of Good Counsel's

Altar Society. Maria helped them make lace-trimmed altar scarves and keep the church immaculate, just as she had done in Italy. The men formed Our Lady of Mount Carmel Society and raised funds for sick and death benefits. Paolo and Maria would one day be grateful for their support.

When a member died, his *fratelli* accompanied him to church in respect-ful procession, to the mournful dirge of funeral music, a custom peculiar to Italians. People of every nationality and color hung over their fences to watch as the men marched solemnly by on the way to Mother of Good Counsel Church. A floral crepe on the front door marked the home where friends came to pray over the corpse and leave donations of food and money.

Each nationality brought its traditions. Among the Irish, of course, wakes became special social events. They drank generous amounts of whiskey, told stories, laughed and wept. Italian funerals were the ultimate sign of honor and respect. Women chanted a long heart-wrenching farewell over the coffin, as they swayed back and forth. Later, their children micheviously mocked them in suitable hyperbole — to the covert amusement of their parents.

Old World customs persisted. Italians had their own kind of Catholicism. Given to honoring the Madonna or special saints, they celebrated special religious holidays differently from the Irish or German Catholics. Across America, villagers transported their own particular saints' *festas* to Italian neighborhoods. In New York, for instance, the Madonna of One-hundred Fifteenth Street has been a long tradition.

In Pittsburgh's Bloomfield, meanwhile, the Saint Rocco *festa* has existed into the millennium. And for over a half-century, in Homewood-Brushton on July 16, the feast of Our Lady of Mount Carmel was celebrated with a Mass and a parade. Children dressed in white marched in two long rows. The *Virginele* carried American flags; the boys carried Italian flags, as parents looked on proudly. Replicating Italian custom, the statue of Our Lady was placed on a beautifully decorated float, preceded by men carrying silk banners of Her Visage. The procession stopped periodically so that Italians could come out of their homes to pin hard-earned $5 and $10 bills to the banners. The money paid for Holy Mass, for music, and a splendorous fireworks display at the end of a day of feasting and dancing in the streets. People of all nationalities looked forward to the *festa* and fireworks.

After the parade, Homewood-Brushton parishioners headed for Mass at Mother of Good Counsel Church, where Father DeFrancesco delivered a dramatic sermon. He elicited passionate tears from the immigrants — and generous donations. One feast day, when he outdid himself in emotional sermonizing, Maria Giuseppa chided him for getting carried away. No one else had ever had the temerity to criticize, let alone scold, the intimidating *Padre*. Nonetheless, Father "D" loved Maria's spirit, and her cooking, when he came to Sunday or Feast Day dinners.

Before the fireworks at the end of the *festa* day, *Maestro* Mezzadeo's band began the evening program of spirited Italian and American music with a rousing rendition of the *Star-Spangled Banner*. Paolo always responded emotionally to the national anthem.

So intertwined with holy feasts was the life of Italians that their children even played *Santa Festa*. Not long after their arrival in America, Domenico and Pietro Palombo organized a *Santa Festa*. They had taken a picture of the Blessed Mother and attached it to a broom. Neighborhood children followed them along, beating with spoons on their mothers' pots and pans. Domenico used his mother's lace table cloth to dress as the priest. As he marched, he chanted in mock Latin: *"Santa Maria, Santa Maria."* The processioners, Black and White, Jew and Gentile, cried back in an attempted imitation of Latin — *"Ora pro nobis."* Up and down Tioga Street they went, amusing Italians and non-Italians alike. When they reached Cox's candy store, a kindly gentleman, convulsed with laughter, bought the whole procession pink ice cream.

As immigrant children became Americanized, they played American games and adapted to all nationalities. Some were slower to assimilate or be accepted; and when arguments erupted among friends, ethnic slurs from Americans flew. Maria and Paolo would not allow the use of those slurs. The Palombo children came to espouse Maria Giuseppa's idea that *"Siamo tutti figli di Dio"* — we are all God's children.

Prejudice had been a "given" in the prewar conservative era of Teddy Roosevelt. The "Old Guard" had believed that immigrants could not be Americanized. But by the time Maria and the children had reached Homewood, the attitude toward aliens had changed, mostly because they were needed when Woodrow Wilson declared war on Germany. Wilson urged all patriotic U.S. male residents, citizens and non-citizens, to volunteer for service. In his heart, Paolo had long ago given his allegiance to America. But regardless of his own sincere belief in the concept of freedom, his fear of the sea overwhelmed him. He had faithfully worked long hours at making war implements for a year. He was torn between honor and duty.

In early April, Congress, in a special session, passed the War Resolution and on April 6, 1917, the United States was at war. September 12, 1918, Paolo reluctantly registered for service at the Homewood Carnegie Library and tucked his Registration Certificate in his *Luisiana Passaporto*. With more faith than courage he said, "I no cana controla destiny. Whata will be will be . . . *Non posso controllare il destino — che será será*." Trusting that Fate would be kind once again, Paolo had finally yielded, seventeen months after his third blonde, blue-eyed son was born on April 17 — the first American. He was named Luigi in honor of Mamma Maria Luigi.

Paolo prayed that he could at least raise a son from start to finish. Faith told him that *Dio* would look after them. And He did. The war ended the next year on November 11, 1918, when the Armistice was signed. They celebrated at Mass and at a community memorial parade for fallen soldiers and returning heroes.

Paolo could now turn to his big dream — to become a *padrone di casa*, a homeowner. Since all their friends lived on or near Tioga Street, he wanted to be near them. On Tioga Street the brick and frame houses were neat and comfortable with 100-foot-deep rear lots. Some held another house. Paolo selected carefully. With the help of a $200 loan from friends and their own savings of $500, Paolo paid $1,500 for a six-room frame house, leaving him an $800 mortgage.

The large lot had one peach tree and one cherry tree. He planted an arbor for table grapes and a fig tree sapling, presented by a friend, that would have to be covered before every winter. Among a variety of garden vegetables, he planted corn, swisschard, zucchini, Italian green beans, tomatoes, and beds of lettuce, escarole, and curly green *radicchio*. One could hardly have *minestra* or *insalata* without these.

Paolo arranged with his Black neighbor, who owned the empty lot next door, to share vegetables in exchange for using his lot. Mr. Turner, a butler in a nearby Homewood mansion, hoped to build a home on his lot one day. There was warm community spirit between Italians and Blacks. Italians did not chose to downgrade Blacks as they themselves sometimes had been downgraded. Maria and Paolo's farming experiences paid off. By October, they had a plentiful harvest to share with Mr. Turner.

From Mrs. Burley, her other Black neighbor, Maria learned to process and preserve fruits and vegetables. They stocked their cold cellar with food. Paolo forgave himself for making wine in America with bought grapes; but he knew how to select the best — and even purchased a wine press and barrels of various sizes, which he scrubbed religiously. In America one did not stomp grapes, but the festivity that went along with wine-making stayed intact.

He had a well-stocked *cantina* to begin the aging process for the distinctive wines that would be used for special occasions. He and Maria made pork sausage, and lye soap from the fat. Nothing was wasted. Taken with American gadgets, Paolo bought a coffee mill, a hand-cranked machine to help cut *pasta fatto a mano,* and a Victorola to play Enrico Caruso's records. He and Maria sang along.

Oh, but they were happy in their little house! The children had chores, and Paolo had begun making improvements — new porcelain sinks replaced the wood-framed ones in the kitchen and upstairs bathroom. Paolo enclosed the side porch and built a second-floor room. There were four coal or wood-burning fireplaces, handsome wall-mounted gas lamps all over the house, and a Franklin wood-burning stove for the parlor.

What a joy American gas lamps were to Maria, accustomed to oil lamps and candles! But Paolo had seen electric lights in the big homes where he gardened. "Soma day we have beeg bright lights — nota gas," he said. Maria smiled. "And soma day we have a beeg brick house," he promised. He had seen such homes in upper Homewood, a low-density, upper middle-class neighborhood.

Paolo and Maria, accustomed to being *padroni,* fit well into homeowner roles. To help them realize their hopes for a "beeg house," Maria took in two boarders who shared a large bedroom with the boys. It held two brass beds, two large chests, and two chairs. Each paid her $10 a month and bought their food for her to cook. At first Maria handwashed and scrubbed their clothes. In a few months, Paolo bought her a wooden washer, which required manual cranking. When poor Maria was worn out from cranking, Paolo and Grazia helped her. Grazia often laughed when she remembered its trade name, Savage, and said, "The name fit. It was a savage because it did a wild dance all over the mud cellar floor."

In fact, most Italian women kept boarders because it was taboo for them to work outside the family — unlike other immigrant women who worked as maids in elite Homewood mansions. Their wealthy owners employed large work forces to maintain their gardens, clean their homes, care for their wardrobes and cook. Black domestic workers settled in lower middle-class Homewood and in this respect were more worldy than their Italian sisters.

There were marked differences among Homewood-Brushton neighborhoods. Poor Blacks and immigrant laborers lived on Finance Street, nearest the railroad tracks, in rented houses with small yards, and an occasional outhouse. Others, mostly Irish Catholics, lived in row houses several blocks away. This clean, lower middle-class neighborhood also housed immigrants from various Italian provinces, who had overcome job discrimination in their own way and saved to buy their little corner of America.

Ethnic neighborhoods were identified by their stores. Homewood-Brushton's Italian bakeries and grocery stores served other Italians who were musicians and music teachers, real estate and insurance agents, barbers and builders — and a refined gardener and chauffeur. The latter were a father and son, who spoke perfect English and worked for the wealthy Hunt family of U.S. Steel.

Italian names were unmistakable. Homewood bakers were Lombardo, and Merlino; grocers were DiLeo, Scuro, Tedesco, Amadeo, and Tucci, all from the lower part of the Italian boot. The builders were the Abruzzi, Ferrante, Palombo, and Donatelli. After Prohibition, two honorable *Napolitani* families, the Capones, opened upscale restaurants that served special *cucina italiana e liquore*. They suffered the unjust stigma left by Al Capone, a prohibition era gangster.

Some Italians changed their last names in order to earn American acceptance. Real Estate Agent Antonio Tomaso became Tony Thomas. The tailor, Nicolo Mastromonico, became Nick Masters. The musicians' names had interesting translations: *Fratangelo*, brother angel; *Mezzodeo*, half god; and *Sapienza*, wise.

And, speaking of translations, there were *paesani* whose nicknames, translated, were hilarious to children who grew up bilingual and did not give up their Italian. For example, Nino *"testadura"* meant hard head. Filomena *"La Strega"* signified the witch, Antonio *"cello d'oro"* meant gold bird, which children knew was really slang for gold penis, and Giovanni *"ooo cuccinello"* was slang for the little dog. The Palombo boys barked when Giovanni approached their front porch, eliciting from Paolo an angry warning and four fingers between clenched teeth: *"Sangue di maialo*! Quiet! Blood of a Peeg! Quiet!" Being Italian was such fun!

Though there was a large Italian population in Pittsburgh, a combination of races and nationalities lived and did business in harmony and with mutual respect throughout the city. Homewood functioned in a comfortable cocoon. Its Jewish business people — who owned dry goods, hardware and clothing stores — lived in upper-class Squirrel Hill. There were grocery stores whose families lived above them, German and Jewish bakeries, and Chinese shirt laundries. The Black families worked as chauffeurs and maids for the nearby rich. Mr. and Mrs. Claybrook were electrician and nurse. Mr. French, half Black and half White and designated mostly as a mulatto, was a successful wallpaper hanger. (Wallpaper was in fashion then.) The Irish were cops. Westinghouse Electric and Manufacturing Company employed Polish, Germans, Irish, Italians, and few, if any, Blacks. None were WASP— that is — ethnically, religiously or politically correct enough to fit the White Anglo-Saxon Protestant mold. Therefore, none were awarded upper-management positions. Yet, within this several square-mile enclave, the so-called American "ideal" of ethnicity functioned well, despite prevailing discrimination.

At the turn of the century of mass immigration groups in large cities — Germans, Chinese, Japanese, Mexicans, Greeks, and Italians relied upon translators. Ethnic contractors, whom historians labeled as *padroni* or bosses, helped foreigners find work. They were often pressured to pay kickbacks to their *padroni*. But the more common practice was that fellow immigrants helped newcomers secure housing, Benefit Society insurance and employment.

Because workers did not have to live in proximity to their work, commuting to their jobs was made easier with the development of mass urban transportation. Neighborhoods from which they came varied in class as well as ethnicity. For instance, railroad and trolley lines divided each section of Homewood-Brushton into sharply different social and ethnic areas.

In the middle-class neighborhoods between the Hamilton and Frankstown trolley lines lived Blacks, Irish, Italians, and Germans. In the new upper middle-class neighborhood, beyond Frankstown, the blue-collar and white-collar Anglo-Saxon Protestants lived in large homes in the Wunderlich and Belmar Plans. As immigrants moved up the economic ladder, they transplanted their large energetic families into these neighborhoods.

Predictably, older families, with more sedate tastes, became offended. They found it hard to accept foreigners. In a White Anglo-Saxon Protestant environment, speaking a foreign language and practicing unconventional cultural customs such as *festa* parades made the newcomers almost as unacceptable as Blacks. And it was of no help that many were working-class Catholics. Prejudices held and shaped by Anglo-Americans, especially against dark-skinned, dark-haired, brown-eyed immigrants persisted. Paolo and his fair-haired, blue-eyed children, often initially mistaken as Nordics, sensed that they were sometimes treated differently from their dark-featured friends — until their religion and nationality surfaced. Kids recognized discrimination and referred to *Americani* bigots as *"Merdi-cani"* (slang for dog's dirt.) Paolo overlooked prejudice. He had a mission — to attain greater economic independence.

Then in 1919, the war was over; there was no more need to manufacture armaments. It was time to move on. Unlike his Polish and Black friends employed in the mills, Paolo had no desire to work in *la bocca d'inferno*. Having become more fluent in English, albeit with an accent, he had no problem getting a job with the Western Pennsylvania Water Company, where he learned more skills to earn a decent income. He took additional side jobs with his builder friends, who valued his talent — and worked so hard that his resistance fell. In February 1919, he became gravely ill.

Upon learning that he had caught the dreaded *pulmonite* that had killed his father, Maria became terrified, because the end result was usually death. A pneumonia epidemic had taken many lives because there were no antibiotics then.

Maria sought help from Doctor Plyer, the community physician. She followed his instructions scrupulously, taking care to keep Paolo's fever down by laying snow-packed cloths across his hot forehead. And she added her own remedies: cherry brandy or *anisetta* to relax and disinfect Paolo's throat, and *minestrone* soup with *pastina* to keep him nourished. She rubbed his chest with *canfora* and washed endless changes of sweat-soaked bed clothes — and prayed to the *Santa Madre*, in colloquial Abruzzese, and to *Dio Omnipotente* in formal Italian.

Maria liked the kindly doctor with the fascinating goatee and offered him soup or *pasta* and a glass of wine on his daily visits, which became remarkably affordable. Father DeFrancesco brought candles for her holy statues. She lit these to the Sacred Heart, and the Holy Mother, and bargained with them to be her emissary to *Dio*. In final desperation, a skeptical Maria consented when certain women, dressed in black, offered to perform an incantation to drive out unwelcomed spirits — *gettatura* — even though Maria was certain that Paolo was not cursed with *malocchio*, the evil eye. It did not matter to Maria that there would be no wages for a long time. If only God would save her Paolo, she would work hard and encourage her children to help.

And work she did, taking in laundry and sewing and writing letters to Italy for illiterate neighbors, who paid her in food and labor that Paolo could not do. Grazia, now sixteen and doing well in English and school subjects, broke tradition and volunteered to quit high school and secure work making cones at the ice cream factory. Her boss permitted her to take home broken cones, which became a welcome treat that held homemade ice cream. The family appreciated the value of Our Lady of Mount Carmel Benefit Society, which paid Paolo $5 a week and paid household expenses; the family ate from their harvest, buying only a little meat and fish. Silvio and Domenico sold newspapers and delivered milk in the cold winter dawn. And the two boarders volunteered an extra two dollars a week — a good sum in those days.

Paolo's illness had required sacrifices. He and Maria sensed what the struggle of working, going to school and learning a new language meant to their children. They sensed that being abusively ridiculed as "dumb dagos" and "wops" hurt their children, who were reared to be proud of their Italian heritage. They encouraged them to speak both languages and not be ashamed of it. Most of their childrens' friends had abandoned their native language to escape intolerance — at the cost of losing their bilingual ability. Mama and Papa comforted them in Italian: "We are foreign, but we are not stupid. We have intelligence. And we have one another. Be brave. Be proud. We will survive anything." And they did survive as Paolo slowly fought his way back to health.

When he had barely regained his strength, he approached his boss to return to work. Paolo had always been hard-working and jovial; everyone liked him — especially his boss, who offered him an easy job as night watchman. It paid more money — another step up. Paolo had been fortunate because illness posed a great threat to immigrants who had so little to sustain them even under the best conditions. It was not uncommon for many to return to Europe after an illness, or after a family death had caused them financial havoc. But regardless of hardships, the Palombo family would adapt. The thought of ever returning to Italy was unthinkable to Maria. She had settled in and come to truly love America, like so many other immigrants who had endured the ordeals of the voyage and Ellis Island to realize their "American Dream."

Now that he was feeling stronger, Paolo decided that they had endured enough pressures. It was time to expose his wife to enjoyable, new American experiences. Since his first trip to America, he had been hatching a mischievous scheme. He anticipated Maria's awe at seeing her first live theater performance. To carry out his plot, he announced that the next Saturday evening they would attend their first Mass at a downtown church.

Maria was bewildered when Paolo bought her a blue silk dress and a hat adorned with an artificial bluebird and matching plumes. Maria scolded him for his extravagance as she tucked her rosary beads into her new silk beaded bag and walked self-consciously to the Hamilton trolley. *Paesani* did not recognize her as they passed.

Never having seen a dazzling theater marquee before, Maria was startled that Paolo hurried her beneath it into the plush brightly-lit theater lobby. She was awe-struck at the elegant chandeliers and deep-red carpet. Paolo hastily explained that in America the central churches were different and more elegant than their own parish church. She had never seen the opulent cathedrals that the wealthy European church hierarchy — Catholic and Protestant — had created on the backs of their impoverished flocks.

Paolo surreptitiously handed the doorman their tickets. *"Dove è l'aqua Santa?"* Maria whispered. Paolo whispered back that there was no Holy Water, and guided her down the aisle to their seats. Maria genuflected respectfully and crossed herself. *"Santa Maria! Che bellezza!"* she exclaimed as she slid along feeling the plush seat backs. She was overwhelmed at the beauty around her.

Anticipating her next question, Paolo explained that the altar was behind the luxurious velvet curtain, and hastily warned her that the spirited music they were hearing was the American-style prelude to the Mass. Suddenly the curtain burst open, and a line of chorus girls dancing the can-can flipped their skirts and revealed their posteriors to the delighted audience. Shocked and mortified, the red-faced Maria shrieked, *"Che potessi schiantar' !!"* This was the ultimate invective she could fling — "I hope you burst!!"

Paulo teased her and remarked that her nickname Rossa was well-earned. For years to come Maria would repeat the farce with great amusement and blush again. And Paolo would leave the white imprint from his forefinger on her crimson cheek to tease her further.

But Maria forgave him. She had many reasons to be grateful. Paolo was alive, baby Luigi and her older children were happy and healthy, her little house and garden were satisfying, and she enjoyed her many new friends and her activity in the church Altar Society. For each of these things, Maria expressed her gratitude with equal fervor in her daily mother-to-mother colloquial conversations with the *Bella Madonna* — whether she prayed in gratitude or supplication. They had a personal relationship.

She needed only to be reunited with Arcangela and little Domenico to make her happiness complete. It was time to appeal to *Dio* Himself, too— in formal Italian. For two years Antonio had sacrificed and saved enough for their voyage. It was time to bring them to America.

They must prepare, she decided. She lit the vigil light on the bedroom mantlepiece, crossed herself and began praying. And then she climbed into her high feather bed, shook Paolo awake, and in her most cajoling voice asked, *"Potrei parlarti, Caro?* Cana we talka, dear?" It would be a long night.

Chapter 10

America Beckons — Family Paths Cross

"We won't be back until it's over, over there," the World War I popular song declared through the voice of Enrico Caruso. In 1917, news that his immigrant ship, the ill-fated *Luisiana*, had been torpedoed and sunk off Spain by a German submarine saddened Paolo. But by 1919, the boys were back. The sea was safe for travel, and another tide of immigrants swelled America's population.

This was the America they found. In a period of rapid industrial growth, new expectations clashed with old traditions, as the country struggled to catch up to modern times. Free speech, curtailed during the War in the name of patriotism, now erupted with a vengeance. America was at the end of innocence and in a period of unrest in the second decade of the new century.

Maria and Paolo were rapidly assimilating into American life, whose social concepts were changing. Militant labor unions made demands against Big Business, protesting against twelve-hour, seven-day work weeks for low wages that immigrants accepted out of necessity. Strident voices fought for democratic rights and liberties: the advancement of colored people, progressive education, and Womens' Suffrage. This last became a reality on June 4, 1919 and won women the right to vote. Hate mongers attacked ethnic and religious minorities. "Prohibition" forbade the consumption of alcohol, and a million Socialists clamored to overthrow Capitalism.

On the positive side, the first decade of the twentieth century brought a discovery that gave mankind its greatest thrust since the wheel — the development of transmitting sound without wires. It happened at the turn of the century in Pittsburgh on the North Side's Observatory Hill, after Italy's Guglielmo Marconi's invention of wireless telegraphy had led to the wireless telephone. Marconi's communication system could transmit and receive only dots and dashes — Morse code. Never before had man been able to hurl into space and retrieve from space the sound of the human voice and music. But Reginald Fessenden, Dean of the Electrical Engineering Department at Western University (now the University of Pittsburgh,) developed the theory of the continuous air wave that superimposed sound onto a radio wave and then into a receiver. The radio wave would then be removed, leaving only the original sound. This concept enabled Fessenden literally to pluck the human voice out of the air and transmit it via wireless telegraph, and suddenly radio transmission was born! On Christmas Eve 1906, putting his theory into practice, Fesenden made the first long-range transmission of voice and sound. Radio operators on ships in the Atlantic, accustomed only to Morse Code, were shocked and frightened. The discovery of radio had made the world smaller.

With the development of aviation and the automobile came the growth of transportation and the expansion of industry and trade. Immigrant labor was welcome again. Those enjoying the benefits and opportunities of life in America after a first decade created a human chain that brought their relatives and friends to the Golden Door. Thus, in the spirit of the times, Paolo and Maria prepared for Arcangela's arrival with little Domenico in 1919, oblivious to ongoing efforts by nativists to restrict entry into the United States.

Immigrant animus was deep. Mistrust of Germans, Irish, Italians and other foreigners motivated nativists to form the pseudo-scientific term "Eugenics" to disguise their blueprint for the biological engineering of American society. The scheme was specifically designed to discriminate against "inferior races." The concept was to evaluate immigrants' suitability for propagating American citizens who would be racially compatible with American ideals. This scheme led to the National Origins Act, which reduced the number of Greek newcomers to one-hundred a year. The Polish immigrant quota dropped 70% to four thousand a year. Without question, Italians were foremost among the races that America assumed to be inferior and was eager to exclude. Their entry quota dropped 90% from forty-two thousand to four thousand a year. After the National Origins Act became law, a Commissioner of Immigration was heard to remark with satisfaction that immigrants disembarking at Ellis Island "looked exactly like Americans." Arcangela and her son were fair, blonde and blue-eyed and would, no doubt, pass through as Nordics.

Arcangela gave away the last possessions from their homes in Italy and came to America. The Palombo parlor became the little family's bedroom. Within three weeks after they arrived, Antonio found them a small row house behind Tucci's grocery store on Tioga Street in Homewood. Next to Tucci's stood a little white wooden church, Pittsburgh's first African Methodist Zion

Church, founded in 1870. Nearby lived a distinguished pillar of the church, Isaac Watson, a descendant of ex-slaves, who went to work for George Westinghouse at his Homewood mansion. Maria loved the little church, and ignoring rules which forbid Catholics to attend non-Catholic services, she stopped to listen and enjoy the spirited worship inside.

Only months after the Palombos brought over Maria's sister and nephew, Sebastiano and Rosa Sapienza added another link in the human chain. They applied for the family's passage to America, specifically to Homewood, just in time; for in 1921 Congress closed the Golden Door by passing the Emergency Quota Act. Thus the Palombos and Sapienzas took their place among the more than four million Italians who came to America between 1820 and 1920. Homewood Italians, unlike their exclusively Abruzzi predecessors in Bloomfield, came from a wide geographical mix from Sicily to Northern Italy.

At the end of August 1920, the Sapienzas would sail from the Port of Palermo, Sicily, on the magnificent *S.S. Belvedere*. Built in 1913 by Cantieri Navali Triestino in Monfalcone, Italy, the 437-foot vessel accommodated 144 first-class passengers and 1400 in third class. After World War I, arrangements for the voyage to America were more efficient. New immigration laws enabled passengers to be cleared at the point of embarkation. Gone were the feared medical exams, the political questions, and the customs inspections. The fear of rejection and deportation at Ellis Island no longer threatened. Unlike conditions suffered by the immigrants who had crossed before them, there was no peril on the sea. Sebastiano's family could travel in peace.

Nonna Marianna was grieved at their decision and wrote from Lentini, pleading that they stay in Sicily. But Rosa Concettina was a commanding woman. Sebastiano could not subdue her demands. He understood. In the end, despite his mother's pleas, he left his grieving family behind. The Sapienzas were scheduled to arrive in America with their three sons, Salvatore, Liborio, and Delifno II on September 6, 1920. While they were the only group from Sebastiano's immediate family to take its place in the history of trans-Atlantic migration, other branches of the family had predated their arrival. Some settled in Zelienople, some on Pittsburgh's South Side, and others in Ohio. In the Sapienza families in Cheyenne, Wyoming, and in Pittsburgh, two carry the same first names — Sebastiano and Salvatore.

Before the end of the twentieth century, according to census, approximately 450 heads of households carried the distinguished Sapienza name, with spelling variations of the last letter.

Sebastiano brought with him superb intelligence and talent and a proud heritage. An established professional musician, he played first clarinet in Termini's opera house orchestra. Silent movies had come to Palermo theaters, where Sebastiano played mood music for silent films, before the "talkies" were invented. Like their American counterparts, Italians had to read fluently in order to understand and enjoy the films.

But music was not Sebastiano's only vocation. In Palermo, he held a position with the *Municipio* as an accountant and calligrapher. His artistic script appeared on legal documents requiring the seal of government. Sebastiano's artistic and musical talents would serve him well; they were, in fact, destined to become an asset to America's history of radio broadcasting.

Rosa packed their best clothing and her most valued belongings in one trunk: the Blessed Mother's statue, Sapienza family portraits, the Christening dress that Vicenzina had sewn for her first born, several beautiful lace collars, embroidered scarves and linens that Marianna had made.

The large framed portraits of her mother and father would be her most prized possessions of all. Sebastiano packed his music, his clarinet, and his other suit.

On the day of their departure, grieving relatives, friends and Sebastiano's music students came to see them off. In the confusion, amid hugs and kisses and tears, someone had forgotten to empty the tall earthenware *pitale* that stood in the corner. Eight-year-old Toto was so distressed that he did not want to leave. In an effort to stay their departure, he threw the house key into the thick stench-filled chamber pot. Sebastiano was aghast. Their efforts to retrieve the elusive key with a stick failed.

The angry, mortified Rosa decided that there was only one thing to do. She commanded Sebastiano to do it: *"Madre d' Dio, solo una cosa si puo' fare. Sebastiano, fa . . . fa!"* Poor Sebastiano removed his coat . . . rolled up his sleeve . . . plunged his arm into the excrement . . . fished around for several minutes . . . and retrieved the errant key. To escape the consequences, Toto sought protection among his relatives.

Now, the chamber pot had been promised to a friend. After it had been emptied, Sebastiano took it and put it behind the neighbor's door. As she flung her door open to say a last goodbye, the ill-fated pot cracked to bits! Little Liborio and Toto remembered the two incidents and repeated the story for years.

In a final *addio,* Rosa went from roof garden to every nook, taking a last look at the beloved Corso home. Down the wide marble stairs she went, stopping at the second-floor balcony where Sebastiano had serenaded her. Each room held joyous and painful memories. Finally, she looked up to the decorative arched window above the front door where two large letters, F.C., marked the home that Frank Corso, her brother, had built. She fixed them in her mind. Rosa brushed her hand slowly across the image of Frank on the massive front door, pulled it shut, and reluctantly relinquished the well-washed key to the new *padrone.*

On their voyage to America, they traveled one class above steerage. On shipboard, Sebastiano read both Italian and English periodicals. To his advantage, he had spoken and translated English during his career at the *Municipio* and his years in military service. As the occasion required, he conversed fluently in English, formal Italian or Sicilian — a peculiar dialect of the Italian language with Spanish influence. During the voyage, Rosa devoted full time to her children — her *piciridi*, pronounced "pee-chee-reed-ee" in Sicilian dialect.

At journey's end, they stood at the great ship's rail to be greeted and overwhelmed by Lady Liberty's welcome. By contrast with the traumas and delays suffered by former immigrants, their stop at Ellis Island was unstress-ful. A new procedure in Europe had cleared them for entry, thereby dissipat-ing any fear of deportation. As they were processed at Ellis Island, a quick inspection of three little boys' shaved heads, Rosa's beautiful hair and clothing, Sebastiano's fluency in English and his music cases gave no cause for delays.

At New York's Grand Central Station, Rosa, unaccustomed to seeing women carry their own luggage, was amazed. The Pennsylvania Railroad took them to Pittsburgh where Sebastiano hired a taxi and directed the driver, in English, to take them to Rosa's brother, Nino Corso, who lived on Hamilton Avenue in Homewood.

The trip was five miles, the fare seventy-five cents. When Sebastiano paid the fare, the cab driver, assuming that he was a greenhorn, kept the entire five-dollar bill. Before Sebastiano could question him or object, the driver was gone. This bit of conniving was a great loss to the little family, who had arrived with one trunk, three suitcases and very little cash. The incident shocked the Sapienzas for many years, because one's honor did not permit such dishonesty among these good people.

Rosa, starved for affection from her distant family, was filled with emotion as her sister-in-law, Carolina, and her brothers took her into their arms. She thought of her only sister Maria Torrido, who had died of influenza in the Pittsburgh epidemic, and wept.

Rosa had come to America with the assurance that her brothers would vouch for their support until Sebastiano found work. The Corso brothers were successful in their own businesses. In her oldest brother, Santo, she saw the resemblance to her father. Santo and Peppino had settled north of Pittsburgh in Parker's Landing, Pennsylvania, "the biggest little city in America." It acquired its nickname when it attracted a large population in the oil boom of the 1880's. The region, rich in coal deposits and vigorous mining activity, fed nearby steel-making furnaces and coal-burning fireplaces and stoves.

The Corsos, like their father in Italy, were natural entrepreneurs. By 1909, Santo owned a one-hundred acre farm at the edge of town. He enjoyed rapid prosperity when coal, oil and gas were discovered on his farm. The location was ideal for commerce. He established a large grocery and meat market, and later opened a five-and-ten-cent store similar to the Woolworth stores. He and his enterprising wife, Maria, and their five children earned considerable wealth. By 1920, when his sister Rosa arrived, he had built two large apartments over his stores, complete with roof gardens embellished with flowers, potted plants and wicker furniture, reminiscent of their rooftops in Sicily.

Peppino engaged in transporting wholesale products from the Pittsburgh produce yards in the Strip District to the businesses in Butler and Armstrong Counties. Later he opened a restaurant and soda parlor that became a favored hangout for the young people. The brothers were fluent in English and commanded high respect. Eventually, their sons flew their own private planes and won elections to local political offices — unheard of for Italians!

Both Santo and Peppino traded with another prosperous brother, Frank, who established the wholesale Pittsburgh Banana Company at the produce yards in the Strip District. Americans nicknamed the red-haired, blue-eyed immigrant the Banana King. At first Frank lived in a comfortable home in Millvale. By now he had acquired a beautiful home in suburban Dormont and a Packard limousine.

Nino Corso, the fourth brother, lived in the developing Homewood suburb where he owned a grocery and produce business. Like Santo and Peppino, he bought bananas from brother Frank, who dealt generously with them, so that their profits would be higher. Their brother-in-law, Nino Torrido, a tradesman who made shoes in Italy, had opened his shop in Homewood not far from Pisani's barbershop, where men of every nationality met on Saturdays to get a shave and a haircut for two bits. News flowed freely, and barbershop quartet harmony erupted when any four Irishmen gathered to sing *Sweet Adaline*, or *Down by the Old Mill Stream*. Like Italians, they loved to sing.

Holding to common practice among all immigrants, Sicilians helped *paesani* make the crossing. They contradicted the popular impression that many Sicilians were dark swarthy types disposed to crime. Given the diverse culture of Sicily, that myth did not apply to the Corso brothers, like the fair-skinned, red-haired Frank. Unfortunately, they and other gifted Southern Italians had been targets of strong prejudice and stereotyping as criminals. The negative mafioso stigma reflected upon honest Italians for several generations.

Nonetheless, gentle-mannered Sebastiano and refined Rosa were offended by newspaper accounts that hammered upon Italian criminal activity. They had come into a loving atmosphere of family success, asking for nothing more than an opportunity to accomplish and prosper. The family was the heart and home of Italian life, much as the Jewish home was its family center of tradition — and worship.

The Corso brothers offered Sebastiano work. But he was not an entrepreneur at heart. He was artistic. And he was proud. He accepted lodging with Nino's family, and looked for temporary work that would sustain them until the right job surfaced. Taking one of the few jobs available to immigrants, he became a janitor in Reymer's candy factory for three weeks.

But news of Sapienza's musical talent spread and soon clarinet students came. He taught for fifty cents an hour — often extending lessons beyond the time limit. In a few weeks, Bartholomew Canistra, an old musician friend from Italy, led him to a position with the Alvin Theater's Pit Orchestra. The grateful Sebastian decided that one day he would honor Bartholomew by asking him to be *padrino* — Godfather — at his oldest son's Confirmation. As his middle name, Salvatore would then carry Bartholomew, his *padrino*'s name.

One night T.J. Vastine, a part-time trumpet player with the Pittsburgh Symphony Orchestra and member of the Westinghouse Electric Company Orchestra and Band, was in the audience at the Alvin Theater. Impressed with Sebastiano's clarinet solos, he urged the immigrant to audition with Victor Saudek, director of the Westinghouse Band and Orchestra. Saudek, too, was impressed. However, to become a Westinghouse musician, one needed to be an employee. T.J. Vastine introduced Sebastiano to the Personnel Director, Mr. Priest, who asked him, "What can you do?"

Nearby, a sign painter was lettering Mr. Priest's door. He was quite surprised to hear Sebastiano reply in perfect English, "I can do what that man is doing. In Italy *calligrafia* was my work." On the spot, he produced, free-hand, precise and eye-appealing showcard posters. Sebastiano immediately won a permanent job doing specialty printing on equipment and fancy lettering on office doors. Saudek awarded Sebastiano "first chair" as solo clarinetist in the company orchestra and band. He made his mark with his superb calligraphy, his performing talents, and his ability to write musical arrangements for the ensembles. Soon his coworkers Americanized his first name, dropping the last vowel.

Not far from Sebastian's home, on the borderline of Pittsburgh and Wilkinsburg, another creative mind had been at work before Sebastian arrived in America. For months, from his own amateur radio station, 8XK, in his garage on Peebles Street, Westinghouse Engineer Frank Conrad had been broadcasting short, semi-weekly radio programs of recorded music, weather reports, baseball scores and the Arlington Time Signals, which listeners utilized to set or check the accuracy of their watches. Amateur radio enthusiasts, accustomed to communicating only in Morse Code, were fascinated with Conrad's programs.

The radio audience grew. To hear his broadcasts on earphones, radio enthusiasts built their own crystal sets, with catwhisker and wire wound around an oatmeal cereal box. One fan, in response to Conrad's request for feedback, sent him a letter making the first radio request: "Coming in loud and clear. Please play *Japanese Sandman*." The radio craze had struck!

At 8 p.m. on November 2, 1920, came a broadcasting "first." From the tallest building at Westinghouse's East Pittsburgh plant, America's Harding-Cox presidential election returns were transmitted over its amateur radio station 8ZZ. Listeners at the nearby Edgewood Club, and Tom and Lee Sapienza listened as Leo Rosenberg announced that Harding had won the election. Meanwhile, a few miles away, Frank Conrad stood ready to take over from his own station, 8XK, in case the new equipment atop the Westinghouse K building failed.

But since that first election, mistaken information created a myth, for although Westinghouse had submitted an early application for a broadcasting license, the company did not receive its *commercial* license as KDKA until two days *after* the election, on November 4, 1920. But later, for publicity purposes, an imitation of the first presidential broadcast was recorded, using KDKA call letters. Eventually, the misinformed public wrongly came to believe that KDKA, not 8ZZ, had aired the first election returns.

Meanwhile, on the roof of the K building in Turtle Creek, electrical engineers had been conducting experiments with various musical sounds for radio broadcasting. Sebastian got involved when they asked Victor Saudek which instrument would give them the widest range of sounds. Without hesitation, he invited Sebastian to join them during his lunch hour, then pressed him into service to play.

The unassuming little man, unaware that he would hold the distinction of being the first musician to perform the first live clarinet selection over the airwaves, chose *Annie Laurie*. Thereafter, before he began practicing or playing for the family's enjoyment, he began the sessions with a formidable series of rapid arpeggios and finished with a pianissimo *Annie Laurie*. The repertoire that followed delighted the ear — and enamored Rosa. Sebastian romanced her with music instead of words.

Conrad, a sleepless genius, experimented into the night with his concept of transmitting sound waves long-distance via radio waves. Flora, his patient wife, brought him hot soup or tea at odd hours. Conrad moved his experiments to the Westinghouse relay station in a Pittsburgh suburb, Forest Hills, where he sent the human voice to the Arctic and around the world for the first time *ever*. At the same time, his colleague Vladmir Zworykin had invented the iconoscope and, on that same site, showed the first electronic television pictures ever.

Eventually, Guglielmo Marconi, along with other noteworthy radio aficionados, visited the site. The inventions and discoveries of Marconi, Reginald Fessenden, Frank Conrad and Vladimir Zworykin had shrunk the globe and given civilization its greatest communication impetus since primitive drums! Conrad and Zworykin had been catalysts for the start of multibillion dollar communication industries — extraordinary twentieth century achievements which, shamefully, have been generally ignored by historians, millennium pundits and Pittsburgh at large!

According to records, by 1921, amateur radio station 8ZAE received the commercial call letters KQV, making it the *second* commercial broadcasting station, and the *first* to be physically located in Pittsburgh. Although KQV has claimed to be the first commercial radio station ever, it was, in fact, Frank Conrad who pioneered the concept of scheduled radio broadcasting, and Conrad who discovered short-wave radio which enabled long-range broadcasting. These two communication developments gave Westinghouse's Vice President, Harry P. Davis, the idea that founded a multibillion dollar industry.

Later, KDKA also broadcast from the Westinghouse plant at Lang and Hamilton Avenues in Homewood, one of several pick-up stations. After 1922, broadcast activity moved to the Pittsburgh Post Building where they regularly broadcast as KDKA, the second commercial radio station to be based in the city of Pittsburgh, Pennsylvania.

The Sapienza boys were familiar with the radio activities in Mr. Conrad's garage. They often met him when they delivered his morning and evening newspapers. Like others along Millionaire's Row, Mr. Conrad preferred that Tom or Lee ring his doorbell and deliver the paper at the door. "He was always dressed up — wore a bow tie. I'll bet he never had to cut their lawn," Lee once remarked. The boys delivered papers twice a day along Millionaire's Row on Penn Avenue. Toto remembered that Conrad was the most generous tipper of the area, especially at Christmas time.

Sebastian's connection with radio made him an early success. Six months after he arrived in America, he moved his family to 7516 Tioga Street, where he purchased two homes on one lot. The larger house accommodated a total of five sons, the last two born there — Santo and Francesco — were eventually called Bill and Frank. Income from the smaller house at the rear, rented by Mr. Claybrook, a successful Black electrician whose wife was a nurse, paid the mortgage. The two Claybrook sons, Fenori and Lucian, and the Sapienza boys were close friends. Sebastian respected Mr. Claybrook's ability and had him wire both of their houses for electricity.

Five doors away lived the Palombo family. In 1920, the Sapienza and Palombo boys became fast friends. They soon learned that Italian boys protected one another, especially by maintaining a code of silence when trouble brewed. Pepperone — the Palombo dog named for the pepper huckster's bellow — lost his best canine friend, who was the Sapienza boys' pet.

The boys' honor would not let Dom and Pete squeal on Toto and Lee when they buried their dog in Paolo's newly-spaded backyard. One morning as Paolo was making furrows to plant early tomatoes, his spade struck and unearthed the dog. "*Sangue di maiale*!!" he thundered. "*Che cos' è questo?*! Blood of a peeg! *Mama Mia!* Whata is thisa thinga?" Of course all of the culprits were baffled, too, as they honored their code of silence. Paolo was never aware of that deception.

Nor was he aware of another ruse to which he fell victim. A neighbor who had a drinking problem was an agnostic and a wife abuser. His wife, a devout Catholic, held sacred the creed of meatless Fridays. One Good Friday, her husband compelled her to cook lamb and forced her to eat it or risk being hit. When the victim confided this to Paolo, he was so angry at the sacrilege that he could never bring himself to eat lamb again.

One day Guy, the butcher, presented Maria with a lamb roast in appreciation of Paolo's generous gift of wine. She did not want to offend Guy and, being frugal, accepted it. At dinner, Maria poured Paolo a large glass of *vino* and delayed serving the soup. Before she served the beautiful roast, generously garnished with garlic and herbs, Maria made small talk as she poured Papa another tall glass of *vino*, and sweetly and pointedly commanded: "Luigi, pleasa passa Papa the veal." She debated whether her deception was a mortal or a venial sin, and planned to "confess" it at the right moment in their bedroom.

Between the Palombo and Sapienza families, in a triple row of houses, lived three Black neighbors: The French family, Miss Lattamore and the Burley family. This little group of neighbors had a few things in common: all were industrious, open-hearted, helpful, compatible, respectful of one another — and victimized by prejudice. In other words, they walked in the same shoes. Their children had fun together. Their parents learned from one another. In the twenties, close relationships were not uncommon between alienated Blacks and multiethnic immigrants.

If sociologists have concluded in retrospect that inter-group tensions were the rule, the Homewood-Brushton community did not seem to fit that pattern. All were under constraint to become like other Americans; but remarkably, they ignored the pressures and held on to their own traditions. They were proud and in the end, rather than yield to mainstream culture, they influenced Americans to bend a little and accept some of their culture: foods, music, celebrations, games, styles, holidays and traditions.

In the twenties, America was still not a utopia of equal opportunities and equal justice. But perhaps Homewood's and America's greatest triumph was the ability of the tenacious underdogs to adapt and succeed, and the determination of their children to keep their parents' dreams alive.

Chapter 11

Tioga Street — New Joys and Sorrows

After 1920, the postwar incoming tide of immigrants dropped significantly, reflecting the attitudes of a society grown skeptical of foreigners. The belief that "our institutions stood diluted by a stream of alien blood" prompted Congressman Albert Johnson to write the Immigration Act of 1924, which reduced quotas by imposing literacy tests and other severe restrictions. President Coolidge signed the Act into law, and the immigrant tide slowed to a trickle. Since 1907, more than one million hopefuls had come through the doors of Ellis Island.

A class system had determined who would have less trouble being admitted. First-class and second-class ticket holders underwent brief inspections aboard ship, and most were allowed to directly enter the United States. Sebastian and Rosa Sapienza's family had been among the fortunate few. But Ellis Island gradually fell into disuse, and in 1954 the Golden Door finally closed.

Nonetheless, immigrants from rural European areas, who had limited education and English-speaking skills, found it a challenging and frightening time. But for Americans educated and socialized in their familiar culture, the Roaring Twenties was a confident, "cocksure" decade that brought new customs and material progress.

Old Victorian values gave way to modern, licentious behavior. The period of technological innovations and industrial growth had been spurred by the pre-1900 electrical revolution. By the end of the third decade, having no electrical lights or telephone was a sign of poverty.

After World War I, the twenties became a highly patriotic era, with Americans celebrating their Fourth of July with greater enthusiasm. No one was more enthusiastic than Paolo Palombo, but his mood of intense patriotism would have a profound effect on his family. Their second decade in America would bring new challenges, new offspring, and new kin. It would be marked by progress, and fraught with tragedy and in spite of the nation's wary attitude toward foreigners, their optimism and indomitable will would enable them to cope.

The combination of work, play and faith sustained the little family. Everyone contributed and saved every penny not needed for basic necessities. With renewed vigor after his illness, Paolo launched new home improvement projects. He chose these prudently, albeit unaware that his first decision would have a profound effect on the family's future. He engaged contractors to insulate his wooden house and roof with fire-proof asbestos shingles, in the fashion of the times. Freshly-painted window frames, doors, and porches made him nearly as proud of his newly-groomed exterior as he had been of his balcony in Italy.

He planted the little plot below the front porch with flowers, and trained morning glories to climb up the symmetrical strands he had strung to form a private porch enclosure. He bought a swing, several porch chairs, and an attractive straw rug. Adapting to the Victorian styles shown in her Sears Roebuck catalog, Maria made hand-lace curtains and trimmed the window shades with wide fringe she had bought from the Syrian door vendor who came by periodically. Her progressive Paolo promised her, "Soon we will have *un telefono, lampioni elettriche, e segge molle*."

Maria would enjoy a telephone, electric lights and soft chairs. "And we will have *un' altra nascita* -- another baby born," she announced.

Paolo had wished for a daughter. On August 9, 1920, they called the midwife, Maria Palmiera, who delivered a blonde blue-eyed baby girl. Paolo and Maria Giuseppa prayed their joy and thanks to the Holy Mother, and reflected upon the sacrifices and separations his older children had endured before they came to America. They prayed their gratitude that their five children would now grow with the love of both parents.

Maria, remembering her good-bye promise to Costanzo, named the baby Elisa Costanza, and later wrote him the good news. The happy father brought an oak, handcranked cradle for his *bambinella;* and Hahn's furniture store gave their loyal customer a sturdy maple rocker for her. There was much to celebrate.

Paolo appreciated and regretted the sacrifice Grazia had made by quitting high school and going to work when he lay gravely ill. The consolation was that she had attended secondary school in Italy and two years of high school in America to give her the benefit of being bilingual, an advantage over young girls of her day. She read and wrote both languages fluently, and used her skill to translate letters for those who needed help. Remembering his own thwarted opportunity to continue his education in Milano, Paolo vowed that his children would finish high school.

Paolo and Maria's attitude toward education, their improving economic status, and the childrens' ability to assimilate and adapt worked to their advantage, along with the opportunities that were available in the Pittsburgh schools. Before World War I, less than one percent of immigrants' children were enrolled in high school. By the twenties, schools had become a vocational training institute that prepared students for office work and other white-collar jobs. Immigrants and first-generation Americans could look forward to progressing as far as their ambition would take them — and ethnic bias would allow. Nonetheless, native Anglo-Americans had the advantage. Many immigrant children did not finish high school.

Within and between middle-class ethnic communities, prejudice was not as strong as the discrimination that came from upper-class and middle-class native-born residents. At first, nationalities tended to socialize only among themselves. But Homewood's diverse population and congenial environment encouraged people to mingle. Families visited each other — Black and White, Jew and Gentile. In summer, after Mass and the traditional Sunday dinner, Italians packed picnic baskets and met their neighbors on the rolling green at Westinghouse Park. Or they boarded trolley cars to go calling, trains to make long-distance sojourns. Visiting was a major pastime and public transportation was readily accessible. Like all others, the Palombo family visited and hosted many visitors.

Maria long wished to visit her cousins in Clyde, New York, from whom she had been painfully separated twenty-two years ago. She dearly loved Lorenzo, Rafaelo and Filomena; but she and Carolina had been especially close. Paolo could not deny her. They took only Luigi and baby Elisa on their trip. *Zia* Arcangela and Grazia would look after the house.

Maria finally saw their farms, which in his letters to Italy, Paolo had described as being like their farm in Abruzzi. The joyous family reunion overwhelmed her. They reminisced about Italy and celebrated with food and wine. There were new children and old *paesani* to meet and embrace; and there was Alessandro, Carolina's handsome oldest son. There was no ocean separating them now, Maria scolded her cousin impishly, and she made Carolina promise to visit Pittsburgh with her husband Nicolo — and Alessandro.

Paolo noticed that his wife was unusually silent when they were homeward bound. Just before the train's rhythmic clack lulled him to sleep, he heard Maria's familiar "Hmmmmm." The pregnant pause that followed was sure to bring a thought-provoking remark. *"Puo' essere un bel' nome, Grazia DiSanto,"* he heard her mutter. "Maybe coulda be beautiful name, Grace Di Santo." Paolo feigned sleep, or it could be another long night.

Several months later there was much feasting and rejoicing in Pittsburgh when Carolina, Nicolo and Alessandro came to meet their long-lost relatives and *paesani.* All of them lived on or near Tioga Street. They chattered in a combination of Abruzzese dialect and English. Maria learned that her cousins' American names were Caroline, Nick and Alexander. Grazia's handsome third cousin came toward her and introduced himself as Alex. She introduced herself as Grace, her American name.

From the first moment, Alex and Grace were strongly attracted to one another. After he left, they corresponded regularly, their letters developing romantic overtones. Grace always included a letter written in Italian for Nicolo and Carolina, whom she respectfully addressed as *Zio* and *Zia,* Uncle and Aunt. Alex was impressed. In return, he sent *Zia* Maria elaborate cards. Maria loved Alessandro's romantic bent. He reminded her of Paolo.

Finally, a very respectful and formal letter arrived. It was addressed to Paolo, asking him for the honor of Grazia's hand. Paolo cleared his throat several times. His blue eyes misted, and Maria wept as they gave Grazia their blessing. The response was swift and affirmative.

According to custom, they gave Grazia a dowry — a modest sum of money, and they filled the huge cherry wood hope chest that Paolo had bought at Hahn's furniture store with embroidered bed linens and scarves. Marriage bans were announced at Mother of Good Counsel Church three weeks before the wedding, scheduled for April 17, 1923.

Ethnic customs die hard. Two weeks prior to the church ceremony, as was the custom in Italy, Alex and Grace were married in civil ceremony at the City County Building in Pittsburgh. But when final details were being prepared, Father DeFrancesco raised the question of the couple's kinship, and the civil ceremony. Grace and Alex were third cousins. By Italian law, they would not be permitted to marry. The couple's civil wedding caused a dilemma. *"Assolutamente non e convenzionale!"* the *Padre* scolded sternly. "This is absolutely unconventional!" he said to Alex.

Maria, unaware of Italian law, responded in amazement, *"Ma davvero?* Rrreeely?"

The good Father understood their confusion; and since the couple was already legally married, there was nothing to do but go through with the ceremony in church. Paolo and Maria accepted their error gracefully.

The wedding party and photographer were selected. The families and wedding party would receive formal photographs. *"Italia! Madonna Mia! Ritratti!"* Maria cried out, remembering that photographs would have to be sent to Italy. When the anticipated parting from Grazia, who would live on the Di Santo farm, brought back painful memories of her separation from Mamma Luigi, she held in her grief. Maria instructed Grazia endlessly on the duties of being a good wife and daughter-in-law and advised: *"Devi guadagnare rispetto."* She counseled her that her main duty would be to earn her mother-in-law's respect, and cautioned Grazia not to torment her husband. *"Un po' di zucchero fa tanto.* A leetla sugara does a lot. You don'ta 'ave to naga heem." Maria winked. Grazia understood Mama's American vocabulary and her flirtatious technique with Papa. Using the Old-World tradition of manipulation, Mama had her own wise way of dealing with the American woman's fight for equal rights.

Final wedding plans fell into place. Celebrations were not strange to Maria and Paolo. Among Italians, aside from baptisms and homecomings, weddings were a major social event. Grazia's white lace wedding dress and long tulle veil hung in Maria's closet. New linoleum covered the parlor and dining room. Paolo braced the floors from the cellar so that added weight would not damage the house. The new leather and mahogany parlor furniture was suitably embellished with hand-crocheted doilies; and the "talking machine" and records were in place on the mahogany Victorian end table.

Furniture was rearranged to make room for long tables laden with roasted chickens, sausage, *polpetti* and *pasta*, Italian cold cuts, pastries, and candy *confetti*. Paolo tapped his best aged white and red *vino*. *Padre* DeFrancesco came to bless — and taste it. Paolo made peach and cherry brandy, and liqueurs from concentrated flavors: *caffè, strega, anisetta*. An array of strong *espresso cappuccino* to clear the head completed the beverages.

Friends and relatives came bearing gifts and money. They feasted until dawn. In a few hours, the newlyweds would be bound for Buffalo and Niagara Falls on the Pennsylvania Railroad "sleeper" to honeymoon for a week. Carolina and Nicolo convinced Maria and Paolo to leave with them three days later to prepare for another celebration. To keep the surprise from the newlyweds, cousin Rafaelo would be their host.

The weary honeymooners arrived in Clyde on the Saturday evening train. Carolina served them a light snack and urged them to get to bed early. They yielded to the suggestion and climbed the stairs to a beautifully furnished bridal bed chamber, the family's gift to them. Grace slipped into her sheer silk and lace nightgown and waited for Alex, who seemed to dally. They had been in bed for a half-hour when an unholy din of horns, singing, and banging on pots and pans erupted. A group of merrymakers burst into their room and pulled them out of bed. Grace was mortified. On the other hand, Alex was highly amused, for he had been expecting his family and friends to carry out this custom of "horning" newlyweds at the "shivaree."

Out in the barn Paolo and Maria waited. Guests and friends had piled the long tables with food. Fiddlers and accordion players greeted the couple with lively music. Revelers frolicked merrily as Uncle Joe called the square dance. In response to his rhythmic hoedown, Alex pulled Maria into the circle:

"Hee haw haw, and a hee haw haw . . .
now don't forget your mother-in-law!
Take her hand . . . now bow down low . . .
twirl her 'round and dosey doe!
Clap your hands . . . hear the call . . .
swing her again and promenade all."

Paolo and Maria delighted the revelers with their performance of *la tarantella*, Abruzzese style. The next day they said their goodbyes and went home exhausted and happy. Remembering the glow on her daughter's face after the honeymoon, Maria said, "Hmmmmm." Paolo waited. *"Puo darsi che siamo Nonno e Nonna subito,"* she said knowingly. "Ees possible we will soon be *Mamu e Tatone* — grandamothera and grandfathera." Paolo nodded and smiled.

Maria loved her new son-in-law, just as Mamma Luigi loved Paolo; and she knew that her daughter's happiness lay with Alessandro, as hers had with Paolo. Though she missed her first-born, there was too much to be done to spend time being unhappy and frustrated. She cooked and baked and scrubbed her little house spotless. Paolo helped her with heavy tasks. The younger children did small chores, while the older boys continued to earn a few dollars delivering papers and milk. Maria sewed sheets and pillow cases from empty flour sacks bleached white, and edged them with crocheted lace. She mended endless piles of socks and torn clothing for her family and two boarders, Martino and Vincenzo, who was nicknamed Jim. Jim became the family's hero.

By now, Paolo spoke reasonably fluent if heavily-accented English — and he had American dreams: "Maybe somma day, I will 'ave my own businessa and bring Alex to work with me, *si vuole Dio*. He'sa smart and knows thisa work." He began studying for his long-awaited citizenship examination. Paolo had become irrevocably American.

He followed American politics and was interested in understanding what each holiday meant. He felt a common bond with the Pilgrims, who had suffered hardships and sacrificed. Although Thanksgiving was a special day, he felt that Americans should give thanks every day for their wonderful country. He tolerated the idea of feasting with traditional turkey; but he reasoned that since Cristoforo Colombo had discovered America, Thanksgiving must have an Italian flair — a side dish of *pasta* and *vino*, at least.

To say that Paolo was a "holiday man" is an understatement. He became totally involved. By 1923, he had caught the full spirit of Independence Day and America's separation from England, draping his big American flag across the front porch railing and anticipating the parade, a big community event, with the excitement of a child.

On Fourth of July morning, he took his family to Homewood Avenue so that he could position them along the front row of people who crowded both sides of the broad street. As the parade marched by, the passing flag and the patriotic band music stirred his emotions. Papa stood at solemn attention, left hand over heart, and right hand in smart salute to the flag he loved, blinking away tears.

At the end of the day, Paolo would join his neighbors along Tioga Street to celebrate in a grand display of fireworks. America had been good to him, and Paolo would show his appreciation. He and Antonio would set off a big rocket first and save the biggest until last. Maria and Arcangela were chattering and watching as each family set off splendiferous bursts of color. "Ooooo! Ahhhh!" people exclaimed in the dark.

No one quite remembers how it happened, but suddenly everyone heard a loud explosion and saw a huge burst of flame set Paolo's clothing on fire. Little Luigi, his father's shadow, caught fire from Paolo's shirt. Uncle Antonio rushed to help him. He and his little Giuseppi, standing close by, caught fire, too, as firecrackers rapidly ignited into bursts of flame. Neighbors came running to help smother the fire with porch rugs.

Jim, the family boarder, scooped Elisa into his arms and ran with her to the rear of the house. He set her down firmly and screamed *"Non ti muovere!! Don't move!!"* She obeyed. He ran back to the fire scene to help. Ambulance sirens wailed. Fire bells clanged as they sped to aid in the disaster. Morning glory vines, flag, and porch rail were consumed by the flames. It was fortunate that Paolo had covered his house with asbestos shingles, for as more powder ignited, sparks flew everywhere.

An ambulance clanged its way to the scene and rushed the four victims to Pittsburgh Hospital. *"Poveri sfortunati!"* onlookers cried. The poor unfortunates had suffered the great pain of third-degree burns. Once again Maria's burdens became oppressive. Once again she called on *Dio Omnipotente* to save her Paolo, beseeched *Santa Maria* to save them all.

Every day she walked two miles to the hospital to comfort and care for her men. She carried homemade chicken soup and *pastina* to them in her big brown china teapot. Neighbors did what they could to help with chores. The boarders just happened to buy and cook too much meat for a few weeks, and insisted that the children help eat the food so it would not spoil.

A week after the disaster, the Palombos' newly-installed telephone jangled. Domenico raised the bell-shaped earpiece from its hook. "Hello, this is Franklin 6518," he said into the black mouthpiece at the end of its stem. It was a frantic Grace calling from Clyde, New York. She had read news of the disaster in their village newspaper, which reported that all four victims had died in the fire. Maria finally managed to convince her of the truth. But the shock had so affected Grace, plagued by the trauma of separation, that she lost the first child she was expecting. For Maria, this miscarriage and death compounded the tragedy.

Seven weeks later, the men came home nearly fully recovered, except for the scars on their arms and backs. Fortunately, none of their faces had been disfigured. After that horrible experience, Independence Day took on a different meaning. Never was another firecracker permitted in the family.

Thereafter, the Fourth of July became an annual day of thanksgiving, commemorated with Holy Mass. For the Palombos, the Fourth of July had become *un giorno maledetto*, a cursed day, bringing even more disasters in the future.

The next year, on May 6, 1924, Maria's sixth and last child was born. Just as she had done before, she summoned a midwife rather than a male physician to assist with the birth. She felt a nagging concern when Maria Palmiera had difficulty getting the newborn to breathe. The midwife declared her to be a "blue baby." The birth crisis passed. Several weeks later at Holy Baptism, the baby was named Yolanda, after the Italian princess. Elisa and Luigi adored their little *sorella.* Grace and Alex, still childless, came home to see her. Alex brought her a huge domed wicker carriage and wheeled her down Tioga Street proudly, wishing she were his baby.

During the three-week visit, Alex and Paolo made plans to found their own construction business with a third partner, Bill Kent. It would be a good partnership, Alex reasoned. Bill and his father-in-law, whom Bill called Paul, had been partners doing side jobs. Working to make profit for someone else seemed pointless when they could earn independent livelihoods from their skills and minimize the struggle against discrimination. The three men shared common traits: honesty, a proud work ethic, and an ability to take sensible risks. To take his place in this partnership, Alex would sell his share of the DiSanto family business and make the transition from Clyde.

Meanwhile Bill's wife, Dorothy Kent, enjoyed the Italian customs and food at Sunday dinners. She admired the ambition, the closeness, and the security that the Italian family offered in a sometime unfriendly environment. Mrs. Kent marveled at the youngest childrens' ability to translate Italian conversations for her. Gradually she and Maria became warm friends.

Paolo and Alex became close companions. They teased each other, played pranks on their wives, and made bets about who could consume more hot dogs. They brought home salted peanuts, Hershey's silvertops and Wrigley's Juicy Fruit gum for the children, and introduced them to silent moving pictures. This time, when Grace and Alex left for Clyde, the parting from Mama and Yolanda was much easier for Grace.

Overall, despite the Independence Day accident, becoming American was still a happy adventure for Paul and Maria. They took their family to band concerts, movies and vaudeville shows. Dressed in their evening best, they left their brood to trusted friends to attend Verdi Operas; they played their favorite arias on the Victorola. On Sunday mornings the happy pair tied on their big white aprons as they prepared dinner. Paolo and Maria became Leonora and Il Trovatore, as they sang their love passionately: *"Non ti scordare di me . . ."* Don't forget me. Their voices and the aroma of chicken soup and spaghetti sauce somehow blended naturally and coaxed the children awake.

Also musically inclined, the boys found pleasure and humor in learning American songs at Brushton School. Pete and Dom Palombo, warbling a tremolo soprano, imitated Miss Killgore's rendition of "Flow Gently Sweet Afton." After school, they joined friends and bellowed the more off-color parodies of World War I songs "Hinkey Dinkey *Parlez-Vous"* -- without a trace of accent. The off-color lyrics would have caused them to see "stars and stripes" had their foreign parents understood them.

Immigrant children had a freedom of bilingual expression that American children lacked. They used the freedom when their friends taunted. The foreigners closed ranks and, in their native language, laid battle strategy before their bewildered enemy. The surprised Americans soon learned that foreigners were not pushovers. They reluctantly endured prejudice, but like their parents, foreign children were determined not to be vanquished. However, sometimes in self-defense, they had to get physical.

Toto Sapienza did just that when, along his newspaper route, a group of boys taunted and threatened him for weeks . "Hey wop! You're a dumb dago!" He had endured their cruel remarks for weeks, but his patience snapped when the biggest bully, urged by several friends, tried to yank his newspapers away. Toto shot a sharp fist at the tormentor's belly and doubled him over, his friend Fenori Claybrook urging him on. Toto turned the shocked ruffian on his face, pushed it into a huge dark brown ball of hot horse manure, recently deposited by the iceman's horse, and rubbed his face in it. The shocked onlookers began to disperse; but when the tyrant raised his dung-smeared head, his friends laughed and yelled, "Nigger, nigger, nigger!" Toto did not forget the hurt on Fenori's face at this versatility in their discrimination.

Young immigrants soon learned that to survive one must fight back. From their parents, they learned that to succeed they must adapt, work, and be proud. Many immigrant children who developed a strong incentive to succeed rose to upper middle-class circles — but not without encountering and rising above anti-ethnic hurdles.

In the twenties, if racism was a sporadic hurdle, diseases were a constant hazard — especially to children who were not immunized until they started first grade. Whooping cough, diphtheria, scarlet fever and measles were so menacing that strict quarantine regulations were imposed. Public health officials posted red signs on front doors, naming the disease within. Children were kept home from school until the peril was over. The Palombo family suffered the consequences of these ailments.

When Elisa was four years old, she developed whooping cough. She and Yolanda had to be kept apart. Her throat filled with mucus, Elisa hacked so violently that she fell breathless — then unconscious. What a fright! Poor Maria imagined the worse. *"Santa Maria! Aiutami!* O Holy Maree Helpa me!" The boarder, quick-witted Jim, seized Elisa, turned her upside down, pounded her back until the mucus gushed out of her mouth, and breathed life into her again.

It was the second time that he had saved her life. Maria thanked him and God profusely. When death seemed ever present, Jim became the family hero. The children loved him and listened with open-mouth awe as he told exciting stories about the Wild West. He and Elisa formed a lasting bond.

The following February 26, 1925 began a bleak year at 7508 Tioga Street. On that morning Elisa was startled awake. From her crib in the bedroom corner, she heard her parents wailing. Elizabeth, a nurse and neighbor, was bathing baby Yolanda — who that same morning sighed her last "Ma-ma, and Ta-ta," as her parents and Dr. Plyer stood helplessly by. Maria's anxiety at having delivered a "blue baby" had not been unfounded, for in those days corrective surgery for a congenitally defective heart was unheard of.

Elisa and Luigi were unhappy and fearful as they waited for John Taylor, the undertaker, to come. Grace and Alex were summoned home. The house soon filled with visitors who brought food and donated $5 or $10 for the funeral and Angel's Mass, since the benefit society did not cover burial costs for children. Lying in her little coffin, with blonde curls framing her beautiful face, Yolanda looked like a Boticelli Angel. Elisa wept and covered her with kisses. Luigi refused to leave her at night.

On the third day, John Taylor arrived to take the casket for the funeral procession. Luigi, upon seeing him claim his little sister, ran frantically for a hatchet. As the undertaker was pushing the casket out the door, an enraged Luigi screamed: "Guddam you! Come back! Come back! Don't take my baby sister!" And he wielded a mighty swipe down the middle of John Taylor's back, ripping his overcoat in half. Had the undertaker not been wearing a heavy wool coat, the result might have been disastrous. Neighbors rescued the grieving little brother and sister from the scene.

After the funeral, the parlor was not the same. Previously the happy setting for a wedding and three Baptisms, it had now been host to the first family death in America. The children fired questions at their saddened parents. "Go get John Taylor! Tell him to bring Yolanda home!" Luigi begged.

Elisa asked, "Where is Heaven, Papa? Will I see God and play with Yolanda?" Paolo and Maria reassured the children patiently that their little sister was now in Heaven with God. "But I want her back!" Elisa wept. She could not understand why Papa held her tight against his wet cheek and rocked her to sleep. Papa's eyes often misted into pools of blue water, but they seldom spilled over. Now the tears flowed freely.

Grace and Alex understood their parents' pain. They went home devastated and determined to have another baby. This time Grace would be carefully supervised so that she would not lose another child. Mama assured them that this time they would succeed.

Paolo made Yolanda's grave marker — a thick cement cross, mounted on a double pedestal. A talented friend carved her name, her birth and death dates, and a small angel across its facade, below a glass-encased bubble for her picture. Paolo rooted it over her grave, built a picket fence around the plot and filled it with perennial flowers, which he and the children tended lovingly.

Yolanda's death had left Papa unsettled. One night he was disturbed by two dreams. In the first dream, he met Saint Anthony, patron of orphans, at the top of the stairs. The saint was holding Yolanda in his arms and Elisa by the hand. Papa was startled awake by his own voice confronting Saint Anthony, *"Non è abbastanza una figlia?* Please, ees nota one leettla girl enough?"

He finally fell asleep again and dreamed of Saint Rocco, patron of the afflicted, again standing at the top of the stairs. The saint was holding Luigi by the hand. Paolo reached to snatch his little sidekick away . . . and sat bolt upright! He broke a cold sweat and told Maria his dream. Maria fetched a towel and a glass of brandy and said comfortingly, "Is a dream, *caro*. Go to sleep, *dormi*. Tomorrow we talk." Paolo had reason to fear.

Both Italian and American newspapers had warned of disease epidemics, advising the public to stay isolated from sick persons, and to keep their bodies and homes clean. Up until 1909, water from the polluted Monongahela River alongside the mills, and waste from outhouses had carried typhoid fever, diptheria and other contagious diseases. Fortunately, in 1909, after political delays, Pittsburgh's public money had finally been used to install a pure water system, to establish a Board of Public Health, and to initiate a mandatory vaccination program for school children, after which the death rate from diseases dropped.

By 1925, though the contagion rate had been lower in Homewood than in crowded city and mill town areas, at least a dozen quarantine signs appeared on doors along Tioga Street, each specifying the communicable disease. Sometimes a floral crepe replaced them when a child died. Maria tried to keep her little ones isolated, but overhead lurked the ubiquitous threat of disease.

The death rate among preschool children was high, partly because immunization serums were limited. The Schick Test shots for Diphtheria and the Dick Test shots for Scarlet Fever were commonly given in first grade, where Luigi, now called Louis, had been inoculated. Elisa, who was pre-school age, had miraculously survived whooping cough without inoculation. But now scarlet fever felled her and challenged poor Maria, who passionately summoned the Holy Mother for support. She willed and nourished her little Elisa back to health.

After Yolanda's death, Paolo was drawn even closer to his *Lisetta*. This little girl was a survivor. By May she had recovered. Maria went to church and lit a candle in thanksgiving. Paul, remembering his dreams, construed them as an omen and prayed his thanks with her.

By mid-summer Papa was his optimistic self again. As he had promised, Independence Day would be a *festa* that called for celebrating American-style — without fireworks at home. He roasted slabs of spare ribs and little chickens, one for each person. He exerted great effort to get the proper trimmings to heap onto his favorite American food — the hot dog. July Fourth called for homemade *gelato*, concocted with rock salt in the hand-turned aluminum ice cream maker. Dom and Pete vied for the privilege of turning the handle. Elisa got to lick her Papa's ice cream-laden forefinger; the homemade rootbeer tickled her nose. Louis was not hungry and would not eat. He had begun showing a rash on his neck and face. By July fourth evening, he had developed a high fever and red open sores; an oozing rash covered his upper body.

Dr. Plyer was summoned. He informed Maria that Louis had contracted the highly-contagious skin infection Erysipilus, and warned that he could suffer a convulsion from the high fever. The family would have to be quarantined and separated from Louis, who was put into Elisa's little bedroom, alone. Maria was to be separated from everyone, too, so that she would not contaminate them while she cared for Louis. The doctor advised her to keep her hands, clothing and house meticulously clean, and gave her a black medicated salve to spread over the sores with a flat wooden stick. Dr. Plyer adamantly instructed Paul to stay away from everyone. He would know in a week if Paul should continue working.

"Four of July," Maria lamented as she scrubbed and boiled and prayed. "*Un altro giorno maledetto.*" She was convinced that it really was a cursed day. "*Santa Madre, ecco io!* It is me again." She beseeched her for the courage and strength to nurse her little *Luigi* well. By midnight, his fever raged until he became delirious and said outrageous things.

A skeptical Maria avoided superstitious, well-meaning *paesani* who offered to perform a *gettatura* ritual to cast off *mal occhio*, the evil eye curse. She was horrified when the delirious Luigi stood on his bed and raised his arms to conduct Maestro Mesdeo's band, using rhythmic, forbidden Italian expletives: "Zzaaa, zzaaa! zzaaaa! Ooo cazzo cazzo cazzo!" A mortified Maria mentally censored the dirty translation, crossed herself, and prayed to the Bella Madonna to forgive him. The off-color words were not amusing at the time; but years later the family found them hilarious.

At midnight, they received an anguished call from Clyde, where Grace had delivered their first grandchild, Anita Yolanda, at eleven p.m. She had lived only a half-hour. Papa cried "*Che giorno maledetto!*"

Several days later, the grief-stricken Maria left for Clyde, leaving Arcangela to care for Louis, now recovering. She took Elisa with her. On the train, Maria scolded her soul mate in exasperation: "*Santa Madre, ma perche mi castiga? . . .* Why? Why you punish me?" She comforted Elisa, assuring her that the two little Angels would play together in Heaven.

A distraught Alex met them at the station in Lyons. He crushed Elisa to him and waited for Maria's comforting hug. At her cousin's casket, Elisa kissed another Botticelli Angel, and wept.

During the long funeral a kindly neighbor, sensing Elisa's grief, diverted her to *Zia* Carolina's piano in the parlor. In the next few hours, Elisa forgot her sorrow as she pressed the keys and discovered that she could play little tunes. Each day, when she was not picking raspberries or finding new amusements on the farm, she slipped quietly into the parlor to play the piano. Soon she was playing tunes she had learned from Mama and Papa when they sang opera songs and Italian folk tunes. The memory of that summer on *Zia* Carolina's farm would endure for a lifetime.

Harvest time had begun, and *Zia* and Mama prepared a hearty farm breakfast for ten or more workers. They served potatoes and eggs, peppers and sausages, and mugs of strong coffee. The two cousins baked twelve loaves of bread twice a week. To Mama this was a touch of her farm in Italy at harvest time.

In late August, Papa came to visit and to accompany them home. Elisa could hardly wait to show him her new-found musical ability. Papa's eyes nearly spilled over from pride and amazement. He hugged her tight and made a firm secret decision. He must do three things when they got home: enroll Elisa in first grade, buy her school clothes, and search for a surprise for her.

Papa loved to dress himself and his family well. He took Elisa to town on the Hamilton streetcar to buy her new school clothes. After several hours, they came home from Kauffman and Baer with several huge boxes filled with a half-dozen dresses, matching knee socks, ribbons, hightop shoes, patent leather slippers, a winter coat, gloves, a scarf and a hat. Papa's extravagance elicited from Mama one of her maxims, "Hmmmm". . . Paolo waited . . . *"Paolo . . . Paolo, dal capo si guasta il pesce.* A fish it spoils froma the head." Papa smiled and thought about another planned extravagance — the surprise that was yet to come.

Although Papa's English was quite good, he still had an accent. When he went to enroll Elisa at school, the teacher misinterpreted his accent, and registered her as Alice. Henceforth, she would be Alice. To her benefit, the Anglicized name, her blonde hair and blue eyes, and the absence of an Italian accent earned her more patient treatment than her dark-featured classmates. Immigrants' children were not oblivious to cultural bias; they had experienced it and heard stories about hurtful incidents.

Alice loved stories at school and enjoyed hearing Miss Groggs read *The Secret Garden*, as she sucked on a throat lozenge. To her delight, some of the stories she read were familiar. Her favorite was *Little Red Riding Hood*. "I know the story in Italian, Miss Groggs," Alice said happily.

A surprised Miss Groggs asked, "Really? What's it called?"

"Cappuccio Rosso. The red hood, and she met the *lupo,* I mean wolf, in the forest."

An astonished Miss Groggs stopped her. "Do you speak Italian?" she asked.

"Yes — and pray — and sing in Italian," Alice answered. Miss Groggs sucked hard on her lozenge and frowned. Alice was confused.

Earlier that day another teacher had smiled at her when she heard Alice singing Italian.

"La donna e mobile'. . ." she sang as she walked along the hall. The teacher stopped her and asked, "Do you know what you're singing, dear?"

Alice replied, "Yes — it's an opera song. Papa sings it when he plays the *Rigoletto* songs on the talking machine."

The astonished teacher asked, "What's your name?"

"My American name is Alice. In Italian, *Mi chiamo Elisa Costanza Palombo.* What's your name?"

"Miss Costanza," she replied. "Why you speak Italian!" She smiled and smiled. Alice knew she had made a friend.

One day, several weeks later, Papa summoned Alice home with a long familiar whistle. By its sound, she knew it was a happy signal. *"Ferma,"* he said, stopping her at the gate. Papa blindfolded her and led her to the parlor door, where he revealed a magnificent surprise! There stood a Remington player piano that he had taken in payment for building a new porch in Shadyside.

Alice cried: "Oh, Papa! *Grazie! Grazie!"* She threw her arms around him, and ran to play the piano — non-stop — through dinner. Now the family had another source of entertainment. Papa had bought music rolls to play that reflected both Italian and American cultures: Verdi operas, and such American popular music as *Shine on Harvest Moon, In the Good Old*

Summertime, Let Me Call You Sweetheart, and other favorites. When any of the family got tired of playing "by ear" — and all of them learned to — they would play the piano rolls.

Until now, the center of their life and socializing had been the dinner table. Like most Italians, they spent much time at the table, solving their problems and comforting their griefs with food. But now there was an extension of that life as family and friends gathered to join in the song fests. Out of their family tragedy, the piano came to brighten their lives again. Grace and Alex were coming home after Christmas! Perhaps 1927 would be a happier year.

Chapter 12

Seasoned With Papa's Love

The Fall harvest had yielded a generous crop of fruits and vegetables for Maria's kitchen. Her neighbor, Mrs. Burley, who cooked for a wealthy family, taught her to bake fruit pies. They shared recipes from Italy and from the Deep South. Their daughters Snooky and Alice shared a close friendship. The canning process she learned from cousins who worked in Clyde's local canneries gave her new ideas. She preserved quince, peaches, spiced pears, pineapple, applesauce, and a variety of fruit jams and jellies. She made sweet and sour pickles, beets, relish, and cauliflower and pickled peppers for salads. Each had a special place on her menus. She put up green beans, peas and corn, and Italian prune tomatoes, dried in the sun, to turn into *salsina*; some she flavored with Italian herbs and preserved in glass jars for spaghetti sauce. She and Paolo made sweet and hot sausage to put into lard, or to hang to dry in the *cantina*.

Whatever they did not grow in their large garden, Paolo bought at the "Yards" in Pittsburgh's distinctive wholesale food Strip District, where fellow Italians shopped, exchanged news, and arranged their *bocce* games. At the Pennsylvania Macaroni Company, Paolo bought a variety of cheeses, olives and pasta — and dried figs and dates. He purchased imported Italian olive oil and *dolci: confetti, torrone,* cinnamon sticks and an assortment of *licori* extracts to make holiday spirits. He selected one crate each of fresh figs, tangerines and oranges, then bought a huge hand of bananas from Frank Corso, the Banana King.

Sometimes Paolo took Louie and Alice to the Italian markets. They loved the smells and atmosphere in the *mercato Italiano*. Papa would allow them to choose special treats from the big square glass jars that held yellow-orange sassafras sticks, or brown *cannella* cinnamon tubes, and other goodies. And they anticipated the hot dog and root beer treat that was sure to follow. Louie and Alice felt sorry for those poor American kids who only knew the local grocery store and A & P market. What a shame!

Paolo thought nostalgically of his olive groves and grape vineyards. With expertise, he chose a variety of grapes to make wine. Italians could be assured of quality in purchasing California grapes to make their wines, because grape-growing immigrants from Northern Italy had brought their experience and formed the Italian-Swiss Colony vineyard and winery at Asti, California, in the 1880's. They established a small wine-making industry, and their vineyards produced more grapes and high-quality wines than there were barrels to hold them.

Each season, Paolo purchased more than a hundred crates of grapes and several new half-barrels and wooden casks to hold last year's aging wines. At wine-making time, the children loved picking raisins from the grapes and making play houses from empty boxes before Paolo broke them up to burn in the fireplaces in every room. The American kids were not so lucky!

Papa promised that after Christmas and before Alex and Grace arrived in April, he would excavate the mud cellar floor and lay cement for the coal furnace he planned to install. The children would no longer need the flannel-wrapped heated brick he tucked in their beds to keep them warm. Alice worried that she would miss the fireplaces — and the smell of crackling pine logs that Papa brought home especially for Christmas.

Then Papa decided that it would not be sensible to have a hot air furnace and only dim gas lights. He promised they would have bright electric lights like the mansions in Pittsburgh. Few people had electric lights, or furnaces, or telephones in their neighborhood. Now the Palombos would have them all.

The harvest was in. Canning and wine-making were finished. And Christmas was coming! Papa and Mama threw themselves with renewed energy into their tasks. Maria was relatively happy with Arcangela's family living on her street. Very early on Christmas Eve, on their way to visit Arcangela, Maria and Alice stopped in the little African Methodist Zion Church on Tioga Street to enjoy the spirited gospel singing and clapping and praying — albeit Catholics were forbidden to go into non-Catholic churches.

But Maria, ecumenical before her time, challenged this dogma. *"Guarda come pregano con tutto il cuore. Dio ascolto.* See howa they pray weeth all their hearts. God, He listena. Yes?" She knew she would have to debate her behavior with Father DeFrancesco. Maria's was an uncommon attitude, when ethnic groups clung exclusively to their own religious practices.

Within the same religion, the Irish of Holy Rosary in Homewood, the Italians of Mother of Good Counsel in Brushton, the Germans of St.

Wolaberg in East Liberty and the Poles of Braddock's Sacred Heart favored their own Christmas hymns and customs. But within their Catholic Faith all shared a common bond of recognition — the Latin Mass and Latin Hymns. *Adeste Fideles* was a universal Latin Christmas favorite.

The Palombo family's favorite Italian carol was *Pastorale*, the story of the Nativity, which the family sang for years after their arrival in America. Miss Mangle, the church organist, played it, emulating the *zampogna* music of shepherd bagpipes. By the time the children sang the story of the poor cold *Bambino Jesu* without clothing to keep Him warm, they wanted to give Him their own wraps. *Santa Natale,* Alice observed, was about loving and giving. Santa Claus was a lesser persona than Jesus.

Growing up Italian was fun. Children knew how fortunate they were to be socially conditioned in two cultures — something social scientists had not figured yet, in their emphasis on cultural patterns, social structure and the dynamics of social change. Not until psychologists formed their theories on patterns of behavior did Americans begin to understand that immigrant children were shaped by many of the values found in dominant American-Nordic culture. The difference was that children of immigrants and slaves understood the hurt caused by bias. They learned their best lessons on open-minded acceptance of all cultures from their parents, for racism in Italy was unknown. There was no racial hierarchy. Fair Italians did not look down upon darker Italians.

An incident that Alice witnessed as a child at Christmas time drove home the meaning of unconditional love for *all* people, and the true meaning of Christmas. In the twenties, life and pleasures were simple. When ethnic bias was strong, a simple act by Papa captured the spirit of Christmas and taught Alice an indelible lesson found in Mama's maxim: *"Siamo tutti figli di Dio."* Many years later, she recorded her "slice of life" in this reminiscence:

<u>Seasoned With Papa's Love</u>

"The dawn was deep red when I awoke. Silver frost leaves had turned the window opaque and a depth of new snow sparkled on the wooden ledge. Lazy flakes swirled like the ones I shook all around in our glass paper weight. The brick at my feet was still warm through the flannel wrapping. Papa's soft familiar whistle floated up the backstairs from the kitchen. Seven-year olds were not supposed to be awake at this hour. But this was a *special* day. It was the day Papa began Christmas giving. I buried my head under the covers to retrieve my woolen socks. Papa had already awakened the fire in the bedroom grate. Pinewood crackled and filled the room with dancing golden light and the fragrant aroma of pine sap. I crept from beneath the warm covers and stole downstairs to enjoy the rare privilege of watching Papa prepare breakfast.

"Buon giorno, Lisetta," he chuckled as he scooped me into his arms, carried me to the tilted wooden rocker and tucked me inside the red and black plaid wool blanket that Mama had brought with her from Italy. Papa moved quickly. He poked the sleeping black iron woodstove and filled it with wood chips and logs. The tea kettle sent out steam and whistled. The aroma of freshly-ground coffee stung my nose as Papa shook it loose from the drawer of the coffee mill. I watched him beat a cupful of eggs and slice thick chunks of Mama's homemade bread — and prepare bits of suet and crumbs for the birds.

I listened to comforting sounds: the muffled "clop-clop" of hoofs on frozen ground, the milk wagon creaking through the snow, footsteps crunching along the walk, and the muted clink of frozen milk bottles. I thought about that night, when we would sit before the great fire and listen to Papa tell the Nativity story in his most picturesque Italian. And we would roast chestnuts and look at leaping flames make weird shadows on the wall.

I snuggled deeper into the itchy blanket and watched Papa agitate the pot-bellied stove until it got red-hot. Softly, he whistled *Adeste Fideles* without seeming to take a breath. Sometimes he would glance at me with his special look and then turn away quickly. A father and his little girl needed no words in moments like these.

Finally, his thick Italian accent broke the silence. "Opena your mouth," he said as he held the stirring fork to my lips. When I swallowed the delicious hot morsel of freshly-cooked eggs, seasoned with Papa's love, I felt warm and happy inside.

Before Mama and the rest of the family were called out of bed, Papa went from room to room and coaxed alive each fireplace. Through the open parlor door, the logs glowed bright orange under the gray ashes. Tom, our fat alley cat, had already taken his spot on the hearth. He performed his morning licking ritual until his fur looked as sleek as Mama's seal hat, then thrummed his thick tail and watched us through amber slits.

The Christmas wreaths were hung and Papa had screwed brass cup hooks into the scarred brown wood chimney piece where we would hang our stockings. Tiny figurines with perfect faces waited on the scalloped ledge to take their vigil around the *presepio*; the manger scene was my most favorite part of Christmas. Covered trays of newly-baked Italian pastries rested on the upright player piano out of the reach of greedy little hands. The ebony clock, pillared like a Greek temple, began its asthmatic gurgle before chiming seven off-key strokes. Christmas was truly coming!

Papa fetched a worn towel and wiped the misted windows. I could barely see the lamplighter lift the metal dome off the frosted glass and snuff out the weak yellow light with his long cupped stick. By now, the fence posts were wearing tall snow hats.

I slid from the cozy blanket and washed at the sink where Papa had poured water from the tea kettle into the chipped porcelain basin. I watched my face wiggle in the water. My feet felt warm and squiggly as I pushed them into the long black stockings and the leather hightops he had toasted before the fire. I stood in silent ecstasy as Papa cupped my chin in his strong warm hand and combed my hair. He was careful to draw a straight part down the middle. I waited for the special squeeze he gave my face when he was finished. He didn't disappoint me. *"Lisetta, mia bella biondina,"* he whispered. I felt special when he called me his beautiful little blonde.

After breakfast, Papa and I went down to the dark cold fruit cellar. We carried up Mama's sturdy wicker garden basket to hold the presents we would give the milkman, the garbage men and the mailman. Our candles made a curious procession of shadows along the stairway wall. *"Lisetta,* you holda the candle so Papa can lighta the gas lamp, eh?"

I felt important. This was the first year I was participating in the ritual. I remembered last year, when I had begun to suspect that Santa Claus (Papa called him "Sundy Close") really did not have an Italian accent and a black mustache over a white beard. Somehow it didn't matter.

We filled the big basket with jars of spiced pears, quince, brandy peaches and grape jelly. Papa carried a crock of homemade Italian sausage preserved in lard. He didn't have to explain about the pleasure of giving. I felt it.

I liked our second trip best. I was allowed to choose a sassafras or cinnamon stick to chew on, or nibble at the raisins and tangerines and fresh figs that Papa had bought for the holidays. Barrels of homemade wine lined the fruit cellar. Sparkling crystal bottles in straw jackets waited to be filled with Papa's clear ruby wine. He reached for his sampling glass. I waited to hear the gurgle from the wooden spigot as the wine dribbled from its huge cask. He offered me a sip. I had known he would. I tried not to screw up my face while tasting.

By the time we had climbed to the kitchen, Mama had already filled the huge black iron skillet with sausages. We wrapped each homemade Christmas treasure in one of Mama's dishtowels, with hand-embroidered words that I had traced for her, "GOD BLESS OUR HOME."

Before the morning passed, Big John and his helper came to empty our great wooden rubbish barrels. I had never seen his helper, who wasn't as big or as black as John. Papa invited them inside to receive his modest gift, a flask of wine. As he carefully stomped the snow from his high galoshes onto the braided oval rug, Big John's nose twitched appreciatively at the spicy fragrance of sizzling sausages.

"Mmm, mmm, Mr. Paul. It's a good batch this year, I can tell." He pulled off his worn black cap and long black gloves and moved toward the round clawfoot table.

Pouring each of his guests a half-full glass of wine, Papa said, "You men still ona the job. But theesa much wine joost warma you eenside." He speared a fat sausage for each of them and invited them to sit. Mama heaped platters full of sausages and crackling-hot chunks of Italian bread, and set them on the table.

The new helper stayed by the kitchen door. Noticing his shyness, Papa coaxed him to the table. "Whatsa th' matter? You no like my sausage? You no like my wine?"

The man shook his head and gravely answered, "Mr. Paul, y' all don't want me to eat at your table. I'm colored folks, you know."

The hurt in Papa's eyes expressed his disappointment. He walked over to his guest and rubbed a stubby forefinger across the brown face. "That'sa funny," he said solemnly examining his finger. "The color no come off. Sita down. Eat. You hurta my heart!"

"Merry Christmas, Mr. Paul!" the man laughed pulling off his gloves. "Merry Christmas everyone!" He blinked away tears. And blew his nose hard. And sat.

I was touched to see his pleasure. I didn't know why. A seven-year old does not stop to think why. I only knew at that moment that my heart brimmed with all the love I had always felt for Papa. "*Lisetta*," he said gruffly, clearing his throat. Papa always cleared his throat when he was about to weep. "*Lisetta*, go find Mama to getta some *biscotti*, eh?"

I flung my arms about his neck. Somehow, when Papa was nearby, the world was beautiful. I could hardly wait for Christmas to come."

* * * * * * * * *

And at last Christmas truly did arrive on that happy December 1927. Every stove had been blackened and polished. The new coal-and-gas kitchen stove was fed generous shovels full of coke and wood chips. Its overhead oven was filled with special Christmas *dolci* for the children: cake dolls for the girls, animal figures for the boys, decorated with colored icing and silver sprinkles.

Paolo had cleaned a variety of seafood for the Christmas Eve Vigil banquet: breaded smelts; *calamari*, squid steamed in basil garlic olive oil; and *baccala,* dried codfish in red sauce. He whistled happily as he sliced a variety of Italian cold meats and cheeses for the *antipasto*. And stopped. "I'm almost afraid to be so happy," Paolo said.

"*Zitto!!* Quiet!!" Maria commanded. She made the sign of the Cross and continued to prepare the other courses from *zuppa minestrone* to *dolci e noci*. Arcangela and Antonio would soon arrive to help. The boarders, Martino and Jim, would join them; and Father De Francesco would come, bringing Miss Mangle to play Christmas music.

Mama prepared a new wicker basket to hold linen embroidered kitchen towels for her dear friend, *Comare* Rachele Capone, and the Christmas *dolci* for her children, Carmen, Joseph, Virginia and Valentino. Maria and Rachele were godparents to one another's children. At noon *Comare* Capone came with arms full of presents and toys. She always knew exactly what to bring. In days when children did not get many toys, *Comare* Capone was like a fairy godmother to Louie and Alice.

At dusk every fireplace in every room crackled and danced merrily. Dom, Joe, and Gina joined their cousins before the fire to roast chestnuts. After the Vigil feast, they gathered around the piano to sing the Italian *Nativity Pastorale*, the Latin *Adeste Fideles* and other carols that were sung in America's Christian churches. Finally, everyone settled down to hear Papa read the Nativity story — by gaslight. Next year there would be electric lights. Next year Grace and Alex would be home at last!

Chapter 13

Goodbye Tioga Street

The Roaring Twenties were labeled the Enlightened Era by some historians. The uncertainties of World War I were over. America had entered a period of new morality. It was the generation of the first Youth Rebellion. Challenged by peer pressure, many children of immigrants raised in Old-World traditions of obedience and modesty were perplexed and frustrated when their strict parents held firm to their values.

American children questioned their elders' authority and rebelled against rigid social customs. Flappers raised their hemlines and used their stockings to "roll 'em down and show their pretty knees." They sported the boyish bob, did the Charleston, imitated Clara Bow, the "It" girl, swooned over Rudolph Valentino, and left home to support the Suffragette Movement.

After the discovery of wireless telegraphy, the telephone and radio, the world globe had shrunk. With the further development of electricity and silent movies, lifestyles changed. The hand-heated flat iron yielded to the electric iron; the ice box gave way to the electric refrigerator, and silent movies evolved into a marvel called "talkies." Innovations in transportation brought new heroes. In 1927, Charles Lindbergh made his famed transatlantic flight in *The Spirit of St. Louis*. Americans took to air travel and started a love affair with the automobile. Young men beckoned in song lyrics: "Won't you come with me, Lucille, in my merry Oldsmobile" and "Come Josephine in my flying machine."

Morals relaxed. Some parents did not, especially if confronted with college boys in raccoon coats who owned automobiles, carried "hooch" in their whiskey flasks, and parked and "necked" on dark roads with their dates. Jazz and cigarettes were in. The Eighteenth Amendment and The Noble Experiment brought in Prohibition and "speakeasies," the hideaways to cover illegal drinking. Families were permitted to make their own wine, but forbidden to sell it for consumption.

Italians in Homewood continued their lifelong tradition of making wine. Curiously, the Irish cops used to stop and visit homes several times a week for a *"social chat"* over a glass of *vino*. Pharmacies sold gallons of alcohol prescribed for "medicinal purposes." Prohibition laws permitted the sale of low-alcohol beverages; and beverage distributor Harry I. Nieman sold "near beer" below his second-floor pool room. One could surmise that hidden speakeasies sold illegal booze and housed slot machines. If raids took place they were discreet, leaving law-abiding Italians to wonder who the local "bootleggers" really were. A popular Louis Jordan song satirized the situation by declaring that *There Ain't Nobody Here But Us Chickens*, when a cop knocked at a speakeasy door.

In the twenties, when prejudice was heavy, Italians were particularly offended by the notoriety of the trial of alleged anarchists Nicola Sacco, an unknown fish peddler, and Bartolomeo Vanzetti, an obscure shoemaker. During the American Radical Movement, protest against government practices and unfair labor bosses was high. Anarchism, the name given to the protest movement, had been mostly related to the German labor movement, whose leaders were prosecuted and executed after the Haymaker Riot in 1886. But somehow, the movement had become a reflection on Italians. The Palombo and Sapienza families, deeply irritated, followed the news.

By 1920, Anarchism had become identified with Italian union organizers and agitators. Though they were not their leaders, Sacco and Vanzetti came to symbolize Anarchism for the world when they spoke against exploitation of the common hardworking man. In a trial reminiscent of the Salem witch hunts, they were convicted for an alleged bank robbery and murder, then languished hopelessly in jail for seven years, protesting their innocence. The notorious case received international radio and newspaper coverage; vaudeville comedians made sport of it. Millions of Americans believed that such foreigners brought in dangerous ideas and activity. Prejudice against these two Italians became blatant when a not-so-impartial Judge Webster Thayer called them "Anarchist bastards" and denied their appeals despite their petitions to him. He sentenced Sacco and Vanzetti to die in the electric chair in 1927.

Some protesters, believing that these men were political scapegoats, demonstrated against their death sentence in front of the courthouse. Ironically, the very tools that had given America her independence — freedom of expression — had failed. After historians tried and re-tried them with different verdicts, it remained debatable whether prejudice had denied them justice. As if the Nordic Nativists were not hurdles enough for Mediterranean immigrants, the stigma left by the case hurt honorable Italians. Throughout the twenties, non-Italian criminals also dominated the news. Bill and Myles O'Donnel, Little Hymie Weiss, Dion O'Banion, Polock Joe Saltis, and other opposing gangs waged turf wars. But Al Capone and the *Mafia* got star billing on radio, in newspapers and in films at the talkies. This emphasis stereotyped Italians, prejudicing Americans even more. Honorable Italians were chagrined. Paolo and Maria, who knew no such characters, were deeply offended. Theirs was the proud world of Columbus, Marconi, DaVinci, Verdi, and so many other world-famous Italians.

Transplanted families from Italy, Ireland, Poland and Germany, alongside Blacks from the South, tried to adapt to changing times as they gradually created a comfortable life, blending age-old ethnic customs with life in Homewood. The children on Tioga Street played happily among moving horse-drawn wagons that delivered milk and ice, with door signs designating "ICE TODAY." And they dodged hucksters peddling vegetables and fruits. Pittsburgh's street sweepers kept busy cleaning up horse manure, and it was not uncommon to see some enterprising gardener shovel it into the garden wheelbarrow.

Airplanes were a novelty to behold. Children stopped at play to point to the sky and shout "Airplane! Airplane!" They pretended to be "Lindy" in imaginary flight. They made paper airplanes; Louie Palombo flew his in the house, where they landed everywhere — even in the spaghetti sauce!

Yes, times were changing and the Palombo family, accustomed to adapting selectively, adjusted to the changes and altered their own little world. Paolo hired laborers to excavate the mud cellar and lay the cement floor in preparation for the new furnace. He had many improvements to complete before Alex and Grace arrived. With their thriving business and a long and trusting relationship, he and Bill Kent were eager for Alex to join them.

Dom and Pete quickly developed American ways. Now teenagers, they were attracted to what interested all American boys — the Model T Ford. Their best buddies, Toto and Lee Sapienza, were equally drawn to America's new craze. By the end of the decade, Ford had nearly four million Model T's rolling around the country. The boys pooled their money and bought an indestructible second-hand "Tin Lizzie," along with a simple tool kit made up of a wrench, a ball-peen hammer, a screw driver, and some wire. They pooled their money for parts. A muffler cost $.25 cents, a new running board $1.25. The Model T was mechanically so simple that almost any handy man could fix it. Every Saturday the boys dismantled their prize, cleaned every part, and re-assembled it. They knew every piece from radiator to rear fender.

Their little brothers, Louie and Duffy, competed for the chance to turn the starting crank below the front hood to coax it into action. After several turns, the flivver spat and coughed, and the engine turned over. Their friends piled into the wide leather front seat and the rear rumble seat. "Aaaaoooogah! Aaaaoooogah!" went the horn as they squeezed the black bulb and rode up and down Formosa Way, Tioga Street, and Brushton Avenue — before drivers' licenses were required. In the early twenties, Grace had adopted some American preferences. She was hopelessly smitten with Rudolph Valentino and tried to learn the Charleston. She wore her dresses shorter — barely to the knee, but stopped short of " . . . turned-down hose, flapper yessir one of those . . . " or cutting her beautiful blonde braids to sport a boyish bob.

Maria's Americanization escalated, too, when she learned to read. It began one day when Alice bounced in from school shouting, *"Mamma, Mamma! Posso leggere!* Mamma, I can read!"

"Allora, anch' io bisogno imparare. Well, then, I must learn, too." The first word Mama learned to read was FREE. The family laughed each time she summoned someone to find out what was being given away. They were quite amused at her musical inflection and Italian way with vowels as she read, "Thay buuk eez on thay daysk. Poot thay buuk ona thay tabla."

Contrary to sociologists' misplaced sympathy for the "marginal man," first-generation Americans who spoke two languages had an advantage. Since many words had Latin roots, they had a better grasp of their meaning. In Alice's case, three things helped with learning to read, spell and define words: assisting Mama to read, being bilingual, and Martino Mariotti, their boarder and mentor. Knowing two languages was such fun!

Martino, a tall, distinguished gentleman with an elegant moustache, wrote editorials for the *Sentinella* newspaper and spoke beautiful formal Italian. The varied discourse and wealth of news he brought home helped speed their Americanization. To the childrens' advantage, they spoke formal Italian to Martino, and Abruzzese dialect to their parents and *paesani*. On Tioga Street, nearly everyone spoke Italian in one dialect or other. Alice and

Louie loved to imitate them. Martino encouraged Alice to read simple Italian words from his newspaper. Church sermons in both Italian and English helped any interested immigrants' children to learn formal Italian, and helped their parents to learn English.

Maria had become enthusiastically American — a socializer. She co-founded and named the women's Italian benefit society, *Stella Guida* (Guiding Star,) destined to be in existence into the twenty-first century. She enjoyed her new non-Italian friends. Mrs. Burley, her Black neighbor, relished her spaghetti; Maria favored her apple pie. Traffic over their back fence was brisk.

Immigrants were amazingly adaptable to their multiethnic communities. The beautiful relationships that developed between children of various cultural backgrounds were a reflection of their parents' attitudes. Johnny and Buddy Burley were Louie's playmates, and Snooky and Alice were very best friends. Children were oblivious to color and nationality, except when victimized by prejudice. And parents found good-humored amusement in their antics.

Their sincerity was revealed one day when their kids decided to have a Tom Thumb wedding, with Johnny Burley as the groom, David Abromovitz the best man, Frances Tedesco the bride, and Snooky Burley her mother. Buddy Burley gave the bride away. Alice was maid of honor, while Louie was the preacher. Dressed in outlandishly appropriate attire, the wedding party marched up and down Tioga Street to the "church," where the ceremony took place on the Burley's front porch. When the wedding was over, Maria fed the party dandelion sandwiches on fresh bread; Mrs. Burley served them applesauce. And the neighbors reacted with veiled amusement.

Since 1926, Snooky and Alice had been walking to school together every day. On the first day of second grade, Alice waited for the knock at her back door. The smell of lilac pomade told her that it was Snooky. There she stood in white starched blouse and blue skirt, waiting to begin their walk to Brushton school. That day they were to share a painful experience that Alice never forgot.

The girls performed their usual ritual as they walked the four blocks to school, pressing their noses against Tedesco's candy store window and drooling over rope licorice, Mary Janes and sour balls. Alice examined the dime in her palm. And closed her fist. Papa had given her a dime to buy a stone for the new University of Pittsburgh that was under construction. Children had been told about the great building that would be the tallest school in Pittsburgh. Banners on the streetcars advertised the new "Cathedral of Learning." Children who gave a dime would have a special certificate to show that their dimes had helped to build the great school that one day they might even attend. Alice clutched her dime. She and Snooky jumped across yesterday's faded hopscotch chalk lines. And giggled. In the distance the huge school bell bonged at the end of Mr. Hissem's rope. They walked faster.

"Let me touch your skin," Snooky said. "It's so soft and pink. It feels like mine, see?" And Alice touched hers. It was warm and brown like Mama's velvet dress. Jet-black wiry plaits and blonde silky hair touched as they put their heads together. And they giggled again. "Let's play house today," Alice said. "You can be the mother this time." Snooky laughed and showed her wide-spaced teeth. The bell bonged louder.

Out of earshot, boys chanted about Mr. Hope, the pot-bellied principal: "Old man Hope with a belly full of soap, went to church on Sunday. He prayed to God to whip his children on Monday." Snooky and Alice stopped and did flips on the black iron monkey bars. "I see your underpants," Snooky giggled. They locked arms across shoulders, pressed their heads together, and counted the twelve steps up to the big stone arched entrance.

They moved past Mr. Hope and walked to room 2B, where Miss Petty stood in the doorway. "Good morning, Miss Petty," they chorused and laughed. She did not laugh back. Alice was bewildered. She was about to experience her first conflict at school, because her values and upbringing clashed with Miss Petty's attitude.

"Go in," she commanded Snooky. Snooky disentangled her chocolate arm and stopped just inside the door. Miss Petty, a product of biased values, scowled, "Don't *ever* walk close like that. Your friend is Negro. She could have lice. Now will you remember not to do it again?"

Alice shrieked "I will do it! Snooky is my friend!" No one ever screamed at Miss Petty —- not ever. Snooky heard and walked droop-shouldered to her desk. Alice felt hot tacks and cold ice chips sting her face. Miss Petty commanded her to stay after school to be punished. Dejected, she walked to the teacher's desk and deposited her dime.

At four o'clock, when they were alone in the cloak room, Alice held her breath. Her parents would never tolerate such disrespect to a teacher.

"You were defiant," Miss Petty said. "Will you be again?"

"Yes!" came the swift reply. The paddle stung hot and beautiful. Alice did not cry. Snooky waited outside the cloakroom door. The two friends walked past Miss Petty, hooked arms, touched heads defiantly and walked home. They did not giggle.

"I wish I could take off my skin," Snooky said. "Did it hurt much?"

"Not much," Alice answered. And together they cried.

When Maria heard the details of the incident, she was horrified. After she scolded Alice for being disrespectful, she folded the two friends in her arms and said, "*Quella maestra era torto!* She wasa wrong!" Snooky loved Mama.

No psychologist could have given a better lesson in human respect and kindness. No historian could have given a more concrete example of American society's misguided attitude toward certain groups. But people saw what they were conditioned to see. The targets of bias had the common bond of understanding one another's frustration. As new immigrants continued to filter into Homewood-Brushton, long-time residents learned and tolerated more about the newcomers and their shared comradeship.

Keeping abreast of progress, Paolo declared it was time to call Mr. Claybrook to install electric lights, a new miracle only several families in the community had. Gas lights had been so gloomy by comparison. At dusk, no matter how high the lamplighter turned up the yellow flame, the street lamp seemed dim. When the houselights were finally lit, *paesani* and friends came to admire their brilliance and lingered to enjoy the warm furnace air. Evenings were longer. They played Italian checkers, *tre-tre*. And they enjoyed an Italian card game called *scopa,* or sweep.

Leisure hours were longer for the children, and Mama read or told them stories as old as Aesop's Fables. To be sure, each tale held a pointed message. And Mama, like Aesop and Jesus, spoke in parables to convey life's lessons. The children had favorites, especially the ones Mama personalized, like Aesop's *La Formica e La Ciccala,* a tale about two friends, an ant and a cricket. Dramatically, Mama told how the industrious ant gathered food every summer day to store for the winter, while her friend the cricket sang her summer away. By winter, the ant had plenty to eat, but the cricket was starving. When she approached her prudent neighbor and asked for food, the ant asked the cricket, "What have you done all summer while I worked so hard, my friend?" The cricket answered, *"Ho cantato e cantato. . . .* I sang and sang.*"* After refusing her request, the ant replied: *"Allora, signora ciccala, continua a cantare!"* ["Well then, Mrs. Cricket, keep singing!"]

With the advent of electricity, the family's lifestyle changed. Papa, the incorrigible gadget consumer, bought an electric iron that became the talk of the block. Mama could retire the heavy hand-heated flat iron on which Alice had learned to iron hankies. Alice had scarcely been able to lift it with two hands, and now she could use the electric iron — with one hand! And if a telephone, a Tappan gas stove, a furnace, a gas water heater, a Ford flivver, a foot-treadle Singer sewing machine and electric lights were not enough, Papa brought home two new marvels: an electric Maytag washing machine to replace the hand-cranked dancing Savage, and the most spectacular invention of all — a radio crystal set.

The children competed to listen to the voices and music that came from earphones, which they had put into a domed butter dish to magnify the sound that originally broadcast from an inventor's garage a few blocks away.

As the craze grew, Joseph Horne's Department Store saw an opportunity and placed a newspaper ad announcing that a radio with a loudspeaker could be purchased for a few dollars. From battery-powered radio evolved electric radio. The craze swept America, launching a multibillion dollar industry. Papa, the addicted gadgeteer, bought an electric table radio. Each night the family listened to news commentator Holy Thomas — Papa's mispronunciation of Lowell Thomas.

At seven o'clock everything stopped, even at movie theaters, while the audience listened to the lovable *Amos n' Andy*, whom Papa called Simminandony. This double-edged satire stereotyped Black characters, but it also poked fun at white society. The next generation of Blacks, not recognizing its satire, would deplore the program's offensiveness and have it disappear from both radio and television. But Amos and Andy's misunderstood loveable antics were far less offensive than the negative programs that would one day evolve and persist about the Italian Mafia, and perpetuate the stereotype of Italians as criminals.

Once the radio craze struck, radios were audible everywhere as one walked the streets. At 7:30 p.m. the KDKA Little Symphony Orchestra presented a program of live music. Commercial jingles sold products: "Socks . . . socks . . . we're the Interwoven pair . . . We're Billy Jones and Ernie Hare

. . . socks . . . socks . . ." And a deep sexy male voice sang about cigars: "When the curling white smoke drifts apart, to the tune of a Spanish guitar; all the world is agleam in that moment supreme, when I'm smoking my Blackstone cigar." Ahhh . . . *Viva l'amore!* America fell in love with Elsie Hitts and Nick Dawson as they dramatized their love affair in *Dangerous Paradise.*

Without question, the radio hastened the Americanization of immigrants. In fact, it helped foreigners learn the English language. Not only did foreign language radio programs develop, but also bilingual announcers played ethnic commercials and music. Antonio Ortalo became an Italian favorite. Maria laughed at humorous commercials about a neighbor's non-stop bubbling coffee pot, *"La caffettiera da mia vicina, ser' e mattina fa 'blu . . . blu . . . blu."* Or, she was amused when a housewife got romantic about Forte Braccio olive oil and declared, "I use you for cooking . . . I never want to leave you." Maria sang along happily, *"Forte Braccio, olio mio, io ti uso per cucinare. Forte Braccio, olio mio, non ti voglio mai lasciare . . ."*

The Palombos became avid listeners of the KDKA Little Symphony and were proud of their neighbor, whom Maria called *Maestro* Sapienza. Every day Sebastian, sometimes dressed in a frock coat, passed the Palombo house on his way to play on the daily radio program with KDKA's Little Symphony orchestra. His oldest son, Toto, accompanied him, sometimes carrying a tall stovepipe hat or an extra band jacket, so that Sebastian could change from his radio broadcast job to play a concert with the Westinghouse Band at the William Penn Hotel ballroom. Many years later when destiny united their families, Alice clearly remembered Sebastian's and Toto's evening trips.

Life was beautiful for both families on Tioga Street. Paolo's business prospered in the twenties. He decided that Calvin Coolidge had been a good Republican president. Money accumulated in the Palombo bank account. The home-buying market was active. Paolo, true to his promise, announced: "We will buy a beeg brick house." He and Maria had already set their hearts on acquiring one of the lovely homes in the North Homewood Belmar Plan, which not long ago had been a race track. They began to house-hunt.

That same year, 1928, brought upward mobility for the now prosperous Sapienza family. They had outgrown their modest four-room frame house on Tioga Street. Adjacent to their old neighborhood, they bought a $10,000 three-story, ten-room brick home at 7506 Hamilton Avenue. The Sapienzas planned to move on May 1. Everyone seemed to move on May 1.

Toto, who had become Tom, and brother Lee acquired a new hobby — raising racing pigeons, known as "the sport of kings." With spare money saved from their school lunches and selling newspapers, they built an elaborate loft in their spacious back yard and bought pigeon feed and vitamins. To prepare for pigeon racing, they purchased several strains of prize-winning birds and crossbred them for competition.

They learned what incentives birds needed to win. The boys knew that when the males were "driving for eggs" and ready to mate, or when a hen was anxious to fly home to her young, these were winners. As a result of their wise care and breeding, the brothers won a number of racing trophies. Once when a mother hen did not return from a race, her babies would have died without her to feed them. Tom raised her squabs by filling his mouth with cooked oatmeal, letting the babies feed from his mouth, just as the mother pigeon would have done. The following year, one of those birds won the biggest racing prize, the $200 Powder Puff Derby. The intelligence, persistence, love and tenderness Tom showed to his birds were strong clues to his exceptional character. When brother "Duffy" also became attracted to the hobby, a strong brotherly bond developed.

Love was an appropriate synonym for Sapienza. And it began with their mother, who enjoyed watching her sons at their hobby. It created a nostalgia for her roof garden with its loft in Palermo, Sicily, where pigeon squabs were raised to cook as a gourmet delicacy. When baby squabs were born defective, rather than throw them away, Rosa prepared them as a delicious tender delicacy, just as she had done in Sicily. To watch her prepare succulent meals with a connoisseur's meticulous care was an expression of her love for her family. But Tom so loved his birds that he would never eat squab. When asked why, he answered: "Would you eat *your* brother?"

Immigrant children learned to work both out of necessity and preference. Like their Corso uncles, the Sapienza boys had an entrepreneurial flair. Like the Palombo boys, they delivered ice and milk, and shoveled snow, and carried grocery bags. They helped food merchants on Saturdays, when trade was good — anything to make a few cents, for a few cents were important when wages were only fifty cents an hour.

Tom and Lee sold papers at the corner of Penn and Braddock Avenues, then the hub of Routes 22 and 30, and also an industrial and affluent residential area. Business was brisk. The brothers bought their papers from C.C. Foster in Homewood — three for a nickel — and sold them for four cents each. Customers tipped them an extra penny. They sold daily papers and the early Bulldog Editions of the *Pittsburgh Press* and *Sun Telegraph* on Saturday evenings. On Sunday mornings they delivered to the prosperous areas of Wilkinsburg, Point Breeze and Fifth Avenue. On Sunday afternoons, they delivered the *New York Times* to the wealthy mansions in "millionaires' row." The Sapienzas' combined earnings were over $20 a week — nearly as much as the head of a household made then.

On Christmas day in 1928, the boys brought home over $10 in tips, a princely sum when $75 bought a Ford Flivver. Rosa was overjoyed at their success and at her newborn sixth son, Julius Aurelius. Intellectual though he was, their father had delivered him when Dr. Conte was late. The boys laid their tips on their mother's bed. Frank Conrad, the radio ham who had brought broadcasting to the world from his garage, had tipped the most. Meanwhile, by October 1929, the Palombos were once again anticipating a grandchild, hoping that this time everything would turn out well. Alex was overjoyed at the prospect. He enjoyed his new life in Pittsburgh. He and Grace took the children to the talkies. Papa treated them to vaudeville, trips to the museum and the zoo. Paul and Alex were close. Business was booming.

But unpredictable Fate stepped in. One morning, Alex could not get out of bed. He was burning with fever. After several visits from the family doctor, the ambulance carried him off to St. Francis Hospital in Lawrenceville. Doctors informed the family that Alex had contracted spinal meningitis, an incurable disease. The grief-stricken Grace and Maria made daily trips to his bedside only to watch him fail. On Christmas Eve 1929, Alex died. Once again the family parlor hosted another body where baby Yolanda's casket had once stood.

The little house at 7508 Tioga overflowed as friends came with food and money. Paolo, Maria, and Bill Kent wept and wept at the loss of their *tesoro*, Alessandro. The children, too, were overcome with grief.

The DiSantos came from Clyde, New York, their anguish indescribable. Carolina was bitter, blaming the smokey *Pittsburgh* and overwork for Alex's death. She vowed never to set foot in the dirty city again. And she did not for many years.

Upstairs, Grace lay seriously ill, having again lost her baby, this time at the shock of losing her handsome Alex. Her mother-in-law was little comfort. When Father DeFrancesco visited Grace, in an effort to console her, he made the unscientific and insensitive observation that perhaps the third-cousin relationship had been ill-fated. This comment haunted the young widow and plunged her deeper into despair. Father "D" officiated at Alex's funeral Mass. Grace, bedridden, was too ill to attend or kiss him goodbye in his coffin.

After his body was transported back to Clyde to the DiSanto's burial plot, insufferable reaction set in. The repeated separations she had endured throughout her young life, culminated by the loss of her babies and husband, caused Grace to have a nervous breakdown. She refused to leave her family to be hospitalized at St. Francis Hospital, where Alex had died. The doctor understood and put her in the care of the family's Black neighbor, Elizabeth, a nurse.

Elizabeth, parents and siblings spared no effort to love and comfort Grace. After her little yellow house was closed, she and Alice shared the little bedroom that Paolo had built. Only Alice heard the depth of her sister's grief during the long lonely nights. The hurt Alice felt for her was deep. It was like watching her own mother suffer. At night when nervous spasms overtook her body, she held and comforted Grace. In turn Grace, eighteen years Alice's senior, showered all her love on her little sister, who became the daughter she had lost. Until she died over fifty years later, Grace was the only one who called her little sister *Elisa*.

Paolo and Maria knew how their Grazia suffered when she looked out the back window at the little yellow home where she and Alex had been so happy. She needed a change. It was time to move. In spite of the much-publicized crash of 1929, Paolo had no fears. With the trade-in of their well-kept, updated home, and with an additional generous downpayment, he could manage. Like many successful immigrants, those who had bread hungered for cake. Those who had a house aspired to have a better house.

Within five months, the Palombos were ready to say goodbye to their life and friends on Tioga Street. They sold their home for a handsome profit to Italian immigrant *paesani* and moved to the upper middle-class neighborhood of Paolo's dream.

Early on May 1, Maria and Grace walked to their new home seven blocks North into the Belmar Plan. The older children stayed to help Paolo and the movers. Louie and Alice stayed to bid their childhood friends goodbye. Louie walked through the empty rooms to retrieve forgotten articles. At the mouth of the parlor fireplace, in front of Dom's sketch of the comics character, Tillie the Toiler, Louie spied his prized toy. It was the typewriter spool whose worn ribbon he had replaced with yards of string wound 'round and 'round. The creative Louie manipulated this spool to roll up and down like a yo-yo — long before a yo-yo ever became an American toy. He tucked it into his pocket and ran out the door.

Alice sat at the top of the stairs and reminisced about her childhood at 7508 Tioga Street. She took a last look at her little bedroom and slid down the bannister for the last time. She kissed it and wept. And the moving van carried them away.

Chapter 14

Moving Up — A New Ethnic Environment

It was a Norman Rockwell morning. Along Tioga Street and Homewood Avenue, boys on their way to school played leapfrog over one another's curved backs. Wives who had stretched their parlor rugs across clotheslines beat the dust out with huge wire whisks. Two elderly gentlemen, intent upon their discussion, stood nose-to-nose at curbside near Homewood Bank, ignoring the approaching D.P.W. water wagon about to spray them. The mover's truck crept slowly toward its destination. Six blocks north on Homewood Avenue, a woman waited patiently at the end of the leash as her dog relieved himself against a helpless fire hydrant. And at the corner of Race Street and Homewood, a circumspect cortege was forming at Fetzer's Funeral Home, without a procession or dirge for the solemn trip by motor car to Homewood Cemetery.

The mover's truck turned right at the next corner to 7208 Monticello Street, at the former residence of Mr. Wunderlich, developer of the Belmar Plan. The home, with its long front porch and fat round columns, was styled after Jefferson's Monticello. Giant maples in full bloom formed a long, cool green arch along the street. Well-kept front lawns and flower gardens welcomed spring.

The Palombo's were the fifth Italian family to come to Monticello Street. In 1917, the "Battle of Monticello Street" had triggered an exodus of older middle-class residents when Robert Vaughn, a Black college graduate and publisher of the widely-read *Pittsburgh Courier*, purchased a house there. Neighbors protested and demanded that the Vaughns move from their block. Vaughn's family refused, thereby making inroads for other incoming middle-class Irish, German and Italian Catholics, who faced the same opposition when they moved to the serene Belmar Plan. Their presence influenced its largely Protestant, old-stock middle class to flee from Homewood.

Oblivious to past prejudice, Paolo and Maria accepted the warm welcome from the Wunderlichs and from their maiden aunt, Miss McCausland, who would be Alice's teacher at Belmar School. The Palombos met their immediate neighbors: Mr. Dixon, General Manager at H.J. Heinz; musician

Ken Bailey and his wife, Virginia, a former Ziegfield Follies dancer; the Sansonetti family, whose son was a graduate Engineer from Carnegie Tech; and the distinguished Reverend and Mrs. Russell, two of several Black neighbors. Paolo and Maria felt at home here.

As a welcoming gift, the Wunderlichs gave the family their large Regency dining room table and buffet, their tall mahogany Victorola, an elegant fringed floor lamp, new awnings, and wicker porch furniture. Miss McCausland gave them a one-foot thick Webster's Dictionary. One day, she and Alice would come to share a warm friendship and a love for poetry.

The family was proud of its new ten-room home. Maria prized the beveled cut glass front doors, the stained glass windows at the stair landings and the unique mantles of carved ebony wood inlaid with imported Venetian tile. Paolo and Maria prayed their thanks for the progress they had made from the small white stone house in Abruzzi to their frame house on Tioga Street and now to this home in the Belmar Plan. The contrast drew a comparison from Paolo: *"Per noi, quest' è un palazzo. It is a palace."*

To satisfy his green thumb, Paolo had plans for the large fenced-in yard behind the privacy of a double garage. It would serve as a hideaway for his vegetable garden and transplanted fig tree. His landscape gardener's eye envisioned the front lawn planted with evergreens, a rose bed and seasonal flowers.

Maria wondered whether the fruit and vegetable huckster, the fish man, the scissors sharpener, and umbrella man would be coming to their door. She would miss the cry of peddlers calling their wares, especially Alivno's familiar call: *"Looo panettero!* Is the bread man!" Upward mobility had its price.

Paolo hired Mr. French to wallpaper the upper dining room wall with scenes of Venetian gardens. Hahn's delivered new maroon parlor furniture, oriental rugs for the living room and dining room, a Hoover electric sweeper to replace the hand sweeper and carpet beater and, to replace their wooden ice box, an ice-making General Electric refrigerator. This newest convenience had changed America's eating habits. Upstairs, Maria's new brass bed sported a Beauty Rest innerspring mattress. But she would miss her feather bed.

Their Remington piano graced the living room corner near the window. Alice eyed it hopefully as her corner to practice piano lessons. If she could have any wish, it would be to have piano lessons. Her other desire was to visit the new Cathedral of Learning and see the stones that the school children's nickels and dimes had bought to help build the University of Pittsburgh.

Her second wish came true one day when Papa kept his promise to take her to see the great edifice. As they rode the 76 Hamilton streetcar to their destination, Alice chattered happily in Italian. When they stood on the great lawn in front of the Cathedral, she held Papa's hand and looked up . . . up, until she nearly fell backwards. She remembered the *exact* day that she had given her dime in second grade — it was the day Miss Petty paddled her about Snooky. Alice dismissed the unpleasant thought. "*Qual e mia pietra,* Papa? Which one is my stone?" she asked.

Pointing high, Papa answered, "*Qella piu alta, Lisetta mia zuccherina.* The highest one ata the top.*"* Alice loved it when Papa called her little sugar girl. That day, a dream was born. She asked Papa if she might come to school here one day: "*Posso venire a scuola qua, qualche giorno?*"

Papa answered, "*Se vuole Dio.*" Paolo had a dream, too. He had long since met the seven-year residence requirement to reach his coveted goal. But in the course of hard work, family sorrows, and personal sufferings, Paolo had deferred his biggest dream — to become a full-fledged United States citizen.

His pride would not allow him to fail the exam required by literacy and citizenship laws before he could receive his final papers. He studied carefully and rehearsed his answers with his children in his best accented English. And finally, more confident with the passage of time, he took the test and came home a proud full citizen on September 2, 1930. That day called for a family feast — with a side dish of pasta to honor *Cristoforo Colombo.*

Paolo was happiest for his wife and immigrant sons. In his heart he was an American patriot and citizen; and now, under the law, so were they. At last they could vote for the president, a right Papa took seriously. For months, he proudly displayed his and Maria's citizenship certificates, before tucking them into a long, leather wallet next to their passports.

For the children, suddenly thrown in with non-Italians, life in the new neighborhood was significantly different. There were no streets filled with noisy kids, no organ grinder and monkey begging for pennies, no kids playing jump rope or hopscotch, and no ethnic slurs, except one. "Garlic-eating dago" taunted a mulatto boy, William Lightfoot. The slur hurt, but Alice found comfort in remembering that Martino Mariotti countered ethnic insults by pointing his forefinger in the air and declaring proudly, "*Ricordati, siamo figli di Rinascimento!*" and reassuring her in English as well: "We are children of the Renaissance!" Alice missed their boarders, Martino and Jim.

That reminder sent the fourth grader to seek out Miss Davis, her friend at Homewood Library, who helped Alice research fifth-grade history books. Proud to learn that the Renaissance began in the 1400's in Northern Italian cities with the Revival of Learning and spread through Europe, Alice read and read.

Indeed, not just for Alice but for all middle-class children in the pre-television era, reading was a crucial form of education and diversion. They especially enjoyed comics and swapped "funnies" on Sunday. The comics had political and philosophical motives for adults, as they took a swipe at the alphabet of give-away Democratic social programs: the NRA, CCC, and PWA. Little Orphan Annie moralized to American kids via anti-Roosevelt conservative cartoonist Harold Gray. Through Daddy Warbucks he said, "You've got to work for what you get." And in the Prohibition era, boys got healthy doses of fair play and bravery, from Jack Armstrong, the all-American Boy, and Dick Tracey, the guy who always caught the criminal and brought him to justice.

Comic pages and movies held adventures and characters that boys imitated. They played cowboys and Indians, and Tarzan. When hard times in the thirties brought a much-publicized boom in crime, boys played G-man and cops and robbers. And they played skate hockey, or rode metal scooters instead of Tioga Street "pushies," handmade from scraps of lumber and discarded roller skates.

Girls roller-skated on sidewalks and sang popular songs from the latest song sheets. They played movie stars. The talkies had become technicolor. Dorothy, Alice's new Italian friend, decided, "I have brown hair, I'll be Janet Gaynor. You be the Blonde Bombshell, Jean Harlowe." Musicals were the rage. They danced and sang *The Lullaby of Broadway*, *Lulu's Back In Town* and *Forty-Second Street*, on the Belmar Theater's amateur hour. Their performance entitled them to see a *free* movie! Twice!

For one thing, life in the new neighborhood was novel and fun. Funny talk was the fad in the thirties. Kids spoke Pig Latin. They put the first letter of a word onto the end and added the letter *a*. "Oda ouya antwa andyca?" ("Do you want candy?") Louie and Alice confounded everyone by speaking Italian Pig Latin because their friends did not understand Italian, and their parents did not understand Pig Latin.

Louie and Alice learned ballroom dancing from brother Tom, who saved his pennies to study at Bowman's Dance Studio in Wilkinsburg. Tall, fair, and graceful, Tom resembled a Swede. His siblings watched as he practiced with Helvi Selmi, his partner in the state's Merry Widow Waltz contest. Soon, the winner's cup became the centerpiece on the living room mantle.

Lou and Alice enjoyed ballroom dancing in the best of two worlds — at Mother of Good Counsel Social Hall, and at Holy Rosary's teen dances, where they mingled with new Irish and German friends. They did the Jitterbug and learned to dance the Swing. Since they looked Irish, Father Carlin, the biased pastor, did not ask them to leave.

Maria attended Mass at Holy Rosary Church sometimes. When retired pastor Italian-friendly Father Malady left, he had been replaced by staunch outspoken Father Carlin, who opposed Italians attending his church. Maria disliked the scolding he gave Mrs. Messina, her new Sicilian friend, when they sat in the pew praying. Overlooking Maria, who could have been mistaken for an Irish woman, said to Mrs. Messina, "Why don't you go to your own Italian church?"

Maria was offended and scolded back in broken English, "Scusa me, *Padre*, but God He isa every place — no?" The stunned *Padre* walked off.

Maria was a nonconformist at a time when the church forbade Catholics to attend non-Catholic services. One summer, Evangelists came to Home-wood and pitched their tent at a nearby lot. Intrigued, Maria wanted to drop by with Alice to investigate. *"Elisa, fa subito, voglio sentire la predica . . .* Hurry, I wanta to hear the sermon." She was amazed to see the congregation solemnly pray for forgiveness for their sins and then go to the altar all together to receive Holy Communion. She liked the idea of mass confession. "Yes, *Dio ascolto loro e perdono*," she decided. "God listena to them and forgive them." Next Sunday dinner, Father DeFrancesco could expect a vigorous debate on the subject of private confession. And he could expect Maria to keep a watchful eye on his helping of *pasta*, for the two were diabetics who had to avoid eating starchy food.

A family friend, Cherokee Indian medicine man, Chief Red Key Loveless, had discovered Maria's diabetes. After he closely observed her, no one knew how he uncannily surmised her problem. His observation was confirmed by the family doctor, who admitted Maria to Pittsburgh Hospital, where the family learned about her starch-free diet and insulin injections. Paolo found her special foods: saccharin for her coffee and tea, spinach noodles to satisfy her desire for macaroni, and gluten flour to make her *pasta fatto a mano* every Sunday. Maria spoke ironically, "Hmmm . . . In Italy where food was simple I coulda eat anything; nowa that I cana get any food I desire, I cannot eat it."

Maria thanked her Indian friend, who dropped by frequently to share stories about his proud Indian heritage and about the suffering the early Americans had inflicted upon his people. The Palombos understood his frustration about rejection and sympathized.

Maria's outlook was multiethnic. In this conservative neighborhood, she made new Black friends and invited them to special family celebrations, not a common practice among the "old-stock." The Reverend and Mrs. Russel were surprised and pleased to be included. Reverend Russell occasionally enjoyed Mr. Palombo's fine wines, respectfully inquiring about the latest vintage. And Paolo respectfully rewarded him. The family appreciated the Reverend's beautifully dressed lady parishioners who promenaded past the house under their elegant hats on their way to church on Sunday mornings — a truly worthy Norman Rockwell scene.

While Homewood had become an ethnic patchquilt with each group living in its own social world, North and South Homewood residents still enjoyed things in common like summer concerts at Westinghouse Park and baseball games at Homewood field. Their swimming pool was for Whites only, while their "colored" friends swam in East Liberty in a ghetto pool called the Inkwell. But on Tioga Street, Black and White friends ignored bias to play games and sports together.

The local YMCA sponsored summer activities for boys who had limited opportunities for outdoor camping during the Depression. Tom Sapienza became a YMCA founding leader at Camp Kon-o-kwee. On his way to the camp, he was surprised to see the name Sapienza on one of the storefronts in nearby Zielenopole. Tom was strict and fair with his charges. They looked up to him, with obvious respect. History repeats. Sixty years later, his son

Tom became a great supporter of the YMCA and Camp Kon-o-kwee, and stood proudly to be photographed by the bench dedicated to his father along one of the camp trails — a monument to the Depression Years.

Despite this idyllic picture of a homogeneous community, the ominous Depression hung over Pittsburgh. Unemployment grew serious in 1930. Jobs ended alarmingly in 1931. True, Paolo and Bill Kent still had abundant work, with Dom, now called Tom by his peers, taking Alex's place in writing and typing bids. He was a bright Commercial Course student at Westinghouse High School and capably handled the accounting.

Soon Paolo and Bill found it difficult to collect monies for some of their work. Businesses closed. Hard times became a catalyst for crime. As legitimate occupations lessened, an alarming number of people looked for easy money through bank robberies. While Italians got star billing for crime, thieves of different nationalities carrying "Tommy guns" robbed banks and post offices, and escaped in speeding cars. Organized crime pulled in millions from prostitution, auto thefts and extortion.

The radio carried a plethora of sensational news. The kidnapping and murder of Charles Lindbergh's baby so frightened Alice that Papa allowed her to sleep with Mama until the trauma passed. A reward was posted for alleged killer John Dillinger: "Get Him Dead or Alive!" By 1935, the Justice Department estimated that outlaws outnumbered carpenters four to one, grocers six to one, and doctors twenty to one!

Meanwhile, after a severe loss in the crash of 1929, banks had stopped making loans, thus putting greater strain on America's war debt. The Depression gained momentum. Paolo and Bill worried about roller coaster headlines that reported: HOOVER SAYS BUSINESS BASIS IS SOUND ... STOCK PRICES SLUMP $14,000,000,000 IN NATION-WIDE STAMPEDE ... STOCKS GAIN AS MARKET IS STEADIED ... BANKERS PLEDGE CONTINUED SUPPORT ... MERCHANT'S SUICIDE LAID TO STOCK LOSSES.

As conditions worsened, men formed bread lines to get daily food handouts and slept under newspaper "Hoover Blankets" in Hooverville Shanty Towns. Women sold apples on street corners. Father Cox's Army marched on Washington from Pittsburgh in protest of poverty. *Brother Can You Spare a Dime?* and *Nobody Knows You When You're Down and Out* became popular songs. "It's just an old shanty in old Shanty Town" were the opening lyrics to another.

People knew that the Depression was serious when the one-armed street singer, a former salesman, sang through a megaphone along Monticello Street to earn pennies, and when housewives fed beggars on their back steps. Families went on the dole, then called welfare. In his campaign for re-election, President Hoover promised "a chicken in every pot" and declared that "prosperity is just around the corner." Paolo asked, "Whose corner? Andy Mellon's corner?" He swore he would not vote for Hoover. Franklin Delano Roosevelt seemed to hold greater promise for America. Like many naturalized Americans, Paolo registered as a Democrat and stayed Democrat until Dwight D. Eisenhower came along.

In March 1933, after his inauguration, Roosevelt woke to the news that the banks had closed. Many of Paolo's friends had panicked and withdrawn their savings. Now Paolo decided to follow their lead and went to the Homewood Bank to withdraw his money. That afternoon as he stood in line waiting to receive his hard-earned savings, the bank teller lowered the iron window bars in his face. A clerk raised a sign that said in ugly black letters, "This Bank is Closed."

Paolo walked and walked, not wanting to go home. An hour later, he walked into the big kitchen of his new home where Alice sat at the table writing. He stood motionless by the kitchen screen door. Alice saw an aged man staring intensely into space, his eyes brimful. They spilled over. She wept for him and Mama, and hugged them both. After the initial shock, she realized that her fervent wish for piano lessons at twenty-five cents a week could not come true now. After all, twenty-five cents would buy five loaves of bread or a large round steak for the family. Her disappointment was deep, but she could forgive Mama and Papa. They would never know. She would learn what music she could on her own. Alice vowed that her own children would never experience her heartache over the loss of studying music.

Gradually, as debtors defaulted, Paolo's cherished business crumbled. He and Bill Kent dissolved their partnership but not their friendship. Paolo decided he would work at anything, but would not accept charity. Although boarders had seemed something of the past, Maria looked for a suitable gentleman to rent one of the six bedrooms. Father DeFrancesco suggested Italian Peter Marino, now called Red Marine, a state inspector and salesman of church wines. But it was not enough to convert two second-floor bedrooms into an apartment, Silvio quit high school in eleventh grade to work full-time at Capone's upscale El Patio restaurant as headwaiter. On weekends, Louie worked at Jake Snyder's Hardware, and Tom at John's Penhurst Fruit Market, whose unsold perishables became family dessert. Maria found an empty plot of ground upon a hill half a mile from home and bargained with the owner for its use in exchange for vegetables.

Eventually, Paolo had to choose between losing his beautiful $12,000 home or working with the Public Works Administration (PWA,) a Roosevelt New Deal recovery plan. Men were put to work making civic improvements on building projects that became a permanent symbol of the Depression. Becoming part of the PWA, Paolo helped build the beautiful stone entrances to Frick Park. Thereafter, each time family members drove or walked past his handiwork, they were reminded that Paul Palombo had built them during the Depression. (Another National Recovery Act project was the Civilian Conservation Corps, CCC, established to provide forestry work for young men.)

Among the less fortunate were Arcangela and Antonio. They had barely surmounted their hardships from immigration when Antonio became ill and died of pneumonia. Domenico, Joe and Gina were now half orphaned. Once again the benefit society provided for burial and a small insurance award. Paolo and Maria and their friends tried to help; but the Depression hit the grieving family too hard. Like many others faced with starving, Arcangela was too proud to accept welfare. But as her nearby garden failed to sustain her family, she capitulated. President Roosevelt had become the savior and hero of the poor.

Once aware of banks' difficulties, the newly inaugurated president declared a national bank holiday, after his inauguration until banks could be fortified by federal loans. Eventually, Homewood Bank reopened. Returned deposits, never fully repaid, came piecemeal over a long period.

Like banks, other businesses suffered. At Westinghouse, employees worked only three days a week: Sebastian Sapienza was fortunate that music jobs and lessons provided him with extra income. Tom, the oldest of six sons, saw the need and quit school for one year to work at Pittsburgh Equitable Meter Company as a storeroom clerk. His brothers inherited the newsboy's corner and paper route.

When Tom returned to school a year later, "Pro" Burton, the football coach, was glad to welcome his star guard back to the football and swimming teams. That year a young teacher developed admiration for her handsome, intelligent student. Tom, more interested in scholastic achievement, ignored her advances. A year later, he graduated with high honor. But because of the Depression, graduates did not rent caps and gowns. The boys wore suits, and Tom himself had to borrow a jacket to wear for the graduation ceremony. The smitten teacher occasionally contacted Tom, but he had a dream — to become a physician.

The Palombo family, like many families of the period, had to set aside cherished dreams. Rebuilding the family business and providing college educations for their sons were now shattered hopes; for their daughter — impossible. Pittsburgh Public Schools took the Utilitarian approach to education. Those who could not afford college were placed into commercial courses to prepare them for jobs. However, students came away commercially skilled and remarkably well-equipped intellectually.

Then on July 4, 1936, the nearly forgotten Independence Day jinx reappeared. After many bouts with strep throat, Alice underwent a tonsillectomy on July 1. Three days later, at home, she suffered a serious hemorrhage. Unable to stop the bleeding, Maria desperately sought help from her dear next-door Black neighbor, "Buttermilk." He had come home for lunch in the limousine he drove for the Frick family. He quickly carried Alice to the limo, propped her on a starched white pillow from his own bed, and drove her to Pittsburgh Hospital. By the time he carried her to the emergency room, his pillow was blood-soaked. Predictably, Maria stormed Heaven and bargained with *Dio* and the saints.

Five days and a blood transfusion later, the bleeder was home again. To help her regain her red blood cells, the doctor recommended a liquid diet containing iron. Maria prepared eggnog and yeast milk shakes. Papa fed her iron-rich homemade beer, which the doctor enjoyed, too. By September, her crisis was over. An overjoyed Papa cooked her a late fourth of July treat — her own little chicken. He treated her to delayed sixteenth-birthday gifts: her first permanent wave and her first opera, *Il Trovatore*. Papa bought her a new dress for the occasion.

Maria smiled proudly at Paolo in his blue serge suit and Chesterfield coat. She gave her daughter a warm embrace and pinned her locket on Alice's maroon velvet dress. Paolo, not really a smoker, pushed his thin cigar into its F.D.R.-style holder, tilted his Homburg hat at a rakish angle, grinned and offered Alice his arm. Maria laughed, "You showoffa! *Tu fa spaccone!*" Alice knew that moment would be forever etched in her memory.

By September 1936, banks were receiving help through federal government loans. They assumed outstanding mortgage loans, lowered interest rates, and granted homeowners extended payments. The Palombos and Sapienzas were among the fortunate who did not lose their homes. Conservatives criticized Roosevelt's New Deal, although his presidential opponent, Wendell Wilkie, had an almost identical social reform platform, whose ideas came from Theodore Roosevelt's Square Deal and Woodrow Wilson's New Freedom Plan.

Many government-instituted reforms had greatly changed the country since the Depression began. Socialist newspapers advocated Industrial Unionism and Socialism. Norman Thomas became the perennial Socialist Party candidate for president. In 1936 and 1940, he received one radical vote from Tom Sapienza, a free-thinking voter in Pittsburgh's 13th ward.

For immigrants, college was the exception. But Tom had exceptional intelligence, motivation, and *moxie*. Like his maternal grandfather and uncles, he became an entrepreneur and opened a deli-sandwich shop to help his family, and to pay college tuition. As a graduate from the top five percent of his class, Tom had been awarded half his tuition to the University of Pittsburgh. To increase his income, he embalmed bodies for the Leslie and Johns Funeral Home and delivered packages for Railways Express. He carried his lunch to Pitt and took only carfare money. His college friends, Eugene and Esther Simon, who were children of the local tailor, had financial support. Jewish families saw education and rigid adherence to their culture as necessities for success. Tom knew and enjoyed their Jewish traditions and holidays and celebrated with his neighbors. Esther had a crush on him — a no-no in those days when romance between Jewish and Gentile young people was rare.

His other college friend was Nick Masters, formerly Nicolo Mastermonico, whose family had purchased the Palombo house. By 1939, they had developed several things in common: both were immigrants, both attended Premed School at the University of Pittsburgh, and both aspired to a medical career. Entry to Medical school was difficult for hard-pressed students, and scholarships were meager. Neither young man could afford the extended years of tuition. Nick quit college and opened a family-run tailor shop. But the realistic, adaptable Tom changed his major from Medicine to Business Administration and continued his round-the-clock work study schedule.

Jobs were scarce. Just as friends helped friends find jobs, relatives helped relatives. Sebastian Sapienza took advantage of a common practice — nepotism. As a company sign maker, Sebastian had wide exposure and had gained respect throughout the Westinghouse plants — enough to get his second and third sons company jobs.

Others found similar opportunities for their relatives and friends. But because of systematic discrimination, Blacks found it difficult to get any new work. Even when trolley transportation was heavy before World War II, not one Black was hired as a streetcar motorman. After great struggle, some managed to work at jobs outside their traditional roles as domestic servants and common laborers. By the 1950's, some became postal clerks, nurses — and even teachers and lawyers. There were a few mill workers from Homewood-Brushton where light industrial factories had sprung up along the train tracks and streetcar tracks. Most people rode the trains or trolleys to their work. Since this kind of industry did not pollute the area, Homewood-Brushton became a desirable working-class place to live.

One did what one could to get and keep jobs. A combination of nepotism and downright nerve worked for the Palombo family. After graduating from Westinghouse High School, Tom Palombo found work at the Rockwell Manufacturing plant, located on the Pittsburgh-Wilkinsburg boundary. His brother Pete was drawn into the company, and Lou was hired after his high school graduation.

The Depression persisted. Men continued to work only three days a week. At Rockwell, the plant manager Carl Dickson, C. D., was drawn to Tom because of his quality work. Tom, sensing his interest, tried to gain favor. He brought C. D. his father's best wine — Prohibition was over by 1933 — and C. D. loved it. Tom kiddingly said, "If you think that's great, you should taste my mother's fabulous Italian cooking!" and invited his boss to dinner. C. D. accepted the invitation for his wife and little "Freddie" Marie, their daughter. Maria Palombo was accustomed to entertaining priests and politician friends of the classy family boarder, Red Marine, who hobnobbed with Justice Musmanno and eventually married the sister of State Representative Marty Mihm. From etiquette columns in the Italian newspaper and the Sears Roebuck wish book, Maria had learned much about hostessing. Now she set a lovely formal table that seated twenty, with tall candles, her best crystal, monogrammed linen and china, and the silverware Pete had given his parents for their twenty-fifth anniversary.

Mrs. Dickson was pleased. She found even greater pleasure when, after dinner, Tom rolled back the dining room rug, shook wax onto the polished floor and cranked the big Victorola. He played the *Merry Widow Waltz* record and pulled Alice to her feet to dance. He and Alice danced the familiar routine he had practiced with her when Helvi Selmi was unavailable — to Mrs. Dickson's amazement. Then he asked his guest to dance. Mrs. D. was entranced as Tom deftly led her through Fox Trots and Tangos. Subsequently, she and C. D. invited Tom to company parties, and Alice became their baby-sitter at their elegant house in Penn Hills. Thereafter, the Palombo boys pulled five-day work weeks, a welcome financial boost for the family.

President Roosevelt's National Recovery Act seemed to be working. The country, concentrating on its domestic woes, could not imagine that it would be given a boost from the gathering forces of World War II. Life abroad seemed remote, despite headlines warning of impending war. The United States kept its policy of isolation, free from foreign political alliances. America was self-contained — indifferent. So was Homewood, with a parochial view of its country.

Homewood belonged to its immigrants now. They attended political lectures at Westinghouse High School, or took evening classes to learn English, study business courses, or polish their Italian. At semester's end, the Italian class produced an all-Italian play and a satire that poked fun at themselves in exaggerated Italian accents — to the delight of their convulsed parents.

Tom and Pete were cast along with a bright young lady, Anne Manella — a first-generation Abruzzese girl. The three became close friends. Anne knew that if friendship should lead to a serious romance and marriage, in the Italian tradition, it was more likely that Pete would receive family approval. Customs die with difficulty: Italians married Italians. First sons or daughters married first.

During their courtship, Anne used Pete's first name, Silvio, which she thought to be even more beautiful than Pietro. Eventually, the family began calling Pete by his first name — Silvio — and his grandfather's name, Pietro, disappeared.

When Anne and Silvio were married at Mother of Good Counsel Church, Paolo and Maria hosted a large *festa* in their spacious home, complete with dancing, Italian *cucina*, and Paolo's special *liquori e vino,* which Father DeFrancesco came to bless — and taste.

The second-floor apartment became the newlyweds' home. By then "Red" Marine had moved to live with Marie, his bride. Breaking custom, Anne continued to work at Potter Title & Trust until her first child was born. He was named for his paternal grandfather, Paul Palombo. Lauretta, her second child, was Grandmother Manella's namesake. Leaving tradition, their third child was named Richard. Anne helped and respected Maria and, like a big sister, listened patiently to Alice's "girl talk," now that Grace had remarried.

Father DeFrancesco, seeing a potential match, had introduced Grace to a refined and kindly Italian widower with a three-year-old son. Little Angelo had been shifted from house to house since infancy. Alice was sent to retrieve him from a kindly relative for his first visit with the family. Sad, bewildered Angelo wrung his little hands — and Alice's emotions. He took her and Grace's heart and sympathy.

When Father "D" married Grace and Mike LaMorte, they settled one block away from her parents' home. The entire family loved little Angelo, especially his new grandparents, who themselves knew the trauma of being orphaned. From a relationship kindled by sympathy grew a deep and genuine love among three people who had suffered much.

The marriage was blessed at last with the birth of their daughter, Rose Marie. Grace was supremely happy to have the child she had so longed for. The little family bought the house next door at 7204 Monticello Street. The two families spent many happy hours together. Paolo and Mike made wine, and gardened, and enjoyed sitting under their fig trees sipping wine.

Having lost Anne to Silvio, Tom continued to pursue his passion for dancing, now a national craze. The Charleston was passé. Café Society was dancing the Tango, Waltz, and Lambeth Walk in posh restaurant clubs that used to be speakeasies before the Eighteenth Amendment was repealed.

Tom's love of ballroom dancing would change his family's lives. Every Saturday, he attended dances at Westview or Kennywood Dancelands, or his favorite ballroom at MacDougal's in East Liberty. In 1934, Tom met a lovely Italian girl, Sophia Belotti, a nanny for Dr. Murray's daughter Betsy. Sophia had only the minimum dance skills, learned from the good nuns who had raised her in the Home of the Good Shepherd, a convent and girls' orphanage. Attracted to her refinement and black-haired beauty, Tom invited her home to meet his parents, and offered her dance lessons to expand her ballroom repertoire.

An immediate love affair developed between Sophia and Maria, who in Sophia's heart became the mother she had missed since childhood. "In my heart you will always be my mother," she declared. Alice and Sophia developed a lifelong affectionate bond. This chance meeting of two young people was like the love story later told in the movie musical, *The Sound of Music:* Leading Lady Maria, like Sophia raised by nuns, left the convent, became a nanny and married the man she loved.

When Tom proposed to Sophia, she was torn between two choices. She had wanted to become a nun. The Sisters of Charity at Good Shepherd Convent had made her novice's habit. But the wise superior, Mother Regis, insisted that before any candidate for the novitiate left the convent, she must spend at least one year outside in the real world in order to be certain that she was not choosing the only secure life she knew.

When Maria and the family visited Sophia's beloved home, they loved the nuns and the whole atmosphere. Sophia was frustrated. Maria and Tom were hopeful. One day Sophia, torn between vocations, asked her superior: "Mother Regis, shall I marry Jesus and become a nun or shall I marry Tom? Will I always wonder about my choice?"

The perceptive Mother Regis helped her decide. "Sophia, you can have two loves forever. Don't be sad if you choose to marry Tom. The world is in need of good Catholic mothers. God may have a plan for you as a wife, a mother and a daughter-in-law." Over the years, her advice proved to be sage and prophetic.

Sophia chose Tom and announced her acceptance to Paolo and Maria. That night they had a long dialogue in thanksgiving to God and the Holy Mother, followed by a celebration Mass the next morning. The wedding was better than any scripted movie could have told it. Maria and Paolo bought Sophia her wedding gown and prepared for two feasts, one at their home and one at the Good Shepherd Home.

On the morning of the wedding, the family went to the Home to escort Sophia to Mother of Good Counsel Church where her groom waited. They carried trays of food, *dolci*, and homemade rootbeer for the nuns and their girls, who were as happy and excited as the bride. After Mass at Mother of Good Counsel Church, the family returned to the convent for an extra ceremonial blessing from the priest and a beautifully chanted program of religious music, sung by the nuns and Sophia's orphan girlfriends. The family took their beloved Sophia and her groom to continue the celebration at her new home on Monticello Street. Sophia's widowed father, Martino Belotti, and her three younger siblings, Amerigo, Teresa and Geneva, who lived at St. Paul's Orphanage, enjoyed the *festa* with their new family. Maria surveyed her table happily. "Hmmmmm . . ." she mused. Paolo waited. *"Ecco la famiglia per orfanelli* — a familee for orphans." Sophia became the family's big sister, nurse, and loyal confidante.

The next year, 1938, was a milestone for Alice Palombo. It was her senior year at Westinghouse High School. Like most of her peers, she had been tracked into the useful "commercial course" and would come to value that training throughout her life. Each year Mr. Dodds, the teacher who sponsored Student Government Activities, selected a top secretarial student to be Secretary of the Student Senate and Cabinet. This time, he chose Alice.

Mr. Dodds was Secretary to the esteemed Homewood-Brushton Board of Trade, who brought the Carnegie Library to Homewood. He took Alice to HBBT business meetings to record and transcribe minutes. That year was a revelation that offered her unique and valuable experience. In a poor job market, those who acquired advance training were given preference. It seemed to be a practical idea when Mr. Dodds recommended that she enroll at Duff's School of Business.

The Duff's representative came to her home to recruit her. After he left, her distressed parents painfully informed Alice that there simply was not enough money for tuition. A recession in 1937 had set back the recovery. The Depression had taken its toll, and climbing out of debt took every available cent. Alice understood, but could not hide her disappointment. Paolo circled her shoulders and cleared his throat several times. "I know howa you feel — firsta your Papa, then your brothers — and nowa you."

Sleep did not come easily that night. Alice stole downstairs to the reception hall mantle where each family member knelt briefly to pray at the little altar before ascending the stairs. Paolo was kneeling, head bowed. Alice knelt beside him. Papa touched her arm. "Soma day, soma day, *Lisetta*," he whispered.

"Some day, Papa," she answered and wept quietly, remembering her other great disappointment — no piano lessons.

When Alice climbed into bed, she thought about her teacher and mentor, Mrs. Parrack, who had given her hope. "Never stop learning," she wrote in the margins of her English themes. "Very fine — continue writing. Aim high — reach for the stars, precious Alice." Oh, how she hated the Depression!

Mrs. P. taught by example and from the Bible verses she read each morning at opening exercises. She personified "love" and conveyed this through Corinthians, Chapter Thirteen. And from Matthew, Chapter Seven, she conveyed the Golden Rule to "do unto others." Before prayer in school was banned, Alice learned more about the Old Testament from the St. James Bible in public school than she had in Catholic Catechism classes.

Ruth K. Parrack had a profound effect on her students. When they entered room 253, they received an immediate education in life by reading the inspiring, character-building quotations she wrote at the top of every blackboard. With a piece of yellow chalk, this little five-foot giant shaped her students' attitudes through the greatest quotations. "Your reach must exceed your grasp, else what's a heaven for?" ". . . OTHERS. Lord, yes OTHERS and none of self for me; help me to live for OTHERS, Lord, that I may live like Thee." Through the words of Mohammed, or Aristotle or other sages, Mrs. Parrack convinced Alice that happiness could best be found in serving OTHERS. This philosophy had an intense effect upon her and directed her actions thereafter. Across every blackboard in angry yellow script their teacher quoted William Sherman's declaration: "WAR IS HELL!" and Neville Chamberlain's: "In war there are no winners." Every day she surveyed her students sadly.

Although the United States had stayed detached from the trouble brewing in Europe, it was clear that Adolph Hitler had an obsession to acquire territory. Mrs. Parrack was distressed at the gathering storm. As war clouds threatened to involve the United States, she feared for the young men who stood at the edge of doom, and encouraged a moment of silent prayer each day. Mrs. Parrack's anxiety, and the menacing war news, prompted Alice to express herself in the way she knew best — poetic supplication. Her poem,

The Herd, in which humanity was a metaphor for sheep being slaughtered, became a plea to God:

" . . . And one by one I see them fall,
while blood and tears are shed;
I ask you, Mighty Shepherd,
If you see your sheep lie dead.

The storm is slow receding,
And some now lie in slumber,
A crippled herd returns to graze,
Indeed decreased in number . . . "

Mrs. Parrack was so moved that the poem became the focus of faculty and English class discussion. One day it appeared on the board — in yellow chalk! Remembering the day her fifth-grade teacher, Miss McCausland, had likewise written one of her poems on the board, Alice smiled.

On graduation night in June 1938 at Soldiers and Sailors Memorial Hall, Mrs. Parrack sat proud. In the lobby, the graduates in suits and white gowns took their places in anticipation of the long march to the great stage. As they chattered, some expressed excitement at the prospect of going to college. Others expressed joy at putting their school years behind them. Unfortunately, some would never attend college or hold a job. The band began playing *Pomp and Circumstance*. The chatter stopped. The graduates started down the long aisle past their proud parents and families.

For Alice this was not a happy occasion, because the ceremony signaled the end of her formal education. "Some day," she thought. Her consolation was that she would be one of the fortunate few who would begin a first job on Monday. She had been hired over twelve applicants to work at Woolworth's 5 & 10 downtown. Alice would come to learn that public school education had served her well after all. The courses in Secretarial Training, Accounting and Sales garnered her a full-time job in which she used these skills.

As her students walked by, Mrs. Parrack's smiling upturned face reflected her pride. "Follow your dream," she had told Alice. Their eyes met briefly, and the two friends shared a special moment. From his aisle seat,

Papa squeezed Alice's hand as she walked by. *"Lisetta,"* he uttered and cleared his throat. She understood.

That night, her class stepped onto the threshold of adulthood. What would Fate ultimately have in store for this generation of youth? Even as their graduation ceremony was in process, Hitler's diabolical plan to send his Panzers into Poland took shape. And Mussolini's young *Fascisti* goose-stepped across Rome, singing their rousing military anthem *Fascetta Nera* [The Black Sash.] By September 1938, Hitler's Nazi troops had seized the Sudetenland of Czechoslovakia. And in November, the anti-Jewish pogrom, *Kristallnacht,* the night of broken glass, clearly defined Hitler's objective. The gathering storm was ominous.

Sicilian donkey cart holds Salvatore Sapienza of Lentini,
and the Corso brothers from Palermo.

Palermo, Sicily. Sebastiano
Sapienza in WWI military uniform, with his wife Rosa and
their first two sons Salvatore
and Liborio.

Santo, the first Corso brother to
come to America in 1904. His
father came in the late 1890s
and returned to Sicily to stay.
He holds Rosette Sapienza.

Courtesy Steamship Historical Society of America Collection, Langsdale Library, University of Baltimore

Sebastiano and Rosa Sapienza sailed with their children, Salvatore, Liborio and Delfino on the *S.S. Belvedere*, built by Cantieri Navali in Triestino, Monfalcone, Italy, 1913. Speed 13 knots; 43 feet long, 51 feet wide. Passenger 1544 (144 first class, 1400 third class). Sold to Cosulich Line in 1919. Seized by U.S. Government in 1941 and renamed *Audocious*. Scuttled off the Normandy coast in 1944.

Courtesy Library of Congress, Prints and Photographs Division, Detroit Publishing Company

By 1920, migrants were processed for entry before they reached Ellis Island. Old fears of rejection at America's doorstep were gone after World War I.

Grazia Palombo poses for her engagement photo in 1920.

Before the funeral, Maria holds her first grandchild, Grazia's baby, who died at birth in 1925.

Maria Giuseppa and Paolo Palombo with Elisa and Luigi, their first children born in America.

Rosa Sapienza and her son Francesco.

Sebastiano Sapienza's talent earned him a position with Westinghouse Electric and a place in broadcasting history when he was selected to play one of the first instrumental music solos on KDKA.

Sebastian played first clarinet with KDKA's Little Symphony Orchestra. Sebastian is fourth from left in the second row.

Courtesy Michael Dalfonso

Mother of Good Counsel Church sponsored Our Lady of Mount Carmel Holy *Festa* from the 1920s-1960s. Here Homewood-Brushton Italians view the Santa Festa parade and anticipate the fireworks to follow later.

Courtesy Michael Dalfonso

Courtesy Michael Dalfonso

Virginelle (Little Virgins) line up for Our Lady of Mount Carmel *Santa Festa* parade.

Our Lady of Mount Carmel members hold Her banner, decorated with donated bills.

MOVING UP! Immigrants left their old homes and moved to middle class neighborhoods. Behind the Sapienza home, three brothers built their pigeon coop and enjoyed breeding and racing pigeons. One year they won the "Powder Puff Derby."

Pigeon racing — the sport of kings — Tom and Lee Sapienza and Joseph Capone standing before the pigeon coop after a Sunday morning race.

Belmar School, Homewood, Pa.

In 1928 the Palombo family moved to the Belmar Plan.
Louis (Luigi) and Alice (Elisa) now attended the Belmar School.

Mike LaMorte moved next door to his Palombo in-laws on Monticello Street
in the Belmar Plan. Mike brought a bit of Italy with him and relaxes beneath
his transplanted fig tree. In Winter, he bent the tree to the ground and covered
it with mulch and burlap to protect it .

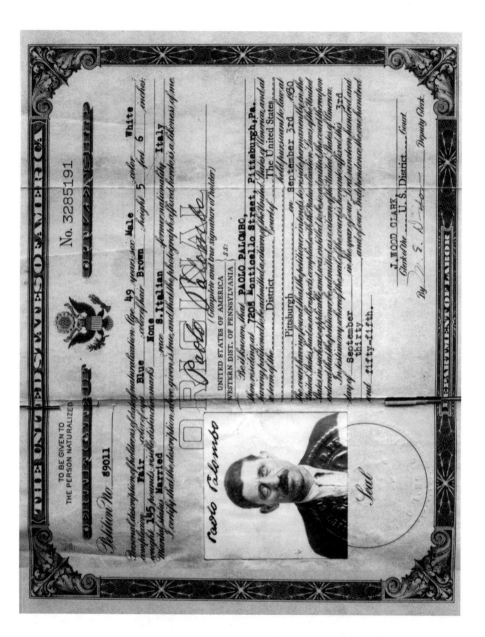

Paolo Palombo became an American citizen in 1930.

Part III — A Changing World

Chapter 15

A Call to Arms

America, preoccupied with its own problems, stayed in its cocoon of isolationism when German tanks effected a quick destruction of Poland in September 1939, thus igniting Europe's "Tinderbox." Barely twenty-five years before, Austria-Hungary had declared war against Serbia to set off World War I on July 28, 1914. Once again, the world was not "safe for democracy." In 1938, Orson Welles had scared the hell out of America with a fictional radio dramatization of the *The War of the Worlds*. But Americans seemed to find the drama more daunting than the real war gaining momentum overseas.

The 1930's had brought innovations in transportation and consumer goods. Entertainment was still in its age of innocence. Hollywood enforced a Production Code of moral purity on movies — no cussing or lustfull kissing —and radio became the moralizing "theater of the mind" and America's political platform. A disheartened populace settled in to hear "Fireside Chats" that united the country. "My friends," President Franklin Delano Roosevelt always began, as he informed Americans and encouraged them to support his New Deal for economic recovery from the Great Depression.

If the 1930's had been the "hungry years" for America, eventually the voracious appetite of war would rage for arms, planes, ships and other sorely needed materials required to sustain the allies abroad. America would literally become an "arsenal of democracy" under her pledge of Lend-Lease aid to Europe. The Allies devoured America's arms and war machines as Hitler became an unstoppable menace.

Now, as this new war started, complacent America — and Homewood for that matter — felt distanced from it. Community and family life functioned routinely. At the Palombo house, 1939 found Maria and Paolo preparing to host another family wedding. Mixed ethnic and religious marriages among first-generation Americans were still an exception rather than the rule. Following tradition, Louis chose for his wife Mary Aiello, an Italian Catholic girl he had met at the Mother of Good Counsel Social Club dance. She and Maria were attracted to each other. Since Mary, the oldest of three, had been orphaned at twelve when her mother died, Paolo and Maria extended their home for the wedding reception. They offered the newlyweds the apartment that Silvio and Anne had vacated when they purchased a home nearby.

Unknown to Louis and his parents, Mary's father, Joe, had become a bitter agnostic when his wife died, and he had quit the church. He reluctantly attended the Mass to give his daughter away. Maria noticed that Joe did not receive Holy Communion at his daughter's wedding. Unsettled, she reasoned that he had accidentally not fasted before Communion and could not, by Catholic Church law, receive the Sacrament.

After the wedding, Mary and Louis greeted friends in the family's large reception hall. When the Reverend and Mrs. Russell arrived, the Reverend briefly bowed his head in respect toward the high mantle where the Sacred Heart and Blessed Mother stood among flowers and candles. And then he turned to Louis and delivered a brief ministerial blessing and lesson: "Louie, you are goin' to walk the path of life alone no more. Marriage is like a loaf of bread. You' gonna get on one end of th' loaf, and she's gonna get on th' other. 'Taint goin' to increase the size of th' loaf, it's gonna increase th' *nutrition.*" And added a secular question: "By the way, m'boy, how's your father's wine this year?" The Russells had kept a benevolent eye on the Palombos from their front porch and happily anticipated their holidays, weddings and baptisms.

One summer evening that same year, Maria fell in love again with a young man who walked into her kitchen. Domenico, now Tom Palombo, had not seen his friend Tom Sapienza for eight years. After a chance meeting and a warm exchange, he invited his friend to come to the Mother of Good Counsel Social Club dance the next night, where he acted as the club's chaperon. With the instincts of a matchmaker, brother Tom said, "Come to the house. We'll go to the dance together. My brother Louie has a terrific collection of dance records that he plays. And Alice is our Social Chairman and loves to dance."

Tom Sapienza accepted. The next evening, a surprised Maria answered the front door and saw the handsome smiling Tom Sapienza, who immediately greeted her with a warm hug and explained the reason for his visit. "Oh come eenside. Tom ees nota home; he had to work late. *Elisa* ees here; she waits to go to a dance."

"*Elisa?* . . . Oh . . . Alice. I'll bet she's grown up by now." Maria laughed and said proudly, "Oh yes, she'sa grown up alright!" Alice, dressed for a special evening out, was standing at the kitchen doorway as Tom Sapienza entered from the hall. His face lit up. His eyes slowly swept her from head to toe and back again — stopping at just the right places in his survey. Then as if coming out of a deep reverie, he burst into a wide dimpled smile, walked over to Maria, crushed her in a strong bear hug, and covered her cheek with kisses. Maria blushed with pleasure. Alice learned much later that at that moment his thought had been, "I've found my wife!" He later explained that his instinctive reaction had been to hug the mother who had produced her for him.

When Paolo entered the kitchen the two men embraced warmly and fell to reminiscing. It was growing late and Tom suggested that he drive Alice to the dance so that they would not be late. As a strict Italian father, Paolo inevitably preferred them to wait. But Maria intervened. "Hmmmmm . . ." Paolo waited through the pregnant pause. "Va . . . va . . . Go. Go now," she said. "*Non credo che è meglio tardi è no mai.* I do not believe that it ees better late than never," she said to Paolo, firmly. Tom Sapienza agreed and he happily escorted Alice to his DeSoto, chattering animatedly with her about various topics, among them English literature.

After several dances, Tom confided to Alice's brother that his dancing skill was limited. Big brother Tom seized the opportunity to invite his friend home for a lesson after the dance. Tom Sapienza proved remarkably, and purposely, retarded in learning. His intentions were clear after the first lesson. Brother Tom colluded. On that hot night when electric fans hardly made a difference, Tom Palombo offered his friend another shirt to replace his damp one. "You can return it tomorrow," he suggested. "You'll need some more lessons." His friend agreed — not so reluctantly.

After each lesson, Maria and Sophia served coffee and home-baked desserts. Their guest enjoyed them as he looked, not so discreetly, at Alice, who felt conspicuous under his glances.

And her oldest brother Silvio reminisced with his boyhood friend and teased Sapienza about urging him to hold little Alice's hand while he took his turn at whatever game the boys were playing on Tioga Street. Alice smiled at their reminiscences. Her gentle big brother Silvio had quietly shown his love and pride in her over the years. And now he and his brother Tom were not so subtly showing their pleasure in Tom Sapienza's attention to their little sister. Alice, embarrassed, feigned annoyance after he left.

Secretly Alice loved their discussions. In a few weeks, Tom did not *ask* Alice to marry him; he *told* her they would be married. "No one will ever love you as deeply as I will," he declared. Alice knew it. She had never experienced such strong, positive vocal affection from any young man before. Nor had she ever met one who was so deeply gentle and perceptive and wise. He did not quite ask her parents' blessing, he firmly informed Paolo and Maria about his intentions. They all knew instinctively that here was born another great and lasting love.

Maria had been shy about discussing the "facts of life," so it was Anne and Sophia who answered Alice's intimate questions about marriage. But Maria had taught Alice, through her unspoken language with Paolo, that unselfish caring for a husband, and a bit of flirting with him, had great rewards. Alice knew that the Italian father may be head of the family, but with tact and strategy, the mother governs it.

Tom was open in his affection for Alice. At Sunday dinner when his left hand reached for her hand, Paolo casually switched their seating. And Tom casually switched from eating with his right hand to his left. A man of his generation, Paolo felt uneasy about embracing and kissing. One night at the front door, when he saw Tom kiss Alice goodnight, he cleared his throat several times and spoke, his accent thick from emotion: "Looka, Tom. I wanta you to knowa — my daughter she don'ta foola 'round. I know you wanta to marry *Elisa* . . . but marriaga itsa lika Chreestmas . . . you don't opena the packeega before Chreestmas . . . you don'ta even shaka th'box!" They understood and loved him for it. Through the years they often laughed about it.

Ironically, only several weeks before Nick Masters had met Alice Palombo at a *paesano*'s house. Thinking of asking her to marry him, he later told his college buddy Tom Sapienza of his plan. And Tom then informed

Nick of his own marriage plan. Neither realized they were speaking about the same girl.

Although he had Americanized his name, Nick was strongly attached to the Italian tradition of arranged marriages. Soon Nick and his mother, bearing gifts, came to make a formal proposal to Maria and Paolo. Maria, considering the bright handsome Tom, was pleased that Alice was out. Casually — and shrewdly — she informed them that in America, young couples make their own decision. And she offered no encouragement. *"Elisa non è pronta . . . non sape bollire aqua.* She'sa nota ready; she can'ta boil water." Her *paesani* left, dissatisfied.

Meanwhile, Rosa was trying to discourage Tom's plan to marry Alice. While she respected the Palombo family, it would be easier for her to relinquish her first son if he were to marry her *Comare* Canistra's Sicilian daughter. But several months later, Tom overcame her resistance.

He and Alice formalized their engagement at a family Christmas dinner, hosted by Paolo and Maria. When they arrived, Rosa and Maria embraced warmly and kissed three times in proper Italian style — alternating cheeks. Rosa removed her hat and gloves. Sebastian removed his hat, shook hands with Paolo and Maria, and shyly looked downward.

After an exquisite Italian dinner, Tom slipped a platinum diamond engagement ring on Alice's finger and kissed her. Paolo squirmed. Sebastian looked away bashfully. Maria and Rosa smiled. The others loved it and raised their glasses . . . *"Buona salute!"*

After dinner, the family gathered at the piano to sing Italian arias, accompanied by the music that came from Paolo's collection of piano music rolls. Sebastian was pleased to see their interest in music, surprised to hear Alice play an Italian song on the keyboard, and astonished that she had not studied music. They bonded immediately. *"Questa signorina é artistica,"* he whispered to Rosa and mused with pleasure, *this young lady is artistic.* Paolo tucked a bottle of his best wine into Sebastian's elbow, after their proper, formal parting *cerimonie.* *"Grazie, Signore Palombo,"* Sebastian said shyly.

For his wedding, Tom asked his friend Nick to be his best man. Nick was stunned when he learned that Alice would be the bride. When his mother heard the news she erupted, *"Sangue di Diavolo!* I thoughta she can'ta boila water!"

A Call to Arms

The new pastor, Father Ceradini, would officiate at their wedding mass at Mother of Good Counsel Church on June 26, 1940. Before their wedding, Alice brought Tom to meet her good friend, Father Pastorius, her religious instructor through high school at Holy Rosary Parish. The name Sapienza impressed and pleased him. He gave Tom and Alice two words of advice that would serve them well for a lifetime: "Remember, if you want a happy marriage you must give each other unselfish devotion. Apply these two words to every task in life and you'll succeed." UNSELFISH DEVOTION was scripted on their modest wedding cake in pink icing. Tom and Alice adopted his words as their credo — and lived them.

Another bit of wise advice came from Maria: "When you eata steak or chickena, wipa your mouth and don'ta tell me. And when you 'ave argumenta, don'ta tell . . . fix it. . . . *'i panni sporco si lavano in casa.* Understanda? Dirty clothes you washa at home." Turning to her daughter she added: "*Elisa,* ifa you 'ave a fight, you can'ta coma home. Fix it." And they did. Unlike today, couples made their marriage work!

On the day before the wedding, Paolo washed Alice's hair, as was his custom. She felt a teardrop on her neck. The next day, when he walked her to the altar, the sharp intake of Papa's breath betrayed his emotions. It was an intimate wedding. Their family, godparents, and a few close friends attended the traditional Latin High Mass. Tom and Alice had to be frugal. Unlike at big spirited Italian weddings, the reception was modest and warm. But in true Italian fashion, the food was delicious and the guests enjoyed Paolo's *vino* and Sebastian's music. The guests sang as his musician friends played lively Italian folk music. Cousin Gina, Alice's maid of honor, caught the wedding bouquet. Maria and Grazia exchanged glances and smiled. Nick's mother and *Comare* Canistra looked on glumly. Rosa scratched her wrist, a nervous habit. Everyone else seemed happy — except Nick.

Later he revealed his emotion and told Alice that being best man at their wedding was the hardest act he had ever had to perform. When Alice disclosed Nick's feelings to Tom, he responded coolly, "Nick has good taste, too." Well, at least Tom could have been jealous, she thought with frustration. And then secretly smiled at his self-confidence.

The newlyweds settled in a two-room apartment one street away from Paolo and Maria. Inevitably, they had their first big argument about going to early Sunday mass so that Tom could go to Rosa's house to see the homing pigeons come in from a race. Alice could not win the argument, so she threatened, "I'm going home to Mama."

"Good," said Tom remembering Maria's words and reached for a suitcase. "I'll help you pack." The dilemma hit Alice, and they both laughed and said: "Fix it!" And they did.

Tom worked part-time delivering Railways Express packages when he was not tending his Deli business. Despite his education, work was still difficult to find. But gathering war clouds in Europe would soon offer opportunity.

Although the United States had declared neutrality on September 5, 1939, Roosevelt did not sit idly watching the Nazis destroy Poland, France and England. He expected the war to reach America. His State of the Union address prepared the country. First he reported the foreign affairs crisis and then asked Congress for over six billion dollars to fund the largest military buildup in United States history. Though most Americans remained opposed to taking sides, F.D.R. mobilized the nation to produce weapons, ships and an average of 60,000 planes a year.

As war became imminent and the U.S. finally recognized its own military weakness, it moved away from isolationism. Legislators Edward Burke and James Wadsworth had no intention of allowing America to remain weak. In June 1940, the same month Hitler's armies entered Paris, they introduced into Congress the Selective Training and Service Bill — the first peacetime draft in the nation's history. On September 16, it became law. America lost her complacency. And Rosa, closely following the news in *Il Progresso* paper, lost her confidence. Within a few months, this legislation would vitally affect the Sapienza family.

Many boys eighteen or over enlisted. Brother Santo [Sundy] left his part-time job at Westinghouse and enlisted in the United States Air Force National Guard. Rosa had misgivings, despite Roosevelt's promise on October 30, 1940: "Your boys are not going to be sent into foreign wars." Before the war spurred an economic upturn in America, jobs were scarce even for the better skilled and better educated.

At his father's urging, Tom applied for a job at Westinghouse Electric and Manufacturing Company in East Pittsburgh. His college background made him desirable material for advancement. At company expense, he seized the opportunity for further training in numerous Electrical Engineering courses and in the Westinghouse Management Training Program.

The era of Scientific Management had arrived. Tom had also completed the curriculum in Cost Accounting, Payroll Accounting, Methods Engineering, Time and Motion Study, Industrial Management and Personnel. Sebastian, Rosa and Alice were proud of him. Evenings, Saturdays and part of Sundays were kept free so that Tom could study. Sunday was family and church day, for Churches were still the centerpiece of Homewood social and family life.

Other areas of community life thrived harmoniously. The thirties were notable for interracial activities, especially community-based sports. Organizations sponsored swimming, basketball, baseball, and football teams. Sports, played on local sandlots, flourished among adults and children. One avid sportsman was fourteen-year-old Frank Sapienza, whose idol had been his big brother Tom, a high school football star.

In a sandlot game in August 1940, Frank's team was scheduled to play its toughest opponent. Frank, the halfback, received the pass that would win or lose the game. He headed for the opening that would get him to the goal line. A husky opponent lunged at him. Several more attacked and crushed him to the ground, after he barely flung himself over the goal line, still in possession of the ball. He had scored the winning touchdown! His last!

An injured victor limped home to help his brothers do Saturday chores. Five tons of coal had to be shoveled into a wheelbarrow and pushed into the cellar coal chute. By the time the job was finished, Frank's leg throbbed with pain. For over a week, he hobbled on his swollen right leg. He did not tell his parents until a fever developed and the pain became so intense that he could no longer withhold his secret. After several examinations, doctors delivered the shocking news that his femur bone had cracked its entire length and was seriously infected.

The diagnosis was Osteomyelitis, for which antibiotics treatment did not yet exist. The week passed. The fever raged. Finally the doctor announced that an operation was crucial for Frank's survival. The infection would have to be scraped clean from the bone, allowing new healthy bone to form.

Brother Tom, a former medical student still attracted to medicine, asked to witness the surgery from the student gallery. From Dr. Markel's expression, he anticipated bad news. "Tom, I don't want to worry your parents, but we may have to amputate Frank's leg. The week's delay after the accident has done great damage. There's one small hope . . . we may be able to stop the infection with a new miracle drug — sulfa. It's in short supply because soldiers get first preference. I'll see what I can do."

Weeks later, Frank still lay gravely ill. Sulfa and drain tubes did not curb the infection. Months passed. A very thin Frank suffered quietly. His mother suffered for him. She devoted every effort to keep his eighteen-inch seeping wound disinfected. She fingered her rosary and bargained with God and the Blessed Mother. And fell asleep exhausted at his bedside, her rosary wrapped around her fingers, only half told. Two more surgeries followed. Amputation was nearly certain. "Tom, I know you and your brothers have given blood, but we'll need more," the surgeon said. Tom assured him they would give it.

"That's not all we'll need," Tom said. "We'll need a lot of faith — and confidence in you, Dr. Markell — and we have both. We won't tell my parents." That night Tom bargained with God. In the days before health insurance, a family closed ranks and helped. Sebastian worked every job he could to meet hospital expenses. Lee, Duffy, and Santo still lived at home and gave their share. Tom gave a week's salary every month. And Julie, the youngest, emptied his piggy bank and offered his father the $93 he had saved from delivering newspapers. When he spilled it on the table, Sebastian blew his nose hard and left the room.

Rosa disinfected Frank's bedroom daily. Alice cleaned halls and stairs weekly in anticipation of the doctor's and the priest's visits. Santo helped his pregnant sister-in-law wash walls. Tony Renda and Joe Pegnato, Frank's closest friend, visited Frank every day. Joe, a successful juggler and entertainer whose stage name was Bobby Jule, practiced juggling at Frank's bedside and promised to buy him a suit when he walked again.

The ray of hope and joy for the family was the expected arrival of their first grandchild. On September 8, 1941, a baby girl was born. Rosa was thrilled. A girl at last — and born on the Blessed Mother's birthday. In keeping with Italian custom and since Rosa had no daughters, Alice was prepared to name the baby Marianna Maria in honor of Sebastian's mother and Santa Maria, the Blessed Mother. Rosa, not inclined to honor her mother-in-law or recognize the September 8 birthdate, adamantly insisted upon her own name.

A Call to Arms

In the hospital, Alice was frustrated. The name Rose, satirized in a song called *Rosie The Riveter*, poked fun at women who had left their kitchens for the first time to go to work. Nurses suggested names, one jokingly calling the baby Rosie the Riveter. Then Tom understood Alice's dilemma.

For three days, she struggled and wept. Finally her solution was to honor both Rosa and the Blessed Mother by naming the baby little Rose — Rosette Marie. Tom told his mother. Rosa, overlooking the honor to the Madonna, was furious because Maria was Alice's mother's name. But Tom held firm. Nonetheless, for Alice it spoiled the joy of her baby's birth. Later, brother-in-law Liborio reminded Alice of the crisis and laughed, "Boy! Mother was tough!"

Soon there would be three girls in the family. Liborio [Lee] married a sweet Italian girl, Lena Martone. Lena was the sister of Italian artist, Atilio Martone, the Michelangelo of Pittsburgh Catholic Churches. His Renaissance paintings graced the roof of Mother of Good Counsel Church. "What talents your children will have — music and art!" Alice happily told Lena.

She and Alice became like sisters, both helping Rosa however they could. If raising six sons during the Depression had kept Rosa cloistered, nursing Frank assured her isolation. Her only contact with the outside world was the Italian Radio Hour and *Il Progresso* newspaper. She spoke little English. Rosa had an extensive Italian vocabulary, but spoke the Sicilian dialect. Fortunately, her daughters-in-law learned to understand this difficult language and accommodated their communication when they spoke with her in their own dialects. This gave Rosa an opportunity to share many stories about life in Sicily. Raised among many Italian dialects, Alice loved the sound of *Siciliano* phrases. And so, within her small world, Rosa kept in touch through Italian newspapers that gave daily war news reports, growing concerned that *Il Duce* Benito Mussolini had allied himself with Hitler.

Patriotic, bewildered American-Italians did not sympathize with the Axis powers and were mortified when the United States asked Italy to close her Consulates in Newark and Detroit. Rosa reminisced about her separation from Sebastian during the "Great War." News of German submarine attacks in the Pacific awakened in Maria Palombo memories of her crossing during World War I.

Perceptive Americans were uneasy about the signing of the Atlantic Charter, when President Roosevelt and Winston Churchill met on the high seas to plan an eight-point program focused upon destroying Nazi tyranny. For frantic Italian-American parents the imminence of war for America meant that their patriotic American sons might have to fight against their relatives in the Italian villages they had left to pursue the American ideal!

Rosa followed the war news closely. It worried her that, as the war across the Atlantic intensified, the conflict in the Pacific theater became more menacing as well, with the U.S. and Japan determined to resolve their long-standing rivalry for Pacific supremacy. When Roosevelt imposed an embargo against Japan on their much-needed scrap metal and American oil, Emperor Hiro Hito sent two Japanese envoys to a Peace Conference with Secretary Cordell Hull. The bumbling, kindly Nomura had worked with Navy Secretary Roosevelt during World War I. Kurusu, Roosevelt's old friend who had an American wife, spoke daily with Secretary Hull.

On November 20, 1941, America relaxed when the media announced that the Japanese envoys had left the Peace Conference smiling, as if resolved on a compromise. But they had disguised their treachery, even as bulletins from Japan were intercepted and decoded. The messages asked Namura and Kurusu to report any balloons above Pearl Harbor. Hearing this, F.D.R. announced to Harry Hopkins, "This means war."

Seventeen days later, on December 7, 1941, Japan leveled a devastating sneak attack on Pearl Harbor, heralded by Roosevelt as "a day that will live in infamy." The U.S. had had plenty of warning, yet when attack came, America's inexcusable indifference to Hitler's atrocities brought stunned surprise. Some thought it was another Orson Welles' *The War of the Worlds* hoax. From that ignoble day until the Korean War, Rosa would see four of her sons go to battle.

The impact of the Great Depression and Franklin Delano Roosevelt's political leadership would change American politics. Suddenly, events reversed the anti-immigrant Nativist viewpoint of the early 1920's. Out of great urgency, a spirit of nationalism developed and immigration quotas became a non-issue. During the war years a labor shortage caused the United States to terminate the Chinese Exclusion Act and stimulate the migration of Asian and Mexican laborers to work in the West on America's railroads and in the agriculture of the Southwest.

Before Roosevelt's election in 1932, the Nativists' restrictive immigration policy of four decades had not considered newcomers to be national assets. Historian Roger Daniels cites the prevalent racism of the 1920's, using as an example vice president Calvin Coolidge's article entitled "Whose Country Is This?" It clearly supported the view of Nordic supremacy and the idea that intermarriage between Nordics and other people produced inferior offspring. Congressman Albert Johnson, who had fought to restrict immigration in 1924, openly proclaimed that ". . . The United States is our land. . . .We intend to maintain it so. The day of unalloyed welcome and indiscriminate acceptance of all races has definitely ended."

Ironically, America's immigrant sons would lay down their lives in World War II to defend the country that had given them such dubious welcome. And even as immigrant animosity lessened in America, anti-Jewish hatred abroad increased and became Hitler's Nazi ideology.

Rosa's sons, two of them immigrants, would surely be drafted to war. Poor Rosa stormed heaven and *Santa Madre*. Alice held three-month-old Rosette and worried that Tom would be conscripted. Despite knowing what to expect, Rosa was shattered when Santo was drafted in 1941 from volunteer National Guard duty into the U.S. Air Force. He served in combat duty in Italy before the Italians, allied with Germany, switched sides in the war. In their very own villages, American-Italian sons saw suffering and atrocities committed by the *Tedesci,* German soldiers purported to be their friends. Santo tried to reach his relatives, but was forbidden to get in touch with them.

Next, Delfino [Duffy] was drafted in 1942 into the Army, where he served first in Okinawa, then in Japan, in anticipation of America's planned invasion of Japan — before the atomic bomb was dropped. After active combat service, he was transferred to the service where homing pigeons were used to send messages over enemy lines.

Lee, like his brother Duffy, served with "the birds." He, too, was transferred in 1943 into the 278th Signal Company in the European theater. His knowledge of homing pigeons placed him in the communication division that sent critical messages, via carrier pigeons, over enemy lines, beyond the reach of war planes and the perils of radio interception. Their youthful hobby probably saved the brothers' lives. Later, they thanked their brother Tom for getting them interested in racing pigeons.

After the invasion of Normandy, Lee's 29th Division fought in the Battle of the Bulge and the St. Lo Battle — then moved across the Ruhr to the Rhine. When they reached the town of Appahousan, Lee witnessed an incredible tragedy. The enemy had set fire to a barn full of Jews and political prisoners. Those who attempted to escape the fire were machine-gunned dead. One poor victim was killed just as he had dug himself through the dirt floor to escape. Lee photographed the horrid site. He smelled the sickening, heavy stench of burning flesh, and saw stiff, dead bodies stacked high in the streets like cordwood. The family never heard the story until years later when the photos were discovered among Lee's war memorabilia.

Unrelenting propaganda against German, Italian, and Japanese atrocities drove patriotic American sons to volunteer to fight Hitler's tyranny. Poor Mama Rosa stormed heaven and *Santa Madre*, and fingered her rosary beads every day. She feared that Toto would be next to go, after married men without children.

The government had frozen workers at their defense jobs, some of which were crucial enought to exempt men from the draft. Anyone who left his employment became eligible for immediate conscription. Because production efficiency was vital to the war effort, Westinghouse had spent time and money training Tom in two fields. He traveled between Westinghouse plants in Eastern cities wherever he was needed, leaving his family behind. His expense account provided perks. Remembering the lessons of the Depression, Alice saved every spare penny.

One day when Tom's induction notice arrived, Alice went with his credentials in hand to answer his draft call at Homewood School. The Draft Board mistook her for a reporter. She explained that she had come to represent Tom, who worked at the Baltimore Westinghouse defense plant. She answered their questions convincingly, but declined to reveal sensitive information. The Board was persuaded that he had a crucial defense job meriting exemption from active duty. Alice walked to nearby Holy Rosary Church, lit a candle, prayed her thanks, and walked four blocks to Hamilton Avenue to share the news with Rosa.

Patriotism was high. Americans were pledged to practice austerity and work hard for victory. To ease the American conscience, all were made to feel that they were contributing to the war effort in the sacrifices they made by giving blood and performing voluntary services. Women stood patiently in line with ration books in hand to buy scarce staples. They left their soap operas and ironing boards to work in defense plants beside the now respected

Rosie the Riveter. Single women, including first-generation American women, joined all branches of service.

While the Sapienza brothers fought overseas, the Palombo boys, married with families, were working overtime at Rockwell Manufacturing Company making ammunition. Maria was grateful that her sons would be home. But she would lose Tom and Alice to "homefront conscription" when Westinghouse transferred Tom to a production management position at the Westinghouse Radio Division in Lansdowne near Baltimore, Maryland. Maria prayed for Rosa. Separation from Tom and Alice was minor compared to the traumas poor Rosa and Sebastian were suffering.

Families were uprooted. People everywhere in the United States were on the move. In Baltimore, Tom settled his family in Brooklyn Park, near the Maryland Yacht Club, not far from the beautiful ocean beaches. Close by were Washington, D.C., and Annapolis, Maryland. Tom, with 200 men under him, worked closely with the Army and Navy Departments. Defense plants were closed to everyone except authorized personnel. Sabotage from within and without was a real fear. On June 28, 1942, the FBI announced that four German saboteurs, deposited in America by Axis submarines, had been captured after slipping onto a beach on Long Island carrying huge crates with enough explosives to sabotage U. S. industry. They were caught, tried and, on August 8, 1942, were electrocuted.

If sabotage was treason, strikes were considered an unpatriotic betrayal. But Tom soon discovered that not all men were patriotic. By slick maneuvering, some workers got overtime incentive pay and early sign-out passes for the Pimlico race track. Tom discovered their scheme, promised to fire them and notify the draft board. Honesty was restored *pronto*!

Tom also contributed to the war effort in the vital area of communication by radio. Environmental hazards of the hot, humid South Pacific posed a threat to radio equipment and required specific protection. Tom's chemistry background enabled him to develop a method for coating, hermetically sealing and packaging valued radio equipment that could endure the perils of any war theater — cspecially the jungles where fungus was an enemy.

The war effort required cooperation and sacrifice on the homefront. Tom wore several hats, working up to eighty hours a week, using many talents. As a salaried supervisor on a fixed income, he worked more and earned less than those under him. But this inequity proved less frustrating than the attitudes he encountered in the prejudiced South. His first experience in Baltimore, Maryland, located just south of the Mason-Dixon line, was startling.

Because leisure time was a precious luxury, Tom tried to spend Sundays with his little family at the ocean beaches. On their first trip to a Baltimore beach, he was appalled to see a sign that read: GENTILES ONLY! He had already seen and deplored NO NEGROES signs at lunch counters and restrooms. He voiced his outrage to Alice that Negro and Jewish sons were dying on foreign beaches to keep bigoted Americans safe. On his next trip, Tom was shocked when he was commanded by the beach supervisor to leave with his family. When Tom asked why, he was told, "You look like a Jew."

Tom unleashed a tirade. "You son-of-a bitch Hitler lover! Throw me off, if you're big enough!" The man backed off. The family opened their beach umbrella and picnic basket and settled in. When they were ready to leave, Tom scornfully showed the angry bigot the Westinghouse I.D. nametag that he always carried. "Oh, you must be an Eyetalian and a Yankee — that isn't much better; but you can come back," said the Baltimorean. Alice hastily pulled little Rosette away. Short of delivering a sock on the jaw, Tom unleashed a set of invectives that are unprintable. For the South, the Civil War and discrimination were not settled. "Negroes" still stood at the back of the bus — even servicemen.

Movement during the war was endless. Baltimore, a port city located at the upper end of the Chesapeake Bay, bustled with commuter trains, buses, and incoming ships. Downtown streets were crowded with servicemen and shipyard employees. It was common to show servicemen appreciation and hospitality — common to find sailors from our Allied countries walking along city streets after their ships had pulled into port. One afternoon, after Alice had finished shopping at the uptown Baltimore fish markets, she encountered two sailors animatedly speaking Italian. She greeted them, *"Benvenuto, Amici!* Welcome!" The sailors were surprised and delighted. As the trio exchanged courtesies and information about their Italian *paesi* of origin, regional traces in their dialects revealed that one was *Abruzzese*, and the other was *Napolitano*. This encounter made Alice miss her family even more. When Tom arrived home from work, Alice announced two guests for dinner. Accustomed to entertaining servicemen stationed in nearby camps, Tom expected to find friends from Pittsburgh. He was thrilled to greet the visitors; the men were pleased to find good food and someone to converse with. Alice was amused that Tom carefully shifted to speaking non-dialect Italian when he sensed that neither of them was Sicilian.

The sailors, happy that Italy was now an American ally, explained that Italy had been strongly anti-Hitler even before abandoning Mussolini and joining the allies. They were pleased to learn that American papers, magazines and newsreels had pictured the Italians' fury at *Il Duce*. What King Emanuel III had not done by demoting him as dictator, the Italians did when they killed Mussolini and hanged him upside-down in the *piazza* to be stoned.

"Quel porco! . . . A pig!" the Italians said. The visitors described the tremendous outpouring of love for American soldiers when Naples fell to Mark Clark's army on October 1, 1943. And they expressed grief that parts of their once-beautiful cities and villages had been reduced to rubble, and many innocents had been killed. After dinner, Tom and Alice drove the pair to their ship and gave them an affectionate send-off and a happy memory despite the somber years.

And generally, although the war years were a dark dismal time, there were light moments. Cartoonists poked fun at shortages: A wife fries an egg white one night and the yolk the next! The comics pushed patriotism. When soldiers went to war, funny-paper characters went to war. They fought "Japs", Orphan Annie collected scrap metal, and Superman hawked blood for the Red Cross.

Fashion stylists captured the mood of the times. In 1929, when the stock market had plunged, skirts had gone above the knees and styles were flamboyant. By contrast, in the forties, the stock market rose and skirts plunged almost ankle length and brought the "new look": the tailored Eisenhower jacket / blouse and big shoulder pads, and Rosie the Riveter's work jeans.

Entertainers wrote and sang the war songs that told the history of those dark years. The bugle call came from Tin Pan Alley: "This is the G. I. Jive, man alive; it starts with the bugle blowing reveille over your head . . ." Americans sang, "Praise the Lord and pass the ammunition," or "Goodbye, dear, I'll be back in a year." In a slap at Hitler, they sang, "Ven Der Fuehrer says, 'Ve iss der master race, den ve'll heil right in der Fuhrer's face . . ." And the brave and beleaguered British sang, "There'll be bluebirds over the white cliffs of Dover tomorrow just you wait and see."

Abroad, the BBC transmitted worldwide newscasts of war activities. Via shortwave radio, Tokyo Rose relentlessly broadcast propaganda designed to undermine allied morale, as American sons of immigrant parents spilled their blood on foreign beaches to uphold the American dream. And back home, their transplanted loved ones, who had endured the trauma of Ellis Island and ethnic bias, mourned. Tom and Alice mourned for them.

Chapter 16

On the Homefront

World War II had taken on the proportions of a massive chess game that preoccupied the nation. Even before television, it had become the most widely reported war in history on radio, in newspapers, and the cinema. Courageous reporters moved with the troops on battleships, in bombers, in muddy foxholes, and on crimson beaches to record the hell of battle.

On the homefront, the war was ultimately won by patriotic zeal and the will of most Americans to put personal desires aside. The ordinary Joe, plumber and farmer, Black and White, Jew and Gentile, picked up a gun and went to war. Other ordinary Americans, soldiers without guns, turned out such a volume of weaponry that the enemy was ultimately crushed beneath the weight of the armaments.

But patriotism was selective. Journalists reported about the profiteering aspects of war. Black market activities brought headlines: RATION STAMP RACKET SMASHED; UNION IS GO-BETWEEN IN BLACK MARKET WHISKEY TRIAL. Wages had been frozen. Without high salary demands and strikes, big businesses, which received millions in war contracts, became bigger and wealthier. Thirty-one enormous companies operated half of the new factories, which they later bought dirt-cheap. Once on a packed railroad train, Alice heard a greedy, well-dressed tycoon boasting : "If this war lasts a couple more years, I'll be walking on Easy Street!"

These were transitory years for many American families who, uprooted at the will of defense demands, moved East, West, North, and South. Consequently, lasting friendships were uncommon. Tom and Alice, however, developed a family-type relationship in Baltimore with their neighbors, "Mom-Mom" Rolle, her daughter Etta and her children.

Mom-Mom's family proved to be of great comfort and value to Tom and Alice when their son was born on May 5, 1944 at Saint Agnes Hospital, located across from the orphanage where famed baseball player, Babe Ruth, had been raised. Affiliated with the renowned Johns Hopkins University, the hospital medical center had an exceptional surgical team who attended wounded soldiers. Tom and Alice would come to feel that Fate had placed them there.

They named their new baby Thomas, his father's American name, and Bartholomew in honor of Tom's godfather and Sebastian's fellow musician. Rosa had been upset when Tom had not married Bartholomew's daughter Josephine. But she was barren, and they would have been childless had Tom yielded to Rosa's wishes. Rosa ignored the topic. Alice, who knew the story, relished the irony that the baby was named after the barren woman's father.

Alice felt desolate when Tom drove Rosette to Pittsburgh to stay with her loving family. In a few days it was clear that baby Tommy was in distress. Alice reported to Dr. Bowe that at each feeding he threw up his milk. In a week he lost weight steadily.

With growing concern about her baby, with the onslaught of war news, and without Tom and Rosette, post-partum depression was tough to battle. Nurses informed Alice about post-partum psychosis, but she rejected this diagnosis. Instead, she found comfort that, unlike many young mothers who yielded their husbands to war, Tom would be home the next day. After all, war was more serious than her own anxiety. "Adjust," Alice reasoned, as she had been taught through her parents' and Tom's attitude.

Distressed families sent loved ones off to war. Americans were absorbed with rationing and the scarcity of certain foods and goods: meat, coffee, sugar, silk undies, hairpins, and childrens' toys. They watched for enemy planes that, fortunately, never reached America. Baltimore, heavily engaged in shipbuilding and located near Washington, D.C., was seriously thought to be vulnerable to attack. Air-raid sirens wailed nightly as people sat in dark houses, and air-raid wardens policed the streets with eyes intent for any shaft of vagrant light. Daytime air-raid drills became routine. At the warning, frightened school children, affecting bravery, headed for corridors and basements.

Their fear was not unfounded, for early in June 1944, the media reported that Germans had launched a second group of potential saboteurs, The Florida Four. These were heavily-armed American deserters who had been trained in methods for sabotage in Germany's Abwehr's dirty tricks school.

On June 5, 1944, General Dwight D. Eisenhower, urging his foot soldiers on to victory in "The Great Crusade," sent his Allied expeditionary force this message: "I have full confidence in your courage, devotion to duty, and skill in battle. We will accept nothing less than full victory! Good luck! And let us all beseech the blessing of Almighty God upon this great and noble undertaking." Next day headlines announced: INVASION IS ON!

"D-Day" had arrived. The Allies swept through France in combined landings by sea and air, and 17,000 troops that had landed on German-held beaches every day of combat pushed ahead inch-by-inch to accomplish their goal.

America was now engaged in full-scale combat with Japan and Germany on the ground, in the air, and on the sea. The first victory came on the European front as the allied assault continued with ordinary foot soldiers, carrying little but survival gear, and heavy doses of personal courage and wit. These brave riflemen, hidden from air attacks, took enemy positions not accessible to tanks. They marched into and captured cities filled with the stench of burning flesh, where hours before Hitler's ovens had annihilated thousands of Jews. With Normandy and battle after battle behind them, they fought, undaunted, toward final victory.

Despite this exciting news, Tom and Alice were fighting their own personal battle at home. Baby Tommy continued to throw up and lose weight. Instinctively, Alice breast-fed him every half-hour in small amounts, and he retained most of his milk. She scheduled an early appointment with pediatrician Dr. Eberly. When the doctor saw the parastolic waves rolling across Tommy's stomach pushing hard to digest his milk, his worse fears were confirmed. The baby had been born with hypertrophic pyloric stenosis, a condition affecting one in ten thousand infants. The doctor explained that the pylorus, the tube between the stomach and large intestine, was being choked by the calcified pyloric ring around it. Tommy would require surgery. To keep him from starving to death, the surgeon would have to slit the ring to allow food to pass through — a delicate and risky operation that only one in four infants survived.

The infant was put in the care of a top-flight surgeon who was engaged full-time performing complex surgery on wounded soldiers. Tommy was scheduled for surgery on the Fourth of July, barely two months after his birth. Uneasily, Alice exclaimed *"Giorno maledetto!* Oh that cursed day!"

On the morning of the operation, Tom and Alice were permitted only a brief look at their son. When they walked away from his crib and through the fourteen-bed ward of wounded soldiers, the patients made encouraging remarks to them. The couple clung together and subdued their emotions. As the surgical team operated upstairs, they knelt in the hospital chapel. A group of nuns prayed the Rosary for them. Alice prayed an emotional appeal to the Bella Madonna, her words lost among the nuns' voices.

Three hours later a nurse came to summon them. Soon the surgical nurse appeared carrying baby Tommy. His pitiful whimper and feeble cry told them that their baby was alive at least! The surgeon came to inform them about the surgery. In emotional relief, Alice thanked him, clutched his hands, kissed them fervently, and collapsed!

The next few days would determine the success of the operation. Because his digestive muscles had developed from overwork, Tommy was put on whole milk laced with powdered food supplement. The decision saved him, because infants cannot normally digest whole milk. Dr. Eberly informed Alice that her feeding instinct had kept Tommy's weight stable enough to endure the operation, and had helped to save him.

Each day as Tom and Alice visited their son, the soldiers in the adjoining ward encouraged them. The couple, in turn, stopped to visit and bring little gifts. The baby began a steady weight gain. After three weeks, they carried Tommy through the ward among cheers and applause. Tom grinned broadly. Alice wept gratefully and heard their ovations for years. Again, contact with servicemen had offered a feeling of community.

Back in Pittsburgh, poor Rosa struggled with Frank's persistent osteo infection, which, despite sulfa drug treatment, had taken its toll and permanently damaged his right leg, arm and jawbone. She fought her fear of hearing bad news about her three sons, and alternately bargained with the Lord, giving Him hell or imploring Him to keep them alive. And she missed Tom, who was the family "rock." Rosa felt lonely. Whereas Sebastian was busy with his work and music activity, Rosa, isolated by her cautious nature, had not readily adjusted to the American language and customs.

Raised as the lonely child of late-in-life parents, she came from a tradition where the youngest child, married or not, stayed to care for elderly parents until their death. In that environment, she had few young friends. Her parents and her husband and children became her whole world and her security base. And anyone who was not her "blood," or anything that threatened the security of that world, was subject to her wrath. Outside of Italian radio and newspaper, she was segregated, by choice, from her neighbors and relatives because Rosa spoke only Italian to her family, her relatives, and very few friends. With three sons at war, and Frank disabled, Rosa's frustrations mounted.

Unfortunately, Lena, who lived in the Sapienza homestead, became the unfair target of those frustrations, plus vague unfounded suspicions. However, reared in the Italian tradition of respect for a mother-in-law, Lena did not challenge Rosa's mounting allegations. Instead, she went quietly in search of a small apartment for herself and baby Louis, gave the post office her change of address, and sought the comfort of her sisters. Because she and Alice had been close, Lena wrote her a worrisome letter about her move, leaving the details to be surmised.

Meanwhile, Alice received another disturbing letter from home — with the frightening news that her mother was going blind from diabetic damage. In view of all this, Tom and Alice chose not to burden their parents, and withheld the news about Tommy's surgery. When Alice finally informed her parents, she was careful to omit the date.

Within a week Paolo and Maria boarded the B & O Railroad to reassure themselves that all was well. Upon his arrival, Paolo intuitively asked if the surgery had been performed on the Fourth of July. Alice nodded. *"Giorno maledetto!"* he exclaimed.

Maria controlled her emotion and, with her limited sight, devoured every feature of Tommy, Rosette, Alice, and Tom, acknowledging that some day she would no longer see them. Maria reasoned that her family would become her eyes.

Paolo would help her adjust. He wanted to show her historic sites, to help her store these in her memory. When Maria saw the warships in Baltimore harbor, a flood of traumatic memories overwhelmed her. She reminisced briefly, then discreetly kissed her forefinger and, just as she had done at Ellis Island, touched it to the ground and said, *"Grazie, Dio."*

In Washington, D.C., Maria marveled at the huge frescoes high in the dome of the Capitol, painted a hundred years before by the Michelangelo of the United States Capitol, seventy-year-old Constantino Brumidi.

A week later, they carried home a comforting report to an anxious Rosa and Sebastiano. Each family reassured the other that God was protecting them and theirs against the perils that threatened their families. Their dauntless courage, adaptability and hell-bent will for their children to survive were awesome.

These attributes were obvious when Tom took the family home in September to celebrate Sebastian's birthday. Rosa, the fierce mother, was an equally fervent *Nonna*. She eagerly cuddled Tommy and within two minutes made her predictable accolades about this baby's intelligence and strength to survive. He was special, and God had spared him for a reason, she declared. Rosa never needed Dr. Spock to teach her about positive bonding and creating a strong self-image in her babies.

But her joy was overshadowed by the cold fear that for three months she had not received a letter from Santo, who was an Air Force Master Sergeant. Although war casualties were daily news fare, she reasoned that D-Day was over. She refused to think the worst. Every day before she went to her mailbox, she stopped before the *Bella Madre's* picture and pleaded, castigated and bargained with her to watch over her three sons and to bring her word from them.

On Sebastian's birthday, before she went to the mailbox, Alice heard Rosa lament to the *Bella Madonna. "Provi la mia pazienza, Bedda Madonna, ma non mi abbandonare!"* Her Sicilian plea was touching: "Test my patience, but don't abandon me!" Suddenly, Rosa swore that today the Blessed Mother had looked at her with the reassurance that Santo's letter would come. She dashed to the front door and tore open the mailbox. Then she came rushing into the kitchen where Alice was feeding the baby, and waved three letters. *"Santa Maria!"* she shrieked. *"Ecco tre lettere da mio Santo!"* Alice's skin erupted in goosebumps as she witnessed this testimony to the power of Faith.

In a few days, Tom and his brood drove back to Baltimore in his precariously operable DeSoto. New cars were not easily available, since the manufacture of every spare vehicle or home appliance was sacrificed for the war effort. Only those engaged in crucial defense jobs would be issued credentials to purchase a new car. The faithful DeSoto broke down half-way home, leaving the family stranded late at night in a remote Maryland town. Tom pushed the vehicle along a cold, lonely highway as Alice held it in neutral and steered — and prayed. A mile later, a small dimly-lit gasoline station came into view. It was closed but the owner, a mechanic who lived on site, agreed to look at the car once he had seen the sleeping babies. The head gasket had blown. Nothing could be done until morning, nor were there any motels close by. But the mechanic's friend happened by to visit and when he learned of the trouble said, "Well hell, friend, I just happen to have the exact spare gasket for that car in my trunk. I collect spare parts, with the war and all."

An hour later Tom thanked their benefactors, paid them, and gave up his ration stamps to fill his tank with gasoline. Clearly, he would have to arrange for another car. Because of his important wartime position, and because the Office of Price Administration [O.P.A.] had frozen prices, Tom was able to buy a new Ford two-door sedan for $1,250. Gasoline rationing limited their travel to two trips home a year and one trip a month to Washington, D.C., areas.

Long work hours and social obligations as a corporate manager kept Tom and Alice busy. Within the corporation, labor and management personnel did not socialize. Even within management circles there was separate socializing, with Catholics and non-Catholics, Italians and non-Italians rarely pursuing close relationships outside of company functions. Tom found pleasure elsewhere with a newly found Jewish friend, Bernie Topaz, who owned a naphtha dry cleaning plant and with whom he shared his experience with racing pigeons. Tom's curiosity and interest in chemistry led him to explore the dry cleaning process which — unknowingly — was to affect his future and shape a new career. Once again, the pigeon fancier hobby affected the destiny of another Sapienza.

Alice, too, found a new interest. Remembering her childhood hurt and disappointment, she held to her vow to encourage her children toward music training. She enrolled Rosette, now five, at the Peabody Conservatory of Music, supervised her piano practice, and studied with Rosette, who was the youngest in her class. When her teacher commented on the little girl's exceptional talent, Alice wanted to live in Baltimore after the war, so that Rosette could continue to study at the Peabody Conservatory. Tom agreed. They invested $1,500 in a Kimball spinet piano and planned to use the rest of their savings for a down payment on a home. But when they found a lovely home in Lansdowne, a Baltimore suburb, the owners refused to sell them the house when they learned that Tom and Alice were "Eyetalian."

This second insult to their ethnicity kindled their anger at prejudice and their urge to move home after the war. But with a war on two fronts, that possibility seemed remote.

With bombs in the news, people took it seriously when Baltimore's air-raid sirens wailed at night. Children sat, bewildered, in the dark with their parents. During one such drill there was not a star in the sky. Tommy peeked out of the corner of his bedroom window and announced, "Look, Mommy, even God's lights are out!"

Patriotism was high: families sewed clothing from yard goods, saved scrap metal for the war cause, and patiently accepted shortages in appliances, imported foods and luxury goods. The war even affected children's play. They pretended to be air-raid wardens instead of cops. And instead of playing cowboys and Indians they played "bombs over Tokyo," as they jumped off their front porches making exploding bomb noises.

One day their playmate, Tony Rolle, developed an extremely high fever and became delirious. The diagnosis was the dreaded disease that had crippled Franklin Roosevelt — polio. The miracle drug to combat it had not yet been developed as a vaccine by Pittsburgh's Jonas Salk. Tony's play-mates were quarantined and examined for the dreaded disease. The two families found comfort together as Tony fought for his life. But after several weeks, he lost the battle. The children were stunned when Tony died. How tragic that science had advanced further in destroying lives than in saving them! Roosevelt's "March of Dimes" to fight polio took on new meaning.

As the war in the Pacific raged, Americans remained prejudiced and unforgiving, especially in their anti-Japanese sentiment. Jewish refugees were accepted in America, but innocent and patriotic Japanese Americans were not welcome to stay. Governor Chase Clark said, "I don't want them coming to Idaho." Governor Payne Ratner ordered patrolmen to bar them from the state highways. "Japs are not wanted and not welcome in Kansas," he said.

Ironically, we were freeing Jews abroad as we incarcerated innocent Japanese Americans at home. In 1942, thousands of Japanese were yanked from their homes in Pacific Coast States and banished, like prisoners of war, to crowded, army-run, barbed wire camps. But many patriotic Nisei men begged to serve in combat to help preserve their treasured principles of freedom. And like Black Americans, they served honorably.

On the Homefront

The war seemed interminable. But in 1945, America was flung into a series of startling events. In January, President Roosevelt had begun an unprecedented fourth term in office. In April, cross-country headlines announced devastating news. The *New York Herald Tribune* declared: PRESIDENT ROOSEVELT IS DEAD; TRUMAN SWORN IN AS SUCCESSOR. A shocked and frightened nation mourned for three days. Flags flew at half-mast. And except for war news and solemn music, radio offered none of the comedy and drama that had boosted American morale.

Harry Truman, the unassuming haberdasher from Missouri, stepped into Roosevelt's big shoes. Would he be equal to the task of dealing with the war against Japan? Speculation and criticism flourished, but Truman stood strong against his detractors. The sign on his desk, "The Buck Stops Here," and his retort to his critics, "If you can't stand the heat, get the hell out of the kitchen!" gave hint of a remarkable, resolute and capable leader.

At last, on May 8, 1945, the Allies proclaimed V-E Day! Victory in Europe! But the nagging horror of the war and Roosevelt's death had consumed the emotions of America. As the Pacific combat intensified, thousands of America's finest were killed. Scarcely four months after Roosevelt's death, the greatest horror of mankind came in August 1945 when Truman made the monumental decision to drop the atomic bomb on Hiroshima and Nagasaki. His decision saved an estimated one million Americans; it obliterated over 100,000 Japanese.

Still smarting from the sneak attack at Pearl Harbor and the loss of American lives in the Pacific, most felt no remorse. But scientists felt guilt about contributing to mass slaughter. The world was no longer the same. If the Depression had not changed America and the world, the new threat of universal annihilation certainly had.

When the news broke on August 14, "V-J Day," that we had won "victory over Japan," uptown Baltimore became a teeming mass of screaming, crying, laughing, kissing humanity. Ear-splitting air-raid sirens wailed; ships' horns and car horns blasted; radios heralded the news; and church bells pealed and pealed and pealed. On the lamppost at the hub of Baltimore and Light Streets, a stuffed body of Japan's Emperor Hirohito had been hanged in effigy.

On their way home from the Peabody Conservatory with their children, Tom and Alice were caught in the mobs. To avoid the crush of joyous celebrants, Tom hoisted Rosette onto his shoulders and Alice lifted Tommy.

But to Alice this was not a happy celebration, given the questionable alliance with Russia. She screamed : "What's wrong with everyone? War is a bunch of crap! We're all idiots!" But no one heard her. Out of habit and frustration, she began praying aloud in Italian. She was sure that back home her mother-in-law was sitting in quiet solemn gratitude and that her parents were kneeling in the reception hall before their beloved statues praying their thanks.

On their way home from war, two of Tom's brothers stopped in Baltimore. What a joyous reunion it was! Before going home to their mother, they wanted to unwind and, like many servicemen, wished to satisfy some of their simple cravings for American food. New radio commercials and new music amused them. There was so much catching-up to do. From their uptight behavior and obvious fatigue, their combat experience was readily noticeable, though they did not discuss it or complain.

What a generation of manhood! They had helped their parents through the Depression and served their country selflessly — scarcely twenty years after they came to America! When the troop ship pulled into New York Harbor and Lee Sapienza saw the Statue of Liberty for the second time in his life, he was overjoyed. When he walked into his house and embraced Lena and Louis, now three, the reunion overwhelmed him. He lifted his son, who cried out joyously to his cousin Billy, "See! Now I have a Daddy, too!"

Postwar America became preoccupied with material necessities. Money was plentiful. Goods were scarce. Appliances were worn. Homes were in demand. In wartime, Truman had instituted the Office of Price Administration to hold the price ceiling. Now that it was abolished, demands for goods and wage increases helped prices to spiral. There was a profusion of marriages and babies. Military Quonset huts were converted to housing and commercial use.

Thousands of war brides and their children clamored for entry into the United States. Thousands more postwar refugees applied for admittance. Initially, American consuls had been ordered to grant visas only to those who would be useful to the United States, but in the last weeks of 1945 President Truman ordered the barriers to be let down. Over 3,000 refugees a month were granted visas, provided they were healthy, non-Nazis and unlikely to become public charges. They would be cleared before they reached Ellis Island.

Defense plants converting to peacetime manufacture sized down. At Baltimore's Westinghouse plant, departments were reorganizing. Union employees with the right skills received priority according to seniority, while plant supervisors were rerouted according to corporate politics. Whereas wartime criteria had rewarded multiple skills, now connections rather than ability earned advancement. Deep-seated anti-Catholic and anti-Italian sentiment and strong Masonic political connections influenced ingrained corporate thinking and decisions.

Among the positions Westinghouse posted, listing desired skills, education and experience, was a management position requiring education and experience in Business Administration, Cost Accounting, Time and Motion Study, and knowledge of specific skills in manufacture. The requirements perfectly suited Tom Sapienza's education and experience. He applied for the job and earned an interview with the Radio and X-ray Division Plant Manager and several department heads. In diminishing order of their importance, they sat like ducks in a row behind their brief cases alongside the conference table, dressed in similar smartly-tailored suits and ties. Tom felt confident.

The manager complimented him highly for the outstanding job he had done during the war. His colleagues concurred and smiled appropriately in unison. The Manager moved toward Tom and put his arm across his shoulders and said patronizingly: "Tom, you're well-qualified for this position, and I like you and the fine work you've done for Westinghouse. You've looked out for the company first. But I have to be honest with you. You're Italian and Catholic and this is as far as you go!" The others in lower pecking order nodded politely through pasted-on smiles.

The comment cut him deeply. Tom's jaw hardened. He stood tall and thundered, "You're right! I've held up the roof when it was about to fall in! No by damn! This is as far as YOU go! I don't need you. Keep your job!" Without waiting for reactions, Tom stormed out — head held high — arms swinging widely.

By the time he arrived home, he had made a decision and had devised a new career plan. That night, Alice saw a grown man weep when he said, "Honey, I quit my job!" And he shared with her the incident and his plan for a new career. "I'll never be humiliated again by any prejudiced bunch of sons-of-bitches! The damned corporation used me, chewed me up and spit me out! I'll make it on my own and we *will* survive!"

Alice never forgot the hurt and anger they shared. Tom's words would stick in her craw for years to come. Rejection at the beach, refusal to sell Italians a house, and now biased denial of an earned promotion were really too much to tolerate, and only strengthened their resolve to leave Baltimore and return to the warmth of their family in Pittsburgh.

A defiant Tom rationalized that in a corporate bureaucracy his talents would be limited and wasted, his ability unchallenged. Tom thrived on challenges. With his new ideas and the confidence and creativity to carry them out, he would live by his wits and start a business. He thought of his Corso uncles. To the boy who had been a mini-entrepreneur at nine and a business owner during his college years, the idea was not new. To start with, Tom had two weeks of vacation pay coming, in addition to their savings. "This has changed our lives forever," he said.

Observing business trends and their relation to the war's end, Tom had noted that service businesses were unaffected by shortages. With limited capital, his options were limited. He recalled his interest in Bernie Topaz' dry cleaning plant, where he had occasionally helped his friend and shared his ideas about the disadvantages of naphtha cleaning solvent. Naphtha held a lingering odor and clothing took longer to dry. A new synthetic rapid-drying cleaning solvent, perchlorethylene, or "perc," had been developed. Tom had formed creative ideas about using "perc" to deliver faster dry cleaning service. With his knowledge of chemistry, his experience in Time and Motion Study, and Industrial Cost Management, Tom reasoned that the dry cleaning business would be inventive and profitable. And Topaz' positive reaction confirmed Tom's resolve.

The pull home was strong. Tom missed his family. Frank was still battling osteo; his brothers were home from war. He felt compelled to return. Despite the advantages of the Peabody Conservatory, Alice wanted her children to grow up among a loving family. The adversities they suffered away from home had bound their close marriage even closer.

When they announced their decision to move home and go into business, Sebastian and Rosa were happy but worried. Maria was cautious and offered this advice: "Hmmm . . . *Il sarto fa cento mesuri e uno taglio,* Tom. The tailor he measura the clotha one hundred times and cuts it only one time," she repeated.

And optimistic Paolo thought of his experience with Alex and said encouragingly: "Looka, Tom, bread you earn witha your owna hands taste better. You needa soma money? I can help you leettle bit." Their siblings and in-laws were excited to have them come home.

With such strong support, Tom put his plans into action in late June 1948. He would establish a one-hour dry cleaning service, the first in Pennsylvania, using the fast-drying "perc" solvent. By the end of their two-week vacation, with the help of Al Gerson, their equipment salesman, they had located a business site on East Ohio Street, the heart of North Side's neat little German community.

When Tom returned to Westinghouse to give his formal two-week resignation notice, his boss was stunned and urged him to reconsider. Tom refused, stifled his anger and said curtly: "When I'm gone you'll find that my quitting is *your* loss and my gain." The comment proved to be prophetic!

But Tom did not leave Westinghouse without regret. The company had been good to his family. Because his father had been a radio broadcasting pioneer, Tom had taken particular interest in following its development. During his work at the Radio Division, Tom had acquired an original manuscript that detailed the birth and progress of radio broadcasting. Its pages revealed each step in the development of communication, and a wealth of technological and broadcasting "firsts." Tom would treasure this piece of history.

Reading the manuscript caused him to reminisce about the twenties, when he and his brother Lee had been Frank Conrad's newspaper carriers, fascinated by his broadcasts from his garage. On the radio crystal set Sebastian had built, Tom remembered hearing Conrad broadcast news items and music on phonograph records, and urging listeners to buy those phonograph records at the Hamilton Music Store in Wilkinsburg. Tom was surprised that Conrad's monumental contributions were barely recognized in the manuscript — especially because he had discovered short-wave radio broadcasting, which sent the human voice around the world for the first time. "Typical corporate ingratitude and exploitation," Tom mused. He wondered whether Conrad, a baptized Catholic married to a non-Catholic, had acknowledged, or denied, his religion. The thought disturbed him. He impatiently cleared his desk, and remembered the hurt he had felt when he heard: "You're Italian and Catholic and this is as far as you go." He piled his records and memorabilia into a carton and resolutely walked away without a backward look — or regret.

That evening Tom's company friends, Tommy Messaraco and Charlie Arceri and their wives, took him and Alice to dinner. Charlie and Alice, avid ballroom dancers, had become great dancing partners. "We'll miss you," Messaraco said, and expressed his anger and insecurity with the company. "Tom, I predict that heads are gonna roll after you're gone. I'll come to Pittsburgh and tell you that myself." And in fact, in one year, the prediction came true. Messaraco relayed the message to Tom with joy!

It was mid-June and Rosette had finished first grade at Saint Agnes School and her second year at the Peabody Conservatory. When her piano teacher bade her goodbye, she predicted that Rosette would have a wonderful career in music. Alice was pleased at the excellent music foundation she had received, but sad to leave the Conservatory.

Tom spent the last two weeks in Baltimore taking his little family swimming in the Chesapeake Bay. They made their last visit to Washington, D. C., and dined in their favorite restaurants, where they got their fill of lobster and hardshell crabs. Alice shopped for the last time at the great outdoor Baltimore markets and cooked varieties of fresh fish nearly every night. The family partied with their neighbors at the regular bimonthly block party. They cooked outdoor feasts, and spun phonograph records from the latest Broadway musicals — *Annie Get Your Gun, Carousel,* and *Kiss Me, Kate.* Their friends expressed their disapproval at the corporate bigotry impelling them to leave Baltimore. And the children said a sad goodbye to their playmates.

On June 30, 1948, the Forest Hills Moving Company from Pittsburgh came to move them home. They retrieved their remaining personal items and packed the car. Alice wondered what new challenges lay ahead of them. She thought of the maxim her mother had quoted to Paolo before he made his first trip to America, and said: "Tom, *Chi lascia la strada vecchia per quello nuova, sa quello che lascia ma non quello che trovo.* " Then rhyming it in English repeated: "He who takes a new road and leaves the old behind, knows what he leaves, but knows not what he will find."

And Tom answered: "Enough! The past is irrevocable. We can't change it. We learn from it and move on!" And they sang their way home to Pittsburgh.

Chapter 17

Home Again

At the end of World War II, returning soldiers brought home invisible emotional scars as a result of atrocities they had seen in the very villages their parents had left to come to America. Italian sons who had come here as children held ideals opposed to those of Hitler and Mussolini, and were particularly disturbed to be sent to fight against their fellow Italians as "the enemy."

But despite their emotional and physical injuries, for most returning veterans postwar readjustment held fewer problems than wives, mothers, and psychologists had anticipated. Although some would undergo long-term damage, government services were there to help them. Under the generous G.I. Bill of Rights, veterans who chose to attend college were awarded college tuition, with paid living expenses. Unlike in the Depression years, jobs were available.

By the end of World War II, it was clear that America had neglected her cities. The need for urban renovation became inextricably bound to the need for better highways. By now the auto craze and the trucking industry had grown considerably. There were over four million cars itching to travel the nation's macadamized roads, if only to the drive-in movie theaters, which had enjoyed instant success. The need for better roads was obvious as war-weary Americans took to their automobiles. In an ambitious program in 1944, the first funds had been assigned for road-building, which included an urban renewal program and plans for building 41,000 miles of interstate highway.

Although America was living under the fearsome cloud of the atomic bomb, Tin Pan Alley and Broadway reflected optimism by creating upbeat musicals. Another opiate to ease anxiety came from entertainers who moved easily from vaudeville and radio to the new kid on the gadgets scene, television. TV's "rrreally big shew" absorbed America, as Ed Sullivan launched the careers of personalities like the hip-swiveling Elvis Presley and the Beatles, who ushered in a dramatic change in music with Rock and Roll.

Home Again

The steady rise of an immigrant son, Frank Sinatra, gave Italians reason to be proud and hopeful that anyone could excel even in the face of ongoing discrimination. Outside of the WASP social circle, where Italians were not accepted, Frank Sinatra, The Voice, was the trailblazer for his fellow Italian singers Dean Martin, Tony Bennet, and others who had Americanized their names to "make it."

It was a new America, welcoming with open arms those patriots who made adjustments from defense lines and defense plants to postwar life. Rosa welcomed each of her sons with a fervent *grazie* to the *Bella Madonna*. Delfino and Liborio returned to work for Westinghouse, where their father still worked and still performed with the orchestra and band.

Santo refused excellent job offers from various airlines because of his traumatic recollection of the sound of warplanes he had serviced for bombing missions. Former high school training led him to purchase a printing press and begin a small side business at home. He finally settled for the quiet atmosphere of the Carnegie Institute, where he worked in its Book Binding Department.

After the war, as Homewood's first-generation Americans became more successful, an ethnic transformation began. They shed some of the age-old customs their parents had brought from Europe, and looked to suburbia. From being Italian-American they became American-Italian, and finally, the new generation became American-American.

Social and moral habits changed. Many women, with new attitudes, wanted equal rights in the market place. Though the conventional stay-at-home wife was still the accepted norm, the seeds of the Women's Liberation Movement were germinating. Women abandoned their ironing boards and soap operas, and sought new roles beyond the world of "kids and kitchens." Anne Palombo, following the trend of wives working to help achieve family goals, resumed her job at the bank, now that her children Paul, Lauretta and Richard were in school. Sophia was happy in her traditional role as stay-at-home Mom for her four sons, Paul Martin, Joseph, Raymond and Michael. She and Grace ultimately became caregivers for Paolo and Maria.

During the forties, attitudes toward marriage and family had had a permanence about them. But after World War II, there was a noticeable decline in the family structure. Divorce rates crept up. In Catholic families divorce was unacceptable. Couples made their marriages work. In the Palombo and Sapienza families divorce was unthinkable! But it happened.

Louis Palombo wanted a traditional stay-at-home wife and mother. Mary sought to be liberated from his dominance. They were on fragile religious and philosophical ground. Mary's agnostic father was indifferent. Maria and Paolo, who were strongly religious, nevertheless hesitated to meddle into the couple's private life. The divorce took an emotional and physical toll on Maria.

When they divorced, recognizing the futility of trying to keep their son, Mary unselfishly relinquished him to Louis' care, remarried and moved away. She knew that little "Sonny" would be raised in a loving atmosphere among his cousins.

If Sonny was unhappy, his quiet demeanor did not reveal it. He and his father were very close. They became a regular part of their extended family, where on Sundays and holidays they shared family fun. Weekdays were devoted to homework and "guy" activities. Eventually, the Catholic Church granted Louis an annulment. He married Jane, a compliant young career woman, whom he controlled.

Conversely, Tom encouraged Alice to be independent. From the outset, even when women played traditional roles at home, they became a close and compatible business team. "A turtle doesn't make progress unless it sticks its neck out," he assured Alice when they opened their business. In a new woman's role, she stuck her neck out.

Progressive, Tom and Alice invested all their savings in equipment and registered their enterprise as *Pennsylvania's Original One Hour Cleaners*. And thus nearly broke, but born of immigrant grit and a will to survive, they embarked on a challenging journey.

To Italians, *la famiglia è tutta,* the family is everything. Tom and Alice had enjoyed a special bond with Sophia and brother Tom, who housed the new entrepreneurs for a few weeks. Brother Tom helped remodel their store. Sophia lovingly cared for the children while Alice worked. Their kids laughed, played, practiced music, loved and scrapped in true sibling fashion. They accepted Sophia's discipline, a spin-off from the good nuns who had raised her.

Tom and Alice rented a house nearby. Paolo and Maria visited them often, Paolo planting a vegetable garden for them around the edges of their large back lawn. One day, the garden drew the attention of a hungry itinerant who begged for food. Alice had just prepared supper and offered him a plate. Just as he was settling near the back door to eat, Tom, on the verge of tears, laid down his fork and said, " I just can't eat. That poor man shouldn't be out there alone." He left the table and brought the stranger inside to have supper with his family. A "good Samaritan" parable from the Bible could not have been a more touching and valuable example. Little Tommy remembered it emotionally years later. Tom's loving gesture had planted the seeds of compassion.

An enthused Tom Sapienza explored the concept of fast-service dry cleaning. Based upon his knowledge of chemistry, he had devised a method to eliminate water and solvent-soluble soil in the same dry cleaning cycle, using a little moisture. Since perchlorethylene dried fast at low temperatures, he could give one-hour service!

Tom was in his glory experimenting! He stood before his spotting board, happily whistling as he challenged difficult stains. He built a still to distill and filter solvents to assure high quality, and used a special ingredient that kept wools soft and unwrinkled. His employees amusedly called him the "mad scientist" when he bought an electric paint can shaker to mix his secret formula. In short, Tom had conceived what, years later, came to be known in the industry as the "charge system," which used a combination of solvent with a small amount of water and detergent. The founding of the *One Hour Martinizing* chain was copied and styled after Tom's idea.

From his management experience, Tom had learned much. He reasoned that because a service business depends largely on labor for its success, its employees are its most valuable asset. His work crew became a family. Seeing a need, Tom helped found the Pennsylvania Retail Dry Cleaners Association, which became a professional and social outlet for members who shared information about the synthetic fabrics market.

But synthetic fabrics and the new "perc" solvent created problems for inexperienced "perc" plant owners and clothing retailers who suffered many damage claims. To combat the trouble, Kaufmann's department store, having heard of Tom's expertise from solvent salesmen, engaged him to test the dry cleaning performance of synthetic fabrics. As a result, Tom, a problem-solver, approached Governor Lawrence in Harrisburg and spearheaded a law requiring manufacturers to attach warning and cleaning direction labels to clothing, thereby limiting the dry cleaners' liabilities. The clothing-labeling practice was born because of Tom's insight.

At that same meeting, he lobbied Governor Lawrence to have the dry cleaning of clothes exempted from the luxury sales tax. In the end, his arguments won over an angry Governor. Tom was satisfied. Fast, safe service was a hit! But the dry cleaning industry was unaware of Tom Sapienza's important contributions.

Life was normal again. Despite their long working hours, Tom and Alice were deeply involved in church affairs — Alice as president of the Parents' Society, Tom as president of the Holy Name Society and chairman of St. Vincent dePaul Society. The latter, a discreetly charitable organization, pledged to keep their work confidential. They helped the poor and buried their dead. But Tom broke that confidence one day when he told Alice that Jim, her beloved childhood hero who had twice saved her life, had died.

At the funeral mass, Tom and Alice knelt in the front pew behind his plain, cheap wooden casket. There were no grieving friends, no family, and no eulogy. Miss Mangle softly played the solemn, high-pitched funeral lament as Father Ceradini quietly performed the Latin Low Mass. As she prayed for Jim's soul, Alice wept and reminisced about her precious Jim. She touched the casket lovingly as Frank LoPresti, the church sexton, wheeled it by on its way to a pauper's grave. A treasured part of her childhood went with her dear Jim. Alice buried her grief in work.

Brother Santo, interchangeably called Bill or Sundy, had broken from Italian custom and married a lovely Irish Catholic girl, Catherine [Kitty] Smith. They moved into the first-floor apartment that brother Lee's wife, Lena, had occupied during the War. Kitty eventually helped Bill Sapienza produce six beautiful children — to Rosa's delight. Their first daughter was named Concetta, Rosa's middle name. Kitty yielded her baby to Rosa's care. They communicated fairly well, as mothers do in any language. But for their remaining children, Bill and Kitty departed from traditional names: William, Michael, Raymond, Carol, and Catherine.

Eventually, three of the six Sapienza sons would marry non-Italian women. The very ethnic Rosa Sapienza made progress toward American customs, but not toward speaking English, so that her family interpreted for her American daughters-in-law.

Home Again

Rosa had accepted the foreign intrusion into her clan. Duffy, her loyal son, married a Polish girl, Emma Liptak, who was equally loyal to her own mother. Sympathetic to Rosa's needs, Delfino, who shopped for her, had been her greatest support. But his loyalty roused competition and animosity between the equally dominant Emma and Rosa. The conflict soon led Duffy to seek a separation, and he moved home. Thereafter, Rosa viewed her other daughters-in-law differently.

Eventually the couple reached an accommodation. Through a common bond, their little Joey, Emma made a tenuous peace with Rosa, who wanted desperately to enjoy her eighth grandson. Joey, seemingly unaffected by the rift, developed a strong and lasting bond of love and respect for the clan.

Rosa's primary worry was that her disabled Frank was not destined to marry. She wondered who would care for him when she was gone. But Frank wasted no pity on himself. Instead, he earned his high school diploma. His dear friends, Joe Pegnato and Tony Renda, had stood by Frank while his brothers were at war. They saw him through five operations and spent long afternoons several times a week helping Frank from his bed, to his wheel chair, to his crutches so that his mother could go about her chores. If anyone was about to relinquish hope, none showed it. How could Rosa not love these boys? They moved his bed to an alcove off the busy dining room where Frank could observe activity. And nearly every day, Tony and Joe closeted themselves with him.

September 17, 1948 had been no different. It was evening and the family had gathered to celebrate grandfather's birthday. Frank's door had been locked for nearly two hours. The boys would admit no one. When Mother and Father tried to enter, they assumed that Frank was indisposed.

Finally, Joe called through the door: "We're ready to open the door. Light the birthday candles and start singing — loud!" Everyone sang.

As the door opened, Frank walked in, without crutches! Mother shrieked: *"Santa Maria!"* Father wept quietly. The family chattered and laughed and cried. At last after eight torturous years, Frank had won his battle! That night was the start of a new series of successes for him.

Through his housebound years, television had brought the world to Frank and to the clan. Every Sunday evening the family had gathered around the twelve-inch DuMont TV screen to enjoy the Ed Sullivan program and other shows. And what a gathering it was! Rosa was in her element, serving coffee, red jello and *biscotti*. Her reaction to television characters and her comprehension were both selective.

She loved wrestling. "Ieeeah!!" she screeched as she cheered Bruno Sammartino, vowing that they were related. Rosa blew kisses to Johnny Carson who was "Junnie Corso," a distant relative who had her maiden name. Who would dare contradict her? And, any female TV performer who was as corpulent as she, was her idol — especially Meeseesa Smeeet, Kate Smith, and Moleee Goldaberg. And how could she not esteem talent scout Ed Sullivan when he featured juggler Joe Pegnato, Frank's faithful friend, as Bobby Jule? Yes, 1948 had been a happy year for Rosa.

That year, a mysterious decision signaled the approaching urban change in Homewood when Father Carlin, without notice, closed Holy Rosary High School, causing its girl students to transfer to other schools and many of the families to move away. Some speculated whether Father Carlin's decision came from his superiors or was driven from his own biased perception of Homewood's changing ethnic makeup. It was no secret that this pastor preferred only the Irish in his parish, unlike Father Malady, who had befriended the Italian Community in establishing their church.

By the 1950's it was certain that a great geographic change would occur. Pittsburgh was at the height of its famed Renaissance I, led by Mayor David Lawrence, who later became Pennsylvania's governor. During his last term, longtime, low-key plans to build a Civic Arena were unveiled in late 1957, and scarcely a year later, ground was broken on April 25, 1958! The plans had called for the destruction of the all-Black Lower Hill.

Pittsburgh was about to undergo a social trauma via massive redevelopment and the Law of Eminent Domain. This law, which originated in England in 1625, gave the government the awesome power to "take" private property for "public use." The concept of the "right of taking" had migrated from Europe to America. The Civic Arena would qualify as "public use," just as another area — the North Side — was soon destined to qualify for "public use."

The intent to demolish all-Black neighborhoods on the Hill would force a vast migration of poor Blacks to other areas. With few communities open to them, multiethnic Homewood and East Liberty were the most likely options. The mostly German North Side, the strongly Italian Bloomfield, and Squirrel Hill, which was solidly Jewish, would not be affected.

Soon visionary and greedy real estate operators stimulated panic by urging East End Whites to sell their homes below value, because of impending neighborhood transformation. In turn, these homes were sold to Blacks at significantly higher cost. Realtors profited big-time while an ordinance, operating under the guise of urban redevelopment and the Law of Eminent Domain, raped the Hill.

Eventually, this unjust Law would play a vital part in American legislation and become a cursed force that would reshape Pittsburgh. It would have an adverse impact on the economic and emotional life of North Side citizens — and Tom and Alice Sapienza. Ironically, they had gone into business to escape the injustice of anti-Italian and anti-Catholic prejudice, only to encounter another form of injustice — legal and political discrimination.

Tom began thinking about owning a home; but he had to fight his strong-willed mother, who objected to his plans for buying a home in the suburbs. The Depression had left Rosa obsessed about losing her home. And the trauma of separations had threatened her security. She objected to their planned move away from Homewood and blamed the idea on Alice, who, like Lena, became the target of her wrath and her litany of undeserved accusations.

Exasperated with Rosa's suspicions, Tom decided to teach her a lesson. "Mother is a fierce mother and I understand; but neither you or Lena deserve to be scapegoats for her frustration. I love her dearly, but I'm going to tell her that I won't visit her 'til she rethinks her behavior." Alice pleaded with him not to be so harsh, but he stayed away for months. "Honey," he said, "When Mohammed won't go to the mountain, the mountain must come to Mohammed. And she will, you'll see when our baby is born."

On August 10, 1949, one day after Alice's birthday, their son Jimmy was born. Two days later, a contrite and tearful Rosa came to the hospital to see her new grandchild. Tom and Alice embraced her warmly and never uttered a word of censure. The matter was permanently dropped. Breaking away from Italian tradition, the baby was given the Biblical name, James Phillip — with no objections from Rosa.

She was overjoyed when a few days later on August 13, Robert Sebastian was born to Lee and Lena. While Lena was a traditional stay-at-home mother, Alice stayed home to care for Jimmy only for the first year. Then he would be introduced to the commercial world and join his mother at work, where accommodations would be made for him.

As a toddler, Jimmy played quietly in his playpen or happily hammered nails into the wooden bottom support of a moveable clothes rack. He became his father's shadow. The Sapienza children literally grew up in "the back room" of their business. Raised in the public world, they became independent and social. They saw their parents at work and helped with chores at the shop and at home. They developed respect for hard work, a value often misunderstood by those whose parents had not known the immigrant experience of learning to live by their wits.

Tom's favorite poem was Henry Van Dyke's *Work*. A trivet on the Sapienza kitchen wall put it best: "The world owes you a living, but you must work hard to collect it." And work they did as they managed household chores and supervised educational and cultural activities. Music was as important as traditional education. The best qualified teacher was sought to teach the children piano, and grandfather Sapienza taught them clarinet, just as his own father had taught him. For years they lovingly remembered his advice: "Don't puffa the cheeks!"

By now, the Sapienza and Palombo families were reasonably content with life. The stresses of World War II were behind them. Notwithstanding an unpredictable Russia, a dim hope for world peace lay ahead. The United Nations had been founded at a world conference in San Francisco and given a permanent home in New York. But the effort at keeping peace was overshadowed by the nagging Red menace. Rosa prayed yards of rosary for world peace.

Since the end of World War II, Russia and the United States had engaged in a cold war of saber rattling, with the atomic threat hanging overhead. In August 1949, America's worse fears were confirmed when Russia exploded its first atomic bomb, named "Joe" for Joseph Stalin. The United States feared that if Russia ever decided to attack our cities, ten to fifteen million people might be wiped out in a single day. Nuclear scientists feared that this bomb could blow the globe to smithereens.

By the mid-fifties, many Americans, gripped with fear, constructed air-raid shelters beneath their homes, equipping these with chemical toilets, protective apparel, respirators, food, water, beverages, Geiger counters to detect radiation, and whatever else a family might need to remain underground.

The world faced an unpredictable future, as two nuclear superpowers competed for supremacy. Few decades in history had witnessed such destruction and enormous global changes. Naziism had brought the Holocaust, while Communism had brought a witch-hunt for "commies" by Senator Joe McCarthy. Despite nuclear fears and the fear of Communism, however, Americans searched for normalcy and tried to live ordinary lives.

But life is not always normal, or ordinary, or free of conflict, as Tom and Alice were to learn. The Greek myths of Sisyphus and of Damocles best describe the struggles that lay ahead for them. Sisyphus, King of Corinth, was condemned to Hades and doomed forever to roll a huge stone uphill, only to have it roll down again each time. And the ebullient Damocles was invited to a lavish banquet, where the tyrant of Syracuse, who wanted to teach him the perilous nature of happiness, seated him under a sword suspended by a hair. Fate likewise held impending doom for Tom and Alice, the unsuspecting victims of North Side's Eminent Domain.

But they had learned that life was a bucking bronco. If they rode deftly, met each challenge and stayed in the saddle, the bronco could be tamed — if not broken. If early 1950 was a precursor of things to come, the rest of the decade would surely challenge them. Indeed a clairvoyant might have advised: "Hold onto your hats, folks, you're in for a helluva ride!"

Chapter 18

The Sword of Damocles

America's response to Communist aggression and Russia's first atomic bomb blast came at the end of January 1950, when Truman announced the development of a new super missile — the Hydrogen bomb. Rosa followed developments in her Italian newspaper, feeling her security threatened by foreboding events in a faraway place called Korea. Would she have to give up another son?

Her concern was confirmed when, on June 25, a massive force from Communist North Korea rolled into South Korea and occupied most of the peninsula. The U.N. Security Council backed Truman when he ordered an American battalion of the 24th Infantry Division to the battlefield. For the second time in five years, America was at war. And once again young men were at risk. Rosa's rosary beads worked overtime.

Conditions worsened when General MacArthur, taking power into his own hands, publicly scorned U.S. policy and advocated the bombing of Communist China. For this unauthorized stance, Truman relieved him of his command. Although Truman's action saved thousands of lives, it caused great public controversy and did not prevent the drafting of young men to war. This time Rosa's youngest, Julius Sapienza, would be called into battle. Poor Rosa! Even her grandchildren were little comfort.

Once again, ironically, a war sustained the economy. For Tom and Alice, business was brisk. For soldiers home on leave who needed immediate service, it worked to their advantage. Tom never charged anyone in service to have their uniforms dry-cleaned. Nor did he charge to dry-clean priests' vestments, nuns' clothing, or altar scarves. Working customers became accustomed to quality and speed. As business prospered, he concluded that Westinghouse had "kicked him upstairs." But he was not complacent. Tom always rose to meet adversity. And it came.

Naphtha dry cleaning plant owners felt threatened by the success of fast service dry cleaning plants, fearing that the new concept would cut into their profits; for their equipment was obsolete and conversion to "perc" would be costly. They pushed for laws banning such dry cleaning plants and appealed to the Laundry and Dry Cleaners Union #209, headed by Bob Ross.

They targeted Tom and Alice. On July 27, 1951, without warning, a union picket appeared in front of their store with a sign announcing: "UNFAIR TO LABOR—SWEAT SHOP WAGES." Tom was furious! Why should he tolerate this lie and intimidation when their employees were being paid nearly twice above the established minimum wage, with overtime pay, volume bonuses and vacations? The union contract offered none of these.

Later that day Bob Ross called and informed Tom that the picket would disappear only when he complied with union demands. Outraged, Tom demanded to know what right they had to picket without first asking to meet. He would never forgive such sneak tactics. He soon learned that an injunction against picketing would not work.

That night Tom asked Sebastian to make a huge double sign. In professional script, it disclaimed the "sweat shop" myth: NO LABOR DISPUTE HERE! The next morning Alice, outwardly calm, hung the sign over her shoulders and picketed the picket — an unconventional behavior that drew public attention.

Traffic stopped on East Ohio Street. For two weeks she dogged the picket. Fellow businessmen came to encourage and cheer the couple on. Newspaper and television cameras appeared, and the incident was recorded on TV's first televised news series, the *Pitt Parade,* written by Bill Beal, and narrated by Bill Burns. Years later, the news item was taken from the KDKA TV archives and televised several times. The *Pittsburgh Press* and the *Post Gazette* tried to be neutral. Mr. Zehner of *The Sun Telegraph* apologized to Mrs. Sapienza for the pro-union slant a reporter had given the story, and secretly admired her spunk.

As the union intimidated Tom's employees, Tom gave them permission to join. He would hold them to the letter of the union contract: only seventy-five cents an hour, no bonuses and no vacations. Of course the employees, whose wages and benefits were much higher, scoffed at the idea and laughed as they passed the picket on their way inside to work. On hot days, Tom brought the weary picket cold drinks. Union customers brought their dry cleaning in the back door. Small plant owners cheered him on for taking up their fight.

The Sword of Damocles

The charade continued for nine months without success until Bob Ross approached Tom with a new ultimatum and threatened to put him out of business. And Tom — rarely a profane man — thundered: "You dumb bastard, I could have helped advance your union slave wages — if you had been gentleman enough to approach me before your sneak picket attack. It's nine months and your baby isn't born yet! Now, you son-of-a bitch, I'll never give in! This is a cock-fight between two game roosters — we fight till one of us dies — and it won't be me, I guarantee it!" Alice was proud. The next morning the picket was gone. The battle was won!

The Korean Battle persisted, however, and as long as Julius was in military service, Rosa stormed heaven. By the Grace of God and the Sicilian threats from Rosa to the *Bella Madonna*, Julius returned home safe. After the war he married a lovely, gentle Irish Catholic girl, Catherine Murphy. For a few years they and the first of their four bright children, Theresa Ann, Charles Sebastian, Gina Rose, and Daniel Edwin, occupied the apartment that Bill, Kitty and their children had outgrown.

Rosa was happy to have her family gathered around the table to enjoy good food and good-natured — but loud — arguments on any subject. Politics always fueled a lively dispute among father, mother and sons. Before the 1952 presidential election, for example, the family was seriously divided between Adlai Stevenson and Ike Eisenhower. Sebastian and Tom favored the intellectual Stevenson. Rosa strongly favored Eisenhower and stood her ground arguing "I like Ike" in near-perfect English. To strangers who did not understand such exchanges, they appeared rude. To the family they were simply spirited, for amid the happy confusion there was *respect.*

Respect was the underlying attitude of growing up Italian-American. Families laughed at themselves and at each other. For instance, Paolo's kids were amused at his fractured English, but dared not show disrespect at his mispronunciations. "Construction" became "scondruction," and "Boy Scout" translated to "boy *scalzo*" or "barefoot boy." And when Paolo pointed to his eyebrow and said "Looka me hona the eye," that meant serious trouble. Italian kids learned to read gestures. Certain looks or gestures spoke volumes. Paolo's non-verbal communication was perfectly clear. If Papa knocked on his head, he was saying: *"Sei testa dura -- you are hard-headed."* If he opened his hand palm up and moved it from side to side, or if he put four fingers between his teeth palm down — look out: *"Non farmi arrabiare!*

Don'ta maka me mad!" And when he brushed four fingers under the chin he meant: *"Non' m' importa.* I don'ta care." A forefinger next to the nose, with the other in the ear, rebuked: "You are a *malandrino* — a ruffian!" But a forefinger twirled into the cheek was the ultimate compliment to the cook. What a repertoire!

Maria was now completely blind. She and Paolo sold their home and moved next door into a second-floor apartment in Grace and Mike's home. The grandchildren, Rose Marie and Angelo, had enjoyed the rich experience of growing up near their *"Mamu"* and *"Tatone"* in a bilingual Italian culture. Both retained their Italianism.

First-generation Americans had the best of two worlds. Those who grew up in Homewood were enriched from the many cultures brought there by their parents. The fabric of the neighborhood was undergoing gradual change. Whites abandoned their community as the influx of Blacks from the Hill moved in. But not everyone fled Homewood simply because of its ethnic change. Children of immigrants, imbued with the spirit of advancement, would have left anyway to build or live in newer homes, just as their parents and American-born forebears had done.

Some residents found it necessary to leave Homewood because community institutions failed them. Without Holy Rosary High School for girls, Catholic families felt deprived and migrated to other parishes like Saint Bede's in Point Breeze. The "browning" of Homewood escalated, changing its racial pattern.

As first-generation Americans went in search of life in suburbia, Mother of Good Counsel's new Church slowly began to lose parishioners. Another volume of residents from the Hill moved in, displaced by the power of the Law of Eminent Domain. Pursuant to this Law came a deluge of national legislation to meet the growing demands for new highways. But America was missing the point, for no one attempted to improve the laws that had victimized those whose properties were impounded to accommodate the demands of progress.

The era of nationalism was alive and well in the 1950's — and so was the economy. By 1953, the building boom was full-blown as families continued their exodus to the Eastern suburbs. Vast wooded areas were cleared to be replaced by whole developments of duplicate "cracker box" houses. Lyrics to a popular song described these homes: "They're all built of ticky-tacky and they all look the same."

Tom and Alice, being mavericks, decided against living in a housing plan. Their business was prosperous. They could look forward to providing their children with university educations and further training in the Arts. It was time to own a home. They found and purchased a half-acre lot in the established upper-middle-class community of Forest Hills and literally carved themselves into its beautiful woods. With their architect, John Pegnato, they designed a split rock home and hired two American-born Italian brothers who had learned their trade in Italy.

The Caretta brothers, who barely spoke English, were anxious to get their start in America. They found Tom Sapienza to be an understanding, astute businessman, who agreed to finance their first business enterprise. Through careful management, in 1952, they built a spacious, uniquely detailed home. When the home was finished, Tom and Alice rewarded the surprised brothers with a $1,000 bonus, a princely sum then. *The following day*, John Caretta left to go fight in the Korean War!

When Tom's family moved into their newly-furnished home in April 1953, Paolo planted a Paul's Scarlet rosebush at the patio's edge. Tom planted the first of one hundred rose bushes nearby, and soon a new hobby was born. The rose was a symbol for Tom; his mother and his Rosette carried that name. From their first anniversary, he sent Alice a rose for each year they were married.

They joined the Pittsburgh Rose Society, and the family became involved, helping Tom prepare for the annual rose shows. Soon his roses began winning ribbons. This led to another hobby — slide photography. Tom, who did nothing half-way, snapped at all hours of the day roses in various stages of bloom. He and Alice became fascinated with their history. When Alice joined International Toastmistress, a speech training program, they shared their hobbies and presented slide programs.

Whereas Tom and Sophia's house had been the center of family activity, the action now moved to Alice's and Tom's home. Although the new generation was American, no self-respecting Italian house was without Frank Sinatra, Dean Martin or Louie Prima records. The talented cousins formed a band and brought their instruments to celebrate holidays. Their love of music would one day launch several professional music careers.

The Sword of Damocles

Life in suburbia attracted other family members. The 1950's drew upwardly mobile city dwellers away from the ethnic patchwork called Homewood as the Hill was torn down. As a result, several factors caused a domino effect that brought massive, devastating changes in Pittsburgh's established business and residential communities.

At the heart of the transformation was the 1951 Highway Trust Fund Act, the first legislation to finance a national Interstate Highway System. Thus began the saga of Interstate Highway 279, and the tragedy of Pittsburgh's East Street "Valley of Indecision" where a new concept of Eminent Domain was born.

Massive urban renewal and super highway building programs were taking shape across America. Major legislation provided a special Trust Fund for construction, but paid little attention to relocation programs and assistance for condemnees whose properties were confiscated. No thought was given to improve the outdated and unjust Law of Eminent Domain to help them.

The extensive road building program, which would link major Northern cities to the St. Lawrence Seaway, began with the 1956 Federal Highway Act. Pittsburgh, a leading steel manufacturer, was the first big city to respond to the proposed highway network, which would both cut through and belt the city, with great impact upon Pittsburgh and the nation in the next two decades.

Undisclosed plans for the East Street Expressway had been on the drawing board since 1951. Studies and preparation for building Interstate Highway 279 were made without notifying or involving the people who would be directly affected. *This was the accepted practice of public works planning in America at the time.* And so in this tradition of *design-first-tell-later*, Richard Gordon and Associates mapped the expressway route and did preliminary soil tests in preparation for construction, and submitted roadway plans to the State Department of Highways. North Side business and home owners were about to become startled casualties of Progress. The North Side was thrown into turmoil. Hundreds of angry residents and business people began a fight against being forcibly displaced to accommodate a highway in the name of Progress! Tom and Alice soon found themselves in the thick of the fray — beneath the Sword of Damocles!

Another problem loomed. Although Paolo had always done a good share of house chores, by now Maria was unable to give their apartment meticulous care. In the true Italian tradition of the close-knit family, Tom and Sophia made room for their parents in their home. Sophia remembered Mother Regis' advice to her when she chose marriage over a religious life: "God may have a different plan for you."

Sophia showered her mother-in-law with love and compassion. Paolo and Maria appreciated the care they received in a loving house filled with four grandsons, visiting family and friends, and Chippy, their mongrel dog. Chippy, walking close by, looked out for Maria as she made her way through the house. He learned to understand commands in Italian, and to lie quietly with chin on his forepaws when the family, surrounded by neighborhood children — Black and White — prayed the Rosary together on the back porch.

The Italian Radio Hour was company for Maria in her hours of darkness. Singer Carlo Buti gave her special pleasure. And Paolo was great comfort. The two sweethearts often sat close, holding hands and reminiscing. Sometimes they sang together — religious hymns now. Maria, always particular about her appearance, would admonish her brood to tell her if she looked presentable when she and Paolo took their daily walk. The children and grandchildren became her eyes. At times, she became despondent. At times, she laughed at herself for doing something clumsy.

She and Paolo looked forward to their biggest goal in life — to celebrate their fiftieth wedding anniversary. Their wish was fulfilled and the family planned a great feast and celebrated at Holy Mass. The women cooked and baked the traditional seven-course celebration dinner from wedding *zuppa* to *dolci e noce*. Each course would be appropriately served with Paolo's red and white wines, and the happy couple would be toasted with special liqueurs. Only one thing would be missing: Father DeFrancesco to bless — and taste — the *vino* beforehand.

For the occasion, Maria wore Paolo's favorite dress and the special wrist watch that he had given her on their silver anniversary. She thought about the feasts that she had prepared with her daughters-in-law and her daughters. She wanted so much to be able to see all her children and grandchildren.

Paolo, still seeing her as his beautiful Red, sensed her gloom and said: *"Tu se ancora mia bella Rossa!"* She rewarded him with a flirtatious comeback and reached for his elbow.

The new Mother of Good Counsel Church was filled with celebrants. Maria looked radiant as Paolo led her to the Altar for a nuptial blessing. The years seemed to fall away, and any stranger who looked into her clear blue eyes might not recognize that she was blind. That day Alice saw a new beauty in aging — a new meaning of love and family. She prayed that her own happy marriage would reach its fiftieth anniversary.

Maria prayed above everything not to become a burden to her loved ones. But it was becoming more difficult for her to move about, for diabetes and hardening of the arteries had taken their toll. At last Maria took to her bed. She reminisced about her precious *Mamma Luigi*. She grieved that she had left her bedridden in Italy in 1916, and beseeched forgiveness. She prayed she would join her *Mamma* before becoming a heavy burden for her family.

Her eldest, Grace, who shared a great bond with her mother, now clung closer. All of her own and in-law children, all her grandchildren visited with her. Tom, Sophia and Grace nursed her tenderly. Alice divided her time between visiting Mama, helping Rosa, and working long hours with Tom, as the Law of Eminent Domain hung over their heads like Damocles' sword. Maria understood. Long ago she had unselfishly advised Alice that, if she had one hour to spare, she should give that hour to her husband, who needed her, and to her mother-in-law, who had no daughters to help her.

As Maria weakened, Paolo scarcely left her side. He spoke tenderly to her and prayed. On Holy Wednesday, April 14, 1955, Maria slipped quietly away, as she had wished, without fuss or mess. Paolo sobbed and sobbed to the very depth of his being, *"Oh Maria Giuseppa! Perche non vuo' fa' la Pasque con me?* Why don'ta you wanta to spend Easter with me?" His words haunted his children as they were consumed with the grief of losing their mother. A great love story ended that day.

Alice became *Elisa* when she walked into the funeral parlor where her mother lay shrouded in blue chiffon and silk. She walked to the casket and knelt to pray an emotional requiem to the *Bella Madonna*, secure that Mama was now with her Best Friend. She absorbed her mother's beautiful features. Maria looked more regal at rest than *Elisa* had ever remembered. Her soft blonde hair, gray-streaked at the temples, was combed back from her forehead. The sausage ringlets were gone.

Elisa heard Mama's laugh echoing through a distant tunnel. She heard her singing bits of opera, and saying nursery rhymes to her grandchildren in broken English, and smiled. "Hickory, dickory, dock; the mouse ran up the clock . . ." became "Deekely, deekely, duck; thay mowsa rrrun upa thay clocka . . ."

Elisa remembered Maria's parables that, like those of Jesus and Aesop, taught by precept and example. And recalled Mama's joy when her son-in-law Tom hugged her, or shared philosophical epigrams in Sicilian dialect. She caressed Mama's hands — the hands that had crocheted laces, woven fabrics, tended flocks, tilled the land, swept, and washed, and baked, and lovingly prepared her family's meals. *Elisa* loved Mama's hands best when they had rested comfortingly on her fevered brow. She felt an intense ache at her enormous loss and wanted to cry out — but sobs and tears would not come. Her throat closed. Deep inside her tortured soul *Elisa* wept. She pulled away from the casket and back to reality as Alice.

At the funeral mass, Paolo, stricken with swollen joints, hobbled on crutches. At the cemetery, he sat in the car with Alice, not far from the graveside. "Mama is in Heaven," he said. He examined familiar tombstones. His sense of humor surfaced as he remembered Jimmy's answer when Alice had eased his worry about dying and going to Heaven. Paolo said reflectively, "Like Jeemee says 'Heaven is nice, but I rather live in America.'"

For nearly a year Paolo showed a relatively cheerful facade before the world. He took long walks. From a friend who worked at the cemetery, the family learned that he visited Maria's grave every day and sobbed his grief. He spent long hours writing his poignant life's story, pouring out the depths of his emotions. His children comforted him. Mother's Day was especially painful for Papa when, on the Italian Hour, Carlo Buti sang *"Mamma, tutta la mia vita bella se tu."* His eyes misted and he whispered, "Maria, you really *were* my whole life." Sophia observed him and worried. The following March, Paolo became ill. Sophia was in his room making his bed as Paolo sat in his chair. Three-year-old Jimmy, whom she was babysitting that day, was nearby. Suddenly Paolo slumped forward, unconscious. Very calm to avoid alarming Jimmy, Sophia gently pushed Paolo back, propped Jimmy against his grandfather's legs and cautioned him to push back and sit still until she came back into the room. She made an emergency call to the doctor and returned to secure Paolo in the chair until she could get help to get him into bed. The doctor diagnosed a stroke.

Paolo remained unconscious as each of his children took turns sitting at his bedside night and day. Each held special memories of his optimism, courage and great love for them and for his *bella Rossa.* Sophia and Tom nursed him tenderly.

When he awakened three days later, the stroke had wrought massive brain damage. His large opaque blue eyes could only turn to Maria's picture and spill over with hot tears that he could no longer control. He spoke garbled sounds as he attempted to convey his thoughts. His facial expression reflected his frustration and his gratitude for little kindnesses. Through gestures, Paolo evoked a bit of humor as he teased little Jimmy that he had caught a rabbit. At every opportunity, he tried to leave the house for an uncertain destination.

Finally, when he became too difficult to manage and close observation failed, Paolo was reluctantly admitted into a sanitarium for his own protection. How distressful it was to see him weep like a lost soul each time the family left to go home after visiting him!

It had been a very painful decade. The family's immigrant ranks were thinning. Before Mama died, death had claimed *Zia* Arcangela and Grace's husband Mike.

A few weeks after Paolo's confinement, they were devastated when on that *maledetto gionoro,* Fourth of July 1956, the Grim Reaper came for Paolo! God had spared his life after the fire on July fourth many years before, and now He reclaimed the spunky immigrant with the spirit of Marco Polo.

The family had endured grief and suffered enormous pain, each in his or her own way. The seemingly stoic Sophia wept inconsolably. The anguish of her accumulated losses caused Alice to develop throat polyps and lose her voice. Doctor DiStio, a throat specialist, ordered a month of complete silence. Alice adapted.

Just as after Maria's death they found comfort in reminiscing about her, at family gatherings, they found solace in sharing priceless memories of Papa. They talked about his habit of whistling as he worked, or singing the *Pange Lingua* as he sat by the window reading his Italian Bible. They reminisced about his duets with Maria on those Sunday mornings, when their beautiful voices, and the aroma of *polpetti* and garlic frying in olive oil, beckoned the family to dress for *Santa Messa*. And recalled how they sang their own love through the opera they loved.

Taking the part of *Il Trovatore*, Paolo's clear tenor voice implored Leonora: " *"Non ti scordare di me . . ."* (" Don't forget me . . .")

And Maria's splendid soprano responded passionately: *"Di te, di te, non mi scorda . . ."* ("I will not forget you . . .")

Like other resilient migrants, Paolo and Maria from Compo Basso, Abruzzi, had succeeded in the face of adversity and discrimination. They made no excuses, placed no blame for their misfortunes. Through their strong faith, hard work and ability to adapt to each new challenge, they survived life beyond the Golden Door and gave America a family which would be an asset to their new country. Foremost, they left their children a legacy of courage and a loving attitude toward people of every nationality, color, religion, and social class. *Ben Fatto! Requiescat in pace!* Well done! May you rest in peace!

Chapter 19

And the Beat Goes On!

"It was the best of times, it was the worst of times . . ." Charles Dickens might have been forecasting the nineteen sixties in America. Where the fifties had been an age of conformity and apathy, the sixties moved to conflict and violence, bringing extreme changes in American traditions and behavior. To the generation of tradition-bound immigrants, America was becoming a fast-changing world, unlike the one they had once known. People raised and challenged all kinds of social issues on brutal streets, on unruly college campuses, and in dissenting government assemblies.

"It was the best of times" when advances in science carried Neil Armstrong, in the Apollo, to man's first walk on the moon, and when advances in equal rights took Marian Anderson, a Black woman, on her first walk across the Metropolitan Opera House stage.

"It was the worst of times" when three American leaders were assassinated: President Kennedy, his brother Robert, and Martin Luther King. These killings prompted an East German newspaper to write: "In the freest nation in the world, murder has become a political tool." The renowned melting pot had not melted and brought national unity. Eleven million Southern Negroes, sons of war heroes, were still deprived of their Constitutional right to vote. And Rosa Parks, a Black woman in Alabama who refused to relinquish her bus seat to a White man, was imprisoned.

But after the Supreme Court upheld her actions, a legal spark ignited the Civil Rights Movement. And Black voting power finally became a reality with the Voting Rights Act of 1964, signed by President Lyndon Johnson after President Kennedy's murder.

Transformation was occurring everywhere. After years of being pushed together, nationalities and races were pulling apart. Longtime residents of the idyllic, multiethnic Homewood community were confused and hurt at the division developing between young Blacks and the White population. Those Italians, who had known the sting of prejudice, did not have the usual biases attributed to Whites. They had broken bread with their Black neighbors; they had celebrated and cried together. Italians understood their fight against discrimination, empathizing when their Black brothers and sisters took to the streets or marched on Washington to demonstrate for their civil rights.

The once-homogenized community continued to lose its White inhabitants, as Pittsburgh's Renaissance moved ahead, and Eminent Domain relentlessly displaced people from the Lower Hill. For numerous reasons, not necessarily racist, Black and White families saw an opportunity to sell their homes and move to nearby boroughs and suburbs.

Rosa and Sebastian moved from Homewood to the Wilkinsburg business district to accomodate Frank's printing business. In their larger Swissvale home, Sophia Palombo took care of her ailing father until he died. In nearby Penn Hills, when Grace lost her husband Mike and her fifty-two-year-old stepson Angelo, she found comfort living under the loving care of her daughter Rosemary and son-in-law Eugene. Nursing homes were the last option for aging parents who had given so much. Given the strength of American-Italian family bonds and parental respect, it was presumed that family members simply took care of one another.

In that same spirit of caring, Italian families of Mother of Good Counsel Church opened their arms to a refugee family, when America's liberal "open-door" immigration policy welcomed the victims of Hitler's atrocities. During the Refugee Year in 1960, the church sponsored Jewish-Italian refugee, Isadore Levi, and his wife and two sons. Tom and Alice offered Isadore a full-time job in the Sapienza business.

Bruises and blue prisoner numbers deeply branded into their arms were mute testimony to the brutalities the Levis had endured in Nazi concentration camps. The grateful couple told how anti-Nazi Italians, priests, and nuns had helped in rescue activities. During the sixties protests, the refugees were astounded that their "Promised Land" could be so fragmented. But even as America appeared to be in upheaval, churches of other faiths accepted oppressed immigrants. Beneath the turmoil, America cared!

The decade "was the best of times" for the Sapienza family. On July 11, 1961, Sebastian and Rosa celebrated their fiftieth wedding anniversary at a special High Mass, surrounded by six sons, their wives, and sixteen grandchildren. As they renewed their wedding vows, their radiant faces belied the anxiety they had endured through the war years and Frank's illness.

And the Beat Goes On!

Son Bill and Kitty hosted an anniversary feast worthy of Italian tradition. Sebastian did what he knew and loved best — played his clarinet. The music that day had a special quality as he serenaded his love for Rosa, just as he had done a half-century ago, across the *strada* from her balcony in Palermo, Sicily. Years washed away as Rosa and Sebastian communicated only as true lovers can.

That time was special for Tom and Alice, too, who were soon to celebrate a bonus birth. In 1961, when Francis Sebastian was born on September 17, grandfather's birthday, their children were twenty-one, eighteen, and thirteen years old. Tom and Alice knew that *Nona* Sapienza would make her usual positive comments about this baby's superior qualities. Rosa, a late-in-life gift and caregiver to her parents, forecast: *"Questo bambino è il bastone da tua vecchiai.* This baby will be the cane for your old age." The prediction would prove to be accurate.

Tom and Alice, having learned much from experience, found new joy in having Frank, but knew that raising him held new challenges. Like Jimmy, his older brother, Frank would be raised in the back room of his parents' business. His values would be shaped in a decade when the youth culture bucked the establishment and wore defiance like a badge of honor. Little Frank, aware that he was a special gift, caught his father's adoring expression one day and said, "I know, Daddy, you're glad God gave me to you!" That perception and mature appreciation of life would one day sustain him through unforeseen boyhood tragedy. For his parents, calamity lay ahead.

Earlier in the year of Frank's birth, the Federal Bureau of Public Roads, without giving the public notice, had approved plans for Highway 79, the East Street Interchange, destined to connect with Interstate Highway 279, then with the St. Lawrence Seaway. But although details for the proposed expressway, the largest single public works project ever to be undertaken in United States history, were begun in 1961, they were not revealed until 1964, when the first public hearing was held on August 1 at the North Side Carnegie Library. Anxious citizens wanted to know when the demolition ball would strike their properties down, and sought assurance that they would be fairly compensated. The unsuspecting people of "Phase I," the first stage of the taking process, would benefit least from Pennsylvania's Eminent Domain Law. Like others, Tom and Alice who were in the Phase I plan, were marked victims of legal highway robbery!

After two years of fruitless protest, the rebellious mood of the sixties erupted when a handful of North Side Pittsburghers, led by optometrist Dr. Martin Krause, formed the Highway Emergency And Relocation Team, HEART, and became the force that challenged the law of Eminent Domain through protests and public meetings. This aroused the anger of President Richard Nixon who scorned protesters. What the team learned was alarming!

Forced to relinquish their properties, people were finding themselves at the mercy of insensitive administrators, whose guidelines determined what would be "fair value" for their real estate. Appeals from HEART for "just compensation" fell on deaf ears. Key properties were forcibly taken piece-meal. Officials were accused of "cherry-picking," that is acquiring properties and letting them deteriorate, thereby devaluing surrounding properties until it was time to negotiate with Highway Officials, who strongly denied these charges. Citizens complained that inflation and low compensation for their properties were causing them deep financial damage. The elderly, too old to fight or begin rebuilding, could not afford higher property replacement costs. Established businesses faced financial ruin. The bankrupted owner of Herman's Funeral Home and Crematorium committed suicide, because new restrictions banned crematoriums.

As forced settlements were made and relocation and legal costs consumed the former property owners' small payment settlements, lawyers and appraisers, builders and political agents got healthy pieces of that government pie. And the beat went on!

But as debates escalated, it was clear that Phase I victims definitely could not let themselves be uprooted without resistance. At angry protest meetings, they demanded that their rights be respected, and threatened to stop the highway! Meanwhile, the fact that over 5,000 families and businesses had fallen victim to forced taking and low settlements became fodder for the national media.

Bureaucracy moved slowly. It was clear that Tom and Alice, at the mercy of highway planners, would soon be forced out of business as promises of settlement fell through. Acquisition officials were suffocating them — figuratively stepping on their financial "air hose." It would take years to begin elsewhere and build a new customer base. Farsighted and realistic Tom began planning ahead, searching for an established business to save the dwindling income from their dying one.

And the Beat Goes On!

With the expectation of being paid the same dislocation damages as other Phase I condemnees, Tom looked to buy a fast service dry cleaning plant and found one in McKeesport. Following acquisition guidelines, he applied for "relocation assistance." But being leaders of the highway protest movement would cost Tom and Alice dearly. When they applied, Highway Acquisition officials denied them, claiming, "You aren't eligible for relocation assistance, you'll be a chain." Tom and Alice were stunned by the clearly discriminatory denial. They found it incredible that the Law of Eminent Domain could be used at the whim of the Urban Redevelopment Authority and Highway Department! Just settlement was not in sight.

Their next hope was a loan from the Small Business Administration. But S.B.A. red tape was also slow. The clock was ticking. Their next and last hope was to remortgage their home. Fortunately, with their excellent credit record, they received their new mortgage without question.

The S.B.A. loan came before the settlement from Eminent Domain. The timing was right, for an attractive building next door to brother Frank's was for sale by the owner, at an appealing price. Close to home, it would make a prime location for a long-cherished idea of a formal wear rental business. Tom and Alice approached Mellon Bank, using their new dry cleaning plant for collateral. Mr. Hallet, the bank manager, approved the transaction without hesitation, admiring the couple's confidence, ability and team work. With a nearly defunct North Side plant, and two new stores, one could now say, ironically, that Eminent Domain had forced them into becoming a "chain."

Tom, capable of working with his brain and his hands, would do the remodeling work in their new building. And Alice would manage the new store. Just as Tommy had done, Jimmy worked after school. Tom's expertise in quality dry cleaning and two seamstress clerks who lived in Wilkinsburg were a combination for success in their new formal wear rental business.

Upstairs, Rosette, newly-married to Bill Hillgrove, lived in the renovated apartment and music studio. They had met as Catholic high school students in television broadcasting at WQED, the world's first educational TV station. Rosette had enjoyed the privilege of being a young WQED TV pioneer, just as her grandfather Sebastian had enjoyed being a radio pioneer over the world's first commercial radio station, KDKA.

Bill and Rosette studied and performed as "television brats" under Sister Rosalie, who taught them at the studio on Clyde Street, before the beloved

Mr. Rogers came to WQED's new Oakland studio. Their careers took them to radio station WDUQ on their Duquesne University Campus, where they broadcast together.

Their career choices would destine them for success. Bill worked in radio and eventually moved to television broadcasting. Rosette taught music in Forest Hills public schools and eventually moved to Duquesne University's Music School, where she taught voice for twelve years. At her home studio, she taught piano privately and held student recitals upstairs. And next door, Sebastian taught clarinet.

Rosa was happy to have her family nearby. *"E bella la famiglia unite."* A united family is beautiful, she thought. The brothers and their families visited several times a week, and the spirited family discussions continued in Wilkinsburg as they once had in Homewood.

Though days were busy, Tom and Alice found time to celebrate their twenty-fifth wedding anniversary in Colonial Williamsburg, Virginia, the Rockefeller Foundation's tribute to Nativist American history. Perfectly manicured English gardens with topiary hedges, furnished period-style houses, both with "colonists" in attendance, were a tribute to Plymouth Rock immigrants. Costumed "slaves" played out the pretense for visitors. Alice wondered and noted that, conspicuous by its absence, was any tribute to the European non-Anglo immigrants who had come through forgotten Ellis Island.

At the hotel, the bellhop delivered twenty-five red roses. Alice hugged Tom hard. "You never forget, Honey. I love you!"

The next morning, they visited President Kennedy's grave at Arlington National Cemetery. With somber faces, people of every class and color from around the world stood at the grave site, captivated by the Eternal Flame. Alice studied each person and thought about another slain president — Abraham Lincoln. "I think Abe Lincoln missed the point," she said. "We really aren't born equal, nor do we stay equal, because in the end even the road to wealth and fame leads to the grave — and then we become equal!"

"That's a profound thought, Honey. I'm sure you'll write a poem about it. We'll do a program about this trip," Tom said, clicking his camera for another potential slide show. His hobby in rose-growing and photography, and Alice's public-speaking skills, made a great combination for a variety of slide shows they presented.

And the Beat Goes On!

Life was full. There was always a rose show, a pigeon race, a speech contest, a high school forensic competition for her and Tom to judge, or some family celebration to attend. On May 16, 1966, at Holy Mass, the Palombo family celebrated the fiftieth anniversary of Maria's arrival at Ellis Island with her children. The sun shone through the stained glass window that Paolo had donated to Mother of Good Counsel's new church, which was not far from the empty little brick church that Paolo had helped to build many years ago. Alice missed the little church of her childhood.

She prayed for her parents' souls, and for the many brave immigrants who had come to America, expecting not a free pass but only an opportunity to achieve. By their example and tenacity, their children had learned and appreciated the merit of hard work, the value of education, and the privilege of living in America. With justifiable pride, Alice smiled as she thought of the Palombo and Sapienza family achievements.

Later that same month, May 1966, there was reason to celebrate again. As winner of the International Toastmistress speech contest in Pittsburgh, Alice was sent to compete at the Regional level in Minneapolis, Minnesota. By coincidence, her second cousin, who had traced the family to Pittsburgh, lived there with her mother Nicola, and her Uncle Pietro Palombo, the children of *Zio* Valentino, who had raised little Paolo when he was orphaned. Alice planned to visit them. The experience shocked, grieved, and thrilled her, for their looks and their mannerisms were exactly like her father's. Oh, how she wished Papa was alive!

What a decade! Later that month, Tom won the "King of the Show" trophy in Pittsburgh's Bicentennial Rose Show. Receiving the trophy prompted an incident that would one day greatly affect young Tommy. Tom studied roses the way he studied homing pigeons. His award taught him a lesson that he shared with Tommy, a spirited late-bloomer who made it into college after four challenging years at Central Catholic High School.

One afternoon when he and Tommy were in the rose garden, Tom shared his thoughts. "Look, Son," he said, "getting through college is tougher than finishing high school. It may take more than four years to graduate, but you'll do it. You could even come out King of the Show like this Christopher Stone rose. It was a runt when I planted that bush. But when it won King of the Show, no one asked me how long it took to develop into a winner." Tommy never forgot.

And the Beat Goes On!

When he graduated from Youngstown University, he stood humbly among the Honor graduates, wearing his gold cord of distinction. After the ceremony, Tommy hurried toward his parents. Remembering his mother's thwarted desire to attend college, he said, "Mother, I told my Dean that for all your help, your name should be on the bottom right side of this diploma. . . . And, Dad, I guess I made King of the Show. You should be wearing this gold honor cord." Tom and Alice never forgot his tribute.

By 1967, the Vietnam War and violent anti-war protests were at their peak. For the first time in American history, thousands of young men refused to be sent overseas to fight a war that was non-threatening to America. Many protesters who fled to Canada were the offspring of grandparents who had struggled to migrate to America.

Ugly war tragedies that were televised every day outraged Tom, who was strongly opposed to the war. He agreed with the young rebels, though he did not voice it publicly. But Frank expressed his father's protest in Bible class and earned a reprimand for it. "Then why do the Bible, and you, teach me 'thou shalt not kill?'" he asked the good nun. She wrote a note home.

His father answered her note curtly. "He's right! I'm proud!"

Jim, now a college student, was also opposed to the unwinnable war. But he did not quite fit the sixties rebellious youth culture. On American campuses many — not all — students were influenced by the doctrine of such men as Dr. Timothy Leary, a Harvard professor drop-out and high priest of the drug cult, who taught a new religion of love and freedom. He convinced his flock that drugs were a spiritual uplift. Their god became Krishna. Rock music became their religious hymns. And drugs their sacrament.

While a student at Kent State University, Jim distanced himself from the angry mobs of chanting anti-Vietnam rebels, who confronted police and National Guards working to control the protesters. America was shocked when the media televised the death of four students shot by peacekeeping National Guards. Among them was Allison Krause, a former student at Jim's high school. The incident turned him against the protest movement.

Since he held high draft status and was eligible for military conscription, he enlisted in the United States Air Force Reserves Air Vac as a Medic, rather than risk being drafted. A mild, compassionate person, he preferred to serve his country not by killing but by taking care of the wounded.

When he left for service, Alice understood Rosa's grief. They would both implore the Madonna's protection. Jim could not believe that he was spending his nineteenth birthday in basic training, alone and sad! On his first Christmas Eve away from home, he called. The stress in his voice was impressive, as he expressed his shock and grief at seeing wounded and dying young men. He asked, "How can I help make them happy?"

"Be yourself. Make them laugh," his mother answered. And he did. From wire clothes hangers he made a Christmas tree and trimmed it with toilet paper and other outrageous ornaments. He led the men in Christmas songs. When he came home New Year's eve, Jim was visibly saddened. When the war ended, he, like other veterans, did not discuss Vietnam.

Since early American history, wars have extracted a great price from patriotic sons of African slaves and sons of European and Asian immigrants, who fought and died for the ideal of freedom. But until the sixties, no generation had so openly and vigorously expressed its revulsion against war. President Nixon had grown progressively angry with protesters of every stripe. He brought that anger to his presidency.

It was later found that, during his election campaign against George McGovern, he had secretly used "dirty tricks" to gain damaging evidence against his opponent. Suspicion and distrust led him to create an official "enemies list" of protestors.

Some of the protestors fighting to change the Law of Eminent Domain suspected themselves to be targets, correctly, they would later learn. By 1967, leaders of HEART, the Highway and Emergency Relocation Team, were so frustrated and angry at delays and unfair settlements that they pressed for a meeting with the City Council. Citizens packed the chamber and demanded solutions and justice.

They stormed City Hall again in 1968. Doc Krause and Alice Sapienza, seasoned public speakers, led the voices of protest. The Chamber was packed with State and Federal highway officials, all discomfitted when Doc and Alice demanded a federal investigation of the Pennsylvania Transportation Department. Doc detailed the injustices and hardships suffered by acquisition victims. Officials sat stone-faced.

When she spoke, Alice did not realize that her tirade would lead to trouble: "It's different when you displace pigs and chickens to build your ribbons of concrete; but when you displace people without giving them just compensation, it's highway robbery! Laws are written for bureaucratic benefit. You've ignored the welfare of condemnees! You may try to rape us in the name of the Law of Eminent Domain, but we refuse to lie quietly and let you finish the job without protest!" Her speech was being tape recorded!

The story had changed little. "Takings" were slow. Offers were low. Across the nation others were suffering the same injustice, as concrete arteries spread across America. Incredible! Pittsburgh's fight gained international attention. A noted surgeon from France, Dr. Bernard Tremeau, a member of the Chamber of Deputies, had come to America to learn about conditions surrounding Eminent Domain procedure. The inhumane process in a "just" society appalled him. He cried, "In France there would be a revolution over this terrible condition!" But the beat went on!

Federal Highway Department representatives from Washington were invited to another protest meeting on January 13, 1969 at St. Boniface Church, where they faced a furious Doc Krause. Alice demanded that crafty highway designers come out of their secret planning sessions and into a socially damaged community. Again, she was tape recorded. Reports of that fateful meeting would reach Secretary John Volpe, Nixon's Federal Secretary of Transportation.

Protestors found every sort of way to unleash their anger, short of riots. Across America, the voices of protest had reached their peak. And so had Nixon's paranoia, which led the president to continue covering up his use of dirty campaign tricks against his opponent, George McGovern. His fears led him to expand his enemies list. Doc Krause and Alice were uneasy, fearing that they had earned the dubious distinction of being on that list. Their fears would prove to be correct.

Intrigued by the history of Eminent Domain, Alice visited the University of Pittsburgh library to learn more. During her inquiry, she learned that Pitt was pioneering a new concept of entrance requirements for enrolling older students in evening college. The librarian gave her a brochure. Alice could dream, at least. During her children's college years, she had enjoyed pouring over their textbooks and typing or helping to write their themes. Of the immigrants' eleven children, only Tom and Julius Sapienza had earned college degrees. The Depression Years had been brutal.

None of Paolo's children had achieved the goal he wished for them, namely, to be educated beyond high school. None, that is, until Fate smiled on Alice in the autumn years of her life. She was forty-nine, and a grand-mother. She weighed matters, then shared her idea with Tommy, her son, who was a Business College Director. He teased her and said she had been to college vicariously through her kids, and encouraged her to enroll.

As she walked across the Pitt campus to her interview with her student adviser, Alice looked up . . . up . . . for her stone. *"Soma day, Lisetta"* said a voice in her head.

Dr. Nancy Caplan examined her transcript and assured an apprehensive Alice that her high school grades, her ITC public speaking and leadership record, and her business experience would be an advantage. She encouraged Alice to take the C.L.E.P. tests to determine her entry level. To her own surprise, Alice earned fifteen credits, and fifteen more after Dr. Mathews had examined her ITC work in areas of Communication and Leadership — a full year of college.

She attacked her studies like someone starved for food, and invited Tom to attend some of her classes. She "hung out" at Gustine's Bar with professors and friends, career professional Lois, and Shulamit, a refugee from the Holocaust.

Life was full; but the prospect of an Eminent Domain settlement was empty. Fortunately there was no financial strain to pay tuition. Alice had earned the first Dean Gow Evening Student Scholarship, followed by the U.S. Association of Evening Students Scholarship. Her Black mentor, Dr. James Frink, who recommended her, wrote her a happy letter: "What a pleasure it was to learn of your scholarship awards in the *Pitt Night Times.* . . . my congratulations and best wishes!" Dr. Frink, aware of her protest activities, liked this maverick who would soon receive another long-antici-pated — and dreaded — NOTICE.

It came one day when she was at the North Side store preparing for another HEART protest meeting. The steady crack of the demolition ball and falling debris could be clearly heard not far away from their renovated building. That day "the other shoe dropped" when the postman pushed open the large glass and steel door of their bright spacious storeroom and handed Tom a large official-looking envelope. He solemnly said, "Looks like this is it for you, too, Tom and Alice." Neither was in the mood for their usual small talk. Before the highway was finished, the postman's ritual would have been repeated for over three hundred displaced business owners, and seventeen hundred uprooted home owners and tenants. They read the document, which they had feared since 1961:

NOTICE TO CONDEMNEE OF CONDEMNATION

In accordance with Section 405 of the Eminent Domain Law of the General Assembly of the Commonwealth of Pennsylvania, the Urban Redevelopment Authority of Pittsburgh hereby gives notice:

1. The Urban Redevelopment Authority of Pittsburgh files Declaration of Taking on the 23rd day of July, 1971, in the Court of Common Pleas of Allegheny County Pennsylvania.

2. Your property has been totally condemned as of the 23rd day of July, 1971, as part of a redevelopment area . . . No.25, East Street Interchange.

3. If you wish to challenge the power or right of the Condemnor, the Redevelopment Authority of Pittsburgh, to appropriate the sufficiency of the section of Taking, you are required to file preliminary objections within thirty (30) days after being served with this NOTICE.

Tom's jaw tightened. "Those thieves!" he thundered, pacing back and forth. "We'll fight the bastards and the law to the death!" Alice dropped to the floor and wept bitterly. She thought of their years of hard work and risk. The waiting was over. They now faced months of endless red tape to get "just compensation."

In the end, their meager settlement would be less than half what it took to buy and enlarge their building. The denied dislocation damages, a percentage that the attorney and appraiser would get, the settlement fees, and loss of an established twenty-five-year business were criminal! To add further insult, because they no longer owned the building, they would now be forced to pay rent, while the "Sovereign" destroyed nearly half-a-lifetime's work!

The unfairness outraged Alice. She thought of the words in the folk ballad: *We owe our souls to the company store*, and exclaimed, "We've given our souls to the Federal Highway!" To vent her frustration, she reached above her for a pen and several dry cleaning slips, and wrote a soulful ballad that she titled *Highway Robbery*. It poured out the cruel fate of victims condemned to be taken. Suiting the mood of the sixties, the song would become significant.

And the Beat Goes On!

In the next few weeks, she and Tom dismantled their business and said the last painful goodbyes to their help, their battle-weary cohorts and longtime friends, and faithful customers. Dr. Krause stood with them as they locked the door at 716 East Ohio Street for the last time. The three pledged to carry on the fight. Dr. Krause remarked: "I'll never travel a highway that I won't wonder how many people made sacrifices so that I could have this convenience. It's a shame, too, because the Law of Eminent Domain could work, if it were rendered with justice."

They nodded solemn agreement, climbed into their car, drove toward the Sixteenth Street bridge, and took the long route home over Polish Hill and through the ethnic neighborhoods that they had traveled over the years. They reminisced about the night they had heard the announcement of man's first walk on the moon . . . and the night Polish people had beat pots and pans when Bill Mazerowski had hit the Pirates' home run that had won the World Series. They laughed about Tom's prank when he had stopped the car in the middle of Polish Hill and yelled out the window, "Yeah *Mazarelli!*"

As they drove through various neighborhoods, they smelled food cooking. Each had an aroma distinct to its own nationality. People sat on their porches, or watered their patches of grass, or stood nose-to-nose on street corners exchanging gossip.

"Not everything has changed," Tom said to comfort himself.

"And the beat goes on," Alice replied.

Chapter 20

And the Music Stopped

Italian author Luigi Barzini lived in the United States briefly as a child. Later, back in Italy, he remembered that the "melting pot" once ruled supreme. "The pot was a great homogenizing machine into which we were all thrown," he said. "Then you turned the crank and out came Anglo-Saxon Americans with Brooks Brothers suits and the same way of speaking and thinking."

Wilkinsburg, a middle-class tightly-knit mostly White suburban community, fit his observation. The "old guard" favored its Anglo-Saxon Protestant values. But in the sixties, unanticipated changes pierced its cocoon and altered its social character as several miles away, on Pittsburgh's Lower Hill, the relentless wrecking ball continued to demolish homes to make way for the construction of the Civic Arena. Forced migration caused an overflow of Blacks into Homewood and Wilkinsburg, increasing Homewood's Black population from twenty-five to eighty-five percent. In a mass exodus, middle-class Whites abandoned their once-beloved neighborhoods and moved to Pittsburgh's outskirts. By 1970, Homewood's established inter-ethnic community and traditions had vanished.

As middle-class Homewood Blacks spilled into Wilkinsburg, "White flight" increased. It was apparent that the town would never be the same conservative WASP community, insulated in its cherished shell. And incoming Blacks would face fewer obstacles than those encountered by such notables as Judge Livingstone Johnson, whose family had settled in Wilkinsburg in 1922. Seventy-eight years later, in a public speech at a Korean Veteran's dedication ceremony, he recalled that, when the family arrived in Wilkinsburg, they had to confront the open objections of the Ku Klux Klan. Judge Johnson told of the days when "you didn't show your black face much in Wilkinsburg."

In the mid-sixties, prejudice was still strong, but mostly covert. In this environment, Tom and Alice, still under financial stress from the pending Eminent Domain settlement, opened their new business next door to brother Frank's print shop. With more courage than money, they began rebuilding what they had lost, while highway bureaucrats continued delaying their settlement.

The first person they hired was Mr. Swan, a kindly old Black immigrant from the South, who earned his living shining the shoes of Wilkinsburg gentlemen and stoking the huge coal furnaces in commercial buildings. Mr. Swan walked with a tilt and wore a cap soiled with coal dust and ashes. But, contrary to appearance and stereotyped thinking, he was a classy gentleman who owned a farm and financed his grandchildren through college. Every day as he watched Tom and Alice remodel their building, he was struck by their warmth and soon found that they shared a bond rooted in discrimination.

Gradually the old man exposed the community's religious, nationality and racial bigotry. His stories were confirmed in a 1987 publication by the Historical Society of Western Pennsylvania. In telling Homewood's history, it reported: "Perhaps the group that hated and feared immigrants and Blacks most was the powerful Ku Klux Klan . . . The fiery crosses and the mass marches of hooded Klansmen were threatening notices to both Catholics and Blacks to stay out of Wilkinsburg and to clear out of Homewood-Brushton." Wilkinsburg's Centennial publication said, "Catholics and Jews in particular were objects of the KKK message."

Swan described the flaming crosses that burned on the Wilkinsburg lawns of Black families who lived on the hills overlooking Homewood-Brushton. He recalled instances when members of the Klan, cloaked in white robes and hoods, had raced menacingly down Wood Street on horseback; or when hundreds of masked members in full regalia, marched down Penn Avenue in broad daylight, led by the mayor and chief of police.

Resident Dorothy Davis Jacobson recalled that the huge black circles cut out around their eyes "made it a most scary thing to watch." But despite their intimidating disguise, dear Mr. Swan did not feel threatened. He knew exactly who they were. He recognized their shoes or boots, which he had often shined. At the memory, he removed his dusty cap, slapped it across his knee, tilted farther right and chuckled.

Mrs. Jacobson humorously recollected that "they came into our store to buy their white sheets — in spite of the fact that we were Jewish — because we sold them two cents cheaper than Caldwell & Graham up the street."

By the 1970's, a few attitudes had begun to change. Protestant middle-class businessmen, ministers and Republican politicians condemned the

Klan's intolerance and helped reduce the animosity. But Swan cautioned Tom and Alice that, appearances aside, Wilkinsburg's middle-class, predominantly White Protestant community still held onto their elitist values and prejudices. "They have twenty-four churches that still aren't Christian," Swan said shaking his head sadly. Aware of this history, Tom Sapienza prudently eliminated his last name when he named his new business "Thomas Barth Formals and Dry Cleaning."

Among the first customers was Mr. Siller, who welcomed Alice to Wilkinsburg. He misjudged her blonde blue-eyed appearance when he said, "It's good to see a new business. We already have enough 'Eyetalian' businesses." And he made reference to the Mafia.

Alice "blew a gasket" and scolded, "Mr. Siller, I feel sorry that God didn't create you Italian. I'm Italian. Please take your business elsewhere, and not to my dry cleaning competitors. I like them!" He left.

Tom and Alice worked long hours. The cost of juggling several businesses was formidable, but their children understood. In the immigrant tradition of *la famiglia*, and a healthy respect for the work ethic, their kids worked after school or on weekends.

Tom's expertise in high-quality dry cleaning was valuable to their formal wear business, and fast service was a welcome convenience for the town and its surrounding communities. At prom and wedding seasons, volume was heavy: hundreds of tuxedos a week went out the door.

High school graduates were a barometer of the times. Early in the sixties they still reflected their parents' conservative values; but by 1970 there was a noticeable change in young attitudes and tastes. The "me-first" generation indulged themselves. Gone were the well-groomed high school and college students. They were busy being different together, as they switched to T-shirts, frumpy hairstyles and torn, bleached jeans. Women gave up wearing dresses for pants. Miraculously though, at prom time, they became well-dressed ladies and gentlemen for a night. Alice, not surprised at the changes around her, bought pants suits to wear on campus. And, bucking the Law of Eminent Domain, did her share of protesting within the Establishment.

Profit-seeking highway boosters pushed for more miles of concrete. But the victims of acquisition felt that they had been financially sacrificed in the name of the "public good." Unrelenting pressure by HEART brought the

Uniform Relocation Assistance Act, passed in January 1970, which allowed some — not all — to claim an increased bonus of up to $15,000 to help pay the higher prices for comparable properties. Unfortunately, the discriminatory Bonus Bill benefitted only Phase II people. Those in Phase I, where most businesses were located, were ineligible! Yet these were the protestors from HEART, who had fought hardest to change a heartless law!

Five hundred outraged citizens staged another mass protest meeting before the City Council on April 1, 1970. The chamber was packed. State highway representatives came but the new Mayor Pete Flaherty was conspicuous by his absence. When citizens presented their litany of felt injustices, Council listened politely, and highway officials squirmed at the charges hurled by the speakers.

Dr. Krause and Alice called for a Congressional investigation. At the same time, Alice took her story to her Social Studies class at Pitt, where her classmates were shocked. The loud-mouthed young protesters, who had considered her to be part of the older indifferent generation, now respected her for bucking the Establishment.

Spurred by citizen protests, Dr. Krause led a crusade to Harrisburg. Rumors of "fixes" and "kickbacks" were rampant, but hard to prove. "We got turned down on everything!" he cried. When the persistent HEART group appealed to Governor Shapp to stop the rape of the North Side Valley, he imposed a moratorium, which went into effect on February 9, 1972. But torn by pressure from highway proponents, he lifted the moratorium in May, and acquisition resumed with the same slow, unjust property settlements.

To further ease their financial load, Tom and Alice rented one of their storerooms to Republican John Heinz, an aspiring candidate for Congress, familiar with the saga of Highway 279. On one of his frequent visits, Heinz hopped up on their counter, swung his legs and asked, "How can I help?" When he had heard the horror stories about condemnees' hardships, he vowed to push for an improved Law of Eminent Domain if he was elected to the House of Representatives in 1971. He kept his promise.

These were the dissident years when, during Nixon's 1972 re-election campaign, five Cubans broke into the Watergate Hotel on June 17 in search of material to be used against his opponents. For nearly two years, while the president was engaged in the cover-up, later investigations revealed that Nixon was so paranoid that he had secretly encouraged a break-in of a psychiatrist's office to get information against his "enemy." When reporters Bob Woodward and Carl Bernstein discovered and broke the story of the cover-up, they concluded that such behavior, if documented, would be impeachable. If Nixon was really involved, it would be the first time known in history that a president had used his office illegally. Some reporters, questioning his knowledge of the "dirty tricks," vilified him.

Nixon's reaction, anger and suspicions were so extreme that he activated his official "enemies list" to investigate anyone and anything. Everyone was suspect in a milieu of political hatred and public protests. President Nixon's generally paranoid attitude would indirectly affect Tom and Alice.

When they were summoned for an IRS audit, they were not surprised. Their protest speeches had been taped, and they suspected that they were targeted for being so vocal. When the tax audit notice came, Tom said proudly, "We made Nixon's 'enemies list,' Honey!" Alice was frightened; Tom was ready and anxious to confront the auditor.

Weeks later when the man came to their home, Tom spread his neatly-printed accounting records across the dining room table. But before he examined the ledgers, the IRS man fired a series of intimidating questions, made negative implications, and dictated specific mandates for operating a corporation. Tom shot to his feet. With each word he angrily jabbed his forefinger under the man's nose and bellowed a staccato, "Look! I'm an independent business owner and not a corporation!" He slapped each pocket hard as he said, "If I take my money in with my right hand and disburse it with my left, you can't tell me how to run my business, so long as I have accurate records and receipts to back up my deductions!" The meticulous Tom slammed his orderly file folder on the table and dumped it upside down, scattering receipts everywhere.

The startled auditor finished his work from Tom's detailed work sheets, gave up on the receipts, and then argued that Tom would still owe over a hundred dollars more, with interest.

And Tom shot back, "Oh, yeah? By the way, here are several deductions that I overlooked. Guess I'll have to file an amended return for my rebate. I don't suppose that will be with interest!" The astonished IRS auditor left without another word.

As the Sapienzas settled into their new business, they were not included in community groups in the early years. Although Alice had presented programs before the tight-knit Historical Society and the Business and Professional Women, she was not invited to join. Similarly, Tom was not invited to join any civic group.

But their customer and business neighbor relationships grew. Tom loved to have philosophical discussions with Marco, the Greek shoemaker. Alice enjoyed shopping on Wood Street at the Sherman family bakery, whose aroma of freshly-baked goodies wafted across to her store, and liked browsing at Danny's home accessories balcony. She patronized Sperling's Furniture Store, James' Flower Shop, and Anderson's Wallpaper and Paint Store. She especially enjoyed her visits to Nick's Shoe Repair shop and the smell of new leather, the whirrrr of the shoemaker's machines, and their small talk. *"Bon giorno, Signora Sapienza. Come va?"* And she liked the way that Mellon Bank Manager, Bill Hallet, frequently called her into his office to talk.

At times Alice wondered whether she was running a business or a social club. The store became a regular stopping-place for friendly customers, for kids after school, and for lonely seniors who liked to linger and chat. Among visitors were Black George, the town's loved eccentric street person, and Charles W. Snarr, a religious octogenarian, who was so fixed in time that he displayed a huge Confederate flag across his living room wall.

Black George was weak-minded, having suffered from a blow to his head, it was rumored. He knew whom to "touch" for a donation inoffensively. Without invitation, he swept the sidewalks erratically in sun and snow, for rewards from merchants. Marco, the shoemaker, gave him unclaimed shoes; Jimmy the barber left money at the local eatery to feed him; Tom Sapienza gave him unclaimed clothing to keep him warm; Rosa Sapienza fed him on Sunday mornings when eateries were closed. As he sat at her back door, he did "'rithmatic" problems on scrap paper from Frank's print shop.

George wore layers of shirts and coats even in summer, and bunked discreetly hidden in the Borough building basement in winter. He knew how to market himself. Even bus drivers patronized George as he traveled between communities to artfully panhandle. One midnight as TV sportscaster Bill Hillgrove was driving around the corner, the bus pulled to the curb. Bill was startled when George unexpectedly loomed out of the parklet gazebo and approached the bus. Without a word, the driver extended a lunchbag through the door and drove off. Hillgrove collapsed in laughter.

On the other hand, mentally sharp for his eighty plus years, Charles W. Snarr made his daily excursion to the library and the business district, walking in measured steps to the "whump, whump" of his cane. "Good morning, George, see you're still at it," he said respectfully maneuvering around a pile of sweepings.

"Yeauh, mm uh huh, sir," came George's respectful response.

"Whump! Whump!" Charles stopped to maneuver his cane and sack of library books. He went into James Floral Shop. "How do, Miss James?" he said ceremoniously lifting his square black Pennsylvania Dutch-style hat. C. W. Snarr made his purchase and left. He adjusted his dark-gray, pin-striped vest over his little round belly, and pushed through the Thomas Barth doorway to drop off his daily, neatly-scripted, two-page religious inspirational messages, duly copied from the King James Bible. He chatted with Tom and Alice through the saliva that filled his throat as he talked. And left a bouquet of flowers for Alice. It was St. Valentine's Day.

Mr. Snarr had an uncanny resemblance to Herbert Hoover — and he knew it. One might suspect that he purposely dressed the part. He wore a high stiffly-starched shirt collar reminiscent of President Hoover's. Charles, a staunch Republican and open admirer of Hoover, did not relate him to the Great Depression — not surprising for a Wilkinsburg gentleman. He was amazingly healthy, despite his daily intake of bacon and eggs and ham. Cholesterol? No problem. He was clearly destined to live to be a hundred. One day as Charles crossed the street in front of the library, a UPS truck swung around the corner and struck him down! He was rushed to nearby Columbia Hospital.

When Tom heard the news, he went to Charles' side every day for nearly a week, at the end of which Charles died. Alice gathered his birthday and holiday cards and tucked them into the fancy box he had given her on Mother's Day. She wept for her friend and the passing of an era. Indeed times had changed. In the span of a single generation, Americans had developed a new character. Victorian values and genteel behavior were gone. A desire for social equality, material wealth and an exploding technology had produced a profound transformation.

Western Pennsylvania had steadily evolved from a no-collar, to a blue-collar, to a white-collar society. As steel mills disappeared, neighborhood business districts declined, while huge shopping malls attracted a growing automobile clientele. Like other neighborhood business areas, Wilkinsburg was in transformation. White residents continued their exodus as more Blacks moved in from the Hill, displaced by the escalating progress of Pittsburgh's Renaissance I. Eminent Domain's compulsory acquisition had already destroyed the inner city.

Meanwhile, during North Side's battle with Eminent Domain, Pittsburgh, in decline as a major industrial center, was emerging as an international corporate center, and farsighted civic and business leaders looked ahead. Although the metamorphosis did not occur overnight, inevitably plans for Renaissance II lay on the horizon, destined in the next decade to fall under the leadership of Mayor Richard Caliguiri.

And on the drawing boards lay designs for constructing upscale skyscrapers to accomodate the new corporate offices. The most imposing would be the black glass PPG building, whose cathedral spires, reminiscent of Italian Renaissance towers to God, were towers to Mammon, the worldly god of profit. One day, under the designation of the "public good," hard-earned businesses and properties would be annihilated and downtown Pittsburgh would emerge with a new image.

To grapple with the problems inherent in dramatic social change, the University of Pittsburgh organized a symposium titled *Renaissance II to What?* As business and educational leaders presented their views on the merits of urban renewal, they paid little attention to the human problems caused by vast social change. The experts had missed the point. Alice, who attended the symposium, came away disappointed and wrote her Sociology theme, *Needed —Human Renewal*, which was judged to be "forceful, perceptive, sensitive."

Like many, she had suffered much, but instead of dwelling upon her own misfortune, she had focused upon a new project. When she was assigned to do a research paper for her Creative Writing class, Alice chose to write about the history of commercial radio broadcasting, because her father-in-law had been a radio pioneer. Her paper, titled *Epitaph or Resurrection?*, led her to a new project and a long-term crusade. While doing research for her paper,

Alice learned that the Frank Conrad garage, birthplace of commercial radio broadcasting, was slated for demolition.

This historic treasure was located on the border of Pittsburgh and Wilkinsburg, on property owned by a local Elks organization. In his garage workroom, Conrad had pioneered radio broadcasting and improved short-wave radio transmission, enabling him to send the human voice around the world from the Westinghouse Hill Station at the apex of Forest Hills. From his work, the globe had shrunk and worldwide communication was born. This Pittsburgh-based miracle, begun when Reginald Fessenden pulled the human voice from the air, ultimately evolved into electronic television when Vladmir Zworykin invented the iconoscope.

Fessenden, Conrad and Zworykin, bright inventors, fell into oblivion because twentieth century history has mistakenly credited David Sarnoff with being the "father of mass media!" Sarnoff, neither a scientist nor an inventor, was a telegraph operator. He was described as a hard-boiled, cigar-chomping, New York super-salesman who convinced capitalists to set up radio and television networks and invest in marketing the sale of radios. The *Time* anthology revealed that Sarnoff proclaimed himself to be the father of the entire electronic communications industry. Said Sarnoff, "In a big ship sailing in an uncharted sea, one fellow needs to be on the bridge. I happen to be that fellow." This had led Alice to remark, "It never occurred to him that without the true radio and television pioneers there would be no bridge!"

To complete her research paper, on June 16, 1972, Alice met with the Elks' Exalted Ruler, Jack McKee; Wilkinsburg Mayor, Edward Daw; Ed Young of KDKA; and Arthur Zeigler of the Pittsburgh History and Landmarks Foundation — and her husband Tom, who had once been Conrad's paper boy. As Jack McKee told her of the impending destruction of the historic garage, Alice argued forcefully for its preservation. And then, fired by her outrage against Interstate Highway 279, threatened, "I'll lie down in front of the wrecking ball to stop its destruction!" The Elks, convinced by her zeal, stopped the razing of the Conrad garage. Tom was proud.

On campus, there were many other crusades. Ardent feminists pushed for equal rights. For some, the women's movement played havoc. Alice's Alpha Sigma Lambda friend, Marla, paid a bitter price for going to college. Her domineering husband felt threatened by her academic achievements and was resentful of her college friends. He had beaten her into mental inferiority, had found a compliant younger woman, and then threatened a divorce. Marla confided her frustration over her pending breakup to Alice, who suggested that the couple go into counseling. The next day Marla's body was discovered in her gas-filled kitchen, with a bullet hole in her head. Her pet dog was found whimpering in the cellar. Crushed over the suicide, Alice appreciated Tom's modern liberal attitude more than ever.

Though she was an open-minded "liberated woman," Alice could not reconcile herself to the moral erosion of young female Baby Boomers who had become blasé about premarital sex. Alice had broken the traditional mold of her generation, but her values about virginity were rock solid. Women who engaged shamelessly in loose sex mortified her. It appalled her that having an affair or becoming an unwed mother held no shame. It angered her that young people who, in circumspect hygiene classes, had once learned about sex and the reproductive system, were now learning how to practice safe sex and use condoms. Despite being modern, this first-generation immigrant's daughter could not accept the topsy-turvy values of the Sexual Revolution.

But essentially Alice had the best of both worlds. For she could also retreat to the comfortable past by visiting her mother-in-law. Now that her parents were gone, Alice treasured Italian conversations with Rosa, whose stories of Italy made her modern day tensions drop away. Sebastian's family still lived in Italy. He had not seen them in fifty years and he longed to fly to Italy to visit with his sister Vicenzina and other relatives. He planned a three-week vacation.

Rosa adored Vicenzina. Their letters and photographs had been a last link to the past. She and her family would travel from Florence to Rome to greet their precious Sebastiano on his arrival, and then be joined by other relatives.

Upon his return home, Sebastiano could not hide his emotions as he described their meeting at the airport, where his enthusiastic sister and the family had waited behind a roped-off passenger section. Sebastian enjoyed telling how Vicenzina recognized him, ran through the barrier past the forceful airport guards, flung herself at him, covered him with kisses, and cried, *"Mio caro Sebastiano!"* Her daughter Anna and her uncle conversed in English and formal Italian. The Sapienzas had abandoned the Sicilian dialect years ago. Anna spoke five languages and traveled internationally as a buyer for America's J.C. Penney Company. She promised to visit Pittsburgh on a company-planned trip to America the following year.

Rosa gave her husband no rest, assailing him with questions. Sebastiano was clearly moved as he relived his visits to Rome and Florence. He had been overwhelmed by the paintings and the sculptures at the Basilica. He described his family's homes — one a villa on the *Italian Riviera*. Rosa enjoyed reliving his experience and sharing his stories with the family when they gathered around her big table to enjoy her *biscotti,* coffee, and whatever other treat she offered.

But on July 2, 1972, the family stories ended. Rosa's grieving sons, Lena, and Alice hovered around her hospital bedside and comforted her until the end. Poor Sebastiano wept quietly.

Rosa Concetta looked regal at rest in her coffin. Her beautiful olive skin belied her years. Circling her hands were the Rosary beads on which she had recited miles of prayers of appeal for her family. Long before the mythical Tevye of *Fiddler on the Roof* conversed with the Almighty, Rosa Sapienza, like her friend Maria Palombo, regularly bargained with God. Rosa was Faith and Love personified. Without the help of Dr. Spock, she had given America six gentle, honest and loving sons who knew unquestionably that they were each special.

Oblivious to America's ethnic preferences, Rosa had come to America with her family not as the "wretched refuse of teaming shores" but as an Italian unwilling to deny or forget her proud roots. This genteel, forceful lady, whose needs and tastes were simple, had found joy in cooking a meal, in sharing stories of bygone days, in cuddling her grandchildren, in reading her Italian newspaper, in listening to her Sebastiano play his clarinet.

Like Paolo earlier, Sebastian was devastated by his beloved Rosa Concettina's death. His Parkinson's condition worsened. He wandered aimlessly around Frank's print shop, walking among his memories. His family visited him often. Then one day when Tom stopped upstairs to see his father, he found Sebastian folding his music stand. He opened his clarinet case and looked at it vacantly. Then put it away — forever. And the music stopped.

Chapter 21

Keep Hoeing Your Garden

So what had become of the Melting Pot by the seventies? Who was in? Who was out? For certain, Blacks had long recognized that they were not welcome into the big kettle. Their ancestors, unwilling emigrants torn from loved ones, were sold into bondage by their greedy African masters and packed into the bowels of slave ships bound for America, where they were used as tools to generate wealth wherever their labor brought profits. During the Civil Rights Movement in the sixties, they challenged the Establishment to recognize their worth, and forced America to change the rules.

Under the impetus of the Black Pride Movement, Blacks led a new ethnic assertiveness and demanded acceptance. They fostered a search for their African roots and spurred other groups to explore their own origins. Across America, universities added courses in History and Sociology. Students interviewed elders, plowed through thousands of microfilm rolls and musty documents in the National Archives, the Chicago and New York Public Libraries, the Mormon Repository, and private libraries.

Young seekers searched family Bibles to reclaim the past that their parents and grandparents had denied them when they sought acceptance into WASP society, for as sociologist William I. Thomas observed, "a destruction of memories was the essence of the Americanization process." The implication was that if you want to be assimilated, forget the past. Deny your roots. Anglicize your name. As a result, he concluded, many young people lost their identity. They grew up ashamed of their ethnicity because assimilationist Americans decided whether immigrant cultures deserved acceptance.

Her resentment against the history of discrimination sparked Alice Palombo Sapienza to pursue a course in Genealogy. Some students took this course to reclaim and justify their identity. Others wanted to vindicate their national origin. Alice, secure rather than uneasy about her heritage, wanted to leave her family a proud legacy. It would not be difficult, for marinated in the tradition of storytelling, she had firsthand resources to trace the family's past. She remembered Martino Mariotti's declaration: "We are children of the Renaissance!" And began the task with zeal.

She wrote into the night, and often until dawn. Her emotions were kaleidoscopic, as she chronicled the family saga. She longed one day to climb the "noisy" slate stairs on Ellis Island that her family and other fearful immigrants had once climbed. She wanted to renew her appreciation of what they had endured to make it to America.

On New Year's Eve 1973, Alice shared her developing story with her family. The clan had gathered around her big dining room table to listen. Ann and Sophia were busy making coffee and heaping platters with traditional Italian foods. Cousins exchanged good-natured banter and childhood memories. Paolo and Maria would have been proud of the bond shared by their family, now into its third generation. As Alice read their story, her sister Grace, and her brothers Silvio and Tom laughed and wept as they heard their past revisited. At times Grace interrupted to ask, "Did you tell about . . ." And Alice reassured her that the incident was included in the story. Alice knew that she would always cherish that New Year's Eve. She had no clue that life-altering challenges lay several years ahead for her family and for Tom and Sophia — challenges that would require dauntless courage.

Despite her ongoing battle with Eminent Domain, there were rewarding projects. In her senior year, Pitt's School of General Studies founded Alpha Sigma Lambda, the Phi Beta Kappa of honor evening students. At the charter banquet, held in the Fall of 1973, Tom sat proudly beside Alice as she was inducted. Then the two were photographed together during dinner in a photo that would mark a sad turning point in their life.

Shortly after, at Tom's urging to contribute her experience to ASL, she helped her peers write the Charter Bylaws. They appointed her ASL Historian. Alice conducted induction ceremonies, made keynote speeches, and volunteered at fund-raising phonothons. Raising thousands of dollars was her way of paying back her tuition-free education. Meanwhile, campus protest activity ended with the Vietnam war in 1973.

The formal wear business was brisk; but behind the activity lay the ubiquitous struggle with Eminent Domain. HEART pressed for an audit of state highway funds. The project had become so costly that highway engineer Anthony Gaeta had to reveal that serious money shortages would prohibit buying more properties. He took with good grace the anger that was meant to be directed at the phantom institution called the "Sovereign."

Arguments bounced back and forth, like a ping-pong ball in perpetual motion, among city, state, federal officials, and dissenting citizens. The issues were basically the same: problems of humane appraisals, relocation assistance, and just compensation.

On and on went the voices of Babel. When the city and state reached an impasse, another meeting ensued, to which Doc Krause invited the media. Tom invited folk singer Lynn DeFalco who sang *Highway Robbery*, the song Alice had written the day their NOTICE came. Announced as a parody to Merle Travis' song, *Sixteen Tons*, the lyrics told the tragic story:

We've done years of work, and what do we get?
Another day older and deeper in debt;
They've killed our business then stole it away,
Now we owe our souls to the Federal Highway!

They took the property that earned our pay,
The work we've done has crumbled away;
No just compensation for the years we've spent,
And to hurt us more, they're charging us rent!

We've done years of work, and where do we go?
The Highway Department doesn't care or know.
We've begged and pleaded several years or more,
And they won't pay enough to replace our store.

They take houses and stores and put in cement,
For ribbons of concrete dollars are spent;
The people it hurts can kick and fuss,
But the roads and cars are more important than us.

We've done years of work, and what do we get?
Nervous frustration and deeper in debt;
For legal advice we've been forced to pay
We've been robbed of our rights by the Federal Highway!

The next night KDKA radio talk show host, Merle Pullis, played it on national radio. Then Michelle Madoff asked Alice to run for City Council. When another tax audit soon followed, Tom was prepared for the challenge, but the conflict had taken its toll.

Barely noticeable physical changes occurred in Tom. His powerful personality mellowed, but not his anger at Eminent Domain. He lost weight. His firm chin, full dimpled face and strong sculptured head became angular. He spent less time with his beloved roses and did not enter the Rose Show. One day, he cut them all down, except Paolo's hardy Paul Scarlet. Puzzled, Frank asked, "What are you doing, Dad?"

"I just don't have time for these anymore," he said indifferently. Their uphill financial battle continued. Family and friends were not aware of their dilemma, nor were their business associates. Tom and Alice had earned strong respect in the business community, especially with Wilkinsburg Mellon Bank Manager, Bill Hallet, who saw them as a successful business team. His impression would benefit Alice at a later date.

Hallet, familiar with the Interstate 279 conflict, nevertheless knew nothing about the hardships caused by bureaucratic delays. Nor was he aware that, when final plans were announced on July 4, 1973 for the eight-lane interstate freeway, the settlements for Phase I condemnees were nowhere in sight. But State bureaucrats, property appraisers, and attorneys had already begun to anticipate their "cut" from the final settlements.

Tom pressed ahead resolutely with business. His annual physical birthday checkup was due on March 24, 1974, one month before his Term Life Insurance Policy was to expire, and in time to submit the required medical report to renew the policy. His physical revealed weight loss. The optimist, seeing this as a positive, proudly thumped his chest and said, "I weigh less than when I played football. How's that for being in condition?"

But three weeks later, he could no longer ignore the malaise that had overtaken him. Tom's voice had become noticeably hoarse. His physical vitality failed him. He scheduled another appointment with Dr. Pagozzi, who it turned out had missed some serious symptoms. After a series of tests, he diagnosed Tom as having cancer in the esophagus and admitted him to McKeesport Hospital. Unfortunately, when the required medical report was submitted to the insurance company, Tom was denied the renewal of his Term Insurance. Quite an emotional and financial blow!

Although he had never been a smoker, it was suspected that years of inhaling dry cleaning chemicals and pesticides from his rose garden had taken their toll. Furthermore, based upon medical research, physicians concluded that anguish over Eminent Domain, and now the denial of his insurance policy, had definitely worsened his condition and prognosis.

Undaunted, Tom said, "Doctor, this may be your verdict, but it's not a sentence." This was not denial. It was defiance! "We'll fight like hell and we'll beat it." And then the philosophical Tom quoted Cervantes, "He that loses wealth loses much; but he that loses courage loses all." And ever aware of his mortality, added Shakespeare's "Tomorrow, and tomorrow, and tomorrow creeps in this petty pace from day to day until the last syllable of recorded time." Sitting bold upright in bed, Tom said, "Let's not waste time, Doc. When do we start treatments? Can I go home and come in for them as they're needed? How long will I be here?" A chemotherapy schedule was arranged, and Tom was discharged.

Rosette insisted that her father stay at her home so that Jim, who had left Kent State, and Alice could handle the business. Tom occupied baby Leah's room, where he could enjoy her crib antics at the foot of his bed, or see little Bill at play, or hear his father, Bill Hillgrove, announce sports on radio and television. Rosette's piano pupils came in for lessons. Between students she prepared liquid nourishment for her father and enjoyed their lifetime closeness. Tom did not lose his sense of humor, and Rosette howled when he said, "Honey, you know that you're sick when your balls hit the commode water. I fixed the problem, though. I lowered the water level!"

A few weeks before, Tom had prepared background slides of religious scenes and of the students Rosette was directing in the musical *Godspell*, which was to be presented for the International Toastmistress Convention. Tom admonished, "No matter what happens, *Godspell* should be produced for your mother's ITC convention as a prayer from me." Rosette promised.

Alice offered to postpone her last semester at school, but Tom rasped his objection and shook his head firmly. "Absolutely not! You have a responsibility to Pitt . . . We both have . . . They gave me a scholarship, too, when I needed it most. Besides, you're only a few months from graduation, and we're going to have a helluva party! No matter what happens, life goes on!" Rosette promised him there would be a party at her house.

On weekends young Tom, a business college Director, came home from his position in Ohio. Thirteen-year-old Frank rode his bike to Wilkinsburg after school to be with his mother, or stayed under the watchful eye of brother Jim, or Uncle Jule — and Chuckie, Frank's older and dearest cousin. Three times a week, Alice's faithful friend, Lois, drove her to classes and then home to Rosette's house to be with Tom. June 26, 1974 was their thirty-fourth anniversary. When Alice came to him that evening, thirty-four fresh red roses greeted her, just as they had every year on their anniversary.

Remaining resolute and optimistic, Tom encouraged Alice: "Honey, you'll never have to scrub floors. You know the business. Our life hasn't always been easy, but aren't we glad we've been a team all these years?" Alice nodded, feigning bravery.

Life had become an unending uphill treadmill. Their compensation from Eminent Domain seemed remote and doubtful. And then one day, attorney Tom Dempsey called Alice to arrange a meeting for them to receive their final settlement. Tom, too ill to travel, requested that Dempsey come to Rosette's house. At Tom's bedside, Dempsey showed little compassion for his client's condition. He was all-business as he explained deduction after deduction from their meager settlement, including his and the appraiser's healthy cut. By the time the calculations were finished, the "just compensation" amounted to less than half the true property market value, with no dislocation damages or compensation for their lost twenty-five-year business. In the end, calculating their settlement, less their indebtedness for survival loans, a $250,000 debt fell on their shoulders, an overwhelming sum in 1974! Alice was furious!

Tom Dempsey left, as impersonally as he had come. She refused to shake his hand, and angrily said, "Tom, I'll tell you what I told those highway bureaucratic bastards. If I were given to curses, the worst curse I could give is — a goddam highway should come through your door! All of you take your pound of flesh and enjoy the spoils!" From that moment on, attorneys became number one on her "shit list," with cunning bureaucrats a close second. The concept of "liberty and justice for all" had failed!

Indeed, Alice was so disillusioned and angry to think that such havoc could befall Americans, that for years afterward she refused to say the Pledge of Allegiance and to salute the American flag! Her last days in school were overwhelming. But with only two business locations to manage, their well-trained employees carried on faithfully — though in sorrow.

As treatments continued, Tom grew weaker and more hoarse. Clearly, he needed to be hospitalized again. But first, he requested to come home for a couple of days — and what precious days they were! The climb up thirty-two front steps was torturous. Tom did not complain. Instead he paused to survey and appreciate the house he had created, and the Paul's Scarlet rose bush, now in full bloom. "Your father planted that bush," he reminisced. Inside, he moved from room to room, drank in every detail, and then went to their spacious downstairs bedroom and lay down.

In the corner was his big desk where Tom did all of his business accounting. Fortunately, Alice had been involved in all phases of the business and was prepared for the succinct twenty-minute lesson in which he clarified his filing system, answered her questions, and gave her this fiscal advice, "Remember, Honey, those IRS bastards might come after us again, and they'll want an explanation for everything. Don't be afraid. This is important. Check for accuracy: Never report less income than the bank deposits you make. And as a safeguard, withhold questionable deductions — and keep fighting — get the s.o.b.'s!"

During that long sleepless night as she and Tom lay close, they reminisced about their own private world. Tom, sensing her grief, comforted her and said, "Honey, when someone once asked Saint Francis of Assisi what he would do if he learned that he would die at sunset that day, Saint Francis answered, 'I would finish hoeing my garden.' Keep hoeing!" Alice tried hard to hold back her sobs. Tom cradled her in his arms. No words were necessary. Their life of "unselfish devotion" had said it all.

The next day Tom was admitted to the University of Pittsburgh Presbyterian Hospital, whose location on the Pitt campus simplified Alice's daily visits and Rosette's commute from the Duquesne University campus where she taught. As chemotherapy treatments escalated and the physical suffering grew more intense, Tom lost more weight, but he never complained. The stream of relatives and friends who came to his room to encourage him expected to meet gloom. Instead, each left surprised, uplifted and impressed because Tom showed courage rather than self-pity.

Just as she had promised her father, Rosette presented the *Godspell* show for the Toastmistress International Convention, making Tom proud. Soon after, an ITC friend who visited was amazed at his attitude when Tom returned to his room after a chemo treatment. He was weeping — for somebody else! "An eleven-year-old boy died down there today and he didn't even get a chance at life. I weep for him — not for me. God has given me a good life, and I thank Him for that and hope I've used his gift wisely." Overcome with grief, Alice's friend left his room.

His roommate, also a cancer patient, was Channel 4 TV sportscaster Ed Conway, married to TV personality Eleanor Schano. In their daily conversations, Tom's calm acceptance and strength left an indelible impression on her. Bill Hillgrove, Tom's son-in-law, was Conway's sports co-anchor. When Ed died, Bill wept and said, "I was hoping to become TV anchor one day, but not now, and not like this. I'd have given it all up, if only Ed Conway had made it."

Bill and Alice had a close relationship, sharing their thoughts and emotions. He listened with empathy — once, half the night — as Alice released her grief. Tom, too, looked upon Bill as his own son and was impatient to see him get his deserved recognition.

That week, Alice was hospitalized for surgery to have a uterine cyst removed. Italian prayers flew at God and the Bella Madonna. Tom mustn't know. His children told him that the busy wedding season demanded her time for several days. God heard. The cyst was benign.

After surgery Alice, alone and lonely, asked for an early release. She spent the next several days recuperating in the visitor's lounge near Tom's room, carefully scheduling early evening visits not to arouse his suspicion.

One evening Tom, an avid news buff, turned their discourse toward the lead TV story of the Watergate break-in and Nixon's cover-up. In the face of more and more damaging evidence, and negative public opinion, political aids had abandoned him. Tom mistrusted Nixon and was annoyed by the pattern of denials, campaign tricks and anger that led him to create his "enemies list." Convinced that they were still victims of that list, Tom snapped, "Fight those highway bastards, Honey!"

The following week, Alice was scheduled to take her final Italian exam. Tom cheered her on, unaware that shortly before class, the doctor had told her that the treatments were useless. The cancer had spread. "It's like spitting in the ocean," the radiologist said.

It was difficult for Alice to take the exam. Her professor, knowing that her husband lay dying not far away, allowed her to take her final in a private room nearby. In her Italian accent she consoled: "I know you want to finish. Now you can cry and write your answers, and no one will know." As she wrote, Alice recalled Tom's words, "Honey, keep hoeing your garden."

The noon news was on TV when Alice visited Tom that day. "How did the Italian exam go, Honey? You've made it to the end." Alice gestured a pseudo brave "thumbs up." His voice was now a hoarse whisper. "I sound like the Godfather," he said and smiled, barely revealing a dimple. "Sounds like they're going to nail the president for that Watergate break-in. He's a liar. He ought to resign." Tom, aware of his prognosis, seemed to rest comfortably under medication. A nurse came to summon Alice to the doctor, who waited for her at the nurses' station.

Dr. Vigianni explained that fluid was steadily building in Tom's chest cavity. If it was not removed regularly, the pressure would become great enough to crush his heart. "He'll last awhile if we keep extracting the fluid. What do you want me to do? Shall we continue extracting?"

Alice erupted at the startled doctor. "How *dare* you ask me to make that decision? Who the hell has the medical degree? What does the Hippocratic Oath require of you? Don't ask *me* whether — when — or if I'll terminate my husband's life! Do your very best for him, and *you* make the decision !" Alice angrily walked away to play out the charade at Tom's bedside.

Tom's Bahamian nurse, who stood nearby, squeezed her arm as she brushed past. "He would be proud," she said.

Days later, it was a hot sultry July 27. Young Tom, home on vacation from Ohio, was doing what came to him naturally — helping tend family business matters. There was always a project waiting to be done at their commercial buildings, and it was normal for the boys to pitch in. Their father had taught them to be proud to work with both their hands, and their minds. "Jesus was a genius — and a carpenter," he had often said. The weather was perfect for Jim and Tom to do roof repairs at the Versailles plant. Frank, Rosette, and Shulamit, were on their way in to visit Tom at the hospital.

When Alice arrived, Tom was agitated at the television pundits, whose hunch about Nixon's attempted cover-up was now a confirmed big story. Tom had stayed interested and analytical. *How tragic*, Alice mused sadly, *that this bright philosophical mind won't be here much longer.* She reflected about their great conversations, the joys of their private world, and their deep mutual trust. She made small talk about business affairs. He stopped her.

"You know, Honey, I really don't care about our business. It's not important." Her heart sank. "Help me to the bathroom please, Honey." They wheeled the I-V bag holder to the bathroom and labored their way back to the bed. Alice stacked his pillows high, and Tom turned his attention to Richard Nixon's television speech. Agitated, he rasped softly — only because he could not boom out his invective — "They ought to impeach the bastard. He's dishonest. He's finished. Where are Tom and Jim?"

"At the Versailles store, tarring the roof," Alice answered.

He whispered, "I'm so proud of them. Regardless of their success, they aren't afraid to dirty their hands." And he began to recite, scarcely above a whisper, his most favorite poem — Henry Van Dyke's *Work*. As he became weaker, he moved only his lips as Alice helped him finish the verse that was so dear to him:

Let me but do my work from day to day
In field or forest at desk or loom,
In roaring marketplace or tranquil room;
Let me but find it in my heart to say,
This is my work — my blessing — and not my doom,
And I am the one by whom this work
Can best be done in the right way . . .

He slumped against Alice, who quickly summoned help. The nurse closed the curtain around his bed. Then remembering that Jimmy had told her that even in apparent oblivion a patient can hear, Alice squeezed his hand and whispered consoling words. "Honey, relax. It's just a weak spell that the doctor said you would feel. I love you, Honey. You'll be okay. I love you. I love you. I love you!" Moments later he was gone! And with him their special private world.

Tom had died as he had lived — unafraid! A strong father who exemplified both traditional and modern values, this immigrant son had left his second-generation children and his beloved America such valuable gifts: a respect for honesty and hard work, the courage to fight for noble principles, and so many other strengths.

In a few minutes, the Bahamian nurse confirmed his death and said to Alice, "This was a rare and courageous man. He knew his end was near and accepted it calmly. Just this morning he told me, 'I have only one regret when I go — that I won't have the privilege of seeing my Frank grow to become a man.'"

Moments later Rosette, Frank, and Shulamit arrived. The medical team herded them into a private room and broke the news. Rosette was devastated. Tom and Jim were summoned. Shulamit took Frank away to spare him the further trauma of seeing their pain — unaware that his father had died.

When the Sapienza brothers were given the news, Lee, his closest brother, rushed to Alice's house. "We've lost our rock!" he cried. Indeed Tom was their strength, their guide; for through the years, the Sicilian immigrant boy had faced and challenged the hurdles that destiny threw at him. He had battled the odds with courage, love, and honor, and left his family a priceless legacy.

When Lee left, Alice sank into Tom's favorite chair and looked around their beautiful living room at the books, the piano, and the art work. Suddenly, things became worthless. "Oh, Tom! Why did you have to leave us? Why? Why?" she shrieked angrily. And then went down to the playroom and stood before the bar where Tom had mixed cocktails for family parties — and screamed — and screamed herself out of energy.

That night at the kitchen table, Tommy and Alice shared their grief and laughed at Tom's habits and quirks. Alice recalled that among the world's great thinkers Tom held the utmost admiration for modern philosopher Eric Hoffer, a dock worker who was not university-educated, and whom academia had not yet fully recognized.

Tommy admitted that his father had been a dominant power in his life. Alice recognized that he had been a forceful yet loving husband and father, using his authority over the family yet giving each a sense of freedom. His children were free to disagree with him. They did not always win, but they could stand up to him. As Tom became weaker, Alice became stronger. He had not only given her a long tether to be the best that she could be, but he had encouraged her independence, too. And she exercised that same independence when her family tried to spare her the ordeal of funeral details. Alice insisted on being involved.

At the funeral home, the mortician gently showed them an array of caskets — in order of diminishing cost — each accompanied with a salesman's tasteful, but subtle sales pitch. Alice, trained to listen, did not need to be persuaded, nor did she feel guilty, or obliged to compensate at Tom's death for any shortcomings she had as a wife. As kindly Mr. Knee expounded on the beauty and price of bronze, Alice saw the equal beauty of wooden caskets and asked their cost. And then she surprised, and probably embarrassed, her family by saying, "Excuse me, sir. Tom loved wood. The price of my love for him can't be measured by the price I pay for his coffin. I'll take that beautiful less costly wooden one which, like the bronze casket, will be wastefully hidden and buried in a cement vault. The price difference will go toward Frank's college education. His father would probably have agreed." Tom had schooled her well.

Knee's funeral home was filled with mourners of various ethnic and social classes on the morning of his funeral — a tribute to Tom's admirable character. Sister-in-law Ann's observation accurately summed up his life: "He was a just man."

Nostalgia triggered Alice's emotions as friends from Homewood-Brushton shared their memories. She longed to go back in time. Sadly, she noted that most of their immigrant parents had died. In their place stood their loyal children, who had survived the prejudices of assimilation, the hardships of the Great Depression, and the perils of World War II.

The mourners knelt to say their final final prayers, and then the morticians conducted the traditional "last viewing" ritual before the casket was closed. Following usual protocol, first the immediate family was directed to say their last painful goodbyes; and then friends were led to file by to pay their "last respects."

Sebastian's wobbly approach toward his son's casket was heart-wrenching. He trembled violently from head to foot, as he stood in stooped misery, issuing a stream of tears. Although his brilliant mind had withdrawn emotionally, Sebastian knew that it was his *"Toto"* in the casket. His grieved sons circled him close.

Alice, equally stricken, knelt and gently caressed the hair on Tom's hands and reflected: *Here lies the man who changed my life, challenged my intellect, took pride in my achievements, loved me passionately and unconditionally. How will I survive without our private world?*

She felt young Frank's comforting, firm hand on her shoulder. And he spoke with his father's wisdom, "Don't cry, Mother. Daddy is just a shell lying there; but his spirit and his words will always be with us. He was such a strong father that he'll be with *me* forever."

What a sage comment, Alice mused as she pushed away from the casket and turned to face the roomful of well-meaning mourners who had watched her anguished farewell. Struggling for control as resentment overtook her, she muttered, "How barbaric!" She felt that the onlookers had invaded the privacy of her bedroom. Mr. Knee would surely get a blunt opinion later.

The funeral was over. The flowers and guests were gone. Frank and Alice sat in their big kitchen remembering Daddy. The floorboards in the hallway creaked, and they heard a familiar off-key whistle. Alice stopped talking. Again a whistle. "It's Daddy!" Frank exclaimed. He had heard it, too. That night Frank insisted on sleeping downstairs on Dad's bed. "I'm not scared — honest, " he said. "I want to sleep on Dad's pillow, so I can smell him." Frank found comfort sleeping on that pillow.

But in 1974 there were no special sensitivity groups to comfort the abandoned mate after the flowers were gone. There was only Tom's reminder to "keep hoeing your garden." Except that it had turned into a vast endless field! There was no time for self-pity. Alice went to Tom's desk to meditate. And penned her thoughts:

REFLECTIONS

I think of his firm chiseled jaw,
The smile on his dimpled face,
His honest dark brown eyes,
And the soft black wave of hair
That never stayed in place.

I hear the off-key whistle
That accompanied his tread,
And think of the love and wisdom,
And the righteous wrath
Reflected in things he said.

I see his manner in my children
And am grateful for his legacy;
Then I pause to smile . . .
For through their clear young eyes,
Their Father looks at me.

Frank had fallen asleep on his father's pillow. Alice kissed his forehead and returned to reality. There was work to do — debts to pay. And bargains to strike with the Bella Madonna. That night, Alice had a long talk with Her.

During World War II, three of Rosa's sons were sent to fight overseas. Liborio (Lee), shown at left with his dog, served in Europe along with his brother Santo while Delfino (Duffy), at right, served in the Pacific Theater.

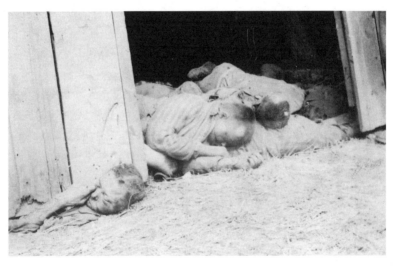

After the Battle of the Bulge, the 279th Signal Company, Lee's division, moved across the Ruhr to the Rhine to the Appahousan. Lee photographed a captive who attempted to crawl from beneath a burned down barn filled with Jews and other political prisoners.

Families were close. Paolo and Maria, who went blind, lived with their children Tom and Sophia.

Sebastiano and Rosa celebrated their fiftieth anniversary at the home of their son Santo, his wife Kitty and their six children.

The Palombo family — Paolo and Maria Giuseppa gave birth to three immigrant children and two first generation American children, who added eight grandchildren to the family tree.

The Sapienza family — Sebastiano and Rosa gave birth to three immigrant sons and three American sons, who gave them fifteen grandchildren — six girls and nine boys.

After World War II, Tom moved his family home from Baltimore, went into business, and built a home in Forest Hills.

Tom enjoyed rose growing as a hobby. His mother Rosa, Rosette and Alice helped gather roses from the Paul's Scarlet rose bush that Paolo planted.

The first generation keeps the music tradition. The children rehearse before grandfather Sebastian's visit. Tom and Alice enjoy as Jimmy and Rosette play piano and Tommy plays clarinet.

When Francis Sebastian was born to Tom and Alice in 1961, grandmother Rosa prophesied that this baby would be the cane for their old age.

After their battle with the unjust Law of Eminent Domain, Tom and Alice moved their business from the North Side to Wilkinsburg.

Tom's last photo with Alice, at her induction into Alpha Sigma Lambda Honor Society at Pitt. Tom, her greatest friend and supporter, died on July 24, 1974, two weeks before she graduated on her birthday.

Part IV — Epilogue

Chapter 22

Ciao Italia! — Roots Revisited

The bizarre seventies began as a drug-addled Hippies Period. Over four million Baby Boomers were college age. Author Tom Wolfe called it the narcissistic Me Decade. In the sixties, dedicated youth had battled in social movements that changed American culture; in the seventies, they were preoccupied with looking good and feeling right rather than with protesting for human rights. Hard-fought social reforms collapsed — along with Nixon's public image.

As a result of the Watergate cover-up, paranoia and conspiracy had reached their limit, fueled by Nixon's suspicious nature. He faced resignation or impeachment — unprecedented for the nation. Nixon chose to resign, and his successor, President Gerald Ford, declared: "Our long national nightmare is over." Alice wished Tom were alive to see the outcome.

Defiant to the end, Nixon flashed a sweeping victory sign as he boarded the presidential aircraft for the last time. Behind his wife Pat's frozen mask, her pain was unmistakable.

The date was August 9, 1974. That same day, her fifty-fourth birthday, Alice graduated from the University of Pittsburgh. Unfortunately, her family could not attend the Commencement. Tommy was working in Ohio, and Jim and Frank were doing necessary business chores. Rosette had promised her father that she would give a graduation party, and was preparing for it.

"*Go get 'em, Tiger!*" Surely Tom walked beside her, she thought. Alice felt her mother's presence when a *summa cum laude* graduate was announced. His last name was Ferrante — Maria's maiden name! "*Somma day, Lisetta,*" her inner voice said, as she received her own *summa cum laude* diploma. The recessional music signaled the graduates out of the great hall. Alice adjusted her cap, stood tall and walked resolutely down the long aisle. Outside in the distance the sun shone brightly on the Cathedral of Learning. She looked for her stone. And smiled.

At Rosette's house, her Alpha Sigma Lambda friends had gathered to help her celebrate. Alice needed them. She remembered Tom's insistence that she stay involved. Pitt activities would help fill the void he had left. She was grateful for the educational opportunity America had given her. She owed a debt and Alpha Sigma Lambda gave her the opportunity to pay it.

She was recruited to plan a series of Business Community Luncheons, to launch an evening school student government, and to revitalize a defunct alumni association. The School of General Studies image was changing. Its name needed to change to reflect its progress. From the suggestions offered, administrators accepted Alice's, in which the word "College" substituted for the word "School" to better define its expanded curriculum and enhance its image. Thus the College of General Studies earned its new name.

Pitt's Bicentennial celebration brought stories, which appeared in campus publications, and a videotaped documentary for the archives. Among them was the story of the Stone at the Top. *"Papa would like that,"* Alice thought.

There was much to accomplish — a big garden to hoe — more goals to reach. Alice accepted a position teaching an evening Speech course that could help finance part of Frank's college education and tuition toward her own Master's Degree. Jim was prepared to help her achieve her determination to pay off the huge debt she had inherited. It made Alice appreciate Mama's work in operating her farm while Papa was away.

Jim and Alice found a new individuality — a new freedom to become their own persons after Tom's death. Artistic Jim made major developments in his music career as a vocalist and songwriter, and established a T-shirt imprint business in their building, upstairs next to his apartment.

But it was still a man's world — for which Alice adopted a new image. She cut her hair short, switched from dresses to wearing pants suits, worked long hours, and grieved privately. Now *she* wore the pants. But soon there would be a new hurdle to overcome.

By 1975 the Equal Rights Amendment was being heavily contested by feminists. Although ERA legislation had passed in the House of Representatives in October 1971, and in the Senate in March 1972, it still lacked eight of the thirty-eight state approvals required to make it a law. Furious ERA activists protested wage and job discrimination and the injustices shown widows in settling their estates. A widow could not claim a 50%

tax-free inheritance from a husband's business or farm, unless she could prove that she had been actively involved with him. Consequently, many women lost their farms and businesses when their husbands died. Alice would have a tough fight ahead.

If tax audits had intimidated her during their Eminent Domain fight, she would have to be ready to face the surprises that IRS auditors had in store. Remembering Tom's fearless behavior and the scene with the IRS auditor in their dining room, she prepared by recruiting help from her nephews — Rosemary's brother Angelo, an IRS auditor, and her husband Eugene, a certified public accountant. Angelo cautioned her to provide enough evidence of her ownership in the business — IF she was denied the exemption.

"T" day came. Alice waited nervously for the auditor. *"Go get 'em, Tiger!"* said an inner voice. When the IRS representative reviewed her estate income tax report, he questioned and challenged her 50% exclusion from tax — and denied her claim. "No, no, lady, you need to show proof that you were an equal partner in the business before you can take this deduction!"

Alice hit the roof! She towered over the startled man, pointed her finger at him — Tom's style — and shrieked, "Dammit! This is robbery! Why doesn't the damned government finish the job? Eminent Domain took my shirt! Here take my pants! I don't even have panty hose on!" she thundered, starting to pull at her slacks.

"No! No! That won't be necessary . . . Just go home and get me some sort of document or written evidence."

Fully prepared, Alice pulled a thick notebook from her briefcase with neatly-mounted pages of newspaper clippings and letters of condolence from business associates. Each of them referred to her interest in the business, and some proved her to be the co-founder. Others showed her actual involvement: battles with the union picket and Eminent Domain.

The IRS rep, showing progressive annoyance as he flipped over each page, finally shoved the notebook across the table. It flew off as he threw up his hands and said, "Okay, okay, lady! You win! You win!" Tom would have been proud. Alice thought about the hours that Eugene and Angelo had unselfishly spent to help their aunt — and blessed *la famiglia* and the little orphan, Angelo, she had loved.

Weeks later, she was invited to speak at the charter meeting of the Executive Womens' Council, along with organizers who were lobbying for the Equal Rights Amendment. Alice's confrontation with the IRS tax auditor was a fit example to include in her talk. When she told the story of her scrap with him, the women leaped to their feet and clapped and whistled and cheered. Kathleen Donnelly reported it in their EWC Newsletter. One day their paths would cross again, and the story would resurface.

Three weeks after Tom died, the Knee Funeral Home received Sebastian, the last surviving parent. The gentle virtuoso had slipped away, grieving quietly for his son and his *cara* Rosa Concettina. But he left an enduring gift. Son Frank designed a beautiful booklet of Sebastian's music, written in his own *calligrafia.* The original compositions revealed through music more than mere language could convey. With his clarinet Sebastian expressed his emotions: love, passion, joy — and sometimes sorrow. What Sebastian could not say with words, he said with music.

As a tribute to his remarkable talent, the Wilkinsburg Symphony Orchestra performed a program of his music. Family and friends listened proudly. As his daughter-in-law Alice announced the program, she felt the spirits of Sebastian, Rosa and Tom offstage. Oh God! They were gone! Suddenly a wave of gloom sucked her into a deep hole. The thought of Christmas without them was bleak.

Big clan parties on each holiday at Maria's and Rosa's houses were over. Families now celebrated separately. However, rooted in family respect, they visited each other. Cousins hugged, reminisced over coffee, Uncle Tom's *vino*, Aunt Anne's and Sophie's *pasticcini,* Aunt Grace's *scarpelli,* and Uncle Silvio's corny jokes. But it was not the same.

For now, these enduring customs bonded them, but when the holidays were over, a strong desire to resurrect the past enveloped Alice. Rosette and Tommy, sensing their mother's misery, remembered that their parents had planned to visit their families in Rome, Florence, and Castellino Sul Biferno. But Alice had abandoned hope of ever seeing Italy, given her pressing financial obligations. To "keep hoeing the garden" in 1975 required determination and fortitude. But her children, Tommy and Rosette, pooled their finances. Jim, Frank and her loyal employees would handle the business. And Alice would maneuver finances to make it through the dead winter months. She approached Mellon Bank manager Bill Hallet with a plan.

When Bill complimented her business skills, Alice was puzzled, unaware that Tom had regularly informed Hallet about her business and academic achievements. Alice asked if she could pay only the interest on her mortgage for a couple of months, so that she could take advantage of an 8%-saving on buying formal wear for the prom season. "Why don't you just borrow the money? Your signature is good for five or six thousand dollars," Hallet suggested.

WOW! Women just can't get this kind of credit! Alice mused. "What? And pay you 8% when I can save as much at no cost? No thanks!" she bluffed. Alice hoped he had not noticed her fright.

Hallet smiled and said, "I like you. You think like a banker! You're on! Tom was right, you're sharp!"

The joyous relief pulled her out of her despair. She could meet her bills and literally not count slices of bread to make it through. Tom's headstone would have to wait, she thought sadly. And then she made the same request to the Small Business Administration and her other mortgage companies. It worked!

The tuxedos? She bought only basic traditional stock on thirty-day discount terms to see her through weddings and the prom season. She subleased flashy novelty tuxedos that would go out of style, eliminated their maintenance cost, made a labor-free profit, and paid her bills with advance deposits. Necessity had taught her how to operate shrewdly. She would order Tom's headstone for his next birthday. It would be engraved UNSELFISH DEVOTION.

And then one Sunday, brother-in-law Lee and Lena came to her house. "I miss Tom," Lee said. "Here. Please take this money. We want to share some of our inheritance that should have been Tom's and yours!" Since Tom had died before his father, his parents' will had excluded Alice, but not her children. Though she understood their reasoning, the exclusion, and not the money, hurt her deeply.

"You deserve it. No one ever worked harder than you with Tom and our family," Lee said, and hugged her. Alice dissolved into tears, not over the money they gave, but over the *inclusion* and the love.

Business was a financial and social education. Dealing with young people during prom season revealed both their best qualities and their moral slide. They shared their college plans with Alice and their startlingly loose attitudes about sex. Mores were changing with this new "permissive" second generation.

Locally, demographics had changed markedly, too. Many ethnic enclaves East of Pittsburgh's inner city were gone, except on Polish Hill, in Italian Bloomfield, and Jewish Squirrel Hill. Homewood now belonged to a new Black generation. Most ethnic churches had disappeared by the mid-seventies.

The passage of the 1965 Immigration Act had brought new waves of Cold War refugees and immigrants from Asia, Latin America and the Philippines. To hopeful oppressed immigrants, America was utopia. But they soon learned that there was a difference between the American ideals they had envisioned at home and the cold reality. Like their forebears, they, too, would have to endure prejudice, struggle to survive, and learn to adapt. Americans who traveled abroad returned with greater appreciation for America, despite her defects. Alice would experience such appreciation upon her return from Europe.

Once prom season was nearly over, it was time to make travel plans. Alice decided to use her Baptismal name, Elisa, when she and Rosette acquired their passports. They would travel with their British friend, Paul. Their three-week itinerary would include three days each in London, Brussels, and Paris. Their final twelve days would be spent visiting relatives in Florence, Rome and Alice's coveted destination, Castellino Sul Biferno. The trio would find that being bilingual was an advantage.

In order to appreciate the ambiance of each country, they stayed in *pensioni* instead of Americanized hotels. In England, they toured the splendid Windsor Castle, walked through modest neighborhoods where sculptured English topiary hedges and formal gardens were in bloom, and visited Windsor's shopping area. At the Scottish Shop Alice informed the proprietor that the first clarinet solo played over the radio had been *Annie Laurie*, a fact confirmed by a news article written when Sebastian retired. The delighted Scotsman recorded the details in his tourists' journal.

The trio commuted to London by train. At Buckingham Palace they saw the changing of the stone-faced Royal Guard. In Hyde Park they heard political rhetoric from improvised soapboxes. They shopped at world-famous retail stores, dined on bland boring food and attended the hit musical *Jesus Christ Super Star*, where they gave the actors a standing ovation as a stoic audience sat.

Their next sojourn was Paris. They stayed at a charming inn located not far from the Eiffel Tower, which rose above them like a huge toy erector set. Nearby, framed by a long row of flags, stood the Arc de Triomphe on the Champs Elysées, where a cacophony of endless traffic and off-key horns bleated incessantly. The concierge appreciated that Paul and Rosette spoke French.

Early in the morning they were awakened by the fishmonger's call, which evoked early memories of hucksters who cried their wares on Tioga Street. The travelers ate hot croissants for breakfast. Later, they dined on luscious French cuisine and Bordeaux wine outdoors on the Champs Elysées, and watched crowds of black, white, yellow, and brown humanity stroll by.

It was Bastille Day — counterpart to America's Fourth of July. The throng, forbidden to move closer, had gathered at the Troccadéro Fountain along its barricades to watch anticipated fireworks. A handsome *gendarme* marching smartly by reminded Alice of Papa. Rosette whistled and exclaimed forcefully in three languages, *"Mon Dieu! Com' è Bello*! I'd like to take him home! I wish he would get us closer!" The gendarme appreciated the remarks — and the beautiful young woman. He straightened tall, stroked his moustache and led them through an opening to a prized spot. Being trilingual was a distinct advantage!

Next morning they packed a lunch with French bread, cheeses, fruits, and bottled water to begin their journey on the crowded train to Florence, Italy. Each train compartment held eight passengers seated on opposite sides. As they traveled South, there were noticeable differences in dialects as families greeted one another at the *stazioni*. Their speech and gestures were animated, their welcomes were emotional. Elisa felt at home — at last!

The trio spoke English as they admired the beauty of tile-roofed chalets and breathtaking mountain scenery. The Italians opposite them surmised that they were *americani* traveling with a chaperone, and made all sorts of speculations about Paul and Rosette and their *scorta*. Some comments were quite hilarious and embarrassing. The Americans understood and feigned ignorance.

As they prepared to leave the compartment when they arrived in Florence, Elisa exclaimed *ad alta voce, "Ehi! Siamo arrivati! Andiamo subito*! Hey! We've arrived. Let's go quickly." The startled Italians were visibly embarrassed as Paul, mother and daughter inched past them begging, *"Scusi, per favore."*

Before their visit, Cousin Anna had arranged for lodging at a charming *pensione* not far from the River Arno. They reached Firenze at one o'clock a.m. and secured a *tassi* to their destination. As they walked across the nearby *piazza* toward their *pensione,* they saw a prostitute coyly plying her charms with a late-night Romeo. They looked away and exchanged amused glances. "It's the oldest profession everywhere. Here's one for the book," said Rosette.

And suddenly they stopped cold. Michelangelo's famed statue of *Davide* loomed majestically over them bigger than life. If *Venus de Medici* was the most beautiful representation of the female form, certainly *Davide* was her male counterpart. Awestruck, they circled the magnificent sculpture and decided they would photograph him in the morning.

The continental breakfast reminded Elisa of similar breakfasts at home with Tom. She remembered the rib-crushing hug he had given Anna when she came to Pittsburgh, and moved quickly to find a telephone. Although Anna spoke four languages, Elisa was grateful for her own ability to speak Italian. After several rings Anna answered, *"Pronto!"* After they had exchanged preliminary greetings, Anna arranged to take them to lunch and visits with the family.

On their way from the *pensione*, they photographed *Davide's* gorgeous body — front and back just as, in France, they had photographed the posterior of Auguste Rodin's *The Thinker,* planning, with their odd sense of humor, to use such shots as "the end" when they showed slides of their trip.

They soon learned that no matter at which *ristorante* they dined, each one made them feel that they were sitting at Maria's or Rosa's table. They could not choose a favorite meal. Typically, Italians ate meat and fish sparingly. Vegetables, abundant and fresh, accompanied a variety of *pasta.* Deserts were often served with huge, succulent fresh fruits.

Firenze, noted for its art and literature, had become the repository of famous statuary and painting masterpieces. Whether in a simple restaurant or an elaborate *albergo*, patrons dined among these works of art, which adorned houses and buildings. The travelers were astounded. After lunch, Anna took them to shop at the straw market for wide-brimmed hats to protect their faces from the hot Italian sun. Along the way, Anna pulled them around the corner and, indicating the beautiful miniature statues atop an ancient brick dwelling, she said, *"Elisa, ecco la casa di Dante.* This is Dante's home."

"Santa Maria! Non ci credo!" Elisa exclaimed and restrained a strong urge to bow respectfully. Magnificent Florence impressed her as a paradox of calm antiquity and modern hubbub, as motor scooters and miniature cars scurried along its narrow streets.

As she conversed with Anna, her husband Sergio, and her sister Aurora, Elisa was struck by the changes that Italian, like English, had undergone over time. New idioms and English-based words and phrases had developed from technology. Italians were pleased that some Americans could speak their mother language. Most could not, having abandoned it to mask their ethnic roots in America.

Rome was their next venue. Romans, like all Italian men, appreciate beautiful women. As Rosette and Elisa tossed their coins into the Trevi Fountain, a group of Italian servicemen surrounded Rosette and looked her over appreciatively, debating her resemblance to two Italian lovelies. *"No—assomiglia Sophia,"* said one.

"No — Liza Minelli," argued another who approached her and asked in perfect but heavily accented English, "You want to come and make a baby weeth me?" The impish Italian removed his hat and bowed. The Americans laughed and walked away.

They crossed the *strada* to the famous Alfredo's Ristorante, to have lunch. The lobby walls were filled with huge framed photos of famous people, including Ike Eisenhower. An Italian violinist moved among the tables as he played a medley of familiar songs. "He reminds me of *Nonno,*" Rosette whispered.

Wherever they went, there were Italian faces as familiar as those in Homewood. He stopped at their table. "Anda wot wood you lika me to play?"

Elisa replied, *"Quest' è Roma. Allora, 'La Bella Romanina' è perfetto."* The trio agreed that *The Beautiful Roman Girl* would be the perfect song to sing. As the violinist played — to his surprise — Elisa sang the lyrics. She and Rosette sang several more songs that delighted diners nearby who, it turned out, were from Squirrel Hill in Pittsburgh.

A handsome gentleman approached their table. Elisa remarked that he resembled her nephew Ricardo, and asked his name. *"Sono Alfredo il secondo.* I am Alfredo's son." He smiled, expressed pleasure at hearing them sing and asked them to be his dinner guests. They had met *the* Alfredo's son!

Speaking Italian held other benefits. Their ride on the autobus to Castello Gondolfo netted them *free* conveyance when Elisa recognized the driver's Abruzzese dialect. Their tour through Rome, via carriage, also came *senza prezzo,* because the driver could share lively Italian conversation with his American guests. Elisa gave the driver *monete* to buy the donkey some food. As they toured, he identified Mussolini's balcony and a Sapienza storefront.

The next day as the trio dined outdoors, the charming carriage driver spied them and issued Elisa an invitation. *"Signora!"* he called. *"Andiamo a fare un giro! Senza prezzo! You no Pay!"* Paul and Rosette teased Elisa.

At Castello Gandolfo, the Pope's guards, somber and strict, controlled the crowd. The Pontiff inspired the throng as he spoke from his balcony in a half-dozen languages, and invoked their response in one, *"Viva il Papa!"*

The visit to St. Peter's Square and the Basilica next day was inspiring. To attend High Mass, hear the majestic choir, see the famed sculpture *Pieta*, and see the beauty of Michelangelo's famous painting of *The Last Judgement* in the Sistine Chapel — all this was awesome. Tourists' upturned faces were transfixed as they viewed angels blowing their trumpets; Christ, the Impartial Judge, weighing the deeds of men; and graves giving up their dead, as archangels waited to convey their souls to salvation or eternal punishment. What a magnificent heritage! How could one not be proud of one's Italian roots?

After more impressive tours and fabulous meals, the visit ended with a tearful *addio* to the Sapienzas. Italians cry easily.

Elisa was eager to meet her family in Castellino Sul Biferno. The train would carry them to Campo Basso, where cousins from Maria's family lived. Mario was a college professor, his brother Franco, a banker. Elisa had met their father Domenico, a builder, who worked summers in Canada and returned home in winter. Many Italians returned regularly to South America, too. The Argentines called them *las golandrinas,* the swallows, because they came to work in their wheat fields after the November European harvest, and returned to Italy in time for spring planting.

Elisa looked for a telephone when they arrived at their *albergo prenotato.* *"Pronto!"* Mario answered. His beautiful Italian made Elisa uneasy. She would have to abandon her dialect. *"Arrivo subito e vi porto a casa e facciamo un bel' pranzo.*" Alice conveyed Mario's message that he would come quickly to take them home, where they would have a beautiful meal. *"Mamma è tanto contenta!"* Mario exclaimed.

At dinner, they exchanged information about their families and friends in America. Since he spoke no English, Mario was pleased that Elisa spoke Italian well enough, *abbastanza bene*. He was also pleased and surprised that she had *un negozio*, and asked many questions about her business practice. Mario proposed that his guests spend the first day at the family *appartamento* overlooking the Adriatic Sea. The next day they would go to Castellino Sul Biferno, her parents' village.

That night Elisa was so excited that she scarcely slept. She was happy when Mario arrived early. On the drive toward the sea, she recollected the stories that her parents had told of their visit there many years ago. Mario coaxed Elisa to stay in Italy now that she was home. He urged her to consider opening her *commercio* there, for a business woman who speaks two languages could have a successful *pratico* near the sea. Elisa loved the idea, but remembering her family and debts, she dismissed a tempting fancy. She was restless to see Castellino Sul Biferno and her beloved roots.

Early the next morning, they began their drive up narrow roads to her *paese*. Campo Basso comprised a series of small towns situated among the hills. As they drove along the foothills, Mario announced the village names and informed them that houses in the older section of Castellino had had to be abandoned and rebuilt in another part of the town.

Elisa reflected on her grandfather Pietro Palombo, who had saved his townsmen and their flocks from the fury of the Biferno. She looked for the river and asked, *"Dov' e il fiume Biferno?"* Elisa felt dismal when Mario answered: *"Il Biferno non c' è piu; è diventato secco."* The Biferno had gone dry.

Sensing her gloom, he contrived a mischievous plan. *"Elisa, perche' non facciamo un grande scherzo allo Zio Giuseppe?"* Mario proposed that they play a big joke and tell her uncle that no one speaks Italian. They agreed. Paul was highly amused.

As they neared the village, Mario said, pointing upward, *"Siamo vicino a Castellino."* Memories flooded Elisa as they drove up the hillside to *Zio* Giuseppe's tiny stone house. The dear little old man came to welcome them arms outstretched. "Ben venuti, cari!"

Mario introduced Elisa, Rosette and Paul. *"Mi dispiace, Zio, Loro non parlano italiano,"* he said, feigning sorrow that they did not speak Italian.

Zio expressed his frustration in Abruzzese dialect — music to Elisa's ears — about Italians who abandoned their native tongue. The poor man tried to recall the English he had hardly spoken since his trip to America in 1910.

A few minutes into the struggle, Mario laughed and told *Zio* that Elisa understood and spoke a few words of Italian. *Zio* then shifted to labored formal Italian. She could hardly contain herself and commanded: *"Va via! Mario, va!"* Mario laughed and stepped outside. When Elisa revealed that she spoke their dialect, the joy on the little man's face was touching. They fell into non-stop Abruzzese discourse as they entered his little stone house where his wife, *Zia* Irene, sat near the chimney corner.

Elisa was amazed to see one wall covered with family photographs that showed their history in America since the early twenties. There were wedding photos, Elisa's Holy Communion photo and much more. *Zio* and *Zia* devoured information about Elisa's siblings: Grazia, Pietro, Domenico and Luigi. They hungered for news about long-lost *paesani* in America — about their families and lifestyles. Elisa enjoyed their nicknames and familiar idioms as they spoke. *Zio* was overjoyed to hear the information — in his own dialect. Paul, who knew some Italian, was puzzled. Rosette understood most of the conversation.

Mario was amused at his cousin's three-way discourse in English, formal Italian and the dialect. And *Zio* Giuseppe was astounded at her detailed knowledge of bygone days. Then, suddenly dubious, he asked: *"Ma fa scerzo? Tu non ti chiami Grazia?"* Elisa assured him that she was not joking and that her name was not Grazia.

Elisa vouched that she was Elisa Costanza, named for *Zio* Costanzo who had taken her family to their port of embarkation when they left Italy. Giuseppe recalled the pitiful day sadly, *"Che giorno pietoso,"* he said wiping a tear. To distract him, Elisa suggested that everyone go outdoors to pose for *a "ritratto."* Paul was confused. Mario was amused.

With exaggerated formality Elisa said: *"Scusi, Mario, andiamo fuori e facciamo una fotografia,"* and directed Mario outside to be photographed. He chuckled. Paul then understood the dialect for the word photograph. *Zio* simply brushed four fingers under his chin and hobbled outside.

Elisa was impatient to see the familiar places that her parents had often vividly described: the *chiesa* where they were married, and the statue of the Madonna where Maria and Grazia had laid their gold necklaces as parting gifts. But most of all she wanted to see the stone house that Paolo had built for his family.

Their first visit would be the village church. As they walked, *Zio* described each holy *festa* from the Nativity of *Bambino Jesu* to the *Via Crucis*, which ended on the little hill that represented Mount Calvary. He told how Maria on *Venerdi Santo*, Good Friday, depicted the Blessed Mother searching frantically for Her Son. Elisa knew exactly what he meant. Back home, during every Holy Week, her mother had sung Mary's part in the story of the *Via Crucis*, passionately asking onlookers, *"Il Figlio mio dov' è?"* As *Zio* Giuseppe described other religious customs, Elisa felt that she had stepped into the past — and loved it.

Rosette later recalled with loving amusement *Zio* Giuseppe's pride as they stopped at each statue on the "grand tour" of the little church. *"Questo è Santo Rocco. Ecco Sant' Antonio,"* he gestured. This was big stuff! And finally, there she was — the Madonna where her mother and sister had prayed and relinquished their jewelry. Elisa became Maria as she wept and, in colloquial Italian, prayed her thanks and a requiem for her mother.

Next they visited the family who had been given her parents' farmland. Elisa realized that the olive oil they had received in America for many years came from her parents' land. She thanked the slender, leather-faced woman who, in return, expressed her gratitude for their gift. She offered her guests wine and crackling-hot bread, fresh-baked in the outdoor oven. *Zio* offered his guests huge figs from the nearby tree and was surprised to learn that Paolo had also grown figs in America.

The town was a contradiction of the old and the new. Atop a few of the little houses, an occasional television antenna appeared. There was a language contrast, too. The senior generation clung to their dialect, despite their education. Their children spoke formal Italian. Language historians had already begun to record and preserve the vanishing dialects, which varied from town to nearby town.

At home, Grazia was the link with the past. She had written her childhood girlfriend and several *paesani* about Elisa's pending visit. When they visited Grazia's *amica,* she reminisced in the local dialect. Her live-in daughter-in-law spoke formal Italian. Their home was simply furnished and equipped with a small television and an electric washer that stood in the corner by the back entry. Elisa recalled the "Savage" and Grazia's description of the family's first washer. It occurred to her that these people were not poor. Instead, they lived simply.

As they began their excursion toward the old section of town to see the stone house and balcony that Paolo had built for his bride, *Zio* reached for a sturdy branch to use as a cane. They came to a mound of stones in the hillside fronted by a heavy latched wooden door. He tapped it and asked, *"Elisa, tu sai cos' è questa?* — You know wotta ees this?" He repeated in his best English.

Complete with inflection and offhand gestures she replied, *"Puo essere la cantina."* To Paul and Rosette she explained, "It's probably the cantine. I'll bet this is where some of the villagers store wine to keep it cold." Astonished, *Zio* asked Elisa how she knew that. She surprised him and sang in raw dialect a rhymed folk ditty about it. Translated it said: "I don't go to Mass because I'm crippled; but to the *cantina* I go — very slow — very slow — *naccata zimma zimma zomma, naccata zimma zimma za!"* *Zio* burst into tears! He had not heard the ditty for years. They sang it together.

As they walked the rim of the hillside, a woman dressed in black balanced a bundle on her head as she rode side-saddle down the hillside on her donkey. Mentally, Elisa saw her mother — and choked up. Looking down toward the vineyards and fig groves below, she asked her uncle to identify Paolo's farm. She looked for the shelter where her grandfather Pietro had died. *Zio* anticipated her question and explained that it had fallen many years ago, *"È caduto tanti anni fa."*

The sun was high and hot when they arrived at the oldest part of the village, where homes were in various stages of decay. There were no little gardens, no smell of baking bread, and except for a snake among the weeds, no signs of life. *Zio* identified the abandoned homes of various people now in America — and finally pointed to the little white stone house and balcony that Paolo had built for his Maria Giuseppa over seventy years ago. It leaned hazardously — the little balcony clinging to its facade. To Elisa it was a shrine.

She dropped to her knees and sobbed — recalling her parents' pride in it. She recalled stories of the struggles and grief of separation they had suffered to reach America. Oh, how far they had progressed! A new wave of gratitude and reverence swept over her. She prayed for their souls! *"Dormite in pace!* Sleep in peace!" At last, she had come home — for them. The experience would remain seared in her memory. Rosette looked on in reverent silence. Nearby *Zio* Giuseppe understood and wept.

In her heart Elisa felt comfortable here. Like her father, she was torn between two loves. She thought about Mario's offer and felt a strong urge to stay in Campo Basso where she would be near the Adriatic Sea and near her roots. Ironically, the magnetic force that had pulled her father away was pulling her back! But it was neither practical nor realistic to leave America and her family, for although Europe had been a stimulating experience, America still held the greater magnetism.

En route home, Elisa's spirit soared when they flew over the Statue of Liberty and Ellis Island. "One day I *must* go there and climb the noisy steps that Grazia described," she decided. And then her emotions plummeted at the thought of going back to a home without Tom, and to the problems she had left behind. But when her sons greeted her at Greater Pittsburgh Airport, their hugs and kisses spoke volumes, and she became Alice again.

A striking surprise waited at home. Tommy had bought her a new electric stove, and Bill and Rosette had bought her a new dishwasher. Frank and Jim had installed these, and painted and wallpapered her tired kitchen walls in sunny colors. "Thank you! I love You! Your father would be so proud. What a family!" she exclaimed.

So, who minded the jet lag she felt the next day as she sat in her tuxedo shop rocking away the memories of Italy? There was much to share with her brothers and sister about the *paese* they had left so long ago. Filled with renewed respect and fond recollections, Alice reflected upon her Italian heritage and the families whose love bound them together. She treasured the sacrifices their immigrant parents had made. Alice loved being Italian. She had come home with new hope. Her heart was full!

The ringing telephone interrupted her reverie. It was Sophia, who, dismissing the ceremonies that normally preceded her conversations with Alice, delivered a devastating message. Tom and Sophia had received a long distance call from their son Raymond in California: His five-year-old son, Tommy, had been struck by a car. He was fighting for his life — a life that would forever be changed. Sophia reported that Tommy had lost use of his limbs, able to move only his head and his tongue. For the rest of his life, bound to a wheelchair and imprisoned in the body of a quadriplegic, he would be dependent upon a respirator to breathe. Tommy's parents and his sister would be condemned to a life of eternal vigil; for "Monster" death lay ever-ready to claim him.

Tom and Sophia stormed Heaven and began a chain of visits to be near Tommy. Many bleak and challenging years lay ahead for their bright, spirited grandson and his family. Their future would be driven by Faith, Courage, Strength, Determination, Tenacity, and Hope!

Truth is often stranger than myth. Could the mythical Cassandra, endowed with the power of prophecy by the god Apollo, and synonymous with all the prophets of doom, have predicted such a Fate?

Chapter 23

The Second Time Around

After Sophia's disastrous news, gloom enveloped Alice again. And although the memories of Italy had eased her grief, with Tom and his parents gone, life seemed empty. The vacant apartment next-door was no longer the family's headquarters. Alice recalled fondly the drop-in visits when the clan gathered over coffee and *biscotti* at Rosa's big table. Five years before, Frank, Sebastian, and Rosa had moved to Butler County. At their lovely country home, in a spacious back yard, stood a large Madonna, palms up, among fresh flowers. Rosa could look out to Her from her window. Optimistic Rosa, who had not faced her mortality, had expected to enjoy many years in her new house. But omnipresent death continued to call frequently after she, Tom, and Sebastian were gone.

Within a decade, the Reaper took eight more from the clan. Santo Sapienza was devastated when his Kitty died. His children mourned deeply for their mother. Baby James Michael followed within days, when death snatched Rosette's newborn son from the very same hospital where Kitty lay dying. And death hovered around little Tommy Palombo, who fought the odds as he bravely adjusted to life in his quadriplegic prison.

With Rosa and Sebastian gone, living in Butler lost its attraction for Frank. He moved back to his Wilkinsburg building, where he and brother Tom had been business neighbors. The family dropped by, but Rosa's once noisy table held less appeal. Bill Sapienza dropped into Alice's shop to share his grief. One day, now less forlorn, he told her that he had been dating Kitty's longtime girlfriend, Mary, and announced that he planned to marry her. He would move his little family into her home. Alice was happy for Bill. She missed the private world that she and Tom had shared, and remembered his advice to her: "Honey, regardless of what challenges or hardships life deals, be like St. Francis. Just keep hoeing your garden!" She decided it was time to put grieving aside and "keep hoeing." Maybe if she worked on her Master's Degree, she could fulfill her desire to learn. There would be less time to grieve. After lunch, she called the university.

At Durante's lunch counter, she sat next to Chamber of Commerce president, Bob Tomnay, who needed a speaker for Wilkinsburg's annual Thanksgiving breakfast. Millie, the waitress, hit on an idea and said, "Hey Bob, here's your replacement. I've heard Alice speak at Pitt banquets many times. She'd be good." That afternoon, Alice accepted Bob's invitation to speak.

The speech, in a traditional WASP town, took "moxie" to deliver. It was more than a customary Thanksgiving platitude about Pilgrims' courage. It was a tribute to all immigrants, including those who were human chattel brought to America in slave ships. It was a reproach to America for not understanding their struggle for human rights. It rebuked bigotry from Plymouth Rock to Ellis Island in a bold appeal for the inclusion of every race, nationality, and religion. She included Papa's view about Thanksgiving: "After all . . . *Cristoforo Colombo* he was *Italiano*, so we must 'ave a deesh of spaghetti to honor him . . . no?"

Some laughed. The ministers were moved. Mellon Bank's Bill Hallet asked her to join the all-male Chamber of Commerce. Since she would definitely be a minority among the "old guard," Alice had reservations. Wilkinsburg's male-dominated attitude toward women was provincial. Until now, the town had been an insulated, conservative, predominantly White community. But change was in the air.

Alice recalled the late sixties, when Civil Rights rioters had spilled into Wilkinsburg and caused fearful merchants to stay behind their endangered glass windows. One day, twelve armed policemen sat on the ledge across her front windows waiting for trouble. They urged Alice to go home. She refused and showed the police a long lead pipe.

"If any nigger gives you trouble, hit him over the head, drag him out the door, and put a tuxedo in his hand," an openly bigoted cop advised. Alice was repulsed and angry!

"I'm not afraid," she said. Just the day before she had confronted an angry Black man who came into her shop to ask how many Black people she employed. "Friend," she had answered, "we're a family. We're Italian and have walked in your shoes. We're your brothers and sisters. Don't break our windows. Go tell it to the Establishment." The man shook her hand and left.

By the seventies, immigration had changed the face of America, literally, and Wilkinsburg's face had changed, too. Until the 1965 Immigration Laws were amended, European Whites accounted for over one-half of the newcomers. After that, Mexicans, Dominicans, Cubans, Jamaicans, and Salvadorans came, followed by Asians. White European foreigners could change their names to gain acceptance; newcomers of color could not change their skins. Old prejudices still classed them as radicals or criminals. All experienced similar rejection and struggle for inclusion. But at least the traumas of Ellis Island and fears of deportation were gone.

Alice admired immigrants who faced the rigors of anti-immigrant attitudes — and made it! Their grit encouraged her to make it. In the Fall, she applied for Graduate School and resumed teaching a Public Speaking course at Pitt. Those decisions were the catalyst for a profound change in her life.

As she walked across the Pitt campus on her way to teach, Alice remembered standing with Papa as she looked up . . . up . . . for her stone. By coincidence she had been assigned to Room 253 in the Cathedral of Learning. Classroom number 253 evoked memories of Mrs. Parrack's room and a blackboard lesson she drove home in bold yellow chalk. It was Socrates' advice: "We serve best when we serve others." Alice wrote one word on the chalkboard. OTHERS. This became her blackboard signature.

When professional students brought challenging topics and questions to class, Alice thought about the lyrics sung to Anna by the King of Siam: "It's a very ancient saying— but a true and honest thought — that if you become a teacher, by your pupils you'll be taught." She had found her niche. Teaching would not only prove to be a financial advantage, but also it would be a coveted academic fulfillment. Lady Fate hovered nearby. And smiled.

A few astute business decisions increased Alice's income. She converted the second-floor front rooms in her building to rentable dance studio and office space. She sold her Versailles cleaning plant, lessening operating expenses and long-term debt. Jim helped her during business hours. At night, combining his singing and comedic talents, he performed with his band *Jimmy and the Dukes*.

Lady Fate had new surprises in store for Alice. When her dance studio tenant learned that Alice loved to dance, she offered her free disco lessons, the latest dance craze. Between college classes, disco lessons, and teaching, Alice made new friends.

A teaching colleague at Pitt, June Kane, was looking for a speaker for her newly formed club of widows and widowers, aptly named *On Our Own*.

Drawn to Alice's speaking activities on campus, June invited her to supper. They laughed and shared ideas. June liked Alice's independence and outlook toward widowhood, and thought her experiences and attitude would be helpful to "helpless" widows. She invited her to come and speak. Alice accepted. Unknown to her, June had formed a plan. This lovable "yenta" also invited John Donnelly, the widower of her longtime friend, Virginia. June thought the two should meet. After much prodding, he came.

At the end of her talk, Alice invited the audience to respond to improvised topics. When tall and distinguished John Donnelly came to the podium, Alice was impressed with his speaking ability and his outrageous humor. At the end of the evening, he escorted her to her car and asked Alice if he might telephone her sometime. *What a perfect gentleman!* she thought.

In a few days, her telephone rang. John announced himself, and Alice responded, "Oh yes, you're that Irish ham who convulsed us a couple of nights ago!" They exchanged some light banter and information. She learned that John was a real estate broker, as Tom had been. She offered little information in return. No matter. June Kane had told it all! Well, not quite.

When his daughter Kathleen heard who her father was going to date, she told him about Alice's speech before the Executive Womens' Council and her gutsy challenge to the IRS auditor. John did not tell that he knew.

"Will you mark June 6 on your calendar and have dinner with me next Wednesday at the Duquesne Club?" he asked.

Who is this guy asking me to the uppity Duquesne Club? . . . "Next Wednesday? No, I can't." He asked why. Alice answered, "I have a disco lesson on Wednesdays."

"What?" he gasped. "You mean you'd give up dinner at the Duquesne Club for a disco lesson? Are you serious?"

"Dead serious, I'm not impressed!" came her answer. The banter continued. Donnelly, not accustomed to "losing a sale," was not about to give up, and he finally convinced Alice to change her mind. They agreed that he would call for her at her tuxedo shop at closing time. When he came into the shop, Jimmy was immediatcly impressed with the well-groomed tall, handsome, assured Irishman.

The doorman at the Duquesne Club escorted John and Alice to the elevator, marked "For ladies only," and pushed the button to take her to the proper floor. John brushed him firmly aside and stepped in. "It may be their rule but, it's not mine. A lady doesn't go unescorted." He reminded her of Tom.

When they approached the huge dining hall, people stood and said, "Good evening, Commissioner." Alice looked around to see who they were greeting, and saw no one. They were escorted to the head table, and everyone sat. Commissioner? The light dawned — it was John. But Commissioner of what? The rogue was thoroughly amused at her reaction when she learned that he was owner of Donnelly Realty and Pennsylvania Real Estate Commissioner.

Dinner conversation was quite interesting — especially when the subject of Eminent Domain surfaced. Her dinner partners were surprised at Alice's in-depth knowledge of the subject and inquired about her background. Donnelly, unknown to Alice, was familiar with her story, but not with her agony and anger.

"Go ahead, Alice, tell them what you do beside run a business and teach," John prodded. She offered little else. "Go ahead. Tell them." Alice did not respond. "No, she's not a lawyer, or in real estate. She's a Rhetorician," he said mischievously. Highly amused, Alice laughed. John's impishness reminded her of her father.

Life had new meaning. They could be great friends. Alice and John, independent entrepreneurs, had much in common: a love of family, friends, fun — and Italian opera. John and his barber — coincidentally, Alice's *paesano* — loved Italian opera. They talked about their mates and shared funny Tom and Virginia stories. Alice soon discovered that John and Tom, both romantics, had many similar traits: integrity, courage, humor, self-confidence, and the courage to fight for their principles.

Eventually, honesty compelled John to reveal something that might militate against a serious relationship. It was August 9, her birthday, two months after their first date. After dinner, John revealed that a romance for them might never happen, because he had undergone triple bypass heart surgery. He was doing well now, but felt his life held no guarantee. He waited for Alice's response.

Momentarily stunned, she thought about Tom and said, "Look, John, no one's life has a guarantee. Tom was the healthiest specimen of manhood, and he's pushing up daisies now. Some little child could go before you do. You're here now, and it doesn't make any difference to me. And if you don't mind, I'll give you the same advice you've given me . . . 'Don't look too far down the road.' " John's reaction was a long, wordless embrace.

That night Alice shared the news with Rosette and later with her sons. Their reactions were like hers. Tom had left his mark with them. Until John came along, no man had seemed to be quite "fit" for their mother.

As their friendship developed, Alice discovered that this gentleman had great respect for women. And women aggressively pursued him. When she heard his story, Alice knew why. He loved and yearned for his mother, who lived in his imagination as God's greatest creation. John, the youngest of four, had been orphaned at two, then cared for by a kindly aunt and his sisters. He longed for a mother, often questioning his father about her.

Necessity finally led his father to remarry; but the little boy inherited the proverbial cruel stepmother. John perceived his father's sorrow when he saw her cruelty. No amount of questioning could induce John to talk about his mean treatment as a stepchild. Only a random expression on his face sometimes revealed it, for he sought to protect the hardworking father he dearly loved. This father was one of millions of Irish who had to escape the famine or the persecution of Irish Catholics. If they did not make it into the police force or politics, they became bottom-of-the-rung laborers, like other immigrants.

But Peter John Donnelly had hopes for his bright, studious son. He worked hard as a mill hand and saved to help him realize his goal. Young John, a product of the good nuns and Catholic school, was attracted to the priesthood. But his negative experiences at the hands of his stepmother drove him far from Pittsburgh after he graduated — to Texas, where the independent adventurer worked for several years at any job to support himself. As a short-order cook, he learned how to season and prepare an iron skillet. He lived frugally and saved his money.

John expressed his feelings in verse in *Thoughts of a Poet*, and *The Traveler*. Upon his return home after his father and stepmother died, he composed *Returning*. For a time, he delivered telegrams for Western Union, where he developed a lifelong bond with Mabel, his motherly supervisor.

John, a private man, kept his early memories locked away; but instead of being bitter from the experience, he developed a deep esteem for women and longed endlessly for his mother. The sentiment and depth of his love for her were found in poems like *The Voice* and *Golden Dreams*. When he was twenty, it was evident that he still yearned to know her. On November 27, 1938, he expressed it poignantly in a five-verse poem titled *To My Mother:*

Mother, where are you tonight,
While winds are cold and strong?
Are you sure that you're alright?
Or, perhaps, has something gone wrong?
. . .
You seem to be my guiding light
Shining from above,
To brighten up the darkest night
With tender Mother's love.

John was perceptive about women. Though he was not romantically talkative, his poetry expressed his love and frustrations: *Eunice McCoy, Dream Girl, The Girl in the Book, Lady Divine, A Toast to the Party Girl, May I Have My Heart Back? Lost Love,* and a soleful plea, *To Lou.* Unknown to Alice, they were both poets.

John loved and cared about people enough to agitate for social change. In 1940, when he sought work in the health care field, he soon discovered that nurses and hospital workers were overworked and underpaid. Seeing this as discrimination, he consulted with head nurse Mary Gerosky and fellow worker Lee Dools about forming a union for hospital workers. Anti-unionists concocted criminal charges and threatened to have John arrested. He went into hiding with a "record" against him, and continued covert activities until the first hospital union in Pittsburgh was organized.

Alice admired John for this. Just as she had fought for fair compensation for displaced property owners, he had fought for fair union wages.

Eventually John married an Irish colleen, Virginia, the orphaned daughter of Pittsburgh Mayor Tom Gallagher. But in 1942, World War II took him off to serve in the United States Army, Second Armored Division, under General Patton, whom he admired and respected.

John achieved the rank of Staff Sergeant and Platoon Sergeant. He wrote and published the first World War II newspaper, *The Daily Dig*, issued for troops in Berlin, Germany. Soldiers eagerly anticipated the "Rag." The years of schooling under the nuns, and serving under Patton, left a clear mark on

John's character: respect for discipline and able leadership. His bearing and demeanor set him apart.

John's most memorable and thrilling war experience occurred one Christmas Eve, while he was on field duty taking a "whore's bath" in his helmet, with pants at half-mast. From the distance a line of jeeps appeared, their waving flags a sign that an important military person was approaching. The convoy stopped. An enormously tall, erect man stepped out and strode firmly toward him. It was General Patton! John, astounded and embarrassed, pulled up his pants, pulled himself to attention and saluted smartly.

"Merry Christmas, sergeant!" Before John could respond, the General let out a one-minute invective of cuss words without repeating himself. "Sergeant, I promise that next year you'll be home for Christmas. We're going to get those @*!%@*!*@*! S.O.B.'S! Now come aboard. Take me to your camp!" John did not remember saluting or zipping his pants. He only remembered the thrill of riding next to this military god-hero.

John was deep, philosophical — an enigma who kept Alice puzzled. Yet he was practical and hardworking as a real estate broker. He and Alice shared the same work ethic. For instance, traveling as the Commissioner kept John very involved. "Busy as I am, I don't like to lose a sale," he once remarked. Alice understood. They were both achievers.

She was busy writing her Master's thesis, and their relationship had reached a standstill. Meanwhile, their sons, Patrick and Tom, had married. Alice attended both their weddings. For herself, however, she saw no marriage on the horizon, so she considered going to Sicily, when her Master's Degree was complete, to see the Plain of the Greeks. Alice suggested that she and John separate. John, quite upset, exclaimed, "Italy! But what if you meet an interested Italian guy?"

"You've lost the sale, John!" Alice wisecracked half-seriously. She tried to distance herself. One night he appeared at her front door with dry cleaning. "I'm your customer," he said impishly. Alice gave up and agreed that they would meet every couple of weeks.

She had new worries. Her urgent goals were to finish her degree and pay her debts before economic conditions worsened. By now, Ronald Reagan was president. The news media revealed that the nation's economy had declined, drug and gun sales had increased, and gang violence was a national scandal. Local gangs shunned each other's turf. Her tuxedo business drew from a wide area; but as gang violence increased, Alice's prom business decreased. Despite the alleged prosperity of "supply-side Reaganomics," her business in Wilkinsburg was in trouble.

It appeared that the eighties were prosperous times. After Reagan restructured the tax code in 1981, some accumulated more luxuries and disposable resources, but the economic gap widened.

The less conservative media reported that a minority of American wage earners were doing only moderately well, while many had hit new depths of poverty. Alice watched "Reaganomics" with skepticism. She feared that the economic trend of the time would adversely affect her tuxedo business; for the reality was that the federal debt soared, the stock market fell, and luxury spending decreased. Tuxedos were a luxury.

Another economic threat lay ahead for her and Frank. Still suffering from the financial havoc caused by the experience of Eminent Domain, their educational goals were in jeopardy. While prosperous yuppies could afford to send their kids to college, many students felt the pinch and dropped out. Ronald Reagan abruptly cut off the partial college scholarship benefits once available for orphaned children who qualified under Social Security. Frank, until his last semester at college, had received these limited scholarship benefits from Social Security to boost his own earned income from on-campus jobs, and whatever help he got from his family.

Now six credits short of graduating, Alice knew that meeting Frank's tuition and paying her own tuition might not be possible. And in fact the deadline for completing her degree expired before she could muster tuition and finish her last two courses. Then, there was still the debt legacy of Eminent Domain. Without an extension, Alice feared she would not get her Master's Degree. She was depressed and avoided seeing John. He was puzzled. She was too proud to complain to anyone. Then the survival bell rang! *Adapt!*

She asked the advice of Dr. Otis Walter, who respected Alice's work. Dr. Walter sent Faculty Dean Dr. Baranger a detailed description of her high academic history, her campus activities, and nonstop teaching record. On November 24, 1982, Otis advised her in a letter to "fill in the application forms for readmission and be sure to enclose your check for $10."

On December 15, 1982, Alice wrote to Dean Baranger, explained her financial crisis, assured him that her self-education had not stopped, and then bargained with the Bella Madonna. Before Christmas, her extension was granted. It was one of her very best Christmases. Alice tucked away her letter of appeal. Her children did not need to know her dilemma. She looked ahead to graduation.

In California, Tommy Palombo, now eighteen, looked forward to his graduation, too. It would be a monumental triumph for Tommy who, like young Frank Sapienza, Alice's brother-in-law, had taken the tragedy life had dealt and surmounted the obstacles. But despite the best physical therapy and the medical care he had received at the renowned Loma Linda Children's Hospital in California, there was no hope for physical recovery. Without use of his limbs, utilizing his tongue and the miracle of technology, the quadraplegic learned to manipulate his wheelchair and computer, typing four words a minute to convey his messages.

From the confines of his bed and wheelchair, Tommy studied and achieved high school status. In a retrospective mood one day the young boy composed an unrhymed poem that graphically revealed his ordeal, his maturity, his determination, and his dependency:

Accident — by Tommy 2
It happened one day. It came out of nowhere.
I could not feel. I could not touch,
except for in my mind.
My life will always be different from that day.
I will always see things from a different view.
I will always look at things more clearly.

People always have to be with me,
because I depend on them for protection from monster death.
The monster is frightening.
It sits on my chest and jumps up and down, making it hard to breathe.
The muscles in my whole body tighten.
The monster starts to suck the air out of my lungs.

I see things more clearly because of the position I'm in,
and the people I'm around.

Because of my accident, I need people and friends around me.
I have to trust them one hundred and ten percent.
When people are drinking and get drunk, I have to be on guard more.
They don't function at 100 percent and they could easily fall asleep
and not wake up to my alarm, signaling that the monster is coming.
Their responses are slower and not as sharp.

The monster gets scared when someone comes to my rescue.
He gets scared because his mission is to kill and take me
from my loved ones,
but he cannot do that while they are with me.
Everyone, no matter how tough or strong,
has their own personal monster of death
that scares them in their own way.

With this faith upon the support of his family and the unusual commitment and help of his loyal high school friend, Ronnie, Tommy fought toward his goal. During school hours when medication and physical stress overtook him, he would sometimes fall asleep. Sacrificing his own grades, Ronnie, two years his junior, tutored Tommy after school each day.

At last graduation day dawned clear and bright. Raymond lifted his son from his automated tilted bed to assist him with his toilette and settle him in his specially equipped wheelchair. The respirator was in place. Connie and his sister Tina waited to help him into his brand-new shoes and suit. Unable to touch or feel the crisp white fabric, Tommy beamed at his reflection in the mirror.

The outdoor ceremony was crowded with family and friends. Sophia sat proudly, anticipating Tommy's coveted moment. It had been a long journey from the San Antonio Hospital to the Loma Linda Rehab Unit where armless and legless children faced their challenging futures.

As the diplomas were presented, Tommy's mentor, Ronnie, was presented a diploma in recognition of his work with Tommy. When his name was called, Tommy commanded and manipulated his wheelchair down the long aisle to receive his diploma. Raymond, Connie, Tina, and Grandmother Sophia stood proudly as the audience applauded him to the dais with a standing ovation. Overhead, an airplane flew low, pulling behind it across the bright blue sky a huge banner proclaiming Tommy's achievement. "CONGRATULATIONS! GO, TOMMY!" Sophia stood emotionally and glanced at those around her. There were few dry eyes in the crowd. She wished desperately that Tom was alive to see his grandson's hard-won triumph.

Back in Pittsburgh, there was another mentor who came to a student's aid. His name was Cowboy. Jimmy's roving musician friend from Wyoming came into their lives with his guitar and unique repertoire of Western folk songs. His cowboy hat and boots dominated his skinny five-foot-two frame. Cowboy needed a place to stay. Jim and Alice provided him with the spare bedroom that had rescued several other musician friends in need. They all had two things in common: all were extremely talented — and nearly broke. In exchange for board, Cowboy offered to watch Alice's store for several hours each morning while she studied for her Master's degree and finished her Thesis. Each day they exchanged stories, had coffee and shared a song or two.

The day Alice announced that she had completed her goal, Cowboy was overjoyed and proud. The next morning, Alice went in to work early. Cowboy had opened the store and was sitting near her desk, strumming his guitar. With his Western twang and happy smile, he sang her a medley of tunes. The last one he sang was Willie Nelson's song *On The Road Again*. The next day he was gone. Alice grieved that she could not express her extreme gratitude to Cowboy.

Otis Walter took Alice to dinner to celebrate her hard-earned achievement and to arrange for her final Master's exam. As they relaxed, Otis announced his pending retirement. He poured Alice a second glass of wine and asked her what she thought about doing a book with him — in California. "I. . . I don't know," she said hesitantly. How did Alice drive home? Verrry carefully — and thoughtfully. She told John about Otis' offer.

"I'll just *bet* he only wants to do a book!" he snapped. Alice was amused.

On the night she finished her finals, John invited her to their favorite restaurant on campus and ordered "crazy cokes" to celebrate. A Manhattan was John's favorite drink. He always kidded her about being a cheap date because one good drink made her tipsy. "Did you think your exams were over? I have a multiple choice question," he said over his third drink.

"Are you going to Italy? To California? Or are you going to marry me?" He had withheld "popping the question" until she finished her finals so that she would not get distracted.

"Are you asking me to *mmmarry* you?" Alice sputtered senselessly, aghast. "You'll have to ask my father!" — then spilled her crazy coke into her book bag and blurted "Yes! Of course, you nutty Irishman!"

Her response must have given him an idea. He marched Alice to Jim's apartment and, standing beneath his porch railing, John ceremoniously asked for his mother's hand. Jim appreciated the moment and just as ceremoniously gave his consent through a mile-wide smile.

At Alice's home, John called Pat and Karen, who knew his plan. "Did she say yes?" Their happy howls conveyed their joy. "Hi Mom! We hoped you'd say yes," Pat said when Alice took the phone.

Kathleen was happy for her father. As nonconformists, she and Alice related well. When John and Alice visited Tommy to tell the news, he pumped his approval with an energetic handshake for John, and a rib-crushing hug for his mother.

"I'm trading my Ms. for a Mrs.," Alice told Frank on the telephone. He liked the trade — and John.

"Hey, a guy who loves Italian opera can't be that bad," Rosette said when she got the news. John had been a proud and faithful fan at all her vocal recitals.

That night Alice tossed restlessly. She dreamed that she was waiting for a bus. When she came aboard, the driver was Tom. She could not believe he was alive! She panicked, thinking that she was being unfaithful to him. Should she tell him about John? She debated as she took her seat. The next passenger to board the bus was John! Her panic grew as John came and sat beside her. She looked toward Tom. He turned his head and gave her a huge, deep-dimpled approving smile, nodded his head yes, twice, and winked.

A few days later she shared her dream with Jim. "He approves of John. I can finally let go of your father," Alice wept.

Jim understood. He had not been able to relinquish his father for a long while. As she revealed her dream, Jim said through tears, "I finally let go of Dad, too. I also had a dream." He could scarcely tell it. "I dreamed I was in an elevator, and standing in front of me was Dad. His full head of hair, his posture and build, his suit was Dad. I didn't believe he was dead. As the elevator traveled interminably upward, I stared and stared at his back until he turned around slowly . . . and looked at me through hollow eyes. His face was the leather-wrinkled ash-gray mask of death! He got off the elevator — and I woke up!" Jim cried and rubbed the goose-bumps on his forearm.

Alice shared her dream with John. Both were ready to let go of the past. Graduation day lay ahead. This graduation ceremony would be different from her last lonely one. John sat proudly as she walked to the dais to receive her Master's Degree. Surely relishing the event with them in spirit were Papa and Tom.

Pat and Karen bought John's home and moved in with their three children, Erin, Maureen, and Brendan. John furnished Alice's house with new rugs and, before their wedding on January 14, moved some of his lovely furniture and antiques.

On her wedding day, the confident public speaker dreaded the thought of walking down the aisle. Her daughter-in-law, Mary, gave her a shot of confidence — Scotch. As she walked toward John at the altar, he recognized the glow and silly smile. "Oh no!" he uttered, taking her arm firmly as he helped her to the kneeler.

Before the wedding, Alice had instructed Father Keane to prepare a memorial altar where they would bring flowers, light candles, and pray for Virginia and Tom. Pat and Kathleen did the video, and brother Tom the audio recording. Rosette and brother Silvio sang the Mass. And her sons Tom, Jim and Frank gave Alice away. Aunt Sophia and John's golf buddy, Jack Little, were proud sponsors.

At their dinner reception, Jimmy sang old and new songs, Irish and Italian songs, as his band played for nearly one hundred close friends and family. For the bridal dance, John requested his favorite, a Polka. And he high-stepped his way joyously around the room. Italians danced the *Irish Jig*. The Irish danced the *Tarantella*. And Frank danced spiritedly, yanking at his coat tail to cover the deep split he had torn in his pants when he slipped on the ice on his way into the church. As he danced by the bridal table, his date lifted Frank's coat. John and Alice were convulsed. "What a happy couple they are!" someone gushed. After John gave a suggestive toast that embarrassed Alice, he pulled her away.

Upon their return from their Bahamian cruise, Alice was inducted as President of the traditionally male-dominated Wilkinsburg Chamber of

Commerce. Although she had doubts at her installation, she "entered laughing." What else would one do when married to a clown?

She began her acceptance speech, "Last year, I accepted office as the Chamber's first woman Vice President, on condition that you would change the title from Vice President to President-of-Vice." She continued after the laughter. "Tonight as the first woman Chamber of Commerce president, I enter office with this warning that I received from Judge Brosky. 'Alice, in order to be a a success as a woman leader, you've got to have gray hair to look *distinguished,* and hemorrhoids to look *concerned.*' Well, folks, I don't have gray hair, but I sure as hell have been concerned!" Women gasped. Men convulsed with laughter. John Donnelly choked on his Manhattan! And loved it!

A few months into her term, the inert coffee-klatch boys were disturbed that she was "making new tracks" for the business district. She faced chauvinist discrimination and knew it. Her dear Black friend Franklin Smith warned Alice that the "good old boys" secretly planned to impeach her.

When Chamber Vice President and School Superintendent Dr. Davis came into her shop, he pompously issued a directive for her to come before the Executive Board. Alice asked why. He said, "It seems you've been making unilateral decisions." Alice recognized the term and source. She was furious, but kept cool.

"If I were a man I guess you'd call it executive *prerogative.* But I'll come and bring my tape measure and black fabric to measure the hood for my inquisition." Using rhetorical repetition, she jabbed her forefinger [Tom's style] and said, "Now, Sir, you won't intimidate me, or manipulate me, or annihilate me. I'll be around long after you're gone, and I'll *piss* on your graves!"

The red-faced Dr. Davis sputtered, bowed meekly, and left. Alice told Harry the barber the story. It spread. The boys bugged off! The maverick Chamber of Commerce president had finally made it into the inner circle of males. "You've made clear tracks for others to follow," Franklin Smith said with satisfaction.

John and Alice enjoyed each other's activities, their fun-loving families and friends. John called Alice the Ayatollah, a nickname he gave her because she kept strict watch over his cholesterol. They laughed together and, unfortunately, mourned together.

Within several years, Death came calling for two more immigrants: "Duffy" Sapienza, the second son to go; and Alice's brother, Tom Palombo, Sophia's dear husband. The following year — as if systematically — the relentless Reaper selected a grandson from each clan: Paul Martin Palombo, who joined his father; and Billy Sapienza, who joined his mother. When Alice became depressed that the ranks were thinning, John said, "Don't dwell on it." His marvelous attitude served him well.

Then in 1985 Alice panicked when a major heart attack hit John. He remained amazingly calm — or resigned. His courage reminded her of Tom when he lay dying. "No, God! Please! Not so soon!" She called Rosette. They followed the ambulance to Mercy Hospital. Dr. Bailey, his longtime heart specialist, told them that John would have to undergo another bypass surgery. Alice did what she did best under duress. Beg! First she implored Dr. Bailey to have his heart team do everything possible to save John. She promised to do whatever she must to give him her best undivided care. Dr. Bailey smiled and pressed her hand. Alice summoned Pat, Karen and Kathleen; then retreated to implore *Dio* and the *Bella Madonna* to guide the doctors to save his life. Nearby, Rosette and John's children waited to comfort her through the ordeal.

In the recovery room several hours later, John lay calmly acceptive among tubes and I-V bags, as a machine purified his blood of cholesterol, and pumped it rhythmically back into his body — "kata . . . clack . . . kata clack . . . kata clack." The miracle of modern science had pulled him through another successful bypass. Alice was amazed at John's attitude. Perceiving her thoughts, he said, "It's not so bad. Don't look too far down the road."

In a few months, John returned to mild activity — golfing and bowling. He enjoyed Jimmy's performances. He sat proudly watching Leah's drama performances, as if she were his very own child. He indulged their grand-children. He stocked Hawaiian Punch for R.J., black olives for Lauren, and green leaves for Leah to "fix" any hurt. He cooked gourmet New York strip steaks for Frank and teased him with an offer of Brussel sprouts, which Frank hated. Yes, John was back to normal mischief.

Two years later, 1987, Wilkinsburg celebrated its Centennial. Mayor Depperman, familiar with Alice's background, appointed her to be Centennial Coordinator. To handle the activities, she organized ten committees of ethnic diversity. The Old Guard and newcomer volunteers, who had many professional talents and skills, worked cooperatively.

She created the theme "Tradition, Unity and Vision," designed to make a statement that spoke her loathing of America's history of prejudice. Bill Hofscher, the Centennial artist, memorialized Alice's creation on the Centennial flag, where a colonial soldier facing left represented Tradition, an astronaut facing right depicted Vision, and in the center, a clasped white hand and black hand represented Unity. At a Borough Council meeting, the Meridian Fife and Drum Corps presented the official flag to the Borough Council.

At the Centennial Parade, commentator Jimmy Sapienza periodically announced a hitch — a snafu! The Borough had lost its seventy-fifth anniversary time capsule, still missing after an intensive search. The lost capsule drew international media attention and fun.

At the Centennial Banquet dance, in its place, Jimmy presented an enormously funny "time capsule" loosely constructed of mismatched wood slats: Among its treasures were: news photos of a search-dog relieving himself against the borough building cornerstone, and a photo of Mayor Depperman leading the Centennial parade on rollerskates, dressed in tuxedo and top hat; a bent, rusty key for the new capsule's proposed hiding place; a street brick and tar pothole, framed with accompanying description; a Centennial flag and T-shirt printed upsidedown; and a "proclamation" that poked fun at local politicians. Revelers were convulsed with laugher!

But for the local media, Wilkinsburg had become a regular target of negative, sensational news. Instead of focusing upon the changing character of the town as a role model of diverse cultures working cooperatively, the media had a field day emphasizing its foibles: devious politics, drug abuse, and youth crimes — which only mirrored the nation's social scene then.

Undaunted, community activists fought back to regain its tarnished image, founding the Wilkinsburg Arts Council and focusing half its productions on Black culture. Professional volunteers wore many hats to stage successful theater productions. The theater attracted critics and fans from the tri-state area, and won numerous awards and critical acclaim for its multicultural plays and musicals. It produced Langston Hughes' Christmas Gospel Musical, *Black Nativity,* and unified classes and faiths — a first in Pittsburgh. The production earned the theater an invitation to perform the musical on Pittsburgh's Fulton playhouse stage. Traditional "Old Wilkinsburg" was gradually transforming.

John brought mischief to the theater scene. One night when the stage was set with some furnishings from their house, John arrived at a dress rehearsal and sat on stage. He unfolded his newspaper and began to read. When Alice questioned his behavior, he feigned surprise. To everyone's complete amusement he said, "Oh my, I thought I was at home!" At another production when the costumes and entire set were created in red, white, and blue, John appeared dressed in red, white, and blue to distribute programs. His merry-making and mischief increased at Christmas time. He came to usher, dressed in a loud patchwork sport coat, a Christmas hat and bow tie which lit up, and socks that played *Jingle Bells* when coaxed.

No less roguish at home, one Christmas morning he planned a special surprise for Alice. A tall, lean man with a small butt, he came downstairs dressed in nothing but huge gift bows attached to his front and rear, with a wide red ribbon stretched horizontally across his chest. "Merrrry Christmas!" he bellowed. "I'm your Christmas present!" Standing nearby was Frank, afraid to look at what the unpredictable rascal might do. Frank dashed for the stairs laughing uproariously and, from the effort, backfired a tremendous blast of air!

John looked upstairs and asked, "Did someone step on a duck?" This threw Frank into convulsive laughter, and he "quacked" again. "Hey Frank," John said. "You can look now," and ripped off the big front bow to reveal outlandish Christmas shorts with Rudolph the red-nosed reindeer pointing his lit-up proboscis in exactly the right spot! Then he turned to Alice and said, *"Buon Natale!* I know, I'm a *ciamentuso,* a teaser like your father was," he said in near-perfect Abruzzese dialect.

When Alice made John repeat the remark at the family Christmas party, Grace said, "He sounds like me." She often mixed Abruzzese and English when she spoke. John laughed when Grace said, as she looked up to the top of his head: "You wouldn't need a stepladder to pick apples." That night she remarked *"Si vuo' Dio.* If God wills, I'd like to see the year 2000 in twelve more years." She was eighty-five years old.

After the holidays Alice and John visited Grace again, to say *"Arrivederci"* until they returned from a two-week vacation in Florida. But Fate disrupted their pleasure. While they vacationed with Uncle Frank, who now lived there with Honey Donley, his care-giver, Grace's health failed. During their visit with Frank and Honey, Alice spent much time helping to pack boxes for his move to another home. After three days, John saw her fatigue and swept her away to visit Jean, her favorite cousin, who lived near Disneyland.

Jean and John bonded immediately through shared humor. They laughed and told outrageous stories. Jean, who made ceramics as a hobby, gave him an immodest statue, *The Secret*. From the front, it was a proper Colonial couple; from the back, the "gentleman" had his hand across her posterior, on her uplifted skirt. Three days later, Jean kissed the couple goodbye and stuffed a bag with oranges for their trip to Disneyland.

Meanwhile, Grace was hospitalized — and on January 24, 1989, lost her hope to see the year 2000. Word reached Alice when it was too late to return for her funeral. Alice was absolutely crushed with remorse! She could not say goodbye! Their vacation lost its joy. John understood. "Don't dwell on it," he said. But she did.

While the train carried them home to Pittsburgh, a movie reel of life with Grace ran through her head, as Alice mourned her surrogate mother. She reminisced from the time Grace and Alex took her to see the first silent movies and the "talkies," to their last visit with her at Christmas. Who would hold Italian conversations with her now? Or call her *Elisa*? No one.

Grace was her mother's generation, holding to the customs of the past. This daughter of two countries and two cultures had bravely endured and conquered much on her journey from the hills of Abruzzi, to Ellis Island, to Pittsburgh. "She's going Home to meet her closest loved ones. She is *Grazia Stella* now," Alice mumbled. John pulled her head onto his shoulder.

In grief, one is likely to have sad thoughts. Alice pondered the number of separations Grazia had endured. She counted thirteen. Suddenly Alice missed her brother Tom. "It's tough to lose a brother — and now my only sister, I'll miss her," she lamented.

John pulled her head onto his shoulder again and said, "I understand. You were fortunate to have two mothers. I never really met mine. I miss her." Alice had never seen John cry openly. They linked arms and retreated to the solace of their "private world." And finally fell asleep.

Chapter 24

"To Everything There is a Season"

On New Year's morning 1990, John was downstairs preparing brunch — as he always did on Sundays and holidays. Last night's party girl enjoyed the aroma of coffee, sizzling bacon, and hotcakes, as she lay in bed. John and Alice had partied with friends and *Five Guys Name Moe*, a band who got its curious label from a Louis Jordan tune.

Jordan's long-forgotten humorous songs appealed to fans in the 1930's and early 1940's. When he broke away from Chick Webb's big band, Louis formed his *Tympany Five* and became recognized as the father of Rhythm 'n' Blues. When Jimmy Sapienza discovered Jordan's musical satire in 1988, it appealed to his sense of humor. It was perfect for the performance style he had acquired as a stand-up comic. He organized a unique group of musicians, and renamed his band *"Jimmy Sapienza's Five Guys Named Moe,"* formerly known as *Jimmy and the Dukes*.

Fans howled when he introduced the fun group: "Hi folks, we're the most politically correct band you'll ever see . . . two Black guys, two blind guys and a fat guy! We're *Jimmy Sapienza's Five Guys Named Moe!"*

John loved it. "The apple didn't fall far from the tree," he said.

Alice reached for her robe and rolled out of bed. John, wearing his tall chef's hat, greeted her with spatula in hand. "Good morning, Ayatollah!" he teased and broke into an off-key fun ditty. Mornings always began with humor.

After breakfast and Mass, they would prepare an Italian buffet for family and visitors and gather around the piano to sing or update their corny jokes. Tomorrow Frank would be gone to his job in Cincinnati. The rest of the family would resume their own routines.

Business would be slow, but community activity would be vigorous, especially with the Wilkinsburg Arts Theater. The theater's committment to presenting multicultural shows drew audiences from the Tri-State area, and consistently earned rave reviews. Its four annual productions of *Black Nativity;* and Gian Carlo Menotti's opera, *Amahl and the Night Visitors,* were Christmas hits. John loved the family's artistry. He sat proudly as

Rosette sang the lead role in the opera and Leah, her daughter, sang and danced in the shepherd's chorus.

The Wilkinsburg Arts Theater attracted professional volunteers who were its lifeblood. Its greatest strength? Multiethnic inclusion. The theater's specific mission was to choose plays that showcased diverse cultures and timely themes, and to arouse sensitivity to anti-racial attitudes.

Nothing was sacred to this community theater. Drug addiction, crooked small-town politics, and other timely themes stirred theater critic Adrian McCoy to write: "Racial stereotypes get a sound trashing." *Post Gazette* drama critic Chris Rawson wrote, "There's a world here that art can help us understand . . . "

"Bull's eye! The Arts understand. The media does not!" Alice exclaimed.

Unfairly, Wilkinsburg was food for sensational news that helped give it a negative image. By now its population had changed significantly with the overflow from the Hill and Homewood. Longtime family-owned businesses were leaving. In their place, a community of Immigrant Orientals and Blacks were developing business enterprises. The Black residential population was now more than half.

Despite First Lady Nancy Reagan's plea, "Just say no to drugs," the national drug problem spread. Pushers were attracted to Wilkinsburg. The community felt threatened. Reacting to the increasing menace, determined residents eventually organized Block Clubs: they walked the streets every night, challenged wrongdoers, and, by the late 90's, swept them out of town. Although there was widespread crime in other communities, the media downplayed these fearless Block Club crime-stoppers, while stereotyping Blacks as criminals, and stigmatizing Wilkinsburg as a community to be feared. The town would soon pay for it.

Unfortunately, anti-racial attitudes and negative publicity, more than crime itself, affected Wilkinsburg's business and social activity. The borough's best kept secret was its many community organizations and its cooperative diversity. Nonetheless, people avoided the town when they could. Alice's business was slowly falling victim to public perception. Fewer theater productions drew fewer nighttime crowds and had to be scheduled for holiday and weekend matinees. Alice expressed her concern to John.

"To everything there is a season," he said and reminded her of the reading in their wedding vows. How prophetic! "Don't dwell on it. Let's enjoy what's happening," he said. And enjoy they did. John's obvious pleasure was Italian opera. They laughed at recognizable human foibles in opera — sometimes their own. They reminisced about Alice's tipsy walk down the aisle — and played their wedding tapes. In January 1992, the happy pair spent their eighth anniversary vacation with son Tom's family at his condo at Hidden Valley ski resort.

But in a few weeks, Alice noticed that her jovial husband had become progressively listless. Regular visits to his new physician, who had replaced the retired Dr. Bailey, showed that his cardiac tests were fine. John was not a complainer; but as he lay around, Alice became uneasy and urged him to revisit the doctor, whose failure to diagnose John's persistent pains reminded her disturbingly of Tom's doctor, who had missed his symptoms. After a series of tests and valuable lost time, John was referred to another physician. The test results were due on March 9. That evening before dinner, Alice asked him about the results.

John, a deeply private man, simply answered, "Let's have dinner." She insisted. He answered, "Don't dwell on it. And don't look too far down the road."

As they sat eating dinner, John suddenly slumped over, and gasping, fell to the floor face down. Alice, unable to turn him over for mouth-to-mouth resuscitation, immediately called 911, whose ambulance crew appeared within minutes. While the emergency team revived John, Alice quickly summoned her friend Rick Harris, Pat and Karen, Bill and Rosette. The paramedics carried John to the ambulance. Rick and Alice followed close behind in her car to Forbes Metropolitan Hospital five miles away.

In his intensive care room, Alice stood by John, as she had stood by Tom, reassuring him and declaring her love. But the tireless unyielding Reaper came again. After midnight John died! And another "private world" had vanished! Parting was no easier the second time.

Their grieving children gathered around Alice, Bill and Rosette insisting that she come home with them. In Rosette's guest room, Alice prayed, scolded the Bella Madonna, and wept the night away. Nearby, Rosette and Bill heard and mourned with her.

Alice hated Knee's Funeral Home and the rituals she had endured so often. Remembering her "last goodbye" to Tom, she insisted, over Mr. Knee's objections, on being alone for her final parting with John.

When they entered the church for the funeral Mass, a strong aroma of cooking bacon filled the air. Frank nudged Alice. "John!" Frank said half-credulously. "I'll bet he's playing his last joke on us." Knowing John, they smiled.

On St. Patrick's Day, a week after he died, came bitter-sweet memories. Loneliness was painful. Alice had unanswered questions about John's death, and was disturbed about the test results that he had concealed. She investigated and learned that he had been diagnosed with prostate cancer! Stunned, horrified and furious, she blamed the new doctor for his death. Alice had the urge to throttle him because, like Tom's doctor, he had missed the early symptoms.

Alice vented her anger: "That dumb idiot! Doctor Bailey was so careful. He wouldn't have let this happen! Enough is enough, God! How will I have courage to continue? I'm sinking into a deep hole. What the hell! I might as well give up!" The telephone rang. It was her dear friend, Harriet Rush, calling to console her.

She repeated her angry tirade. Harriet, herself widowed, listened patiently and then calmly said, "Alice, my friend, don't allow yourself to get down into that deep hole. The farther down you go, the harder it is to pull up. What did you do when Tom died? You found something worthwhile to do. Didn't you go back to school? Come on, friend, don't give in . . . Hey, I'm like Lucy in the Peanuts comics. Think I'll hang out my psychiatrist's shingle. That'll be five cents for the advice."

"Socrates went around giving advice, and they poisoned him," Alice laughed. She weighed Harriet's suggestion. It was a turning point. She respected Harriet. They shared the same sense of humor, the same birthday, and the same love for music and writing.

Fortunately, Jimmy lived above Alice's shop. He and his mother had much in common, including creativity. Many mornings when she came to work, she could hear Jimmy rehearsing or composing another song, and knew that he had been up all night. She did not disturb him, understanding that creative people needed time and freedom to be alone. But he always found time to share his latest song. The inclusion eased her loneliness.

As Jimmy's repertoire gained popularity, fans nominated him Pittsburgh's "best vocalist" and the *Five Guys Named Moe* "best band." When John Cigna of KDKA saw their performance, he was impressed. He booked the group for his annual Spaghetti Breakfast. "Jimmy, I'm going to make you a household word," he said. And he did.

Cigna continued booking the *Five Guys Named Moe* for over sixteen years. Fans who listened on radio called in. Some remembered Sebastian Sapienza, Jimmy's grandfather, who had played with the KDKA Little Symphony Orchestra in the early twenties! The station's radio music past had come full circle. At one Spaghetti Breakfast performance, the band came at seven a.m. dressed in pajamas and convulsed John Cigna with laughter. The internet audience who logged on loved it, too.

Audiences loved the Louis Jordan songs, which received more exposure through Tony Mowad's programs on Duquesne University's radio station WDUQ and *Five Guys'* performances with Mowad's Jazz Society audiences. Between performances, Jimmy kept composing. He collected records and stories about Jordan and shared these with Alice. Their common creative bond lifted her from her depression. One day as she read about Jordan's private life, and the history of exclusion and prejudice endured by Black musicians, she identified with them and became irate.

"What a crock of crap," she stormed. "My God, Jimmy, this would make a great musical drama! We could really kick ass! Your band does great Jordan stuff and would be perfect for it." She remembered her friend's advice after John died, "Find something worthwhile to do," and decided to write a musical drama. Because of her experience as the theater's Executive Director, she became its producer.

Grief diminished as mother and son consulted and enjoyed achieving their common goal. Jimmy became script adviser. Bobby Boswell, Jimmy's friend, had played bass in Jordan's band. Alice interviewed him and gained firsthand knowledge about Jordan, his associates, and Fleecie, his scheming, nagging first wife. With this insight, Alice developed their characters.

Jimmy selected the title *Brother Beware* from a Jordan tune that fit the story. The script consistently traveled from Alice's tuxedo shop to Jim's music studio upstairs. Knowing the vernacular of the era helped her craft authentic dialogue. They laughed and exchanged ideas and played out parts. Then they applied to New York for the necessary royalty rights to music. To their disappointment, they found that royalty rights were restricted because a new group from London, who had only recently taken the name *Five Guys Named Moe*, was slated to come to America. Undaunted, Jimmy composed two special Jordanesque show tunes, *"No Good Woman"* and *"Little Rock Shuffle"* — in reference to Little Rock, Arkansas, Jordan's home. Jimmy's compositions enhanced the script perfectly, and became immediate and lasting hits wherever he performed.

In addition, Alice's grandson, R.J., and his parents traveled to St. Louis to Jordan's grave. R.J. took slide photos of his tombstone to include with the show's scenery.

When Director Lamont Arnold read the script, he exclaimed, "My God, Alice, I love it! I never knew this guy existed. Thank you for giving our kids a Black hero. If I weren't looking at a White face, I'd swear a Black playwright wrote this!" He hugged her spontaneously.

"Well a pissed-off Italian woman wrote it!" Alice laughed.

Lamont was pleased to discover Jimmy's musical and acting talent, and cast him in two parts: as himself, the lead singer of his band and as Lou Levy, Jordan's slick agent. When Boswell saw the performance, he remarked, "Alice, you nailed the story just right!"

Writing *Brother Beware* gave Alice an excuse to spend long hours at her shop, comforted by Jimmy's presence. Going home to an empty house was painful. Her children knew it. Rosette, though busy with her family and a successful music career, kept in close touch with her mother. Frank, who still lived in Cincinnati, came home at every opportunity. Tom, sensing his mother's loneliness, and holding to the character of Italian family loyalty, devised a plan to bring Frank home.

Tom had become president and co-owner of the Sawyer Business School, and cofounder of the Pennsylvania Culinary Institute. Reflecting his father's business genius, he had helped spiral these schools to multimillion dollar successes. A humble and quietly generous man, he had been a patron to underprivileged students, and a discreet and generous financial benefactor to his clan.

Though the idea of bringing Frank home was typical of his generosity and caring, behind the plan lay an attitude that the family lived by. It was spelled out on the trivet that hung on their kitchen wall: "The world owes you a living, but you must work hard to collect it."

Confident about Frank's success in management positions, his positive attitude and his family work ethic, Tom offered him a job interview with the Sawyer Business School Employment Director. The brothers, conscious of nepotism, expected no special consideration. Frank was hired and soon proved his value.

Alice, respecting Frank's independence, invited him to live at home until he found an apartment. He accepted. They were happy in the assurance that their non-interfering living style was a perfect fit. He resumed contact with cousins and old friends, and she looked forward to the opening of her play.

But a cloud hung over the theater, forced to its knees by the media's relentless focus on Wilkinsburg's eroding reputation. Unfortunately, *Brother Beware* would be its final production, scheduled for three weeks of weekend matinees that included Friday evening performances. In the Christmas season of 1992, *Brother Beware* drew large audiences, including numerous known actors, radio and television personalities, and a charming "Moe" fan, Paula, who would add some new drama to the clan's story.

Brother Beware earned several news features and critical acclaim as a musical drama. Among these was a favorable review by respected *Post Gazette* theater critic Chris Rawson, who appreciated both the play's ethnic story line and the acting and musical talents of its performers. Its staff writer Marlo Verilla wrote: "To people who wonder why she is writing about a Black man she says, 'Because I am your sister. Forget the color of my skin, look at the color of my heart.' " The *Tribune Review* theater critic Ed Blank wrote: "Play mixes writer's and Jordan's lives . . . To look for the differences between Sapienza-Donnelly and Jordan is to miss the point of the oneness she feels with him." Bingo!

After the final curtain, the theater's eight-year history drew to a close. Amid a standing ovation for cast and crew and calls of "author, author," Alice scarcely remembered the congratulations and good wishes. She remembered the sad farewells at the final cast party. Tonight she had closed her play. Tomorrow, after forty-five years, she would close her business. *"To everything there is a season,"* she mused sadly, remembering John.

But a surprise came when Alice was chosen VITA (Volunteer In The Arts) awardee of the year at the Awards Luncheon at Heinz Hall. Her Arts colleague, Jeanne McNutt, who had nominated her, smiled like *Alice in Wonderland's* Cheshire Cat. Stunned at the honor, the winner said to her fellow nominees, "You are each deserving of this honor. No one earns an award in isolation. There are invisible hands who earned this with me." God, how she wished John was there!

At home, her family rallied close. Brother Lou, who had always kept a "mothering" eye on her, came by — without Jane. Alice learned that Lou's Jane had suffered a nervous breakdown and was confined to Pitt's Western Psychiatric Hospital. After several weeks at home, and after many more agonizing weeks of emotional turmoil, the stress took its toll on Lou. He suffered a heart attack and was rushed to Forbes Metropolitan Hospital. "I hate this damned hospital!" Alice complained.

When she arrived, Lou was unconscious. His son and wife Donna waited helplessly. Jane, hysterical, fell apart screaming. Alice found herself once again in the same intensive care room where John had died. Childhood memories of her close bond to Lou flooded her. And she remembered the love he expressed in the poems he'd written for her sixty-fifth birthday and for the eve of her wedding to John. And wept. "Dear God, not again," she pleaded, as she watched the monitor above Lou's bed.

By now she knew the routine. Lou could surely hear her. She stood beside him, as she had stood beside Tom and John, and spoke loving words. The lifeline on the monitor quivered across the screen and flattened. And Lou was gone! It was April 1993, near his seventy-sixth birthday. Alice hated this room. She took mental inventory of this generation's family survivors. The ranks were diminishing. "Two Palombo and four Sapienza siblings are left," she lamented.

Nearby, Lou's son and his wife Donna wept inconsolably. Jane relapsed into another breakdown and had to be confined to Western Psych immediately. She never saw Lou again — not even at his funeral. She retreated to the cloister of her troubled mind. What would be her fate now?

At her brother's funeral, Alice gave an upbeat eulogy about the well-meaning, take-charge brother who had cared for and loved his family too well. Alice watched the hurt on his son's face, glad to see that the tribute to his father made him smile through tears.

With each family member's death, material things became less important and the family became more precious. At the cemetery Alice walked among family graves and stopped before Tom's tombstone, and read: UNSELFISH DEVOTION. A chill ran down her spine as she looked at her own grave.

That evening as she lay in bed deep in thought, grim reality and gloom hit her. *We have no choice; we will be gone and buried one by one in an overpriced useless fancy coffin, and be missed for a while. And overhead, life will go on without us! Yes, to everything there is a season.*

To her empty bedroom she said, "What a humbling sad thought! Only Silvio and I are left! An uncommon generation is dying." She remembered the family history she had written for Dr. Levine's Genealogy course. "The road ahead is short. I should finish that history. It's time," she mumbled into her pillow and prayed herself to oblivion.

Chapter 25

Denouement

"What the son wishes to forget, the grandson wishes to remember," observed Immigration Research Historian Marcus Lee Hansen. Before the nineteen sixties, many immigrant sons and daughters renounced their roots, until the Civil Rights Movement triggered appreciation for, and interest in, ethnic culture. With new-found pride and an unprecedented ethnic revival in the nineteen seventies, Americans went in search of their heritage. The catalyst was the Black Power Movement.

Traditionally, America celebrated only the Colonial past and its English-speaking Anglo settlers, who came before 1880. They spoke one language and were one religion — Protestant. They assimilated easily. People who came later from the British Isles and North Western Europe spoke many languages and worshipped differently. They met economic, political, educational, and religious barriers that persisted until Black pride gained momentum in the seventies and changed tradition. Colleges developed Genealogy courses as many students aspired to reclaim their roots.

Alice had begun her story in Genealogy class in 1972. Five busy years and several attempts after her retirement, she resumed writing the family story that she had chronicled over many years. Her manuscript rested in her briefcase among her other valued compositions.

The suitcase also held a treasured manila envelope that contained her parents' precious past: Mama's *Passaporto Per Il Duca d' Aosta* and Papa's *Passaporto Per Luisiana* -- the Boarding Pass from his last crossing. Alice pressed the passport to her heart, in gratitude for Papa's survival of that last perilous voyage. Among the treasures were two savings booklets from *Casa Di Risparmio, Provincia di Campobasso,* a bilingual Catechism that helped them understand their religion in English, and Paolo's U. S. registration card for service in World War I were among the treasures. In Papa's wallet was a photo of his cousin Carmelina, the nun, and his prized U.S. Democratic Voter's Club card. Papa had loved politics and had taken an active part in the election campaigns.

Denouement

The memento that made her parents proudest was the brown leather folder that held their treasured American Citizenship Certificates. The memorabilia represented their story of courage and sacrifice. God, how she missed them! They would be proud of their progeny.

Alice reflected with pride that more than half of three generations of Palombos and Sapienzas had successfully pursued business careers, college degrees, and professional careers in Education, Law, Medicine, and the Arts. She concluded that their success was Italy's legacy to America, just as the contributions of all immigrants, since Plymouth Rock, are part of America's legacy. She considered herself fortunate and enriched for having been raised to respect people of all races and nationalities; and believed that those in prior generations who had given up their ethnicity in order to "fit in" were truly impoverished.

Seated comfortably in her big chair, Alice began to meditate — a luxury she treasured. *I feel like a rider astride two horses. I'm torn between two cultures, and I've chosen the best of both. But in my heart, I'll always be a daughter of the Renaissance. "Figlia di Rinascimento,"* she declared.

Martino Mariotti had made her proud to be Italian-American at a time when many denied their nationality in order to be assimilated or to escape prejudice. *"Caro Martino, requiescat in pace!"* she exclaimed. Alice was grateful that the Italian-American was no longer stereotyped as a pushcart vendor or organ grinder with monkey, and pleased that Italians were no longer doomed to work only as common laborers. Those jobs now fell to new immigrants, Asian and South American.

Continuing her reflections, Alice was torn between two eras. She looked Janus-faced to the calm, decent epoch before the sixties and the new liberated generation. Although Alice considered herself a contemporary woman, she had been raised in the old-fashioned tradition where Italian daughters knew what was morally expected of them. And her thoughts turned to the disturbing changes in contemporary American values, where modern daughters had no shame about living with lovers, aborting their babies, or conceiving babies out of wedlock. Most disturbing to her was the growing trend of single women shopping for super male genes at sperm banks to bear children who were deprived of fathers. An appalling thought gripped her, and she grumbled: "How can a boy play football with test tube number 950? Or a girl dance with her father on her wedding day? How sad!"

Denouement

Alice had seen Victorian standards of morality vanish, and mourned the passing of immigrant values. She decided that, if being modern required her to change or corrupt her beliefs, she would stay old-fashioned. She looked at Mama's citizenship photo and smiled.

She gently folded it into its brown pouch with Papa's photo. Emotional and inspired by the precious artifacts of her heritage, she became *Elisa*. She laughed as she remembered how her mother and Rosa communicated with their Friend, the Holy Mother. Rosa beseeched the *Bedda Madonna* in Sicilian dialect. Maria bargained with Her in Abruzzeze. "What a relationship!" Alice exclaimed as she retrieved her notes and manuscript and closed her briefcase.

Until now, Alice had postponed writing. She and a faithful few supporters had devoted many years toward helping to save a national historic treasure — the Frank Conrad garage, birthplace of the radio broadcasting industry. But their attempts had failed to gain the interest and financial support of the broadcasting media and philanthropists. And now, Conrad's creative haven was about to be demolished to make way for a fast-food eatery — and lost to history!

Appeals to private and government funders to help find it a home at another historic site had met with indifference, or outright refusal! "What will be its destiny? It seems there is no room at the Inn for the Bethlehem of Broadcasting!" Alice exclaimed. Time was passing swiftly. Finally, she had to revise her priorities and turn toward her postponed writing effort.

Between a schedule of full activities, her story gradually developed. She decided that she would finish the final chapter after she had visited Ellis Island. It had been nearly ninety-six years since Paolo's first crossing to America in 1904. The decade and the twentieth century were ending.

The year 2000 had been labeled "Y2K" by the media. With the advent of the new millennium came incessant warnings about impending disasters that would occur if intercontinental computers — sabotaged by their own date lines — were to shut down. How had the world survived for centuries before technology?

Comedians, reeling between comedy and tragedy, had a field day with millennium jokes, kidding that the world could *virtually stop at midnight*. For weeks, Jimmy Sapienza drew laughter as he rehearsed audiences to sing *Auld Lang Syne*, Y2K-style, "Should auld acquaint . . ."

Denouement

It was December 31, 1999. Jim's children, Mia Rose and Keely Elise, and baby Michael Sebastian, Frank's son, were visiting Nunnie for a New Year's Eve sleep-over in her big bedroom. Their parents would ring in the millenium with Jimmy's band. Alice watched her grandchildren happy at play. They rehearsed endlessly "Happy Birthday to baby Michael" and blew candles on an imaginary cake for their cousin's first birthday. Each time they repeated the chorus, Michael reacted with a hearty laugh that left him breathless — and anticipating more. Alice, proud that at least one of her grandchildren would carry the Sapienza name, laughed with them.

Y2K did not mean much to these third-generation babies. Alice could not imagine what new marvels they would live to see in the twenty-first century — and thought briefly — and sadly, of her own mortality. After Michael was settled in his crib and the girls were tucked into Nunnie's big bed, Alice sang a lullaby and waited for the giggles and squeals to stop as they drifted off to sleep.

She speculated what an exciting tomorrow lay ahead for Michael Sebastian. But alas, had doom's prophet, Cassandra, been availabe to reveal his future, she would have prophesied that, after his second birthday, Death would come calling for his mother! The Reaper's excuse? A cerebral hemorrhage and blood clot. Unaware of the new role Destiny would soon give her as Michael's mother, a happy grandmother sank into her big, tilt-back chair to watch television as each country welcomed the new millenium.

She had been skeptical about the overblown hype that fueled the nation. As Father Time made his journey country by country, she expected to hear about technological disasters. However, the wonderful miracle of television brought beautiful scenes and celebrations from civilizations around the globe. Instead of thinking about New Year's resolutions or disasters, Alice, completely relaxed, allowed her imagination to carry her back in time. In a world of memories and fantasy, the mind wanders its aimless course.

She reflected upon the enormous changes that progress had brought in her lifetime. Some changes were exciting. Some were puzzling and made her feel like a stranger in a new world. "I feel like Gregor Samsa," she said as her thoughts turned to Franz Kafka's allegory, *The Metamorphosis*. Kafka described in painful detail how Gregor Samsa went to bed feeling insecure in his real world and awoke next morning from a troubled dream to discover that he had been transformed into a giant cockroach! "He examined his great corrugated brown belly and spindly legs fluttering helplessly before him." Suddenly, Gregor felt alien in his environment.

And here the analogy ends, except to say that Alice's world, like Gregor's, had altered significantly and she sometimes felt alien in it. Her saving grace was her ability to adapt to life's perpetual changes and challenges.

In nearly eight decades, she had seen a great transformation in science, and an unholy change in human character. This first-generation Italian daughter looked at the world of her lifetime, altered by a progression of miracles in technology from the age of electricity to the age of computers. In the twenties life had been simple. She reminisced about the developments she had seen in a world of new consumer commodities: the evolution of the telephone, when a living "operator" instead of an impersonal recording answered a call, to the intercontinental telephone fax machines that abolished time and space.

She thought about "moving pictures" that had developed into "talkies," and television images that now brought the world into her home. Her manual typewriter had evolved to an electric one, and then to the unimaginable feats of the computer, linked worldwide via the Internet, where buyers who once shopped through the Sears Roebuck catalog, like Maria and Rosa, now shopped "on-line."

Memory carried her back to Mama's Tappan gas range that had succeeded their coal-burning cooking stove, just as electric lamps had followed oil lamps and dim gas lights. And now even her electric stove was outranked by the microwave oven.

Alice recalled her curiosity at hearing music from big platters installed on Papa's "talking machine," and the leap from records to tapes to compact discs — and her awe at sounds of voices and music that came through earphones and loudspeakers. She had been only five when Mama's electric iron replaced the heavy flat-irons that had to be heated on the coal stove. And nine, when the wooden icebox gave way to the refrigerator. Oh, how she missed the iceman's truck where she and brother Louie swiped chunks of ice! Technology had its shortcomings!

She relived the joy of turning the crank on the aluminum ice cream bucket filled with rock salt as it magically produced luscious flavors. And remembered her joy at the arrival of the Maytag washer that eliminated turning the hand-cranked wringer on the "Savage" that danced across the cellar floor. *Elisa* — she was not Alice then — recalled her big brothers' pride in their Ford "Tin Lizzie" as they cranked the handle below the front hood to get the motor running. She concluded that hand cranks were the technology then.

There had been great changes in transportation from horse and wagon to delivery truck, to giant motor trailer and a great variety of modern vehicles to suit every individual preference. She missed the iron monsters that spewed steam and belched smoke as they hissed to a deafening stop at the Homewood Railroad Station — and remembered wistfully that before locomotives had become streamlined electric trains, children waited by the tracks to wave to the engineer. And who could know the excitement of stopping play to point upward and shout "Airplane! Airplane!" at the contraption that miraculously flew like a bird?

Alice thought about the jumbo jets that have diminished the globe, the rockets that have hurled men to the moon, and the destructive air power that lurks behind threatening guided missiles. Her reflection shifted to men's inventive genius that moved civilization from the bow and arrow to gunpowder, and from cannons to the atomic bomb capable of annihilating the vulnerable planet. She reflected upon the Biblical prophecy, which forecast that a great battle between the forces of good and evil would occur at the end of the world, and worried that deranged human beings might devise new tools for evil and bring on Armageddon. Alice shuddered, and, like Gregor Samsa, she felt somewhat insecure in her world. It had been a revolutionary century like none before it!

She stared reflectively at the television set, presenting Millennium celebrations from everywhere, and remembered that her sister Grace had wished she could live to see this new century. Their ninety-five-year-old brother Silvio would see it. He had moved with Anne, his wife, to the Catholic senior care home near their daughter Lauretta. Alice's brothers-in-law Lee, Bill, Frank, and Jule would surely celebrate the finale of the century their parents had brought them into. Alice looked around her den at family pictures and, in thanksgiving, exclaimed *"Ti ringrazio, Dio!"*

As the twentieth century was approaching its finale, television cameras swept the mob celebrating on Times Square. The countdown was about to begin: 10-9-8-7-6-5-4-3-2-1. The din was deafening! The millennium had arrived! And nothing catastrophic had happened. Alice missed Tom — and John — and once again thought sadly of her own mortality and the short road ahead.

"I wonder what the Y2K media hype will be today," she said as she flipped her big calendar to Saturday January 1, 2000.

Sunday afternoon brought a welcome visit from son Tom. Alice poured them coffee and they sat at the kitchen table to visit. On the stove meatballs were simmering in Frank's basil-garlic garden tomato sauce. Alice thought briefly about her Sunday visits to Tommy's house, where the arias from a favorite opera flooded the kitchen; and he, the happy cook, seasoned the spaghetti sauce, as he waved his spoon, singing *alta voce*. He reminded her of Papa.

After the small talk, he said, "I have some news to share with you, Mother. You, Rosette, my Lauren, and I are going to Ellis Island this summer. I know how much it means to you."

Alice was pleased and grateful to her kids, as well as to the two Italians, Peter Sammartino and famed auto magnate Lee Iacocca, and the New Jersey's Bicentennial Commission, who had initiated the renovation of Ellis Island. Until 1990, it had remained trashed and neglected for nearly forty years.

"I want to walk where my parents walked when they came to America." Alice could scarcely get the words out without emotion. "I want to climb the noisy stairs that my sister Grace remembered so vividly. And then I can finish the family story." Alice poured them a second cup of coffee and sliced a chunk of freshly-baked bread. She knew Tom would dip it in the spaghetti sauce. And he did. They shared plans for their trip, and Alice sent him off with a container of homemade tomato sauce.

To appreciate fully her visit to Ellis Island, Alice turned to her history books. Her research revealed that immigration had always caused great controversy in America, and that discrimination against Italians was not unique. Historians confirmed that all nationalities had struggled for acceptance since English culture dominated America before the end of the seventeenth century. Its language, its racial and religious attitudes, its laws and economic power left lasting marks on American society.

Alice could scarcely wait to get to Ellis Island to honor those immigrants who had survived those ordeals. She would visit there with greater appreciation. According to numerous historians, there had never been a time without stereotyped negative impressions in American society. They existed in the Colonial period, and they exist today — as Alice was soon to learn.

She worked diligently to complete all but the last chapter of her story before her trip. In early June, she had done just that moments before she walked into Mellon Bank in Forest Hills. Her happy expression forced the curiosity of the bank teller: "Why Mrs. Donnelly, you look so happy! Something good must have happened."

Alice briefly explained that she was nearly finished writing her family's story and looked forward to visiting Ellis Island in two weeks. The teller was clearly surprised and asked her what the story was about. Alice explained that it was a narrative about the family's immigrant crossing. "And where were they from, Mrs. Donnelly?"

"Italy," Alice answered.

The teller smiled and asked in melodic sugar tones: "And did you write about the Maaaafeeeaah?" The rude comment was an insult to Italians and an offense to her family honor.

The remark brought back a flood of resentment. Alice was startled, crushed — then angry at this *Americana*'s condescending, insensitive insult and answered, "I'm Italian. Look at my full name — Alice Sapienza-Donnelly. My nephew Joseph calls me a hyphenated woman." Then, pretending humor, she said: "To anyone who is a bigot it becomes Alice — up-yours — Donnelly," and mentally gave the woman the palm-in-elbow "Italian salute." The embarrassed teller's expression froze.

Alice concluded that the movies and television had succeeded. The nativist superior attitude that has stereotyped and linked crime to certain immigrants lives on! She understood the anger that the word "Nigger" arouses from Black people. Alice came home livid and related the incident to her children and the Sapienza clan. The incident reinforced the point of the family story. Alice wondered if Americans would ever drop anti-immigrant, anti-racial and anti-Semitic bigotry, and rise above prejudice. She tried to shake her anger and focus on her decades-old desire to visit Ellis Island.

The happy day came at the end of June. A forest of New York skyscrapers, dominated by the World Trade Center's imposing Twin Towers, rose to meet the huge airliner as it descended from the bright summer evening sky and touched down at La Guardia Airport. Barely an hour after the foursome arrived at their hotel, they were on their way to Mosconi's Italian *ristorante* in the Village.

When they walked into the *trattoria,* the aroma of familiar herbs and Italian *cucina* and the mingling of various dialects made Alice feel that she had come home. The opportunity to speak Italian with master chef Mosconi was a happy bonus.

Pietro Mosconi, *il padrone,* was particularly proud to say that his guests included some of the Pittsburgh Steelers football team. He was surprised to learn that among them was "the Voice of the Steelers," Rosette's husband Bill Hillgrove. *Signore* Mosconi spent nearly a half-hour conversing with his guests, now in accented English, now in Italian. And then, with typical Italian generosity reminiscent of Alice's Papa, he ordered a complimentary bottle of the exquisite *vino rosso* his guests had been drinking at dinner. Yes, they had come home!

Another surprise greeted them when the happy travelers were beckoned into the hotel bar by "Papa George," who recognized Rosette. She was an occasional visitor there with Bill when they stayed as hotel guests. Georgio, who was Italian and Greek, presided over his bar with the flair of an artist — no a virtuoso — of "mixology," and the gift of a raconteur whose stories were rich in Greek history, sprinkled with Italian or Greek, as the telling required. Papa George had come to America through Ellis Island.

Astonishment and pleasure — short of ecstasy — filled Alice's evening as she and Papa George shared Italian conversation and Greek history, which was the basis of her Master's Thesis. Papa George plied his guests with a variety of "sample" after-dinner drinks, taking discreet care to serve Lauren only soft drinks.

"It pays to be bilingual — first Pietro Mosconi and now Papa George," Alice said facetiously sipping another complimentary after-dinner liqueur. Except for special occasions, Alice rarely drank. This had been a special fun-filled evening. Everyone anticipated a fun-filled day on tomorrow's trip to Ellis Island.

Their hotel, located away from midtown, was closer to their destination at the tip of Manhattan. With notebook and cameras in hand, the tourists hopped the cab that would take them to New York Harbor. The Nigerian cab driver, an interesting recent immigrant, darted deftly in and out of congested traffic. A forest of amazing, colorful graffiti and slogans, created by gang members' spray cans, identified their turf. Today there were no clothes hanging awesomely from the sky between *un bosco di grandi edifici* such as Papa had seen in 1904. Stacks and stacks of apartments rose against an imposing skyline. Alice wondered how many people were packed into them.

The cabbie stopped at Battery Park, where they could purchase ferryboat tickets. He waited for his fare and anticipated tip. Alice made a mental note to include a generous budget for perpetual tips, if she ever visited New York again. Free admission to the "Gateway to America" was provided by the Statue of Liberty-Ellis Island Foundation, operated through the National Parks Service.

As they stood among the sightseers on the Staten Island Ferry, the Statue of Liberty came into view. When she appeared larger than life, Alice's throat tightened as she recalled the emotional stories told by her parents when they saw the magnificent Lady Liberty "lift [her] lamp beside the Golden Door." She understood their emotions. And smiled at the memory of Mama's description of little Domenico kneeling and crossing himself in holy respect when she cried *"Santa Maria!"*

The ferry stopped at her pedestal. Alice looked up at the statue's spiked crown and down to Emma Lazarus' words imbedded in bronze: 'Wretched refuse!' "An insult," she said. "Those two words ought to be changed to *hopeful migrants!"*

Her thoughts shifted to those who came from England to Plymouth Rock, and to those slaves who were torn from their roots, sold by their African masters, and forceably brought to America in slave ships to toil wherever their labor brought profits. Alice, knowing that no group of immigrants had suffered greater abuse, was annoyed that historians had seen slaves as property, never as immigrants.

The ferry sailed slowly toward Ellis Island. Still deep in meditation, Alice reflected: *However our ancestors got to America is secondary to the fact that we, children of survivors, are the beneficiaries. And regardless of our religious, racial or ethnic backgrounds, "Siamo tutti figli di Dio," as Mama used to say. So why are we humans at odds with one another about our genetic differences? When will we ever learn?*

Rosette startled Alice out of her daydream. "There it is!" she shouted. One-half mile away on Ellis Island stood the cluster of red brick Victorian and Byzantine structures where immigrants were once processed for admission or deportation. Alice fought back tears at the prospect of walking where her parents and thousands of expectant immigrants had walked. And she remembered the stories Papa had told of frightened passengers who were deported because they had failed physical exams or questions.

A blast from the ferry's horn signaled their arrival. Overhead, alert seagulls darted gracefully over the water's crest to retrieve unsuspecting fish or scraps that passengers had deliberately tossed into the water.

On their way into the main building, they passed the Immigrant Wall of Honor and joined the tourists who searched for their ancestors' names among thousands engraved there for posterity.

Alice's children thoughtfully anticipated her every need or pleasure. They arranged for a wheelchair so that she would not have to walk the long guided tour. Lauren, Tom, and Rosette took turns pushing. Alice, deeply moved by her role reversal from caretaker to spoiled mother, tried not to show her emotions.

When they entered the Great Hall, Alice remembered her father's description of its enormously high ceiling and recalled Grace's vivid impression of the "noisy steps" where millions of immigrant feet clanged their way up to reach the dreaded examining stations. Wheelchair or no, Alice wanted to climb the "noisy steps" — and would have tried — but could not find them in the center of the hall where Grace had described them to be. A guide informed them that the originals had been recreated, using suitable materials, and moved to the side. Alice was disappointed. She understood that so much had deteriorated, and appreciated the recreation; at least someone cared! But she opted not to climb the imitation structure, for it would *not* be Grazia's stairs.

Gone were the rows of iron bars that, like a cattle yard, had encased immigrants on wooden benches, waiting to be processed. She remembered how Papa described in detail why immigrants feared being separated from loved ones who were approved for entry, and feared being deported if they did not pass medical examinations or customs inspectors' questions.

Without success, she looked for the "green door" that had once admitted those who were approved to enter America. No green door? Again she was disappointed, remembering Mama's emotions when she described pushing through "*la porta verde*" to her new home.

Denouement

As the tour and a live play took visitors back in time to the immigrants' experiences on Ellis Island, Alice relived the stories of her own family's Italian past and the story she had recorded.

Before they relinquished the wheelchair, Tom and Rosette registered the Palombo and Sapienza family names that had yet to be inscribed on the Immigrant Wall of Honor. With that gesture and a walk into the Ellis Island past, Alice found closure.

Obviously, the appropriate way to end their sojourn was to dine in Little Italy. They hailed one of the cabs that seemed to be in perpetual motion, round-the-clock. The cabbie darted from lane to lane with amazing agility and haste along streets lined with crowded outdoor cafés. The aroma along the way was distinctly Italian. And their meal and the *vino* were distinctly excellent. Alice remembered the ridicule once suffered by garlic-eating Italians, and noted that now Italian cuisine is widely imitated, and popular.

Back at their hotel, Papa George waited to indulge them with a new variety of mixed drinks and a new variety of bilingual stories. Rosette assured him that she had found his name on the Wall of Honor. And, in a last *addio*, he sent them to their rooms with complimentary nightcaps. The desk clerks laughed as they passed by with their drinks and chorused, "I know, it pays to speak Italian!"

When they climbed into the cab the next day, Alice thanked Rosette, Tom, and Lauren for the happy trip and their tender loving care. The airliner reduced the New York skyline to a miniature Christmas tree village. Alice reclined in her seat with renewed appreciation and gratitude for the life her parents had made possible beyond the Golden Door.

As she pushed her way into the house, the telephone rang. It was Paula welcoming her home. A few minutes into the conversation, she said, "Hey, Nunnie, you're coming with us to the Italian Day Picnic at Kennywood Park next week." Her German-Irish daughter-in-law, who loves Italian culture, continued, "And there's a Saint Rocco festival the week after that. Do you want to go?" Alice accepted and said, "By then I'll need an Italian fix."

As Paula drove Alice and her little granddaughters Mia and Keely to see Daddy perform at the Italian Sons and Daughters festivities, Paula said, "Say something Italian, Nunnie. I love to hear you talk." She and the girls sang a favorite little song, *Farfallina,* Little Butterfly.

Denouement

The sound of music pulled them to the center of activity. Alice looked for long-lost familiar faces and shared memories with old friends. On the main stage, Italian singer Jimmy Sapienza and his *Five Guys Named Moe* entertained the crowd with Louie Prima, Frank Sinatra, Dean Martin, and Tony Bennet hits. What else?

A playwright with a vivid imagination could not have created a more touching episode than what happened next. Jimmy's performance was interrupted when the Blue Coats, a brass band of costumed musicians, approached playing a crescendo of Italian music. As the *festa* parade circled the main stage, the onstage band joined in. Spirited dancers in the crowd broke into the *Tarantella* -- and stopped respectfully when a float came by. The float was the parade's main feature. Italian customs persist. Without a parade and a statue honoring the occasion — the *Madonna*, or *Santo Rocco*, or *Sant' Antonio* -- no Italian *festa* is complete.

Alice had eagerly anticipated her Italian fix, but she was not prepared for what came next. She had scarcely shed the memory of the Lady of Mount Carmel parade of her childhood, when a sizable green miniature of the Statue of Liberty floated by. It *appeared* the Italians had deified and given her all the honor of a saint! Alice mistakenly concluded that the only thing missing was a traditional holy banner where immigrants had once pinned $5 and $10 bills.

Amusing? Corny? To some Americans, perhaps. But, despite its similarity to traditional custom, this was not a religious *festa* parade. More telling was the patriotism and emotion that reflected Italian gratitude and high esteem for what the Statue of Liberty represents. Alice was touched by the spectacle. Her generation would understand and appreciate this adulation, for until the nineteen seventies, appreciation of *all* immigrant roots and ethnicity had been largely overlooked.

By coincidence, her curiosity about the miniature statue's origin led her to question an American-born Italian patriot, Art Trunzo, an activist in Italian celebrations. It was he who had helped find a replica of Lady Liberty to honor the occasion of her centennial in July 1986. He and the Glassport Pennsylvania Lions Club wrote a letter of inquiry to the Statue of Liberty Ellis Island Foundation. By fortunate circumstance, there was one statue available. It was offered as a donation to Glassport's celebration of Lady Liberty's Centennial, provided someone went to New York Harbor to claim her.

Denouement

Transporting her would be risky. A gentleman, who was headed for New York to pick up a shipment of toys, volunteered to convey the statue back to Glassport. It arrived home safely without a dent or bruise. The man had cleverly transported it nestled among a huge shipment of stuffed animals!

A month after the Italian Day picnic, the Annual Italian Festival broke loose for three days. Jimmy and Paula invited Alice to go. The night before, Jimmy and his band had entertained the audience. Familiar aromas of traditional Italian dishes, and trays of *pasticcini* and *dolci* were waiting to delight and gratify hundreds of Italian revelers with healthy appetites.

Alice surveyed the tables lined with Italian faces. She envisioned the hardships their courageous immigrant parents had experienced to cross the Atlantic in steerage. Alice wondered how many of their youngest descendants knew their stories, or understood and spoke their beautiful language. How could they? Most in her own generation did not speak it either. They had abandoned their language in their concern to be accepted by the *Americani*. But, thankfully, at least this generation still respected their splendid Italian heritage. Suddenly, she heard an emotional outburst of *God Bless America*, sung *ad alta voce*.

On two stages, decorated in red, white and green, costumed folk dancers and singers, and round-the-hour bands performed Italian love songs and lively dances. Ah, but on the main stage, in a central position of honor, stood the green toga-clad *Statua di Liberta!*

Now Alice, hopelessly addicted to ethnic customs, had been to many different festivals, but never had she seen Lady Liberty shown the respect and esteem Italians showed her. With the celebration of her centennial, the Statue had finally become the symbol of immigration, representing immigrants of every ethnic background — all God's children — *tutti figli di Dio.* For Italians, Lady Liberty became strikingly significant, and they have used her as a way of showing *amore di patria* — love of country. It is the Italian way of saying to America, *"Tante grazie!"*

From their example, we might learn that perhaps it is past time for Americans to rise above their prejudices and thank people of every race and ethnicity who came with hopes high, endured hardships, made sacrifices, and made America a beautiful and mighty nation that can justly proclaim — *"Liberta e giustizia per tutti!"* — "Liberty and justice for all!"

In 1975, cousin Mario Palombo accompanied Elisa along the foothills of Campo Basso to visit her roots at Castellino Sul Biferno. Here Elisa poses with Zio Giuseppe and Zia Irene.

The village pathway leads to the *capella* — the little village church.

Courtesy Domenic Palombo

Bargaining with an Italian *zingara* — gypsy.

A proud Abruzzese peasant poses with her prized goats.

John Donnelly drinks a toast to Alice at their wedding.

Ten years after Tom Sapienza died, Alice met and married Pennsylvania Real Estate Commissioner, John Donnelly. John, a mischevious clown, loved all things Italian — especially opera.

Pittsburgh is still an ethnic patchquilt. Italians from Abruzzi (now called Abruzzo) settled in Bloomfield section of Pittsburgh, Pa., where they have lived since early 1900.

Italians are true patriots. At Italian festivals and parades, this miniature Statue of Liberty holds a place of honor. Through her, Italians show *Amore di patria*. Love of country! She was donated by the Statue of Liberty Ellis Island Foundation to the Lions Club of Glassport, Pennsylvania, where she is proudly displayed in the Glassport Library window.

Pittsburgh loves ethnic events. John Cigna, morning KDKA radio host, has drawn large crowds to the annual spaghetti breakfast. Before his retirement in 2001, John and many contributing sponsors fed hundreds of fans who came to enjoy Italian cuisine and lively musical performances.

Jimmy Sapienza and the Five Guys Named Moe. Jimmy is KDKA radio pioneer Sebastian Sapienza's grandson and often performs at KDKA events.

Inventor Frank Conrad's home and garage workshop, located at the border of Pittsburgh and Wilkinsburg, Pa., as it appeared in July 1920.

The walls came tumbling down in September 2001 as the historic Frank Conrad homesite made way for a fast food restaurant. Sadly, the Conrad garage, the "Bethlehem" of radio broadcasting, was dismantled and now waits for new home.

Courtesy Library of Congress, Prints and Photographs Division, Detroit Publishing Company Collection

After foreign terrorists attacked and destroyed New York City's World Trade Center on September 11, 2001, the Lady in the Harbor, with her torch held high, stood in stark contrast beyond the smoking ruins, a silent sentinel still welcoming immigrants to America's Golden Door.

AFTERWORD

And the Walls Came Tumbling Down!

In her effort to recover the past, Alice realized, as did author Thomas Wolfe, that "you can't go home again." People constantly try to go back to one or another kind of home to revisit their roots. She had revisited hers by narrating the family's story, and now she prepared to recover the past through photographs. But when she returned to her hometown, the place had changed so much as to prohibit any real "going home."

As she approached Mother of Good Counsel church, where she was baptized in 1920, she heard sounds of spirited clapping and Gospel hymns, reminiscent of those she and her mother had once enjoyed as they walked along Tioga Street. The pastor invited her in when she told him that her father had helped build this church. A shocking discovery brought Alice to tears when she saw the steeple ceiling painted a bright white. Gone was the precious Renaissance religious art painted by Pittsburgh's own Michelangelo, Attilo Martone, the brother of Lena Sapienza. She wondered if anyone had realized its value.

Favored childhood spots, Brushton School and other treasured landmarks, were gone; the house on Tioga Street, where she was born, had been transformed beyond the point of evoking nostalgia. Alice reflected: *Can one really recover the past? People cannot go back because the world is constantly changing, and we must be ready to change.*

She had accepted the idea as she drove onto Monticello Street to revisit the lovely Jeffersonian home that her parents had sacrificed to own. She looked along the once maple-lined street, now nearly bare of trees, and saw once elegant homes in various stages of disrepair. She turned to focus her camera on 7208, her home, and 7206, Grazia's home, and made a shocking discovery. They were gone! In their place were two empty, overgrown lots.

Overcome with sadness, she wondered: *Why did this happen to only these homes on the block? Did some developer or antique buff recover the stained glass windows at the stair landings, and the beautiful ebony wood mantles, adorned with Venitian tiles? Or, like many precious landmarks, had the indifferent wreckers reduced them to masses of dust and rubble?*

A heartsick Alice had finally discovered that you really can't go home again. As she drove away, her thoughts turned to the destruction of another home — a historic treasure — and she remembered September 27, 2001.

That day, sounds from the steady pounding of demolition equipment pierced the autumn morning air, and the walls of the Frank Conrad house came tumbling down! As they watched in disheartened, helpless silence, Rick Harris' photo lens and Lee Schaeffer's video camera recorded the tragic destruction. Alice winced as the Conrad piano, which had entertained the first radio listeners over his amateur station 8XK, crashed upon the rubble with a final discordant groan.

The little garage behind Conrad's home, where he had pioneered radio broadcasting, had already been carefully dismantled. Each section had been accurately documented and stored for future reconstruction at a yet unknown location. Although a substantial gift from Interep CEO Ralph Guild had temporarily saved the ill-fated garage, the birthplace of commercial radio broadcasting was about to become a fast-food pleasure ground, and only a few people faithful to radio history had seemed to care. Their fifteen-year struggle to preserve it had failed, along with their appeals to the broadcasting industry, to philanthropists and to wealthy corporate America! There was no fanfare, no news coverage to report the sad fate of this historically significant site where the genesis of *worldwide communication* had occurred.

By contrast, reports of events on September 11, 2001 made this demolition seem insignificant after a complacent America had been taken by surprise when two American commercial airliners crashed through the Twin Towers of New York City's famed World Trade Center. Soon *those* walls came tumbling down, killing nearly three thousand innocent people and hundreds of rescue workers trapped inside the burning inferno!

America was horrified when, within the hour, another highjacked plane attacked the Pentagon; and still another, United Airlines Flight 93, had been commandeered to attack Washington, D. C., where the White House stood vulnerable. Resolute heroes on board had communicated their horrific dilemma to loved ones via cell phones and then, sacrificing themselves, attacked the terrorists, aborted the ill-fated human missile and perished with everyone on board.

The first attacks ever unleashed on American soil had been accomplished by religious fanatics who, in the avowed name of Islam, believed themselves to be martyrs. And suddenly, good and evil were at war. Clearly, Americans and the structures symbolic of American life were the targets for the Muslims' holy war — their Jihad. Moreover, ominous terroristic threats of nuclear, biological, and chemical warfare drove fear into American hearts, arousing deep concern and speculation that this might be the prelude to Armageddon!

Abruptly, American thinking changed, and anti-immigrant attitudes, inactive since the Immigration Act of 1986, surfaced again. Despite government appeals to Americans not to show anti-Arab bigotry, cries for deportation of questionable Arab foreign visitors came from some Americans whose own parents had once suffered racial profiling and immigrant prejudice.

Rescue teams — heroes all — worked nonstop to reclaim precious humans, dead or alive, from the enormous rubble. As families and friends grieved for their luckless victims, national leaders, attempting to calm America's phobia, rebuked the evil-doers, vowed to hunt them down and "bring them to justice." Just as the free world had once pursued Adolph Hitler and the Nazis in Europe, it now pursued Osama Bin Laden and Taliban henchmen, who lurked worldwide as a global threat.

Refusing to be intimidated by terrorism, a united nation responded to its leaders' moving appeals. Televised for the world to see, patriots representing every nationality, color, and religion stood on the decimated site at New York's Ground Zero, raised their voices in patrotic songs, and prayed their thanks to the country that had traditionally opened its arms to the world's downtrodden.

In harsh contrast beyond the smoking ruins, the Lady in the harbor, a symbolic terrorists' target, stood with her torch held high, as a stark reminder that many had emigrated to America to escape their evil tyrants. Not far away at her feet, Ellis Island lay as a memento of the hopeful millions who had sought refuge here to fulfill their dreams beyond the Golden Door.

Gone was the "land of the free" where Americans had once felt secure; for although the Taliban had collapsed after several weeks of war, America had been paralyzed! Despite the appeals for bravery and the encouraging patriotic rhetoric from political leaders and media analysts, the greatest tragedy that had emerged on September 11, 2001, was the reality that America was no longer the same safe haven that its immigrants had once known — since the walls came tumbling down!

SELECTED BIBLIOGRAPHY

Beal, William G.; Donnelly, Alice Sapienza; Harris, Richard. *When Radio Was Young*. Publisher, Wilkinsburg Commission, U.S.A., 1995.

Bodnar, John; Simon, Roger; Weber, Michael. *Lives of Their Own*. University of Illinois Press, 1982.

Clough, Shepard B. General Editor, Columbia University; *A History of the Western World*. Second Edition, D.C. Heath & Company, Lexington, Massachusetts, 1969.

Cox, Vic. *The Challenge of Immigration*. Enslow Publishers, Inc. Springfield, N.J., 1995.

Daniels, Roger. *Coming to America/A History of Immigration and Ethnicity in American Life*. Harper Collins Publishers First Edition, 1990.

Kleinberg, S.J. *Shadow of the Mills*. University of Pittsburgh Press. 1989.

Kraut, Alan M. *The Huddled Masses; The immigrant in American Society 1880-1921*. Basic Books, New York, 1989.

Ravenstein, Earnest George, 1844-1913. *Essay: Laws of Migration*, 1889, (Keith Johnston, 1890), East Stanford, London.

Roselli, Bart & Sapolsky, Steven. *Homewood-Brushton— A Century of Community-Making*. Publisher Howard Heinz History Center, Pgh., Pa. 1987. (contributor, Alice Sapienza Donnelly, 1985).

Sapienza, Alice. University of Pittsburgh Themes, Manuscript, Masters Thesis. *Epitaph or Resurrection?*; *Valley of Indecision*; *The Golden Door*; *Needed Human Renewal*; *Highway Robbery*; *Across The Ionian Sea*; 1972, 1973, 1974, 1984, 1997.

Traverso, Edmund. *Critique of Madison Grant — The Passing of a Great Race*. Charles Scribner & Sons; Lexington, Mass., 1968.

Wilkinsburg Centennial Publication Committee, Editor Marjorie Michaux. *Historic Wilkinsburg 1887-1987*. Walsworth Press, 1988. (contributor, Alice Sapienza Donnelly)

About the Author

Marjorie Michaux, whose poetry series, *The Dream Weaver*, was an early KDKA radio favorite in the nineteen sixties, interviewed and wrote this article about the author: "Her pen name is Elisa Palombo Sapienza, but she is better known as Alice Sapienza Donnelly. Her friends will henceforth also know her as an award-winning poet, playwright and public speaker. To her, words are the key to the mysteries of the creative mind. Since she was a blue-eyed, blonde *bambina* growing up in the Palombo family home, she grasped at the lyrical Italian words and their sister words in English. They became the rich source of the river that runs through her life -- her love of learning and reading.

Alice talks about how her parents enjoyed working together and singing some glorious refrain from a favorite opera as they prepared the pasta or washed the dishes. 'I learned to speak Italian while they cooked and prayed,' Alice muses.

Twice widowed, she owned and managed Thomas Barth Formals and Dry Cleaning Shops and has been a speaking instructor at the University of Pittsburgh for twenty-eight years. She has served on many fronts as a business woman, as first woman President of the Wilkinsburg Chamber of Commerce, as Wilkinsburg's 1987 Centennial Coordinator, and co-founder of the Wilkinsburg Cultural Commission.

During the golden period of local theater in the 1980's, the Cultural Commission sponsored The Wilkinsburg Arts Theater, naming her its Executive Director. The theater was the stage for her musical about Louis Jordan, the father of Rhythm and Blues, for which her musical drama, *Brother Beware,* won critical acclaim.

What does Alice consider her greatest achievement aside from raising her family? Her answer is quick and concise. She views her fight to help change the Law of Eminent Domain as a blessing for future generations, abolishing the practice, Alice exclaims, *'when the state could come in and literally steal your property!'*

Today the battle she fights has a brighter hue. As President of the nonprofit National Museum of Broadcasting, she, her Executive Committee and project Chairman Rick Harris have strived to rescue the Frank Conrad garage where radio broadcasting was born. This historic treasure will honor the Electronic Communication field."

Amidst all this, Alice has raised four children who have become successful professionals in business and the arts. They have rewarded her by presenting her with eight grandchildren and three great grandchildren.

The year 2006 held a remarkable surprise! For several years Alice had experienced progressively worse leg and chest pains. By mid-April she became aware of occasional memory lapses. Her doctor admitted her to UPMC Shadyside Hospital. A series of tests revealed that a large, non-malignant brain tumor had grown in her forehead. On May 22, 2006, her surgeon, Doctor Ghassan Bejjani, successfully removed it. A grateful lady daily prays and thanks him and God for her survival. Today, she has some short-term memory loss -- a small price to pay for a large miracle. .

What is the greatest lesson to learn from this experience? **Life is fragile and short. Each day is a gift to be treasured.**